Imagined Economies

This book examines the economic bases of regional sovereignty movements in the Russian Federation from 1990 through 1993. Based on an original data set of Russian regional sovereignty movements, Herrera's analysis employs a variety of methods including both qualitative case studies of Sverdlovsk and Samara oblasts using systematic content analysis of local newspaper articles and quantitative statistical analysis. The central finding of the book is that variation in Russian regional activism is explained not by differences in economic conditions but by differences in the construction or imagination of economic interests; in the language of other contemporary debates, economic advantage and disadvantage are as imagined as nations. In arguing that regional economic interests are intersubjective, contingent, and institutionally specific, the book addresses a major question in political economy, namely the origin of economic interests. In addition, by engaging the nationalism literature, the book expands the constructivist paradigm to the development of economic interests.

Yoshiko M. Herrera is an associate professor in the Government Department, in the Faculty of Arts and Sciences at Harvard University. She is a faculty associate of the Weatherhead Center for International Affairs and a faculty associate and Executive Committee member of the Davis Center for Russian and Eurasian Studies. She is also a member of the Program on New Approaches to Russian Security at the Center for Strategic & International Studies.

Cambridge Studies in Comparative Politics

General Editor
Margaret Levi   *University of Washington, Seattle*

Assistant General Editor
Stephen Hanson   *University of Washington, Seattle*

Associate Editors
Robert H. Bates   *Harvard University*
Peter Hall   *Harvard University*
Peter Lange   *Duke University*
Helen Milner   *Columbia University*
Frances Rosenbluth   *Yale University*
Susan Stokes   *University of Chicago*
Sidney Tarrow   *Cornell University*

Other Books in the Series

Lisa Baldez, *Why Women Protest: Women's Movements in Chile*
Stefano Bartolini, *The Political Mobilization of the European Left,*
     1860–1980: The Class Cleavage
Mark Beissinger, *Nationalist Mobilization and the Collapse of the Soviet State*
Nancy Bermeo, ed., *Unemployment in the New Europe*
Carles Boix, *Democracy and Redistribution*
Carles Boix, *Political Parties, Growth, and Equality: Conservative and Social*
     Democratic Economic Strategies in the World Economy
Catherine Boone, *Merchant Capital and the Roots of State Power in Senegal,*
     1930–1985
Catherine Boone, *Political Topographies of the African State: Territorial*
     Authority and Institutional Change
Michael Bratton and Nicolas van de Walle, *Democratic Experiments in*
     Africa: Regime Transitions in Comparative Perspective
Valerie Bunce, *Leaving Socialism and Leaving the State: The End of*
     Yugoslavia, the Soviet Union, and Czechoslovakia

Continued after the Index

Imagined Economies

THE SOURCES OF RUSSIAN REGIONALISM

YOSHIKO M. HERRERA

Harvard University

CAMBRIDGE
UNIVERSITY PRESS

PUBLISHED BY THE PRESS SYNDICATE OF THE UNIVERSITY OF CAMBRIDGE
The Pitt Building, Trumpington Street, Cambridge, United Kingdom

CAMBRIDGE UNIVERSITY PRESS
The Edinburgh Building, Cambridge CB2 2RU, UK
40 West 20th Street, New York, NY 10011-4211, USA
477 Williamstown Road, Port Melbourne, VIC 3207, Australia
Ruiz de Alarcón 13, 28014 Madrid, Spain
Dock House, The Waterfront, Cape Town 8001, South Africa

http://www.cambridge.org

First published 2005

Printed in the United States of America

Typeface Janson Text Roman 10/13 pt.   *System* LaTeX 2_ε [TB]

A catalog record for this book is available from the British Library.

Library of Congress Cataloging in Publication Data

Herrera, Yoshiko M., 1970–
Imagined economies : the sources of Russian regionalism / Yoshiko M. Herrera.
    p.   cm. – (Cambridge studies in comparative politics)
Includes bibliographical references and index.
ISBN 0-521-82736-1
1. Russia (Federation) – Economic conditions – 1991 – Regional disparities.
2. Regionalism – Russia (Federation)   I. Title.   II. Series.
HC340.12H47   2004
330.947–dc22   2004049267

ISBN 0 521 82736 1 hardback

*This book is dedicated to the loving memory of
my grandfather Robert B. Herrera (1913–2000)
and my father Leonard B. Herrera (1944–2001).*

Contents

List of Tables

List of Tables

List of Figures and Maps

Figures

Maps

List of Acronyms

AECORU	*Assotsiatsii ekonomicheskogo vzaimodeistviia oblastei i respublik Urala* (Association for Economic Cooperation of Oblasts and Republics of the Urals)
AO	*avtonomnaia oblast'* (autonomous oblast) and *avtonomnyi okrug* (autonomous okrug)
ASSR	*avtonomnaia Sovetskaia Sotsialisticheskaia respublika* (Autonomous Soviet Socialist Republic)
CPD	*S"ezd narodnykh deputatov* (Congress of People's Deputies)
CPSU	*Kommunisticheskaia partiia Sovetskogo Soiuza* (Communist Party of the Soviet Union)
DVR	*Demokraticheskii vybor Rossii* (Democratic Choice of Russia)
FFSR	*Fond finansovoi podderzhki sub"ektov Rossiiskoi Federatsii* or *Fond finansovoi podderzhki regionov* (Fund for Financial Support of Regions)
FSU	Former Soviet Union
GDP	Gross Domestic Product
GRP	Gross Regional Product
GKChP	*Gosudarstvennyi komitet po chrezvychainomu polozheniiu* (State Committee on the State of Emergency)
Gosplan	*Gosudarstvennyi planovyi komitet* (State Planning Committee)
Gossnab	*Gosudarstvennyi komitet SSSR po material'no-tekhnicheskomu snabzheniiu* (State Committee of the USSR for Material-Technical Supplies)
ILO	International Labor Organization

INDEM   *Tsentr prikladnykh politicheskikh issledovanii* (Center for Applied Political Research); formerly *Informatika dlia demokratii* (Information for Democracy)

ispolkom   *ispolnitel'nyi komitet soveta* (executive committee of the soviet)

Kommsomol *Vsesoiuznyi Leninskii Kommunisticheskii soiuz molodezhi* (All-Union Lenin Communist Youth League)

LDPR   *Liberal'no-demokraticheskaia partiia Rossii* (Liberal-Democratic Party of Russia)

MGO   *mezhotraslevoe gosudarstvennoe ob"edinenie* (interbranch state association)

NAACP   National Association for the Advancement of Colored People

NDR   *Nash Dom–Rossiia* (Our Home Is Russia)

obkom   *oblastnoi komitet* (oblast committee)

RSFSR   *Rossiiskaia Sovetskaia Federativnaiia Sotsialisticheskaia Respublika* (Russian Soviet Federated Socialist Republic)

SEU   subjective expected utility

SNA   System of National Accounts

Sovnarkhoz *Sovet narodnogo khoziaistva* (Council of the National Economy)

SSR   *Sovetskaia Sotsialisticheskaia respublika* (Soviet Socialist Republic)

TsSU   *Tsentral'noe statisticheskoe upravlenie SSSR* (Central Statistical Administration of the USSR)

USSR   *Soiuz Sovetskikh Sotsialisticheskikh Respublik* (Union of Soviet Socialist Republics)

VAT   Value-Added Tax

VAZ   *Vozhskii avtomobil'nyi zavod* (Volga Automobile Factory)

VSNKh   *Vysshii sovet narodnogo khoziaistva* (Supreme Economic Council)

VTsIOM   *Vserossiiskii tsentr izucheniia obshchestvennogo mneniia* (All-Russian Center for the Study of Public Opinion); formerly (until 1992) *Vsesoiuznyi tsentr izucheniia obshchestvennogo mneniia* (All-Union Center for the Study of Public Opinion)

Note on Transliteration

For transliteration of Russian words, the Library of Congress (LOC) transliteration system has been used with a few exceptions: Words that happen to be conventionally transliterated in English under a different system have been transliterated according to such conventions when used in the text (for example, "Yeltsin" instead of "El'tsin," "soviet" instead of "sovet," "Yakovlev" instead of "Iakovlev," Moscow instead of "Moskva," and St. Petersburg instead of "Sankt Peterburg"); when such words appear in Russian titles in citations they are transliterated according to LOC. References to Russian words that have been published in English are left as transliterated in the publication. For concision, the soft sign, signified under the LOC system with an apostrophe, has been omitted from the end of very frequently cited words in the text (such as "oblast" and "Rossel"); when such words appear in Russian titles in citations they are transliterated according to LOC. Finally, the plural of certain Russian words has been anglicized (e.g., "oblasts," rather than the Russian "oblasti").

Most Russian regional names are the same as the regional capital city names, except that regional names are adjectives rather than nouns. In Table 1.3, for concision, in lieu of adjectival regional names, I have listed the shorter regional capital city names except where the capital city name differs from the region name; in those cases the regional name is given in adjectival form (for example, Kamchatskaia). Exceptions include "Nizhegorodskaia Oblast," which appears as "Nizhnii Novgorod" owing to common usage, and "Moskovskaia Oblast" and "Leningradskaia Oblast," which are spelled out in full to lessen confusion with the cities. Finally, because they appear so frequently in the text, for concision, "Sverdlovsk" and "Samara" rather than "Sverdlovskaia" and "Samarskaia" have been used throughout the text to refer to the oblasts.

Acknowledgments

This book grew out of two experiences in the mid-1990s: traveling around Russian regions, asking questions, and following interesting leads; and being a graduate student at the University of Chicago, surrounded by even more questions. Turning those questions into a dissertation, as well as its subsequent transformation into this book, would not have been possible without the support along the way of many wonderful friends, colleagues, teachers, and generous research-supporting organizations.

As a graduate student in the Department of Political Science at the University of Chicago, I could not have asked for a more stimulating and intellectually engaging environment. My dissertation committee chair, David D. Laitin, was consistently a strong supporter, and he allocated countless hours of his time to listening to my thoughts, ideas, and problems related to this project, while also providing detailed comments at a moment's notice – no graduate student could have asked for more. The other members of my committee – Gary Herrigel, Susanne Rudolph, and Ronald G. Suny – also all generously and continuously over the years offered both intellectual and moral support without which I would not have been able to complete this project. In particular I am thankful to Gary Herrigel for his excellent teaching, for introducing me to constructivist political economy, and in general for taking the time to discuss so many issues with me. In addition, Adam Przeworski played a crucial role in the formulation and development of this project. The personal and professional examples set by each member of my committee exemplify standards of brilliance in scholarship and spirit; I am grateful for having had the opportunity to work with each of them.

Harvard University, and in particular the Government Department; the Weatherhead Center for International Affairs under the direction of Jorge Domínguez; and the Davis Center for Russian and Eurasian Studies have been tremendously supportive in providing the resources and opportunity to transform the dissertation into a book. I am especially grateful to Timothy Colton and Lisbeth Tarlow of the Davis Center for their continued institutional and intellectual support. In addition, my colleagues in the Government Department are a source of friendship and intellectual engagement for which I am deeply appreciative.

Most of all, in acknowledging assistance in completing this book, I am thankful to those who read and commented on all or part of the manuscript. Rawi Abdelal, Yitzhak Brudny, Timothy Colton, Stephen E. Hanson, Jacques Hymans, Andrew Kydd, David Laitin, Gerald McDermott, Jeff Strabone, and David Woodruff all read the entire manuscript at various stages and generously offered detailed and constructive advice. Several other kind individuals including Bear Braumoeller, Gerald Easter, Grzegorz Ekiert, Timothy Frye, Vladimir Gel'man, Kimberly K. Germain, Elise Giuliano, Julian Go, Peter Hall, Gary Herrigel, Stephen Herschler, Ted Hopf, Brett Klopp, John LeDonne, Will Lowe, Rory MacFarquhar, Philip Paolino, Timothy Snyder, Steve Solnick, and Konstantin Sonin read and commented on various chapters, and I am grateful to them all. In the final stretch, Rawi, David W., Andy, David L., Jacques, Bear, Gary, and Jeff gave me valuable concrete assistance as well as encouragement, which allowed me to finally part with the last revisions.

The manuscript also benefited from the contributions of a number of excellent research assistants. First and foremost, George Georgiev did a masterful job in gathering data on regional sovereignty movements and in helping me compile the quantitative data sets. Roman Kassianov assisted me with selecting and copying articles from the newspapers in Samara. Liudmila Amerik and Irina Ruvinsky were helpful and committed in the coding of articles. Darya Nachinkina provided excellent assistance in the final stages of preparing the manuscript. And last but not least, Jeff Strabone provided insightful editorial assistance.

I received financial support for this book from a number of sources over the years. First, the National Science Foundation (Three Year Graduate Fellowship Award), IREX (Individual Advanced Research/Research Resident Grant), Fulbright-Hays (Doctoral Dissertation Research Abroad Fellowship), and the University of Chicago allowed me to do the initial research for this project while I was in graduate school. Later, faculty support from Harvard University allowed me to carry out revisions of the manuscript. In particular I would like to thank Jack Cogan for his generosity and sponsorship of the Davis Center Junior Faculty Leave Grants.

Acknowledgments

I also am very grateful to Cambridge University Press and in particular Lewis Bateman, Margaret Levi, and Stephen Hanson for generously and patiently guiding me through the revision process.

My family and friends have also been fantastically helpful in the course of this project. In a way that I don't think is typical, my parents and grandparents were very supportive at consequential moments in my intellectual and professional development – even when they had no idea what I was doing. As time goes by, I appreciate more and more their dedication to free thinking and the pursuit of what's interesting. The friends who have been there for me during the time it has taken to complete this book are too numerous to mention all by name, but I especially thank Elise Giuliano, Farnaz Fardad, and Pushpita Casey for their warm and optimistic encouragement over the years.

I also am indebted to my many friends in Russia, especially Alevtina Gavrilova and Aleksei Kilin and their families. Alya is the nicest and most helpful person anyone could hope to meet; luckily for me, we were next-door neighbors in Moscow. Aleksei saved me many times in Ekaterinburg – first by helping me find an apartment (so I would not have to live in the mental hospital in which I'd been assigned housing!) and then also by showing me how to navigate the libraries and archives. Alya and Aleksei helped me tremendously with my research, but also, thanks to them, I thoroughly enjoyed my years in Russia. I'm glad the research for this book gave me the chance to meet such wonderful people.

Finally, returning home, Andy and Katya deserve special mention. They have been totally supportive at the most critical and irrational moments in this book process; I am so grateful to have them in my life.

As is evident from these comments, no one could ask for a better set of advisors or context for intellectual development than I have received at the University of Chicago and at Harvard University, as well as by my family and friends. I was surrounded by people who cared and people who gave all they could; the rest was up to me. So, of course, I take all responsibility for any errors or shortcomings.

Imagined Economies

Introduction

In December 1991, seventy years of communist rule in the Soviet Union came to an abrupt end. The center could not hold, things fell apart, and it was not clear what new beast was slouching towards Bethlehem to be born. As the Communist Party ceded executive functions to newly emerging state institutions, regional elites within the Russian Federation, the largest of the fifteen Soviet republics, suddenly found key roles available to them in the active building of a new Russian federal state. The future seemed to be wide open, and several regions seized the opportunity to make political and economic demands on the center in the form of movements for greater autonomy and sovereignty.

Yet not all regions of the Russian Federation sought greater autonomy, and this diversity of outcomes poses important questions which the scholarly literature has, for the most part, neglected. Put most generally, why did some regions come to believe that greater autonomy or full sovereignty was the best way to fulfill regional political and economic interests, while others did not? The experience of Russia's 89 regions in the early 1990s presents a puzzling pattern of variation in autonomy and sovereignty movements. The apparent role of economic factors in autonomy and sovereignty movements is particularly intriguing. There was remarkable heterogeneity in expressed economic interests, even though many regions bore striking similarities in their structural economic conditions, institutional configuration, and political history. Some regions understood greater autonomy or sovereignty to be in their economic interests, while others did not find material advantage in the possibility of more political authority. This issue – the economic basis of sovereignty movements – asks questions at the very core of political economy: What are the origins of economic interests and what explains their development and influence on political action?

1

In this book, I analyze the experience of autonomy movements in the Russian Federation in the early 1990s in order to explain the development of regional economic interests and movements for greater sovereignty. This analysis will shed much needed light on a critical phase in the development of Russian federalism and will also add to our understanding of the development of economic interests and sovereignty movements in general. By combining theoretical insights from a literature I term *constructivist political economy* with the scholarly literature on nationalism, and by empirically analyzing Russian regionalism in general as well as through the detailed experience of the development of an autonomy movement for a Urals Republic in Sverdlovsk Oblast, I have developed an imagined economies analytical framework that relies on the interaction of particular institutional contexts and local understandings of the economy to explain the development of economic interests in greater sovereignty.[1] The results are both theoretical and empirical: I argue that the imagined economies framework not only provides a better explanation of the pattern of regionalism in the Russian Federation but may also be applicable to other cases of economic-based sovereignty movements. In addition, it makes a critical contribution to the scholarly literature on nationalism by extending the historical constructivist approach to the economy. Finally, the imagined economies framework adds to the growing constructivist political economy literature in ways that build on understanding the origins and development of economic interests.

Regionalism in the Russian Federation

In *Imagined Communities*, Benedict Anderson posits certain necessary conditions, in the sense of "conceptual events," for the imagination of nations.[2] In the Russian context of the early 1990s, glasnost, perestroika, and the breakup of the Soviet Union were the critical context for the imagination

---

[1] The term "imagined economies" is derived from the work of Benedict Anderson. Although Anderson used the term *imagination* to refer to "communities" in the sense of linkages between people who don't know each other, I am using the term to refer to shared, local, non-objectivist understandings of regional economies. The relevant noun is different (communities vs. economies) but the sense of shared, non-objective, historically constructed entities is preserved. See Benedict Anderson, *Imagined Communities: Reflections on the Origin and Spread of Nationalism*, rev. ed. (London: Verso, 1996).

[2] Anderson, 1996.

of post-Soviet regional political and economic interests.[3] The end of the Soviet Union brought about an absolute change in rules that destroyed Soviet political and economic authority and allowed for the serious questioning of Moscow-based authority. What the breakdown in belief in the divine right of kings was to the French or American Revolutions, the breakdown in the authority of the Communist Party of the Soviet Union was to the regions of Russia. The cosmology of the socialist universe was signed away, and the history of Russia was to be written by erstwhile unremarkable apparatchiks like Boris Yeltsin. The career paths of regional elites were thoroughly upset by the institutional breakdown of the Communist Party. Russian regional leaders could still look to Moscow as the center, but it was unclear how long that would last. This disruption in career trajectories made regional elites aware of their new location as leaders of regions within the Russian Federation, but ordinary people also became acutely aware of their territorial location because the place where they happened to be living in 1991 signified a new basis for future citizenship.

The first Russian Republic, which began in the fall of 1991 and lasted until December 1993, was outside the organizing framework of Soviet political and economic categories of understanding. Instead, this was a period of contestation over power and the system of authority that would structure political and economic relations in the Russian Federation. Politically, it was a game of musical chairs: All the rules and paths to power had been upset and no one knew which institution would turn out to be the relevant one. The Federation Treaty and the Constitution were works-in-progress, and political actors faced many organizational choices including multiple seats of authority in the region. No one knew which chair would be left when the music stopped – would it be the executive or the legislature, the oblasts or the republics? On the economic side, the de facto decentralization of economic resources that began under perestroika and accelerated with the decline of the Communist Party of the Soviet Union (CPSU) represented the transformation from Soviet principles of redistribution to a Hobbesian every-region-for-itself state of anarchy that exacerbated regional inequality.

The outcomes of these processes created a scenario in which political and economic categories had become sufficiently fluid so as to allow for novel

---

[3] *Glasnost* refers to "openness" mainly in the press, while *perestroika* refers to "restructuring" of political and economic governance organizations. I will elaborate on these concepts and the context for imagination of the regional economy in greater detail in Chapter 3.

types of interaction between regional actors adhering to particular ideas about the economy and events. During this period, regions came to appreciate both the new opportunities that had opened up to them and the urgency of making choices; additionally, *some* regions came to see greater autonomy or sovereignty as the only way to solve regional economic problems.

The "parade of sovereignties" during the early 1990s in which region after region declared sovereignty following the collapse of the Communist Party and precipitating the end of the USSR (Union of Soviet Socialist Republics or *Soiuz Sotsialisticheskikh Respublik*) gave rise to nationalist demands by ethnically defined territories, such as Tatarstan and Chechnia. Within Russia, there arose "non-nationalist" movements for greater autonomy, which were driven mainly by economic grievances rather than ethnic claims, from regions with populations overwhelmingly self-identified as ethnically Russian. Out of the 89 regions of the Russian Federation, there were 55 so-called *Russian regions'* made up of 49 oblasts and 6 krais.[4] Of these, approximately 40% pressed for greater autonomy, while the remaining 60% had little or no activism toward sovereignty.[5]

This variation in autonomy movements among the Russian regions presents an unusual opportunity for the systematic analysis of the economic bases of sovereignty movements. The absence of ethnicized political demands among these regions, combined with their institutional similarity, allows for comparative analysis of economic factors that is uncomplicated by variance in national identity, nationalist mobilization, or institutional configurations. Admittedly, most of these autonomy movements in Russia were not aimed at full sovereignty. Nevertheless, because interests in sovereignty are not primordial, and because separatist movements nearly always start out as movements with lower-level demands for autonomy, understanding the dynamic development of autonomy movements and the expression of economic interests in greater sovereignty will inform the analysis of sovereignty and separatist movements more generally.

---

[4] The Russian Federation is divided into several types of administrative units: republics, oblasts, krais, federal cities, autonomous okrugs, and one autonomous oblast. In brief, republics, autonomous okrugs, and the one autonomous oblast are ethnically defined, symbolically and institutionally privileging the titular ethnic group (e.g., Tatars in Tatarstan). The other administrative units – the oblasts, krais, and federal cities – have not been defined by ethnic criteria, do not privilege any particular ethnic group, and have populations overwhelmingly self-identified as "Russian." Consequently, these oblasts, krais, and federal cities are considered "Russian regions." The definitions, ethnic distinctions, and history of the regions of the Federation are discussed in greater detail in Chapter 1.

[5] In Chapter 1, I present an original data set that elaborates on this claim.

This project began in 1994 when I was in Ekaterinburg interviewing regional officials regarding federal relations. There I noticed something startling: The rhetoric of regional officials in discussing the *economic* claims of their region, Sverdlovsk Oblast, resembled nationalist discourse, except that it was about economic rather than ethnic claims. These economic claims, moreover, formed the core of the region's movement for greater sovereignty. I investigated the nature of Sverdlovsk's economic claims and found that, surprisingly, there was little in the structure of Sverdlovsk's economy that would explain the level and intensity of activism toward greater sovereignty. To better understand the material basis of Sverdlovsk's economic claims, I considered the experience of other regional autonomy movements and other regions that were economically similar to Sverdlovsk.

I constructed a data set of regional movements for greater sovereignty for all 55 oblasts and krais in the Russian Federation from 1990 to 1993 that could be used to test quantitatively a number of factors (economic, geographic, demographic, and historical) on all Russian regions.[6] And, in order to push the analysis of the material basis for regional economic claims further, I compared the economy and expressed economic interests of Sverdlovsk with that of an economically similar region, Samara Oblast.[7]

The comparison of Sverdlovsk and Samara Oblasts illustrates well the puzzle of the economic basis of sovereignty movements in the Russian Federation. Both regions share the same institutional legal status as oblasts and have a history of peaceful relations with the Russian center and no experience of independent statehood. The ethnic composition of both regions is strongly Russian, 83% in Samara and 89% in Sverdlovsk.[8] Both regions also have populations far above the Russian regional average and are among the most populous regions in the Russian Federation.[9] They are also similar in terms of their relative distance from Moscow and in territorial size.[10]

Economically, both Samara and Sverdlovsk, like the rest of Russia, were hit hard by the economic decline of the perestroika era and by the cuts to the defense industry in particular, and production in the early 1990s in both

---

[6] See Chapter 1 for discussion and analysis of this data set.

[7] See Chapter 5 for an extended discussion of this comparison.

[8] Valerii A. Tishkov, ed., *Narody Rossii entsiklopedia* (Moscow: Nauchnoe izdatel'stvo, Bol'shaia Rossiiskaia entsiklopedia, 1994), pp. 439–40.

[9] Among all 89 subjects, Sverdlovsk was the fifth most populous (as of 1993) and Samara was ranked eleventh. Among the oblasts and krais, Sverdlovsk is third, and Samara is seventh.

[10] Sverdlovsk is 1,667 kilometers from Moscow and 194,800 square kilometers in size. Samara is 1,098 kilometers from Moscow and 53,600 square kilometers in size.

regions plummeted. In recent years, however, both regions have turned out to be among the economically strongest in the entire Russian Federation. The one significant economic difference between Samara and Sverdlovsk in the early 1990s concerned net tax payments: Samara paid significantly more into the federal budget per capita than Sverdlovsk.

On the face of it, one might expect net tax payments to be correlated with greater demands for autonomy or sovereignty, suggesting that Samara, rather than Sverdlovsk would be more likely to make economic demands against the center. Yet, despite the fact that the two regions were very similar economically, there was virtually no regional activism in Samara, while Sverdlovsk had one of the strongest movements for greater sovereignty in the entire Federation, and economic claims formed the basis of Sverdlovsk's activism.

The Economic Basis of Regional Sovereignty Movements

If we consider the scholarly literature on sovereignty movements, we see that there is a curious disjuncture between the nationalism literature on the one hand, and the political economy literature on the other. As is well known, nationalist movements can no longer be explained by "ethnicity" because scholars of nationalism have long ago undertaken the investigation and de-essentialization of ethnic identity and have convincingly historicized the construction of ethnicity, showing it to have imaginative, non-biological origins.[11] But this literature gives us little guidance on economic questions because – although ethnic, linguistic, and cultural demands are approached as historically constructed phenomena involving interpretation, institutional contexts, and particular actors – economic claims, with very few exceptions in that same scholarly literature on nationalism, have been largely treated as simple reflections of observable, objective facts.[12] Consequently, for understandings of the economic basis of sovereignty movements,

[11] See, for example, Anderson, 1996; and Ronald G. Suny, *The Revenge of the Past: Nationalism, Revolution, and the Collapse of the Soviet Union* (Stanford, CA: Stanford Univ. Press, 1993).

[12] Some notable exceptions that treat economic factors from a constructivist perspective in the nationalism literature include Rawi Abdelal, *National Purpose in the World Economy: Post-Soviet States in Comparative Perspective* (Ithaca, NY: Cornell Univ. Press, 2001); and Liah Greenfeld, *The Spirit of Capitalism: Nationalism and Economic Growth*, (Cambridge, MA: Harvard Univ. Press, 2001). Greenfeld's work draws of course on Max Weber. See Max Weber, *The Protestant Ethic and the Spirit of Capitalism*, translated by Talcott Parsons, (London: Routledge, 2001). I discuss the vast literature on constructivist approaches to the economy (more generally, beyond nationalism) in Chapter 2.

we tend to turn (in)to economists. This disjuncture is borne out in explanations of Soviet and Russian sovereignty movements, which can be divided into constructivist nationalist explanations that tend not to focus on economic factors and non-constructivist political economy explanations that primarily focus on economic factors.

One of the most prominent arguments in the political economy literature on the economic basis of sovereignty movements in the Russian Federation is that regional activism was a bargaining strategy used by regions in order to extract resources from the center.[13] There is no doubt that bargaining was going on between the center and the regions in Russia in the early 1990s. However, the bargaining literature does not explain variation in regional interests in greater sovereignty per se because it sidesteps the question of interests in sovereignty by treating sovereignty claims as a hollow vehicle for realizing other economic interests. To the extent that these bargaining models consider variation in regional actions, differences in regional economic resources may allow for differences in the types of demands that regions make, but all economically similar regions are expected to act alike. Indeed, in many cases, bargaining models of sovereignty posit structural economic variables as the essential basis for regional demands.[14] Yet most Russian regions did not seek separatism or greater autonomy, and more importantly, economically similar regions, such as Sverdlovsk and Samara, did not behave alike with respect to bargaining demands or to sovereignty claims.

If we consider structural economic arguments for sovereignty in general, we see that scholars have disagreed about the influence of relative wealth and resources. Some argue that richer regions are the most likely to seek greater sovereignty, while others argue that poorer regions will press hardest for more autonomy. In the case of sovereignty movements among the ethnic republics in the Soviet Union and Russian Federation, the consensus is that, ceteris paribus, the most economically advanced regions fought hardest for greater sovereignty.[15] This structural economic advantage argument,

---

[13] Steven Solnick, "Will Russia Survive? Center and Periphery in the Russian Federation," in Barnett Rubin and Jack Snyder, eds., *Post-Soviet Political Order: Conflict and State Building* (New York: Routledge, 1998); and Daniel S. Treisman, *After the Deluge: Regional Crises and Political Consolidation in Russia* (Ann Arbor, MI: Univ. of Michigan Press, 1999).

[14] Daniel S. Treisman, "Russia's 'Ethnic Revival': The Separatist Activism of Regional Leaders in a Postcommunist Order," *World Politics* 49:2 (1997), pp. 212–49.

[15] For example, Philip G. Roeder, "Soviet Federalism and Ethnic Mobilization," *World Politics* 43:2 (January 1991), pp. 196–232; and Henry Hale, "The Parade of Sovereignties: Testing

however, does not hold up when considering the autonomy movements among the Russian regions.

I quantitatively evaluated the effect of several economic variables on regional activism, but the results did not suggest a clear relationship between structural economic conditions and Russian regional autonomy movements. Most of the economic variables were not significant, the coefficients were low, and the adjusted R-squared values were extremely low. The most surprising and interesting finding was the direction and significance of net tax payments across all the model specifications.[16] Bargaining and structural economic models of movements for greater sovereignty would have predicted a positive relationship, that is, that the higher the net tax payments, the more likely the regional activism. In the case of the Russian regions, however, the regression results suggested the opposite – a puzzling finding that is also consistent with the comparison of Sverdlovsk and Samara. The general conclusion from the quantitative analysis, however, is that the pattern of autonomy movements within the Russian Federation does not follow from any obvious economic, demographic, or geographic relationship.

How do these findings regarding the experience of the Russian regions affect our understanding of the relationship between structural economic conditions and sovereignty movements? The argument that the wealthiest regions would be most likely to seek greater sovereignty was not confirmed, but so too was there a lack of support for the argument that the poorest regions would seek greater autonomy. Given the growing literature in political economy that considers how economic claims and interests may be mediated and therefore may differ from the structural material conditions on which they are based, it seems necessary to consider the economic basis of sovereignty movements from a different angle.

The objectivity of the economy has been questioned in a range of disciplines, including cognitive science, psychology, economics, political science, sociology, and history.[17] Work in these fields provides overwhelming support for the idea that expressed economic interests are shaped by political, social, and cultural contexts, including particular configurations of

Theories of Secession in the Soviet Setting," *British Journal of Political Science* 30 (2000), pp. 31–56.

[16] Net tax payments are the amount, per capita, that regional citizens contribute to the federal budget in tax payments, minus the amount they receive back in federal subventions.

[17] See Chapter 2 for extended discussion of this point.

actors and institutions. To put it another way, economic interests are inter-subjectively constructed.

Based on this emerging research tradition as well as on my own empirical analysis of Russian regions, I argue that the economic claims advanced by regional movements share with nationalist claims a non-essentialist nature. I use the term *constructivist political economy* to refer to an approach to the economy that advances an argument for the intersubjectivity of economic interests based on insights from cognitive psychology, historical institutionalism, economic sociology, and social theory. Thus, returning to the debate over whether the richest or the poorest regions are most likely to seek greater sovereignty, I say both arguments are correct, or, if you like, they are both incorrect, because the sense of exploitation that drives economic claims for sovereignty, while not wholly divorced from material facts, is mediated by institutions and shared understandings of economic conditions.

If we consider the quantitative analysis of Russian regionalism in light of constructivist political economy, we can see how the same economic conditions might lead to different regional activism outcomes because the relevant aspect of the economic conditions – the *understanding* of the economic conditions – may not be the same as what is being picked up in data sets that focus only on unmediated structural conditions. In other words, there may be *multiple local interpretations* of economic conditions, which do indeed affect sovereignty movements, but the multiplicity of meanings muddles the effect of particular structural variables on sovereignty movements across all regions.

Imagined Economies

In trying to account for regional activism in Russia, one cannot escape the suggestion that in many cases regional elites did not see the same economic conditions and prospects for the regional economy as "objective" analysis would suggest. Over and over, regional leaders made statements about the economy that did not seem to match the observations of outside analysts. Instead, the expressed economic interests advanced by regional elites corresponded somewhat tenuously to the economic indicators contained for example in the data sets of the Russian State Statistical Committee (Goskomstat) or the Ministry of Finance. Yet these expressed economic interests were crucial to the development of regional political movements, regardless of their uncertain relationship to structural economic conditions.

In order to systematically analyze the existence of specifically *local* understandings of the economy, I collected nearly two thousand newspaper articles related to economic events in Samara and Sverdlovsk from over thirty local newspapers and journals covering the period of 1990 to 1993. By the early 1990s, Soviet central censorship had been nearly eliminated, and regional publications were increasingly able to give voice to local concerns and issues, including criticism of the central government. For these reasons, local newspapers in the early 1990s are an excellent source for documenting the ways in which local actors understood the world. Using discourse and quantitative content analysis, I documented interpretations in Samara and Sverdlovsk, and I compared those understandings with accounts of economic conditions found in quantitative data sets.

The findings from this systematic analysis were that, although data on structural economic conditions predict some regional understandings of the economy, the observed variance in understandings of the economy found in Samara and Sverdlovsk – and in particular greater negativity in Sverdlovsk compared to Samara – was not predicted by "objective" data on economic conditions.

I followed the analysis of economic understandings in Sverdlovsk and Samara with additional extensive content analysis of the movement for a Urals Republic in Sverdlovsk Oblast in order to examine whether and how the economic pessimism in Sverdlovsk was related to the region's autonomy movement.[18] That analysis clearly establishes that the movement for a Urals Republic was driven by negative interpretations of economic conditions, and, in particular, concerns over constitutional inequality and economic autonomy. My content analysis also provides evidence of a particularly *regional* understanding of the economy, in the sense that Sverdlovsk actors, in comparison with non-Sverdlovsk actors, share particular beliefs about the economy. That is, location was a significant predictor of the understanding of the basis for the sovereignty movement.

Thus, despite the prevailing certainty regarding the provenance of economic interests and economic claims, in my research I found that the relationship between economic conditions and expressed economic claims was not an expected one. The content analysis provides strong evidence that the assumed transparency and universality of data upon which most economic theories of sovereignty are based did not hold up to empirical

---

[18] Because there was no sovereignty movement in Samara, I could not analyze the discourse of claims for regional autonomy there, as I did for Sverdlovsk.

10

scrutiny. This finding of territorialized divergence between objective conditions and regional understandings suggests that differences in regional understandings of the economy can be considered a possible source of explanation of how similar economic conditions lead to different political outcomes.

The central argument of this book is that variation in regional activism is explained not by differences in structural economic conditions but by differences in understandings of the economy, which, in particular institutional contexts, resulted in differences in the imagination of economic interests. In the process of imagination, there is dynamic interaction between institutional context, events, and ideas in which understandings are activated and developed in response to certain experiences, and those understandings then themselves become the fuel for further action.

Returning to the initial empirical puzzle that motivated this analysis, in the case of Sverdlovsk, the rewriting of the oblast charter and the federal Constitution ignited the debate over inequality toward the region. This debate resonated with the already existing pessimism in understandings of local economic conditions held by actors in the region; negative understandings of the economy further exacerbated the sense of unacceptable constitutional and economic inequality toward the region. Moreover, the particular institutional context of fluid political and economic categories made some alternatives for action seem necessary and others impossible. In short, the movement for the Urals Republic can be explained by the institutional context of perestroika that opened up the conceptual possibilities for reconsidering the region's place in the Federation, the existence of negative local understandings of the economy, and the transformation of those understandings in the context of the institutional events of 1992–3.

By contrast, in the case of Samara Oblast, a movement for greater sovereignty simply did not occur. True, the idea of regional inequality did surface, especially when Samara's leaders were asked to comment on events in Sverdlovsk. Yet the idea of regional inequality had no apparent motive force toward initiating a movement. Pessimistic local understandings of the economy, the potential seedlings from which the idea of regional inequality could be cultivated into an interest in greater sovereignty, barely circulated in Samara, as opposed to Sverdlovsk. The difference between outcomes in Sverdlovsk and Samara regarding movements for greater sovereignty ultimately depended on the propensity of local actors in Samara for more positive understandings of their own regional economic conditions.

11

The case of Samara is an absence and, as such, offers an interpretive challenge. In terms of a sovereignty movement, there is simply nothing there, or at least nothing substantial. The chief value of this absence in Samara is that it functions to throw into greater relief the movement that did occur in Sverdlovsk. The case of Samara compels us to ask, all the more zealously: Why did Sverdlovsk, otherwise Samara's comparative twin, experience such a movement?

The fundamental argument that I make in opposition to earlier theorists is that objective economic conditions underdetermine regionalist outcomes; to put it in the language of other contemporary debates, economic advantage and disadvantage are as imagined as nations. In the literature on nationalism, which focuses mainly on the historical construction of ethnic and nationalist movements, the relative economic situation comes in as a deus ex machina to explain the variation. Scholars assume that ethnicity is fluid but that economic interests are definite and real. In contrast, I argue that expressed economic interests may well be as fluid as ethnicity, and the regional economy may be as imagined as the nation. Just as ethnic solidarity is an important social force weakly connected, if at all, to biological facts, so these collective economic claims may have a powerful impact on political life even if they are only weakly connected to "objective" economic facts. And, just as imagined communities are the relevant reality for nationalist movements, the imagination of the regional economy was the reality for regional movements in the Russian Federation.

The approach to the analysis of the economy in this book offers an alternative to the treatment of regional economic claims as simply the direct, mistaken, or purposefully manipulated representation of "objective" economic conditions. This conception of imagined economies differs significantly from others in the nationalism literature in that the economy is understood to be a set of multiple, locally legitimate, historically based understandings, rather than consisting of a "real" economy and then "false" or "mistaken" interpretations. The de-naturalization of economic data entails the acknowledgment that there is always mediation between the represented data and some kind of empirical reality. This mediation occurs as particular institutions, organizations, and actors influence, shape, and interact with the data.

The principal theoretical claim of my analysis is that it is necessary to make a crucial extension to the work on nationalism – broadly conceived to include nationalist, regionalist, and separatist movements – by bringing constructivist political economy approaches, including social theory, to the

Table I.1 *Summary of Imagined Economies Framework*

Material "facts"	→	Cognition and interpretation	→	Mediation of interpretations	→	Development of intersubjective understandings of the economy	→	Development of specific economic and political interests

scholarly literature on nationalism. This merging of constructivist political economy and nationalism, I call *imagined economies*. Building on the work of constructivist political economy with insights from schema theory and Bourdieu, my imagined economies framework suggests that (1) economic structural variables alone do not determine economic interests; (2) economic facts are subject to multiple understandings; and (3) interests and external conditions are mutually constituting. The imagined economies framework can be represented as shown in Table I.1.

Rather than assuming direct, unmediated, objective understanding of external reality, cognitive and constructivist models account for the heterogeneity of interpretations of the economy. The cognitive model is based on schema theory and relies on experience-based patterns to process new information. These experience-based patterns suggest local sources for specific understandings of economic conditions that may differ from an assumed universal objective economic reality. The constructivist approach to economic interpretations, which works in conjunction with the cognitive model, incorporates not only findings from economic sociology that treat the economy as a system embedded in broader political and social relations but also findings from historical institutionalism that consider the role of ideas, networks, and timing in shaping economic interests and institutions. Constructivist approaches to the economy suggest institutional mechanisms by which particular understandings come about. In addition, interpretations of economic reality are mediated by the social context. This process is based on insights from social theory, and in particular Pierre Bourdieu's concept of *habitus*, which represents the concept of systemic, naturalized power hierarchies that shape understandings in particular times and places. Through these cognitive, constructivist, and social processes, we can identify a set of particular local understandings of the economy.

Finally, the interplay of these intersubjective understandings of the economy in the institutional context of the time then produces specific articulated economic interests and demands for greater sovereignty, or the economic basis of sovereignty movements, which constitutes the final step in the analytical framework. In terms of the puzzle of Russian regionalism, the analytical framework of imagined economies suggests a research agenda that begins with identification of local interpretations of external economic conditions, and then analyzes those local understandings in particular social and institutional contexts.

Implications for Russian Federalism

The first Russian Republic, which extended from the end of the USSR in late fall 1991 to the formal adoption of the Federation's first constitution in December 1993, was a crucial period in the institutionalization of federal relations. The adoption of the December 1993 Constitution, which was the culminating event of the period, was a critical juncture in federal relations and continues to shape Russian politics today. In this respect, analysis of the events of 1991–3 is crucial to any understanding of the subsequent boundaries of political and economic life in the Russian Federation.

The movements for greater sovereignty among the Russian regions, such as Sverdlovsk's attempt to create a Urals Republic, deserve special attention in any analysis of the development of federalism in Russia for several reasons. First, Sverdlovsk's sustained efforts to gain political and economic equality were important in eventually changing the way all oblasts and krais were treated in the Constitution, that is, they were finally granted full equality with republics and other subjects of the Federation.[19] Second, on the basis of demands for the Urals Republic, Sverdlovsk played an important role in achieving elections at the regional and local level.[20] Finally, the Urals Republic experience highlights the institutionally contingent nature of sovereignty movements because it illustrates both the development of interests in sovereignty movements and the transformation of sovereignty demands into regional claims within existing institutional structures.

---

[19] De facto inequality persists, but the de jure recognition of equality paved the way for practical struggles over implementation within the existing institutional framework.

[20] Although the election of governors was a compromise between the federal executive and the legislature that was part of the debate over the composition of the Federation Council (upper house of parliament), Sverdlovsk's successful legal battle to have a popularly elected executive, like republics, was an important element in this outcome.

14

Implications of the Imagined Economies Framework

In addition to contributing to a better understanding of the development of federalism in Russia, analysis of the Sverdlovsk and Samara cases using the imagined economies framework also has implications for the study of nationalism and political economy. The central contribution of the imagined economies framework to the scholarly literature on nationalism is the idea that, like the nation, the economy is an imagined entity based on data that are subject to historical experience, institutional constraints, local interpretation, and power hierarchies. In brief, the imagined economies framework extends constructivism of the economy to the scholarly literature on nationalism.

Although in the empirical chapters that follow I focus on regional movements for greater sovereignty rather than nationalist or separatist movements per se, the imagined economies framework should apply to studies of nationalism more broadly because economic claims play a role in many, if not most, nationalist and secessionist movements. That is, by contributing to an understanding of the development of expressed economic interests and the economic bases of sovereignty movements in general, the imagined economies framework addresses an extensive range of sovereignty movements.

In addition, by explicitly denying primordial interests in sovereignty, and instead treating interests in greater sovereignty as historically and institutionally contingent, the imagined economies framework can contribute to a better understanding of secessionist movements. By positing that separatist movements never start out fully formed, and acknowledging fluidity in the goals and aspirations of sovereignty movements which are subject to change owing to the introduction of factors including major events such as war or violence, institutions, social mobilization, and new identity formation the imagined economies framework suggests a way to understand the development of extreme and costly interests, such as separatism.

Finally, the imagined economies framework should contribute to understanding the development of interests in the political economy literature. The analytical framework is a theoretical apparatus that can accommodate individual-level processing of information while remaining attentive to institutional context and the set of socially shared categories through which external reality is understood and interests are developed. In this way, the imagined economies framework follows on the growing political economy literature that goes beyond structural variables to problematize the relationship between economic conditions and economic interests and considers ways in which economic understandings are mediated by information effects, elite manipulation, framing, institutions, and social context. In other words, the imagined economies framework contributes to a better understanding of the development of economic interests and the ways in which politics and economics are related.

Chapter Outline

In Chapter 1, I present an analysis of regionalism in the Russian Federation from 1990 to 1993. I discuss the context of federalism and sovereignty movements, and I present an original data set on regional activism that I constructed on the basis of systematic content analysis of newspapers. The data set treats sovereignty as a continuum and is intended to capture the spectrum of sovereignty-oriented activism among the Russian regions. I also review existing theories of regionalism and sovereignty movements in the Russian Federation and USSR, and I use statistical analysis to test those theories. The conclusion of the quantitative analysis is that traditional economic variables do not explain Russian regionalism very well. However, I also discuss the issue of data complexity in order to suggest a continued focus on, and novel approach to, the role of economic factors in sovereignty movements.

In Chapter 2, I present a theoretical discussion of the imagined economies framework through a three-part analysis of the role of economic factors in the scholarly literature on nationalism by discussing, in turn, objectivist approaches to the economy, orthodox critiques of objectivism, and heterodox constructivist approaches to the economy. In the analysis of each approach to the economy, I discuss economic-based theories of nationalism consistent with each perspective. In the end, I combine insights from constructivist political economy, broadly construed, that is, contributions from cognitive science, economic sociology, historical institutionalism, and social theory, notably Bourdieu's concept of *habitus*, to arrive at the imagined economies framework, which I argue can make a contribution to the scholarly literature on nationalism.

In Chapter 3, I use Bourdieu's concept of *habitus* to consider the timing and differential development of regional understandings of the economy in Russia. Using habitus as a framework, I analyze the conceptualization of the massive changes in political and economic institutions from the Soviet

16

period to 1991 as a struggle between orthodox and heterodox projects. I argue that the doxa was the concept of a centrally controlled USSR and that perestroika ought to be considered an orthodox project aimed at propping up the crisis-ridden doxa of centralized Soviet political and economic power. Furthermore, I suggest that perestroika, which literally means "restructuring," produced a heterodox project that I term *rasstroika*.

I begin by briefly outlining the doxic conception of Soviet economic and political power and the challenges to the doxa presented by the stagnation of the late Brezhnev era. I then chronologically trace the events of 1985 to 1991, showing how orthodox perestroika actions by Gorbachev and his allies, aimed at strengthening the Soviet system, created opportunities for and were met by heterodox reactions aimed against the Soviet system. By examining the arena of political and economic governance during this period, I demonstrate that the conceptualization of political and economic categories by Russian actors underwent a radical transformation from a doxic position of central homogeneous control to heterogeneous open-ended possibility.

In Chapter 4, I provide an account of the institutional landscape of the first Russian Republic, from fall 1991 to December 1993. I detail both political institutional developments and the growing variance in regional economic conditions and inequality. I argue that the heterogeneity of categories and understandings made possible by rasstroika provided the conceptual and institutional context for the development of different understandings of regional economic interests and variance in regional strategies for political action.

In Chapter 5, I present a quantitative content analysis of regional understandings of the economy. This chapter focuses on two regions, Sverdlovsk and Samara Oblasts, in order to investigate the relationship between "objective" economic conditions and regional understandings of the economy. I situate the comparison of economic understandings by first outlining historical, geographic, and political conditions in the regions. Next I discuss the objective economic conditions of the regions and outline what one would expect in terms of understandings of the economy based on objective differences.

Using content analysis, I then systematically compare local representations of economic conditions with "objective" indicators. The analysis expands the intuition from Chapter 1 to demonstrate that local understandings of the economy are underdetermined by material conditions and cannot be readily predicted by objective accounts of economic conditions. I provide evidence for the claim that regional understandings of the economy in Sverdlovsk and Samara differ significantly despite similarity in objective conditions, and I show in particular that regional understandings of the economy in Sverdlovsk were more negative than in Samara.

To explain the relationship between regional understandings of the economy and movements for greater sovereignty, in Chapter 6 I outline the discourse of the movement for a Urals Republic through an analysis of newspaper articles published in Sverdlovsk. I examine the arguments for and against the Urals Republic in order to demonstrate that the idea that Sverdlovsk was subject to constitutional and economic inequality was at the heart of the sovereignty movement. The presentation of arguments in favor of the Urals Republic demonstrates that among Sverdlovsk actors there was a widely shared idea of inequality toward Sverdlovsk in comparison with other regions in the Russian Federation. And the presentation of arguments against the Urals Republic also suggests that the idea of inequality seemed to be particular to Sverdlovsk actors.

The data in this chapter suggest that, in attempting to create a Urals Republic, Sverdlovsk actors were voicing their demand that there should be economic and political equality among all subjects in the Federation, and that greater economic autonomy was the solution to the economic crisis facing the region. These findings are consistent with the evidence presented in Chapter 5 regarding the more negative understandings of the economy in Sverdlovsk compared to Samara. Thus, the analysis in the chapter demonstrates the relationship between particular understandings of the economy and movements for greater sovereignty.

Chapter 7 combines the findings of the content analysis in Chapters 5 and 6 with the analysis of institutional context in Chapters 3 and 4 to present a narrative of the movement for a Urals Republic. The discussion is arranged chronologically according to the major institutional events in the Russian Federation and supports the claim that, in regard to movements for greater sovereignty in the Russian Federation, the expression of economic and political interests arose out of the interaction between regionally shared understandings of the economy and the experience of regional actors in working through particular institutional contexts. In this way, the analysis highlights the role of institutional contingency and supports the concept of mutual constitution of local understandings and institutional and experiential contexts. That is, the creation and denouement of the Urals Republic and the few sparks of activity toward a movement for greater sovereignty in Samara were determined both by the particular underlying ideas about the regional economy and understandings of political and economic categories, and by the experience of regional actors within the institutional context of 1992–3. Finally, in the conclusion, I consider post-1993 developments in Russian federalism and extensions of the imagined economies framework.

1

Regionalism in the Russian Federation

THEORIES AND EVIDENCE

Federalism and sovereignty movements in Russia during 1990–3 have mainly been examined in terms of the actions of non-Russian ethnic republics. To gain a deeper understanding of the economic basis of sovereignty and autonomy movements for all regions of Russia, in this chapter I test existing explanations on an original data set that captures the spectrum of sovereignty-oriented activism among the *Russian* regions (oblasts and krais). I show that economic variables found in traditional quantitative data sets and used in previous explanations do not explain the pattern of *Russian* regionalism very well, but I analyze the complexity of economic data in Russia to suggest a different approach to the role of economic factors in sovereignty movements.

Regions and Federalism in the USSR and Russia

Any discussion of regionalism and federalism in the USSR and Russia must begin with an acknowledgment of the fact that the USSR was territorially divided in a very complicated way. The administrative and ethnic territorial divisions that constituted the state were irregular, uneven, and subject to change over the course of Soviet history. They were also fundamental in making and breaking the Soviet state.

Beyond urban and rural districts, there were, broadly speaking, three main administrative levels in the USSR, although not all levels existed in every territorial unit. As shown in Table 1.1, as of 1989, there were 15 union republics (*Sovetskaia Sotsialisticheskaia respublika* or Soviet Socialist Republic, SSR), whose specific names and institutional structures corresponded to ethnic groups (e.g., Estonian SSR, Ukrainian SSR). These ethnic groups, after whom the territorial units were named, had the status

Table 1.1 *Administrative-Territorial Units of the USSR, 1989*[a]

English Name	Russian Name	Number of Units	Ethnically Defined	Institutional Hierarchy Level
Union Republic (SSR)	*Sovetskaia sotsialisticheskaia respublika (SSR)*	15	Yes	Highest
Autonomous Republic (ASSR)	*Avtonomnaia SSR (ASSR)*	20	Yes	Middle
Oblast (or Region)	*Oblast'*	122	No	Middle
Krai (or Region)	*Krai*	6	No	Middle
Autonomous Oblast (AO)	*Avtonomnaia oblast' (AO)*	8	Yes	Lowest
Autonomous Okrug (AO)	*Avtonomnyi okrug (AO)*	10	Yes	Lowest

[a] Derived from "Soviet Union," *Library of Congress Country Studies*, available at *http://lcweb2. loc.gov/frd/cs/sutoc.html* (20 May 2004).

of "titular" (title) groups (e.g., Estonians in the Estonian SSR). Russians did not have their own republic; instead Russia was a federation called the Russian Soviet Federated Socialist Republic (*Rossiiskaia Sovetskaia Federativnaia Sotsialisticheskaia Respublika* or RSFSR).[1] All the union republics were subdivided into smaller territorial units that might have had either an ethnic or non-ethnic administrative basis. However, not every union republic contained the same types of subunits.

The second-level ethnic territorial units were called autonomous soviet socialist republics (*avtonomnaia Sovetskaia Sotsialisticheskaia respublika*, or ASSR), and there were a total of 20 ASSRs (as of 1989). But these ASSRs existed in only 5 of the 15 union republics.[2] The second-level non-ethnic units consisted of oblasts and krais, now commonly called

---

[1] The terms *Rossiiskaia* and *Russkaia* both translate into English as "Russian," but whereas *Russkaia* refers to Russian ethnicity, *Rossiiskaia* is a non-ethnic designation for the territorial state of Russia. An analogy might be *British* versus *English* (i.e., *English* referring to English ethnicity and *British* accommodating non-English groups such as Welsh, Scottish, or Irish). The RSFSR in the Soviet Union and the subsequent Russian Federation both officially use the non-ethnic term *Rossiiskaia*.

[2] The RSFSR contained 13 ASSRs; Azerbaijan had 2 (Nagorno-Karabakh and Nakhichevan); Georgia had 3 (Abkhazia, Ajaria, and South Ossetia); Tajikistan had 1 (Gorno-Badakhshan); and Uzbekistan had 1 (Karakalpak). Jeffrey Kahn, *Federalism, Democratization, and the Rule of Law in Russia* (New York: Oxford Univ. Press, 2002), p. 12.

regions.[3] However, 5 of the smaller union republics did not contain any oblasts, and krais existed only in the RSFSR.[4]

At the next level in the institutional hierarchy were two more types of ethnically defined units: the 8 autonomous oblasts (*avtonomnaia oblast*, or AO) and the 10 autonomous okrugs (*avtonomnyi okrug*, also AO), all of which were named after a specific ethnic group (e.g., Nenetskii AO). The 6 RSFSR krais contained both oblasts and autonomous oblasts or autonomous okrugs, but some AOs were located in oblasts as well. Regarding the ethnic territorial units, it should be noted that these were politically constructed units, and more often than not, the titles of the units did not accurately reflect the demographic concentration of ethnic populations. Many of the ethnic territories (republics and AOs) were home to more Russians than members of the titular groups; for example, of the 20 ASSRs only 8 did not have Russian majorities.

The next administrative level (which was actually the second level for those union republics that lacked ASSRs, oblasts, krais, and AOs) was the district (*raion*). In the case of large cities, these non-ethnically defined administrative units were further divided into city districts (*gorodskii raion*). And finally, there were thousands of villages and settlements.

Much of the history of the Soviet Union revolves around the evolution of this ethnic and territorial administrative system. The consolidation of the state entailed a lengthy process of establishing territorial control over one sixth of the world's land mass. In 1922, the Soviet Union consisted of four republics: the RSFSR, the Ukrainian Republic, the Belorussian Republic, and the Transcaucasian Soviet Federated Socialist Republic. From the RSFSR, five new union republics (Soviet Socialist Republics) were later created in the late 1920s and 1930s: The Turkmen SSR and the Uzbek SSR in 1924; the Tajik SSR, split off from the Uzbek SSR in 1929; and the Kazakh SSR and Kyrgyz SSR in 1936. Also in 1936, the Transcaucasian SFSR was split into the Armenian SSR, the Georgian SSR, and the Azerbaijanian SSR.

Beyond the union republics, Soviet history is also marked by many changes to lower-level territorial units. Because of changes in regional administrative principles, including the evolving policy toward nationalities

---

[3] Oblasts and krais probably should be called *provinces*, but the most commonly used term, especially in the post-Soviet period, is *region*. Therefore, to avoid confusion, throughout the book I use the term region to refer to oblasts and krais.

[4] Estonia, Latvia, Lithuania, Armenia, and Moldova had no oblasts.

as well as state goals of industrialization, the ASSRs, AOs, and oblasts were also consolidated and divided at various points.[5] For example, during the 1920s, many oblasts were reorganized; one of the first to be created was the Urals Oblast, which included the former Ekaterinburg, Perm', Tiumen', and Cheliabinsk *guberniias*.[6] Similarly, in 1934, right before the seventeenth Party Congress, the Urals Oblast was split into Sverdlovsk, Cheliabinsk, and Obsko-Irtyshsk Oblasts.[7]

In the 1940s, several changes related to the USSR's wartime territorial acquisitions occurred: Estonia, Latvia, and Lithuania were added as union republics (SSRs). In addition, territory from Germany created Kaliningrad, which became part of the RSFSR, and territory from Poland and Czechoslovakia was added to the Belorussian and Ukrainian Republics. Territory from Romania, called Bessarabia, was merged with territory from the Moldovan ASSR in Ukraine to create a union-level Moldovan SSR. Finnish territory was incorporated into the Karelo-Finnish Republic (a union republic); however, in 1956 this Republic was downgraded to an ASSR, the Karelian Autonomous Republic (within the RSFSR).[8] And finally, in the east, southern Sakhalin and the Kuril Islands were "returned" from Japan to the Soviet Union, becoming part of the RSFSR.

After the end of the Soviet Union, when the Russian Federation was established in December 1991, it consisted of the units that had been part of the RSFSR, including 16 ASSRs, 49 oblasts, 6 krais, 5 autonomous oblasts, and 10 autonomous okrugs. The ASSRs became simply "republics" (losing the "autonomous soviet socialist" prefix), and within the first few months of 1992, 4 of the 5 autonomous oblasts had been designated republics as well, bringing the number of republics to 20. Because Chechnia declared independence from the RSFSR in December 1991, the Republic of Checheno-Ingushetia was de facto split up, although Chechnia and Ingushetia were officially separated into 2 republics only a year later, which brought the total number of republics to its current number

---

[5] For an extended discussion of this phenomenon, especially regarding Soviet policy toward ethnic groups, see Terry Martin, *The Affirmative Action Empire: Nations and Nationalism in the Soviet Union, 1923–1939* (Ithaca, NY: Cornell Univ. Press, 2001).

[6] *Guberniia* was a prerevolutionary administrative-territorial unit. James R. Harris, *The Great Urals: Regionalism and the Evolution of the Soviet System* (Ithaca, NY: Cornell Univ. Press, 1999), p. 47.

[7] Harris, 1999, p. 144, archival reference in footnote 90.

[8] "Soviet Union," *Library of Congress Country Studies*, available at *http://lcweb2.loc.gov/frd/cs/sutoc.html* (20 May 2004).

Table 1.2 *Subjects of the Russian Federation, as of December 1993*

English Name	Russian Name	Number of Units	Ethnically Defined	De facto Institutional Hierarchy Level
Republic	*Respublika*	21	Yes	Highest
Oblast or Region	*Oblast'*	49	No	Middle
Krai or Region	*Krai*	6	No	Middle
Federal City	*Gorod federal'nogo znacheniia*	2	No	Middle
Autonomous Oblast (AO)	*Avtonomnaia oblast'*	1	Yes	Lowest
Autonomous Okrug (AO)	*Avtonomnyi okrug*	10	Yes	Lowest

of 21.[9] Another change from the RSFSR constituent units was the 2 "federal cities" of Moscow and St. Petersburg, created as such in 1993. Thus, as shown in Table 1.2, the Russian Federation is currently composed of 89 administrative units, now collectively called *subjects*. Among these subjects, there are six legal categories: 21 republics; 49 oblasts; 6 krais; 10 autonomous okrugs; 1 autonomous oblast; and 2 federal cities.

In the initial 1992 Federation Treaty, consistent with the Soviet experience of asymmetry, the republics were given more political and economic rights than other units. However, all 89 of these different territorial units were made de jure equal under the December 1993 Russian Constitution. Nevertheless, there are significant and persistent institutionalized social, economic, and political differences between the constituent territorial units. Indeed, the different types of subjects remain asymmetrical in almost every way: institutionally, ethnically, economically, geographically, and politically. (See Map 1.)

Institutionally, the republics have historically been and continue to be the most developed in terms of autonomous governance organizations. All the republics, for example, have elected "presidents" and their own "constitutions," most of which were ratified by the middle of 1994. All the other subjects have "governors" (except in the case of Moscow, which has a mayor), and instead of "constitutions," the other subjects each have a "charter" (*ustav*), the vast majority of which were ratified after mid-1995.[10]

---

[9] Edward Walker, "The Neglected Dimension: Russian Federalism and Its Implications for Constitution-making," *East European Constitutional Review* 2:2 (Spring 1993), p. 24.

[10] Kahn, 2002, p. 6.

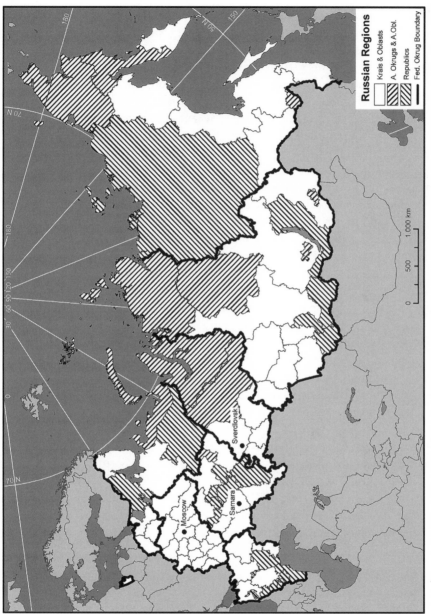

Map 1   Map of Russia's Regions. Map created by Y. M. Herrera using *ESRI Data & Maps*, 2000, and *World Complete GfK Macon*, 2003.

Oblasts and krais are institutionally almost exactly alike and are frequently grouped together in terms of institutional type (as I do in this study). The 2 federal cities, Moscow and St. Petersburg, each have a distinct institutional design and their status as subjects is relatively new.

The 10 autonomous okrugs and the 1 autonomous oblast are the least institutionally developed, having been under the tutelage of a particular oblast or krai for most of their administrative existence. Even more than ten years after they were supposedly made constitutionally equal to other subjects of the Federation, the legislation that would institutionalize autonomy from the host krais and oblasts has by and large still not been completed. An example of the persistent administrative-institutional interconnection is the fact that for many of these AOs, economic and demographic official state statistics still have not been disaggregated from the data of the host krai or oblast; this is a straightforward continuation of the Soviet practice, which combined the data. For example, very frequently the data for Tiumen' Oblast contains data for Khanty-Mansiisk and Iamalo-Nenets AOs.[11]

In terms of ethnicity and national identity, there is a great deal of variation across type of subjects within the Federation. In almost all the oblasts and krais, 80–90% of residents describe themselves as ethnically "Russian," and the non-Russian residents are not politically mobilized along ethnic lines.[12] Moreover, the oblasts and krais have been named after geographical or historical figures or events rather than after particular ethnic groups. Hence, oblasts and krais are often referred to as *Russian regions*. In contrast, the ethnic populations of republics and AOs vary considerably. According to the 1989 census, of the 31 republics and AOs, only 8 had titular group majorities, and Russians constituted a majority in 18, and a plurality in 3.[13] The remaining two had non-Russian and non-titular majorities.

Economically, the subjects of the Federation differ markedly, and this variance has increased since 1991. The one factor that is relatively similar across all subjects of the Federation is education, but levels of real income, unemployment, industrialization, raw materials extraction, exports,

[11] In the data I present in Table 1.3, I also had to include AO data in the host krai or oblast data because disaggregated data were largely unavailable for the 1990–3 period.
[12] Of course, the category of "ethnic Russian" is a constructed one and has changed over time. The demographic information presented here is based on responses to the 1989 census.
[13] At that time, the 31 ethnic units in the RSFSR included 16 ASSRs, 5 autonomous oblasts, and 10 autonomous okrugs. Today those same regions comprise 32 units: 21 republics, 10 autonomous okrugs, and 1 autonomous oblast. (Chechnia and Ingushetia had been 1 republic, hence the number 31 instead of 32.)

and urbanization all vary considerably.[14] Politically, there is a high degree of variation in terms of levels of democracy, as well as other more discrete institutio-nal factors such as regional party development or support for particular parties.[15]

Given the size of the Russian Federation, it is no surprise that, geographically, the subjects of the Federation vary in terms of climate and physical characteristics, but they also vary greatly in size, with the federal cities on one end of the spectrum and the Republic of Sakha at the other. At 3,103,200 square kilometers, Sakha would be the sixth largest country in the world, larger even than India. Neither is the population evenly distributed among the territorial units: The 32 republics and AOs constitute more than 50% of the territory of the Federation but only about 15% of the population.

Another relevant geographical and political distinction is the existence of historic, primarily geographically defined areas, which I term *macro-regions* that encompass a number of subjects. These include, for example, the Central Black-Earth region, the Volga region, the Caucasus, the Urals, Siberia, and the Far East. These historic areas roughly correspond to the macro-regions used by Goskomstat for regional statistical aggregation. And more recently, under President Putin, seven *federal districts*, based on existing military districts, were created. These federal districts, like the Goskomstat macro-regions, are in most cases similar to historic geographical divisions.[16]

The Parade of Sovereignties

The decline in the power of the Communist Party of the Soviet Union – the primary institution of power in the USSR – occurred in tandem with the rise of sovereignty movements among the union and autonomous republics throughout the Union.[17] The "parade of sovereignties" refers to the period

---

[14] In Chapter 4, I discuss the issue of growing regional inequality in more detail.

[15] On measuring regional democracy, see Kelly McMann and Nikolai Petrov, "A Survey of Democracy in Russia's Regions," *Post-Soviet Geography and Economics* 41:3 (2000), pp. 155–82; Vladimir Gel'man, "Regime Transition, Uncertainty and Prospects for Democratisation: The Politics of Russia's Regions in a Comparative Perspective," *Europe-Asia Studies* 51:6 (1999), pp. 939–56. On regional party development, see Vladimir Gel'man and Grigorii Golosov, "Regional Party System Formation in Russia: The Deviant Case of Sverdlovsk Oblast," *The Journal of Communist Studies and Transition Politics* 14:1–2 (March–June 1998), pp. 31–53; and Grigorii Golosov, *Political Parties in the Regions of Russia: Democracy* (Boulder, CO: Lynne Rienner Publishers, 2003).

[16] All subjects of the Federation and their corresponding macro-region and federal district are listed in the appendix in Table A1.

[17] The end of the Soviet Union is discussed in detail in Chapter 3.

of November 1988 to July 1991, when all 15 union republics and all the republics and most AOs within the RSFSR declared sovereignty.[18] Within the RSFSR, in an attempt to shift power away from union-level institutions, in 1990 Boris Yeltsin, then chairman of the RSFSR Supreme Soviet, famously called on constituent regions within the RSFSR to "take all the sovereignty you can swallow."

Despite the uniformity of declarations, Jeffrey Kahn's study of federalism and sovereignty in Russia made the very insightful argument that the meaning of sovereignty was not uniformly understood by the political elites across the Soviet Union.[19] That elites used the term to mean different things is not so surprising given the relatively novel and unpredictable process of state formation in which elites found themselves. However, the phenomenon of multiple meanings of sovereignty in the context of state fluidity illustrates the fact that the concept of sovereignty is bound up with the definition of the state.

Some scholars of international relations have argued that state sovereignty is a continuum and that levels of sovereignty vary among states.[20] The concept of federalism suggests that the same may apply to regions within states. In considering the structure of the Soviet Union and the issue of sovereignty and federalism, Kahn has conceptualized the sovereignty continuum as running between self-determination at one end, and full subordination at the other, with federalism occupying a middle ground.[21] Secession is the extreme of self-determination, taking a region outside the state altogether, but there are more intermediate positions, including "nullification" or the rejection of certain aspects of central rule, protection of certain spheres of autonomy, and allowance for local administration.[22] I have adapted Kahn's continuum in Figure 1.1. The main

---

[18] There are many sources for these declarations. For a collection of all declarations, see Kahn, 2002, p. 105, Table 5.1.

[19] Kahn, 2002, p. 89.

[20] David A. Lake, *Entangling Relations: American Foreign Policy in Its Century* (Princeton, NJ: Princeton Univ. Press, 1999); and Stephen D. Krasner, *Sovereignty: Organized Hypocrisy* (Princeton, NJ: Princeton Univ. Press, 1999). For analyses of post-Soviet Russian sovereignty, see Michael McFaul, "The Sovereignty Script: Red Book for Russian Revolutionaries," in Stephen D. Krasner, ed., *Problematic Sovereignty: Contested Rules and Political Possibilities* (New York: Columbia Univ. Press, 2001) pp. 194–223; and Alexander Cooley, "Imperial Wreckage: Property Rights, Sovereignty, and Security in the Post-Soviet Space," *International Security* 25:3 (winter 2000–1) pp. 100–27.

[21] For an excellent discussion of federalism and where Russia fits in comparative perspective, see Kahn, 2002.

[22] Kahn, 2002, Chapter 2.

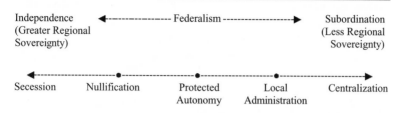

Figure 1.1 *Sovereignty Continuum* (Adapted from Kahn, 2002, p. 33)

addition is the concept of greater or less *regional* sovereignty corresponding to the independence–subordination dimension.

At the regional level, sovereignty is a measure of the degree of institution-alized control by specific actors (regional governments) over exchanges and agreements in or related to their own territory. In the modern era, virtually all governments must engage in thousands of agreements with other gov-ernments and organizations in order to regulate the spheres of political, economic, and social life in their territory. The more a regional govern-ment is able to control or regulate such agreements, the more sovereign one may consider it. Sovereignty then can be measured in degrees rather than as simply existing or not. Moreover, regional sub-state governments may also seek to increase their own sovereignty vis-à-vis the central government and other regions. One implication of this understanding is that if sovereignty is measured by degrees of control over regional decision-making, rather than necessarily as an attempt to gain statehood, then independent statehood is only one possible outcome for a movement for greater sovereignty.

Secession merits special attention. As Figure 1.1 suggests, the distinc-tion between secession and movements for greater sovereignty is a matter of degree. However, it is important to emphasize that secession differs from other points along the continuum in that it is an endgame move. It calls for the formation of a new state, rather than just evolution or change within the state and, therefore, is somewhat different from other attempts to gain greater sovereignty. In the Russian Federation, only Chechnia has contin-ued to pursue secession. All the other regions and republics either never wanted secession or have since scaled back their claims to greater autonomy.

Separatist movements rarely, if ever, start out as movements fully com-mitted to secession; rather, interest in secession builds as a result of failed, or at times successful, attempts to gain greater sovereignty. Despite the undeniable relationship between identity concerns or nationalism and secessionist movements, interests in secession are not primordially given.

29

Moreover, no movement for greater sovereignty can ever articulate consistently – from start to finish – the goals to which it aspires or the goals for which it will settle because these goals may change along the way owing to a range of factors that are not necessarily in the control of the proponents of a sovereignty movement. These types of factors may include, for example, major events such as war or violence, institutional changes, social mobilization, and new identity formation.

Given the fluidity of goals and aspirations of sovereignty movements, to focus only on those rare movements that turn out to be bona fide secessionist, would be to ignore the range of cases which could have sought secession, but ultimately did not. And due to this selection bias, one could gain only a very limited understanding of the origins of interests in greater sovereignty, or secession. Therefore, the question of why regions seek greater autonomy rather than full statehood, though limited in some ways, may still shed light on the overall question of movements for greater sovereignty, including secessionist movements.

Regionalism in the Russian Federation

In considering the broader question of sovereignty movements in the Russian Federation, the majority of scholarly attention has focused on the republics. This is reasonable insofar as republics such as Chechnia or Tatarstan appeared to pose the greatest threat to the integrity of the Federation. However, among the Russian regions, that is, the oblasts and krais and federal cities, there also was a significant degree of regional activism in the form of movements for greater sovereignty.[23] Moreover, the oblasts and krais provide an unusually good opportunity for the analysis of the development of interests in sovereignty movements. Among the Russian regions, there is variation in outcomes – many regions had sovereignty movements and many did not – but there also is stability in two of the main factors related to sovereignty movements, namely nationalist mobilization and institutional context.

As I discussed earlier, most of the Russian regions are over 80% ethnically Russian, and almost none had serious ethnic tensions. In addition, even though there were colossal institutional changes related to perestroika, the

---

[23] The two federal cities of Moscow and St. Petersburg are institutionally quite different from the oblasts and krais; therefore, even though they have predominantly Russian populations and had a high degree of activism toward greater sovereignty, I do not include them in the quantitative analysis with the other oblasts and krais.

breakup of the USSR, and the formation of the new Russian state, the oblasts and krais were institutionally similar with regard to the governance organizations necessary for political and economic autonomy. One can control, therefore, for two significant factors related to sovereignty movements – nationalism and institutions – by focusing specifically on Russian regions. This allows for systematic analysis of another important factor related to regionalism, namely economic interests.

To take advantage of the opportunities offered by the variety of Russian regions for the study of sovereignty movements, I sought comprehensive data on the level of regional movements for greater sovereignty in oblasts and krais. Although there are many case studies and scattered reports of regional attempts at greater sovereignty, there was no systematic source for measuring Russian regional activism. I therefore constructed a data set that treats sovereignty as a continuum and is intended to capture the spectrum of sovereignty-oriented activism among the Russian regions.[24] I included five weighted indicators of regional activism toward greater sovereignty and, on the basis of those indicators, compiled an "index of regional activism" for all of the oblasts and krais of the Federation during 1990–3. (See Table 1.3.)[25] The five indicators include:

1. A unilateral declaration of change in a region's administrative status before October 1993;
2. The adoption of a regional "constitution";
3. A non-binding referendum on sovereignty;
4. Assertions that regional law takes precedence over federal law; and
5. Assertions of economic autonomy.

The first indicator, unilateral change in administrative status, was the clearest and strongest signal of regional activism toward greater sovereignty and was therefore weighted most heavily: 3 in the index. This indicator marks a public unilateral declaration of the intent to change a region's

---

[24] For the republics and AOs, Daniel Treisman constructed a scale of separatist activism according to eleven indicators. His scale included: "Declared Sovereignty," "Raised Administrative Status," "Adopted Own Constitution," "Asserted Legal Supremacy," "Held Referendum on Supremacy," "Turnout <25% in Federal Election, 12/93," "Declared Independence," "Refused to Send Conscripts," "Independent Foreign Policy," "Asserted Right to Natural Resources," and "Asserted Right to Own Currency." Russian regions (oblasts, krais, and federal cities) are excluded from his study. Daniel Treisman, "Russia's 'Ethnic Revival': The Separatist Activism of Regional Leaders in a Postcommunist Order," *World Politics* 49:2 (1997), pp. 226–8.

[25] See Table A2 in appendix for source citations.

administrative status, that is, from "oblast" or "krai" to "republic."[26] The declaration had to have occurred before October 1993 in order to be counted in the index because, in the institutional chaos that followed violent conflict between President Yeltsin and the parliament in early October 1993, there were several declarations of changes in status. However, most of these decisions taken at that time were very short-lived (less than one week), and they indicated more about the uncertain political situation, especially tension between the legislative and executive institutions, than the strength or existence of a regional movement for greater sovereignty.

The second and third indicators, "adoption of a regional 'constitution'" and "non-binding referendum on sovereignty," constituted two of the three legal measures that oblasts or krais had to take to change their status in the Federation (the third was approval by the Supreme Soviet). Each of these steps was given a weight of 2 in the index because they were important formal steps on the path toward greater sovereignty. Interestingly, both of these legal measures were technically illegal. According the Federation Treaty of 1992, every oblast and krai was supposed to formulate a "charter" (*ustav*), but only republics were allowed to have "constitutions." Also, oblasts and krais were not allowed to have referenda on sovereignty. Several oblasts and krais nevertheless adopted "constitutions" and held non-binding referenda or "polls" (*opros*) on sovereignty. These acts were clearly attempts toward formally upgrading the region's administrative status and autonomy.

Finally, the fourth and fifth indicators measure less formal regional assertiveness toward greater sovereignty. Because these indicators included assertions and declarations that may or may not have actually been realized, and because there may have been other goals besides sovereignty involved in these declarations, these indicators were given a weight of 1 in the activism index. The assertion that regional law takes precedence over federal law is different from mere violations of federal law. As is well-known, there were thousands and thousands of violations of federal law by regions throughout the 1990s, and this process was only significantly reversed under President Putin. But in the 1990–3 period, there were specific declarations that regional law would take precedence over federal law, and

---

[26] These were *declarations* of changes in status rather than actual changes because since 1991 very few constituent units in the Russian Federation were actually able to change their status. The only actual changes were the four AOs that became republics and the division of Chechnia and Ingushetia into two separate republics in 1992. The creation in 1993 of the federal cities of Moscow and St. Petersburg was also a change in status for those cities, which had previously been oblast capitals.

this was, therefore, an assertion of regional sovereignty, rather than just a sign of confusion or ignorance of federal law. The assertion of economic autonomy included declarations of free economic zones, assertions of independent foreign economic policy, declarations of control over territorial natural resources, declarations of fiscal disobedience, and issuance of a regional currency. In contrast to mere rent-seeking or other types of unilateral economic actions by regional elites, the actions counted in this indicator were aimed at regional versus central control of the economy.

The data set and regional activism index are based on events from 1990 to 1993.[27] This period was chosen because it represents the period in which there were formal attempts to increase political sovereignty. Regional activism among the Russian regions began in approximately 1990, and the actual movements for greater sovereignty (i.e., regional social movements aimed at formally changing a region's legal status in the Federation) largely ended in December 1993 with the adoption of a new federal constitution. After 1993, regions did not stop making demands, but the parade of sovereignties and the regional movements for greater sovereignty were transformed into the more "normal" politics of debates over federalism. The actions noted in the first three indicators of the regional activism index (unilateral declarations, adoptions of "constitutions," and sovereignty referendums) stopped occurring after 1993. The last two indicators concerning declarations of increased legal and economic autonomy continued throughout the 1990s, but the rhetoric took a more muted form insofar as it was a call to further debate rather than a declaration of unilateral action.

The data in this table are derived from a systematic content analysis of *Izvestiia* and *Kommersant'-Daily* newspapers over four years, 1990–3. During this period, the newspapers were not indexed, nor available electronically, and thus I had to visually search daily papers for articles relating to the sovereignty indicators. Where possible, I also supplemented the data set with reports by other scholarly sources.[28]

The principal results of the analysis are presented in the second column on the left in Table 1.3, where an index score for regional activism based on

---

[27] The "parade of sovereignties" refers to sovereignty moments in the USSR. This regional activism index tracks sovereignty movements in *Russia*.

[28] The other two sources were Michael McFaul and Nikolai Petrov, eds., *Politicheskii al'manakh Rossii 1997*, vol. 1 (Washington, DC: Carnegie Endowment for International Peace, 1998), pp. 125–32, Table 1.3; and Beth Mitchneck, "An Assessment of the Growing Local Economic Development Function of Local Authorities in Russia," *Economic Geography* 71:2 (April 1995), pp. 150–70.

Table 1.3 *Indicators of Regional Activism Among Russian Regions, 1990–1993*

Region	Regional Activism Index Total Score	1. Unilateral Change in Administrative Status Before 10/93	2. Adoption of Regional "Constitution"	3. Non-binding Referendum on Sovereignty	4. Assertion that Regional Law Takes Precedence over Federal Law	5. Assertion of Economic Autonomy
	Total possible: 9	*Point weight:3*	*Point weight: 2*	*Point weight:2*	*Point weight:1*	*Point weight:1*
Altaiskii	1					1
Amurskaia	1					1
Arkhangel'sk	5	3			1	1
Astrakhan'	0					
Belgorod	1					1
Briansk	1					1
Cheliabinsk	7	3		2	1	1
Chita	6	3		2		1
Iaroslavl'	1					1
Irkutsk	4	3				1
Ivanovo	0					
Kaliningrad	1					1
Kaluga	0					
Kamchatskaia	1					1
Kemerovo	1					1
Khabarovsk	1					1
Kirov	0					
Kostroma	0					
Krasnodar	0					
Krasnoiarsk	7	3	2		1	1
Kurgan	3	3				
Kursk	1					1
Leningradskaia Oblast	6	3		2		1

Lipetsk	1					1
Magadan	1					1
Moskovskaia Oblast	7	3		2	1	1
Murmansk	0					
Nizhnii Novgorod	3	3				
Novgorod	1					1
Novosibirsk	1					1
Omsk	1					1
Orel	2					1
Orenburg	3	3			1	
Penza	0					
Perm'	3	3				
Primorskii	4	3		2		1
Pskov	2			2		
Riazan'	1				1	
Rostovskaia	1			2		1
Sakhalinskaia	3			2		1
Samara	0					
Saratov	4		2	2		
Smolensk	1				1	
Stavropol'	0					
Sverdlovsk	8	3	2	2	1	
Tambov	1					1
Tiumen'	4	3				1
Tomsk	6	3		2		1
Tula	0					
Tver'	0					
Ul'ianovsk	0					
Vladimir	0					
Volgograd	1					1
Vologda	9	3	2	2	1	1
Voronezh	4	3				

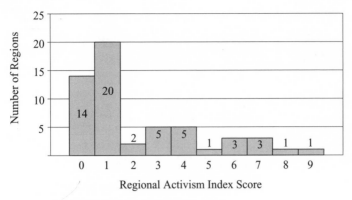

Figure 1.2 Regional Activism Distribution.

the sum of the weighted indicators is listed. From Table 1.3, we find that among the 55 Russian regions, 9 regions had scores of 5 or more in regional activism, 10 had scores between 3 and 4, 22 had scores of 1 or 2, and 14 regions had scores of zero. The total number represents an approximate measure of the strength of regional activism toward greater sovereignty and can be used to present an outline of the pattern of regionalism in the Russian Federation. Figure 1.2 shows the distribution of the regional activism index scores. From this figure, it is clear that many regions, over 60% (34 out of 55), had little or no activism toward greater sovereignty. Nevertheless, there was significant activism among the remaining 40%. Through further consideration of this pattern, we can gain a sense of how to approach the general question of the causes of regional movements for greater sovereignty in the Russian Federation, and also the more specific question of the economic basis for sovereignty.

Explaining Regional Movements for Greater Sovereignty

Given the results presented in Table 1.3 and Figure 1.2, we can turn to a number of explanations of sovereignty movements in the USSR and Russian Federation to analyze the observed pattern of regional activism. I will discuss theories related to nationalism, institutions, elite mobility, bargaining, and structural economic factors to provide theoretical justification for the further quantitative analysis of the regional activism data that follow.

As I noted in the preceding discussion of types of subjects of the Russian Federation, the oblasts and krais are overwhelmingly ethnically Russian, and there has not been significant nationalist activity, either Russian or non-Russian, in any of the oblasts and krais.[29] Therefore, although nationalism is one of the primary explanations for separatist actions of the union republics of the USSR and some of the republics of the Russian Federation, it was not a factor in movements for greater sovereignty among the Russian regions.[30]

Along with nationalism, state-level and regional-level institutional factors were also important variables in the development of sovereignty movements in the USSR.[31] At the state level, the institutional configuration of the USSR, and in particular the non-integrative federalized system that relied on the Communist Party for cohesion, turned out to be remarkably unstable after the destruction of the CPSU.[32] In the case of the Russian Federation, the weakness of the new state was undoubtedly a factor in regional and

---

[29] For an analysis of the development of Russian nationalism in general, see Yitzhak Brudny, *Reinventing Russia: Russian Nationalism and the Soviet State, 1953–1991* (Cambridge, MA: Harvard Univ. Press, 1998).

[30] The literature on nationalism in the USSR is well-developed. Two studies that stand out are Ronald G. Suny, *Revenge of the Past: Nationalism, Revolution, and the Collapse of the Soviet Union* (Stanford, CA: Stanford Univ. Press, 1993); and Mark Beissinger, *Nationalist Mobilization and the Collapse of the Soviet State* (New York: Cambridge Univ. Press, 2002). For noteworthy analyses of nationalist mobilization in the Russian Federation, see Elise Giuliano, "Who Determines the Self in the Politics of Self-Determination? Identity and Preference Formation in Tatarstan's Nationalist Mobilization," *Comparative Politics* 32:3 (April 2000), pp. 295–316; Rogers Brubaker, *Nationalism Reframed: Nationhood and the National Question in the New Europe* (Cambridge Univ. Press, 1996), pp. 23–54; Dmitry Gorenburg, *Minority Ethnic Mobilization in the Russian Federation* (New York: Cambridge Univ. Press, 2003); and Dmitry Gorenburg, "Regional Separatism in Russia: Ethnic Mobilisation or Power Grab?" *Europe-Asia Studies* 51:2 (1999), pp. 245–74. In contrast to others who argued that cultural claims were actually attempts to get more economic power or resources, Gorenburg argues instead that a review of the discourse of republican elites shows that they used the rhetoric of economic claims to increase cultural autonomy quietly. For an analysis of ethnic violence in the post-Soviet states, see Monica Duffy Toft, *The Geography of Ethnic Violence* (Princeton, NJ: Princeton Univ. Press, 2003).

[31] Some prominent analyses that focus on institutional factors in examining the breakup of the USSR (in comparison to other cases, e.g., Yugoslavia or the Russian Federation) include Valerie Bunce, *Subversive Institutions: The Design and the Destruction of Socialism and the State* (New York: Cambridge Univ. Press, 1999); and Gail W. Lapidus, "Asymmetrical Federalism and State Breakdown in Russia," *Post-Soviet Affairs* 15:1 (1999), pp. 74–82. Bunce considers state disintegration (in Yugoslavia, the USSR, and Czechoslovakia) and argues that institutional design and opportunities for change in the 1980s (both domestic and international) explain the differences in how states disintegrated (i.e., peace versus war). Lapidus analyzes the differences between the Russian Federation and Soviet cases. She cites differences in geography and ethnicity but argues that institutional and historical factors were especially important insofar as none of the Russian republics had the experience of independent statehood or as much institutional autonomy as the union republics.

[32] I analyze this process in more detail in Chapter 3.

State S
as foster

republican assertiveness.[33] Yet the general context of state weakness cannot explain the *variation* in levels of sovereignty demands among the Federation's constituent units. Looking to the sub-state level, however, the institutional context was a significant variable in sovereignty outcomes. The only constituent units of the USSR that gained full independence and statehood were the union republics – and this was despite large differences in ethnic mobilization, economic resources, and geography. Given this experience, by focusing on only oblasts and krais, and thus holding the variable of institutional type constant, I am able to consider the effect of other, namely economic, variables on the observed variation in regional activism.

Sov on bargain
Steal.

With regard to oblasts and krais, perhaps the most prominent explanation for movements for greater sovereignty in the scholarly literature is that regional activism was actually just a bargaining strategy used by regions to extract resources from the center. Steven Solnick was among the first to articulate this argument.[34] On the face of it, this is correct insofar as there is no doubt that negotiation over federal political and economic boundaries – indeed bargaining – was going on in the early 1990s. Moreover, central bargaining with regions as well as nations and national elites in times of state crisis was part and parcel of the Russian Revolution and the formation and development of the USSR.[35] Thus, it really is not especially surprising to see federal bargaining again at the end of the USSR in conjunction with the formation of the new Russian state.

There are now several varieties of bargaining arguments aimed at explaining regional activism.[36] Solnick considered the issue of collective action and argued that there was greater collective action among the republics,

---

[33] For more on this point, see Lapidus, 1999.

[34] Steven L. Solnick, "Federal Bargaining in Russia," *East European Constitutional Review* 4:4 (Fall 1995), pp. 52–8.

[35] For work on the relationship between war and concessions to non-Russian nations after the revolution, see Jurij Borys, *Sovietization of Ukraine, 1917–1923: The Communist Doctrine and Practice of Self-Determination* (Edmonton: Canadian Institute of Ukrainian Studies, 1980); and Mark von Hagen, "The Great War and the Mobilization of Ethnicity in the Russian Empire," in Barnett R. Rubin and Jack L. Snyder, eds., *Post-Soviet Political Order: Conflict and State-Building* (New York: Routledge, 1998), pp. 34–57. On regional bargaining in the early Soviet and Stalin period, see Harris, 1999. For the postwar period, see Donna Bahry, *Outside Moscow: Power, Politics, and Budgetary Policy in the Soviet Republics* (New York: Columbia Univ. Press, 1987); and Jerry Hough, *The Soviet Prefects: The Local Party Organs in Industrial Decision-Making* (Cambridge, MA: Harvard Univ. Press, 1969).

[36] Steven Solnick, "Will Russia Survive? Center and Periphery in the Russian Federation," in Rubin and Snyder, 1998; Mikhail Alexseev, "Decentralization Versus State Collapse: Explaining Russia's Endurance," *Journal of Peace Research* 38:1 (2001), pp. 101–6; and Daniel

as opposed to the Russian regions (oblasts and krais). He also argued in particular that the movement for a Urals Republic was a mechanism for collective action among five Urals oblasts, but that ultimately the center was able to effectively block collective action among the oblasts by offering financial rewards to specific regions. Daniel Treisman largely repeated these earlier bargaining arguments in his study of region-center relations in 1992–6, arguing that the center pursued a strategy of selective fiscal appeasement, economically paying off demanding regions in exchange for political support.[37]

The fundamental problem with the bargaining literature as an explanation for sovereignty movements – among either the Russian regions or republics in both the Russian Federation and the USSR – is that it does not address the specificity of sovereignty claims per se, and it does not explain regional *variation* in interests for greater sovereignty because bargaining models are essentially structural economic arguments. Bargaining models tend to treat sovereignty claims as a mechanism for realizing other interests in that a region's claim for greater sovereignty is treated as a hollow shell concealing other, mainly economic, interests. If sovereignty claims are treated this way, then the question of why regions pursue greater sovereignty rather than some other political or economic demand is sidestepped because, following a functionalist logic, sovereignty claims should arise whenever they would seem to be an effective means to achieving other regional economic or political goals.

A second problem with bargaining models is that they assume that structurally similar regions will behave in similar ways. In the Russian case, however, not all economically similar regions sought separatism or greater autonomy. Returning to the observations in Table 1.3 and Figure 1.2, the question of what explains the pattern remains. To the extent that bargaining arguments recognize variation in regional strategies, they tend to focus on underlying economic structural variables as the basis for regions' ability to make demands on the center.[38] This move essentially changes the explanation for sovereignty movements to an argument based on economic structural variables.

Along these lines, in examining nationalism in the Soviet Union, several authors have argued that the most economically advanced regions were

S. Treisman *After the Deluge: Regional Crises and Political Consolidation in Russia* (Ann Arbor, MI: Univ. of Michigan Press, 1999).

[37] Treisman, 1999.

[38] Treisman, 1997.

the most separatist.[39] Henry Hale argued that separatism in the USSR was driven by economic concerns, and specifically that the wealthy regions were likely to secede first. The logic of his argument was that, in an ethnically diverse state, there is a potential for exploitation, and "rich regions have the most to lose in case of exploitation, while, conversely, poor regions only risk cutting themselves off from technology transfer, access to high value-added jobs and development subsidies."[40] Similarly, Daniel Treisman examined republics within the Russian Federation and argued that underlying economic variables (industrial wealth, export capacity, natural resource base, tax base, and population) provide regions with bargaining power vis-à-vis the center and therefore are the strongest predictors of separatist activism.[41]

In an extension of economic conditions to include the attributes of modernization, Philip Roeder, in his study of the republics of the Soviet Union, argued that the most modernized regions were the ones most likely to seek greater sovereignty. He wrote, "it is the nationalities with the highest levels of educational, occupational, and often political attainment, rather than the disadvantaged or marginal ones, that have advanced the most ambitious agendas for change and engaged in the most extensive protest."[42] In many ways, the focus on the attributes of modernization and development is consistent with theories, such as Ernest Gellner's, which link the development of nationalism and the nation-state to processes of economic development and industrialization.[43]

Quantitative Analysis of Existing Theories

To evaluate existing explanations for movements for greater sovereignty, I analyzed the effects of several variables suggested by the theories on the dependent variable of regional activism. Because the variables of ethnicity and institutional type have been held constant by the selection of only Russian regions (oblasts and krais) in the pool of cases, I was able to focus on and evaluate the effects of several economic variables.

---

[39] See for example, Philip G. Roeder, "Soviet Federalism and Ethnic Mobilization," *World Politics* 43:2 (January 1991), pp. 196–232; Henry Hale, "The Parade of Sovereignties: Testing Theories of Secession in the Soviet Setting," *British Journal of Political Science* 30 (2000), pp. 31–56; and Treisman, 1997.

[40] Hale, 2000, p. 34.

[41] Treisman, 1997.

[42] Roeder, 1991, p. 197.

[43] Ernest Gellner, *Nations and Nationalism* (Ithaca, NY: Cornell Univ. Press, 1983).

I constructed two basic models: a static model based on the average values of twelve indicators for each of the regions for the four years of 1990–3, and a model of the change in seven variables from 1990 to 1993 (i.e., 1993 as a percent of 1990). The variables in the first model, the *Regional Conditions* model, are based on theories of modernization, economic structure, and bargaining and indicate the economic conditions of the region during the period under study. The variables in the *Regional Change* model indicate how economic conditions changed, either declined or improved, during same period. The Regional Change model is motivated by the idea of relative deprivation and expectations. To date, no one has applied this theory to Russian regionalism, but it seemed worth considering the idea that economic conditions might influence regional activism, not via recognition of current endowment but instead via recognition of how economic conditions have changed during the transition to a market economy and what conditions should be, given past economic conditions.

In some cases, data for all four years were not available, and so, as noted, available data were used instead. Similarly, there were cases where data either did not change over time (e.g., distance from Moscow) or where data for more than one year were not available (e.g., net tax payments); therefore, those variables were not included in the Regional Change model. Many of the economic variables were given in current rubles without the relevant price deflators. In order to average values across the four-year period, I normalized individual regional ruble values for each year into a percent of the Russian average (except exports and raw materials, which are a percent of the Russian total). For example, if the Russian average per capita income in 1990 were 200 rubles and the regional monthly income were 180, the region would be at 90% of the Russian average. I then averaged those percentages to arrive at an "average percent of the Russian average" (e.g., if regional income were 90%, 85%, 95%, and 90% of the Russian average for the four years, the average would be 90% for the 1990–3 period). Most of the data come from Goskomstat, but the exceptions as well as all other source details are discussed in the appendix.[44]

The averaged variables that measure economic conditions include real income, per capita industrial production, regional raw materials production,

---

[44] Goskomstat is the Russian State Statistical Committee. Owing to the historic practice of combining AO data with the host krai or oblast data, I have been forced to include AO data in the data for the host krai or oblast. This is disappointing because it greatly increases the values for certain oblasts or krais (notably Tiumen'), but it was impossible to avoid because the data were not disaggregated by Goskomstat.

Table 1.4 *Regional Conditions Model: Expected Relationships Between Independent Variables and Regional Activism, According to Select Theories*

Variables in Modernization Theory (Roeder)	Expected Effect on Regionalism	Variables in Economic Structural Theories (Hale, Treisman)	Expected Effect on Regionalism	Variables in Bargaining Theories (Treisman)	Expected Effect on Regionalism
Real income	+	Real income	+		
Industrial production	+	Industrial production	+	Industrial production	+
Raw materials	+	Raw materials	+	Raw materials	+
Exports	+	Exports	+	Exports	+
Defense employment	+	Defense employment	+		
Unemployment	−	Unemployment	−		
Net tax payments	+	Net tax payments	+	Net tax payments	+
Urbanization	+				
Education	+				
				Population	+

regional export values, defense employment, unemployment, and per capita net tax payments. The variables that measure socioeconomic conditions include urbanization and education. Other variables included as controls include population, distance from Moscow, and strike activity.[45]

The variables that measure changes in economic conditions from 1990 to 1993 include real income change, per capita industrial production change, regional raw materials production change, regional value of exports change, and unemployment change.[46] Change in socioeconomic conditions is indicated by change in the level of urbanization. Population change is included as a control variable.

The bargaining, structural economic, and modernization arguments overlap and are similar in their predicted directionality of economic variables. It is useful, however, to separate them analytically in order to test different economic-based models of regionalism. As outlined in Table 1.4, if the argument for economic structural variables articulated by Hale and Treisman is correct, real income, industrial production, raw materials

---

[45] See Table A3 in the appendix for a full description of the variables and source citations.
[46] See Table A4 in the appendix for a full description of the variables and source citations.

production, and export values should have a positive effect on regional activism. Defense employment, as a signal of industrial strength, should also be positive.[47] Unemployment, signaling a depressed regional economy, should have a negative effect. And finally, assuming taxes and federal transfers are based in some way on economic revenues and needs, net tax payments should have a positive effect because those regions that pay the highest taxes (signaling a strong tax base) and receive the fewest federal subsidies should be the wealthiest regions. If Roeder's modernization argument holds, the variables associated with increasing modernization (i.e., urbanization and education) should also both have a positive effect on regional activism. Treisman's 1997 bargaining model is quite close to the economic structural model and posits a positive relationship between regional activism and industrial production, raw materials, exports, net tax payments, and population.[48]

Regionalism might be a function of economic decline in that those regions that suffer the most might be the most likely to seek greater sovereignty in order to attempt to improve their economies on their own. We can call this the "economic downturn" argument. Similarly, regionalism might result not just from structural economic decline but also from decline in the level of development of the economy more broadly construed – we can call this the "demodernization" thesis. The years between 1990 and 1993 may seem like a short period to measure change, but in those years Russian gross domestic product (GDP) continued its spiral downward inherited from the late Soviet period falling –4.0%, –5.0%, –14.5%, and –8.7%, respectively, and Russian life expectancy declined by 6% (4.24 years) in those four years.[49]

Table 1.5 illustrates the predicted relationships between regional activism and change in economic conditions. If the economic downturn thesis is correct, decreasing real income, per capita industrial production, regional raw materials production, and regional value of exports should be correlated with more regional activism; in other words, the relationship should be negative. Conversely, increasing unemployment should be positively

---

[47] One might argue that defense employment should be negative according to economic structural models, but that would depend on the assumption that defense industries have negative economic value for a region. A more conventional view is that the defense industry was a major component of Soviet industrialization and therefore those regions with extensive defense industries were more industrialized, and hence economically stronger.

[48] Treisman, 1997.

[49] European Bank for Reconstruction and Development (EBRD), *Transition Report 1999* (London: EBRD, 1999), p. 73, and Goskomstat.

Table 1.5 *Regional Change Model: Expected Relationships Between Independent Variables and Regional Activism, According to Select Theories*

Variables in Demodernization Theory	Expected Effect on Regionalism	Variables in Economic Downturn Theory	Expected Effect on Regionalism
Real income change	–	Real income change	–
Industrial production change	–	Industrial production change	–
Raw materials production change	–	Raw materials production change	–
Exports change	–	Exports change	–
Unemployment change	+	Unemployment change	+
Urbanization change	–		

correlated with regional activism. For the demodernization argument, the same relationships should hold, but decreasing urbanization should also be correlated with increasing regional activism.

To test these relationships I regressed the variables according to the theoretical models on the logged dependent variable of regional activism.[50] The results of the Economic Change models are not very informative. None of the variables in any of the specifications turned out to be significant.[51]

In the Regional Conditions models, displayed in Table 1.6, overall the results are rather weak: Almost all the variables are not significant, the coefficients are low, and the adjusted R-squared values are very low – in one case negative. Population turns out to be significant in the bargaining specification and the specification with all the variables.[52] However, the most surprising and interesting finding is the direction and significance of net tax payments across all the model specifications. Net tax payments is the

---

[50] I used the natural log of the scores on the Index of Regional Activism [log (1 + activism)] to get a more normal distribution of the dependent variable. Also, I was not able to get data for all four years and thus have used what was available as noted in Table A4 in the appendix.

[51] The regression results are listed in Table A5 in the appendix.

[52] As a check, I tried the modernization and economic structure specifications with population as a control variable. The results were just about the same: Only net tax payments was significant, and the coefficient and standard errors were very similar. In the modernization specification with population, the coefficient was −0.0011286, and the standard error was 0.000544, significant at the 0.05 level; in the economic structural specification with population, the coefficient was −0.0009886, and the standard error was 0.0005236, significant at the 0.10 level.

Table 1.6 *The Effect of Economic Conditions on Regional Activism (OLS regression coefficients, standard errors in parentheses)*

	All	Modernization	Economic Structure	Bargaining
Real income	0.0030892	0.0015106	0.0017873	
	(0.006819)	(0.0067282)	(0.0065438)	
Industrial production	0.6812877	0.4355962	0.1488653	0.2451135
	(0.5177489)	(0.4912504)	(0.3767089)	(0.3502726)
Raw materials	0.0176576	0.0037579	0.0026322	0.0011606
	(0.0212881)	(0.0153405)	(0.0149918)	(0.0132746)
Exports	−0.0023483	0.1044443	0.1200215	0.0803728
	(0.103894)	(0.0899885)	(0.0829978)	(0.0799302)
Defense employment	0.0872371	0.1511512	0.1050818	
	(0.1316799)	(0.1265165)	(0.1142429)	
Unemployment	−0.0034816	−0.0000938	−0.0012469	
	(0.0072427)	(0.0071982)	(0.0062653)	
Net tax payments	**− 0.0010711**[*][a]	**−0.0011759**[**]	**−0.0010443**[**]	**−0.0009165**[**]
	(0.0006463)	(0.0005537)	(0.0005288)	(0.000498)
Urbanization	−0.0125025	−0.0123844		
	(0.0136666)	(0.013361)		
Education	0.0058063	0.0055929		
	(0.018727)	(0.0171013)		
Population	**0.0036585**[**]			**0.0025942**[**]
	(0.0018269)			(0.0014819)
Distance from Moscow	0.001085			
	(0.0011758)			
Strike activity	−0.0003962			
	(0.000372)			
Constant	0.6285774	1.052028	0.7109146	0.4531214
	(1.651857)	(1.434981)	(0.8439012)	(0.3586306)
Number of obs =	55	55	55	55
F =	(12, 42) 1.16	(9, 45) 0.94	(7, 47) 1.10	(5, 49) 2.04
Prob > F =	0.345	0.5028	0.3787	0.0897
R-squared =	0.2482	0.1579	0.1408	0.1721
Adj R-squared =	0.0334	−0.0105	0.0128	0.0876
Root MSE =	0.71006	0.726	0.71756	0.68985

[a] significant at the 0.105 level, *significant at the 0.10 level, ** significant at the 0.05 level.

amount, per capita, that regional citizens contribute to the federal budget in tax payments, minus the amount they receive back in federal subventions. All three of the previous models of the economic basis of movements for greater sovereignty (i.e., the modernization, economic structure, and bargaining models) would have predicted a positive relationship; in other words, the higher the net tax payments are, the more likely regional activism is. However, here in the case of the Russian regions, the regression results suggest, controlling for a range of other variables, that the relationship is negative, namely, ceteris paribus, the higher net tax payments are, the lower the level of regional activism is.

The net tax payments coefficients refer to a unit change in the regional per capita net tax payment, as a percent of the Russian average; that is, a one percent change in the per capita net tax payment in a given region would result in approximately one-tenth of a percent unit change in the log-activism value.[53] While the coefficients indeed are relatively small, the directionality, given the predictions of existing theories, is interesting nonetheless.

In order to probe this relationship further, I did a bivariate regression of net tax payments on regional activism, and I plotted the relationship in Figure 1.3. In the bivariate regression, net tax payment turns out to be both insignificant and *positive*, and the adjusted R-squared is negative.[54] However, Figure 1.3 shows that one region, Tiumen', is a rather extreme outlier, and by eliminating Tiumen' the bivariate coefficient becomes negative, though still insignificant.[55] These bivariate regressions suggest that there must be other variables seriously confounding the relationship between net tax payments and regional activism, and it is only by holding those constant, as in the multiple regression models, that the effect of net tax payments on regional activism becomes significant (and negative when all cases are included).

One point that is clear from Figure 1.3 and Table 1.6 is that, at a minimum, the interpretation of the effect of economic conditions on regional activism is not simple. Net tax payments, the only variable besides population that had a significant effect, was negative, but previous theories predicted it would be positive. Moreover, the effect of this variable is only

---

[53] The log-activism values range from 0 to 2.30, with a mean of 0.90 and a standard deviation of 0.72.

[54] The coefficient was 0.0000388; the standard error was 0.0003398.

[55] The coefficient was −0.0004816; the standard error was 0.0005094. It should be noted that these Tiumen' data include the net tax contributions of the two very wealthy AOs Khanty-Mansiisk and Iamalo-Nenets.

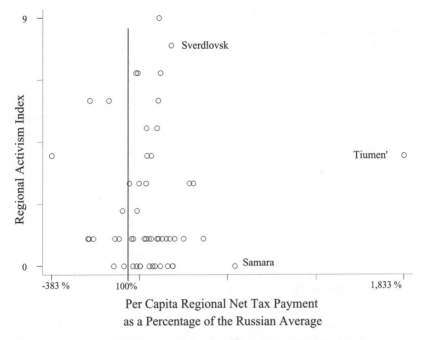

Per Capita Regional Net Tax Payment
as a Percentage of the Russian Average

Figure 1.3   Regional Activism and Regional Per Capita Net Tax Payment

significant when other variables, such as population and exports in particular, are held constant.

In considering the theoretical interpretation of these findings, we might conclude that previous theories (e.g., Hale, Roeder, and Treisman), which considered separatist activism in the USSR and ethnic republics of the Russian Federation, did not hold up when extended to the Russian regions. This is somewhat surprising because, given the fact that ethnicity and institutions have been held constant, one might argue that the Russian regions are a relatively more likely site for economic-based sovereignty movements. Nevertheless, the modernization and structural economic variables suggested by previous theories did not hold up among these Russian regional cases.

Data Complexity and Multiple Local Understandings of the Economy

Toward a more complete understanding of the relationship between economic factors and political action, and in particular the negative relationship between net tax payments and regional activism, it is worth considering the nature of economic information in the late Soviet and post-Soviet period, as well as the relationship between the economy and variables used to describe it. Perestroika began the process of restructuring the system of political and economic authority in the Soviet Union, and this process continues into the present through the continual development of new state political and economic institutions.[56] This process of state restructuring had a major impact on the measurement and conceptualization of economic indicators. The primary institution for economic (and demographic) data, the USSR Central Statistics Administration (*Tsentral'noe Statisticheskoe Upravlenie SSSR*, or TsSU), was both organizationally and conceptually transformed.[57] Organizationally, in 1987, TsSU was transformed into Goskomstat USSR (*Gosudarstvennyi Komitet SSSR po Statistike*), and with the breakup of the USSR in 1991, Goskomstat USSR became Goskomstat of the Russian Federation. However, the conceptual changes in Russian economic statistics following the end of the USSR were just as, if not more, consequential for economic understandings than the organizational changes.

The shift to a market-oriented economy entailed much more than a change in the ownership of property. The end of state planning as a concept removed one of the central functions of state statistical agencies – tracking plan fulfillment – and replaced it instead with the construction of Western types of market-based value indicators consistent with the development of a system of national accounts (SNA). This shift coincided with the goal of standardization of Russian economic information with international norms.

But market-based value indicators require prices. The move to market-based value indicators could only take place with the introduction, in 1992, of free prices on most goods, energy excepted.[58] The introduction of Western types of value indicators and the shift to a system of national accounts (SNA) then made Russian-produced estimates of GDP possible. The establishment of a SNA represents a major step toward bringing the content and categories of Russian economic statistics in line with international norms, and it would be hard to overstate the scale of change in conceptual categories

---

[56] See Chapter 3 for a more detailed discussion of perestroika.

[57] *Goskomstat Rossii, Rossiiskaia gosudarstvennaia statistika, 1802–1996* (Moscow: Izdat tsentr, 1996).

[58] However, some monetary reforms as well as the imposition of sales taxes in the late 1980s caused consumer prices to rise even in 1990.

and importance of this change in terms of its effect on understandings of the Russian economy.[59]

The move to international economic indicators was rapid but did not happen overnight. The first estimates of gross regional product (GRP) began in 1994 and were published officially in 1998.[60] For the 1990–3 period, there are no official estimates of GRP. And, even with these newer GRP estimates, the understanding of regional contributions to overall Soviet or Russian GDP remains very complicated, and much of this is owing to the difficulty of assessing the relevant prices. For example, Richard Ericson's work on Soviet input-output tables suggests that the true costs of production were concealed as a result of underpricing of energy supplies and overvaluing of manufactured goods.[61] The effect of this price difference is that in industrial regions, such as Sverdlovsk, which essentially had been receiving subsidized energy inputs, the region's contribution to overall GDP would have been overvalued. Moreover, even when using the partially liberalized energy prices of the post-1992 era, the construction of GRP during the inflationary 1990s remains very complicated because small differences in price deflators have large effects on calculating changes in GRP and GDP.[62]

Another indicator that would seem very important to regional activism, which was also only available officially after 1994, was federal transfers (and thus net tax payments). During Soviet times, it was impossible for any

[59] For analyses of the shift to a SNA, see Shinichiro Tabata, "Changes in the Structure and Distribution of Russian GDP in the 1990s," *Post-Soviet Geography and Economics* 37:3 (1996), pp. 129–44; Pavel Guzhvin, "Rossiiskaia statistika segodnia zavtra," *Voprosy ekonomiki*, no. 5 (May 1993), pp. 4–13; and James Noren, "Statistical Reporting in the States of the Former USSR," *Post-Soviet Geography and Economics* 35:1 (1994), pp. 13–37.

[60] For official sources, see Goskomstat Rossii, *Rossiiskii statisticheskii ezhegodnik 1998* (Moscow: Informatika, 1998). For an early unofficial source, see E. Chistiakov and T. Teplukhina, "Valovoi vnutrenii produkt regionov-sub"ektov RF," *Ekonomist*, no. 4 (1996), pp. 16–18. They calculated per capita GRP for 1993–5 and divided regions into ten ranked categories. Tiumen' was alone in category one, with 800% of the Russian Federation average, while both Samara and Sverdlovsk, along with seven other regions, were in the second highest group with a range of 125–190% of the average.

[61] Richard Ericson, "The Structural Barrier to Transition Hidden in Input-Output Tables of Centrally Planned Economies," *Economic Systems* 23:3 (September 1999), pp. 199–244. This is very interesting because it suggests the problem of value distortions in the input-output tables themselves, predating the value problems associated with the introduction of prices in 1992.

[62] Moreover, inflation as a concept is hard to understand in the absence of free prices. If the change in prices is a function of central fiat rather than market forces, then inflation does not have the same meaning as it does in a market economy.

region to calculate how much it paid into the federal center and how much it received back because regional and federal obligations and responsibilities were not sufficiently disaggregated. The Fund for Financial Support of Regions (FFSR), which documents federal subsidies to regions, was created only in 1994.[63] The concept of "donor" region is, therefore, a post-1994 development and refers to those regions that do not receive FFSR resources. One might have expected that the status of a "donor region" would have figured prominently in sovereignty and federalism debates in the early 1990s, but it did not because it did not yet exist. However, this does not mean there were no donor regions before 1994, only that at the time it would have been very difficult, if not impossible, to know which regions they were.

GRP and net taxes were only the tip of the iceberg in terms of the range of opportunities for the reconceptualization of regional economic conditions that were made possible by the introduction of prices and market-based value indicators. During Soviet times, because prices were set by central planners, there was not very much variation in regional prices (the variation was in terms of supply and availability of goods, but not in terms of price). However, after 1992, the variance in regional prices steeply increased.[64] Wages did differ during Soviet times, but owing to the relative uniformity of prices, higher wages generally meant higher real income. As both wages and costs of living began to vary across regions, calculation of real income became much more complicated.[65] For example, in Sverdlovsk, wages were higher than in Samara for 1990, 1991, and 1992 but were lower in 1993.[66] At the same time, food prices in Sverdlovsk were higher than Samara in 1992, but lower in 1993.[67] Between 1992 and 1993, prices in Samara rose by 10.6 times, while prices in Sverdlovsk rose by only 8.5 times.[68] But

---

[63] For an analysis of this fund and the difficulty of calculating federal support for regions prior to 1994, see Shinichiro Tabata, "Transfers from Federal to Regional Budgets in Russia: A Statistical Analysis," *Post-Soviet Geography and Economics* 39:8 (1998), pp. 447–60. For an assessment of regional budgetary revenues and expenditures, see Philip Hanson, *Regions, Local Power and Economic Change in Russia* (London: Royal Institute of International Affairs, 1994), pp. 48–50, Appendix Table A2.

[64] Further analysis of regional inequality follows in Chapter 4.

[65] For one of the earliest assessments of regional real income, see L. A. Nemova, "Rynok truda," *EKO*, no.10 (October 1993), p. 39. See also Hanson, 1994, p. 17.

[66] Calculated from Goskomstat Rossii, *Rossiiskii statisticheskii ezhegodnik 1995* (Moscow: Goskomstat Rossii, 1995), pp. 610–11.

[67] Goskomstat Rossii, *Tseny v Rossii 1995* (Moscow: Goskomstat Rossii, 1995), p. 33.

[68] Calculated from data given by Goskomstat Rossii, *Tseny v Rossii 1995* (Moscow: Goskomstat Rossii, 1995), pp. 24 and 33. The index of prices in the entire Russian Federation during the same period rose by 9.4 times.

price increases between 1992 and 1993 may have been lower in Sverdlovsk because the prices there were already high in 1992, relative to Samara. And the higher food prices in Sverdlovsk in 1992 coincided with higher wages during the same period; the lower food prices in 1993 coincided with lower wages. From this example, it is difficult to know which region was better off in terms of real income during 1990–3.

Similarly, the value of regional foreign trade, imports and exports, is difficult to comprehend because of the way it is calculated and again because of complicated price issues.[69] Foreign trade is reported according to place of shipment or location of importer, but any value added along the way and final user location are not included. Thus, a region like Samara would appear to have very high export values because it exports cars, whose inputs from other regions (energy, steel, rubber, plastics, etc., as well as the capital and labor which went into those products) are not counted. Similarly, with imports, only the location of the importing firm, usually Moscow or St. Petersburg, is counted, even though many goods imported into those two cities end up in other regions.[70] In addition, there is much unreported trade, which would tend to decrease the trade values for regions that lie on border or transit routes.

Another major issue that complicates the interpretation of foreign trade data is that regional trade figures are given in current rubles, which are only loosely, if at all, connected to world prices. For example, if one compares the sum of regional ruble trade values in 1992 with the stated dollar value of trade for the same year, the exchange rate would be 38 rubles to the dollar for exports and 26 for imports – but the actual rate was 180 in January and went up to 418 by December 1992.[71] Thus, somewhere along the way, a range of products was seriously undervalued, relative to world prices, and that under-valuation affects measures purporting to compare regional trade values, for example in Tiumen', where the dollar values of its main exports, oil and gas, are understated. Similarly, other regions' exports, like Samara's, are overstated. Thus, it is difficult to use the ruble-denominated regional trade to figure out the weight of the region in the overall dollar value of Russia's foreign trade.

[69] For an excellent analysis, see Hanson, 1994. See also Shinichiro Tabata, "The Anatomy of Russian Foreign Trade Statistics," *Post-Soviet Geography* 35:8 (1994), pp. 433–54; and Misha Belkindas and Olga Ivanova, *Foreign Trade Statistics in the USSR and Successor States* (Washington, DC: The World Bank, 1995).

[70] Hanson, 1994, p. 34.

[71] Ibid.

Beyond the matter of the complexity of value indicators, the post-Soviet period also brought into focus the need for conceptualization of new categories of economic indicators. Unemployment, for example, was not a category of analysis during Soviet times.[72] Like other indicators discussed previously, measurement error is a serious issue.[73] However, the debate over unemployment and especially the definition of *job seekers* highlights a deeper question of the meaning of unemployment in the post-Soviet context. For example, in the early 1990s context of massive nonpayment of wages, what does it mean to be "unemployed"? Should those who work but do not get paid (for several months) be considered employed? And should those who don't work, don't get paid, but still receive social services from a firm be considered employed? Or should "unemployed" only refer to those who are officially cut off from work (and firm-provided services)? There are also issues of classifying reduced-time workers. Goskomstat provides two measures of unemployment, one according to those economically active members of the population who are seeking work (the International Labor Organization or ILO definition), and one of official, registered unemployment. However, neither Goskomstat measure takes into account the issues of reduced-time work or nonpayments.[74] Given differences in nonpayments and reduced-time work across regions, it is possible to see how regional comparisons of unemployment in the early 1990s might not have converged on a single understanding of the term.

The context of organizational and conceptual reconfiguration of statistics that marked the early 1990s suggests another issue in the interpretation of economic data, namely, the problem of assessing change over time. Changes in methodology may cause the appearance of changes in the real world, when in fact the "change" is just the result of new (and perhaps

---

[72] The nonexistence of unemployment during Soviet times is symptomatic of one of the traditional problems with Goskomstat and its Soviet predecessors, namely, the ignorance (both deliberate and unintentional) of whole classes of activity. Some areas were specifically ignored, such as prison and military activity, but others, such as the informal economy, were not captured owing both to methodological issues and to political or ideological debates over the existence of such activity.

[73] Some argue that the unemployed in Russia are undercounted because undercounting hinges on the definition of job seekers versus discouraged workers. See, for example, Steven Rosefielde, "The Civilian Labour Force and Unemployment in the Russian Federation," *Europe-Asia Studies* 52:8 (December 2000), pp. 1433–47.

[74] Michael Bradshaw developed a measure of regional unemployment for 1993, which combines official unemployment with reduced-time working. See Hanson, 1994, Appendix Table 1.

improved) methodology. For example, in discussing the apparent increase in infant mortality in the 1970s, Victoria Velkoff and Jane Miller argue that improvements in the way infant mortality was measured made it seem like there was an increase in the 1970s, when in fact the real rate probably did not actually change.[75] Moreover, whereas there were well-known incentives for overestimation of production to fulfill plan targets during the Soviet period, in the post-Soviet period, the opposite incentives have been in place because the institutional fluidity between the tax authorities and statistical agencies makes underreporting desirable.[76] The change in incentives not only would affect yearly estimates but would also affect apparent changes over time. For example, the incentive shift alone (i.e., from over-reporting to under-reporting), may be responsible for at least some fraction of the level of the decline in production.

Thus far, I have outlined the complexity involved in assessing regional economic conditions from the point of view of the outside observer who has access to the latest data on regional conditions, in some cases more than ten years after the fact. However, a conceptual issue from the point of view of assessing regional understandings of the economy is to consider that the data that regional actors had available to them at the time of their decision to pursue greater sovereignty (i.e., the available data in 1990–3) is much more limited than what is available here. Published sources came to a halt in 1990, stopping with Soviet data from 1989. Later, all-Russian statistical yearbooks with what comparative data existed for 1990–3 were only published in 1994, although regional statistical offices had their own, mostly unpublished, records of regional statistics for the 1990–3 period. On the one hand, if we assume that published data represent phenomena that regional actors knew about at time t_1, and that the publication at time t_2 of data regarding conditions at time t_1 is simply an after-the-fact account of the phenomena, then the delay in publication has no effect on what regional actors understood about the economy at time t_1. On the other hand, if we assume that published data are sources of information for regional actors, then the relevant published sources for regional understandings of

---

[75] Victoria A. Velkoff and Jane E. Miller, "Trends and Differentials in Infant Mortality in the Soviet Union, 1970–90: How Much Is Due to Misreporting?" *Population Studies* 49:2 (July 1995), pp. 241–58.

[76] That is, the tax authorities and Goskomstat (the state statistical committee) are rumored to share information; therefore, firm data reported to Goskomstat may be used by the tax authorities to collect revenue from firms, resulting in incentives for firms to under-report to Goskomstat.

the economy would be those which were in print during time t_1, perhaps containing information on economic conditions of time t_0.

One final point in interpreting objective indicators of regional economic conditions concerns the ecological inference problem; in other words, aggregate regional data might not reflect the interests of regional elites or groups of relevant citizens influential in movements for greater sovereignty. Indeed, political institutional complexity and within-region individual and group interests are not captured by most of the structural economic variables considered in the quantitative analysis here or in previous analyses.

Conclusion

Quantitative analysis of regionalism within the Russian Federation, undertaken in light of existing theories and the available economic data, shows that several variables, supposed by said theories to be explanatory, did not have the expected effect on sovereignty movements. In particular, my findings for the Russian regions suggest that, in contrast to earlier studies that focused on the ethnic republics within Russia, higher net tax payments had a negative effect on movements for greater sovereignty.

In order to explain this quantitative finding, I analyzed the economic variables that went into the analysis here and in previous studies. Essentially, there are two main findings from this qualitative analysis: Measurement and conceptual issues shape the effect of economic factors. Measurement issues, broadly conceived, concern the quality of information captured in quantitative data sets as well as the quality of information available to relevant political actors. As I have outlined earlier, these measurement issues appear in a variety of forms and may explain some of the gap between objective economic conditions and information about those conditions. Simple measurement error in the independent variables is an obvious possibility. The complexity of the economy, including the measurement of value indicators in inflationary times or the measurement of regional contributions to export values, for example, is technically complicated.

But, there are many more ways in which reality may differ from actors' understanding of conditions. For example, the timing of data publication may be at odds with the timing of decision-making. In other words, today's information about the economy, captured in quantitative data sets, might not fully capture regional understandings of the 1990–3 period. In addition, incentives for reporting and the inference problem of discerning regional elite preferences from aggregate data add to the difficulty of ascertaining the true state of regional economic conditions. The discussion of these measurement issues supports the argument that the economic variables tested in the foregoing analysis and in previous theories have not captured the aspects of the regional economy relevant to political activism toward greater sovereignty.

A second finding from the qualitative analysis of economic variables is that beyond measurement issues, there are conceptual differences in the definition of variables as well as in the value of those variables for regional economic and political conditions. For example, the discussion of unemployment highlights the possibility of reasonable disagreements over the definition and measurement of regional unemployment. An additional conceptual issue is the idea that there is a range of potential interpretations of regional economic conditions. In other words, the fluidity of categories of economic knowledge represents a possibility for variation in the way regional actors process data and, consequently, a possibility for differential development of meaning according to region. Moreover, the scholarly debate over economic indicators should form a critical part of the understanding of economic interests because it reflects of potential interpretive opportunities facing regional actors. The interconnectedness of underlying conceptual complexity and measurement issues suggests that establishing "the truth" or a single legitimate assessment of regional economic conditions is rather difficult.

The conclusion of this qualitative and quantitative analysis of the role of economic factors in regional sovereignty movements in Russia is that economic conditions matter, but not in the systematic and objective way that most quantitative studies assume. Even though this conclusion suggests that a focus on rich versus poor regions in the explanation of regionalism or separatism may be missing the essential explanatory mechanism, it does not imply that economic variables do not matter or that economic factors are irrelevant. Rather, the discussion of the measurement and conceptual issues behind the economic variables suggests that objective understanding of the economy is hard to come by, both in quantitative data sets and among relevant political actors.

A second key point is that the effect of economic variables may not be systematic or uniform. In other words, the same economic conditions might lead to different regional activism outcomes because the relevant aspect of the economic conditions – the *understanding* of the economic conditions – may not be the same as what is being picked up in traditional variables. In addition, the meaning of economic conditions and their indicators may vary across regions as a result of conceptual differences. If we return to Table 1.4 and reconsider the "expected value" of the independent variables, we can see that, in light of the qualitative analysis, the table is too constraining because both the magnitude and sign of the variables may differ according to local regional understandings of what are normatively acceptable values of the variables as well as relationships between variables.

Even though the immediate post-Soviet context may particularly lend itself to a great deal of diversity in economic understandings, consideration of each of the economic variables in a variety of contexts suggests that, in every economy, despite attempts at systematic measurement and disciplined interpretation, economic reality is chaotic enough to allow for alternative interpretations. The argument then is that economic factors in the study of political movements should be treated like biological or demographic factors in studies of nationalism: They matter, but they don't have an unmediated objective effect on outcomes. Rather, the facts are products of objective reality and social construction; therefore, their effect may differ across contexts of time and space.

Analysis that treats economic factors as subject to serious measurement and conceptual issues as well as multiple local interpretations, is a core part of the imagined economies framework (which I discuss in greater detail in the next chapter). The basic insight of this framework is that scholars must go beyond off-the-shelf data sets to understand the economic basis of political movements. Further inquiry into both the construction of data sets and local interpretations of economic circumstances may yield a more satisfactory explanation of the relationship between the economy and political action.

One of the main advantages of the imagined economies framework is that it can address variation among economically similar regions, without throwing out either economic factors or instrumental rationality. The idea of mediated economic understanding, or imagined economies, does not deny instrumental rationality or the idea that regions can be expected to fight for what they think they deserve – but it does ask a crucial question that is often ignored when preferences are taken for granted: Why do regions think they deserve what they do, and how is it that economic interests become interests in greater sovereignty?

The point is not that in developing local understandings regions make up stories about the economy out of thin air or that underlying economic facts have no meaning; nor is it that some regions were wrong, and some were correct in their assessments of economic conditions. Rather, the argument is that meanings of economic facts, like other political, demographic, or other scientific facts, are socially held and may vary over time and place, and according to group interpretations. In other words, there is room for different assessments of economic facts, and this process of mediation deserves scholarly attention.

↳ subjectivly of ∈ 'facts'.

2

Imagined Economies

CONSTRUCTIVIST POLITICAL ECONOMY AND NATIONALISM

How are regional movements for greater sovereignty related to objective economic conditions? The findings in Chapter 1 suggested that the relationship is not simply reflective; that is, Russian regions with comparable economic conditions did not have similar levels of activism toward greater sovereignty. And, analysis of specific cases shows that many regional movements for greater sovereignty were motivated by economic demands. We therefore face the question of how similar economic conditions could produce different economic interests.

In this chapter, I outline and support the case for an imagined economies framework through a three-part analysis of the role of economic factors in the nationalism literature, by discussing in turn objectivist approaches to the economy, orthodox critiques of objectivism, and heterodox constructivist approaches to the economy. In the analysis of these approaches to the economy, I discuss economic-based theories of nationalism consistent with each approach. In the end, I combine insights from constructivist political economy – cognitive science, economic sociology, historical institutionalism, and social theory – to arrive at the imagined economies framework, which I argue productively expands the nationalism literature.

Objectivism

An analysis of objectivism begins with a particular model of cognition because cognition addresses the issue of how human beings, including economic actors, understand their surroundings. The *classic* view of cognition is of rule-based manipulation of symbols.[1] In this view, thought is abstract

---

[1] For discussion of this and other views, see Roy D'Andrade, *The Development of Cognitive Anthropology* (Cambridge: Cambridge Univ. Press, 1995), p. 136.

58

and unconnected to the particularity of bodies, minds, or souls. Rather than enhancing, adapting, or interfering with external reality, the brain functions like a calculator – simply manipulating and processing symbols that neatly correspond to reality.

In the discipline of economics and among political scientists and sociologists who have sought to extend the empirical domain of economists' mode of reasoning, cognition of economic conditions by rational actors is largely treated as a process of receiving information about the world followed by calculation according to a set of rules or preferences. This understanding of economic cognition is consistent with the classic view of cognition and is based on an assumed objectivity in understanding economic conditions. According to this view, economic information, once discovered, has independent and universal meaning.[2] Individual understandings of economic reality simply reflect external economic conditions, or at least the available information about them. The origins of economic interests need not be investigated because economic interests are assumed to arise directly out of economic conditions.

A model of how actors use economic information to make choices, in other words, a model of decision-making, also follows from the objectivist view of cognition. In traditional economic models this decision-making process has been described as utility maximization.[3] According to this model, individuals, given information, make choices that maximize utility by calculating the value of alternatives. The set of rules that guides calculation (and choice) is an individual's ordered set of preferences. Choices are purposeful in that they are undertaken to achieve some goal (utility), and this assumption of purposeful action is fundamental to rational choice theory. The utility maximization formulation was presumed adequate for economic decision-making, except where information about economic conditions was uncertain. In response to these conditions, economists and

---

[2] This is not to suggest that objective economic data are easy to come by; on the contrary, even for objectivists, raw data are almost always considered imperfect, and it takes careful and concerted efforts (including international standardization) to arrive at data sets that can be considered reflective of real economic conditions. However, the cleansing of raw data does not suggest that mediation by human beings of data is to be encouraged; rather, it implies that some effort may be required in the process of uncovering or discovering objective economic information.

[3] The process of choice, as opposed to just the results of choice, can be studied under the term *procedural rationality*. See Herbert Simon, "Rationality as Process and Product of Thought," *The American Economic Review: Papers and Proceedings of the 90th Meeting of the American Economic Association, New York Dec. 28–30, 1977*, 68:2 (May 1978), pp. 1–16.

statisticians developed the notion of *subjective expected utility* (SEU), which substituted expected values for known values.[4]

The conclusion to be drawn from objectivist models of the economy, such as SEU, is that the principal problem of economic decision-making lies not in understanding some sort of mediated interpretation but rather in simply gathering accurate information (or expected values) about the external environment. Where the relationship between economic conditions and economic interests is assumed to follow directly, the approach to the economy can be called objectivist.[5]

Objectivism in Nationalism Studies

The objectivist position is well-represented in the scholarly literature on nationalism where it has been repeatedly argued that structural economic conditions in some way drive movements for greater sovereignty. In these analyses, external reality, with very minimal mediation, produces economic interests that are pursued by various groups. The economic basis for separatism or nationalism, however, varies. On the one hand, regional endowment arguments suggest that wealth and development may lead to greater support for separatism because well-off regions would be better able to survive and perhaps be better off on their own.[6] For example, as we saw in Chapter 1, Hale and Treisman argued that wealthy regions in the Soviet Union and Russia were the most likely to seek greater sovereignty. Following a similar logic, Ronald Rogowski argued that advanced groups within states would be the most likely to seek secession, because it would

---

[4] A classic work on SEU, especially as related to probability estimates, is Leonard J. Savage, *The Foundations of Statistics*, 2nd rev. ed. (New York: Dover, 1972).

[5] The concept of "objectivism" is to some degree an ideal-type, and there is of course some overlap with the orthodox and heterodox critiques of objectivism, which I discuss later.

[6] See Henry Hale, "The Parade of Sovereignties: Testing Theories of Secession in the Soviet Setting," *British Journal of Political Science* 30 (2000), pp. 31–56; and Daniel S. Treisman, "Russia's 'Ethnic Revival': The Separatist Activism of Regional Leaders in a Postcommunist Order," *World Politics* 49:2 (1997), pp. 212–49. Similarly, for a study done to calculate "Independence Potential" or the economic viability of Soviet republics by defining "Independence Criteria," which were in fact structural economic criteria, see Jurgen Corbet, *The Soviet Union at the Crossroads: Facts and Figures on the Soviet Republics* (Frankfurt Am Main: Deutsche Bank, 1991). Other examples of the argument that wealthy regions would be most separatist include Milica Zarkovic Bookman, *The Economics of Secession* (New York: St. Martin's Press, 1993); Milica Zarkovic Bookman, *The Political Economy of Discontinuous Development* (New York: Praeger, 1991); and Immanuel Wallerstein, *Africa: The Politics of Independence* (New York: Vintage, 1961).

be irrational for groups without skills to seek statehood.[7] Likewise, Eric Hobsbawm argued that the condition of underdevelopment makes poorer regions want to remain part of the state in order to be associated with the advanced regions.[8]

On the other hand, some underdevelopment arguments suggest that poor regions may be poor as a result of exploitation by the state, and therefore poor regions may have incentives to pursue greater sovereignty.[9] For example, Michael Hechter argues that economic power asymmetries and, especially, exploitation of peripheral regions by the center will lead to separatist movements.[10] Donald Horowitz focuses on "antipathy" as the source of ethnic conflict, but to the extent that he considers economic factors in separatist movements, he argues that secession is most likely to come from the "backward groups in backward regions."[11] His reasoning is that given uncertainty over control of the state and fear of other groups, "backward groups" not benefiting by participation in the state will have little to lose by fighting. All the same, Horowitz cautions that because of their "backward" condition, such groups are unlikely to succeed, and thus secession is improbable. Finally, beyond specific regional economic conditions, arguments that focus on the international trade environment suggest that changes in

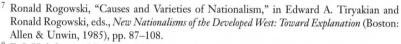

[7] Ronald Rogowski, "Causes and Varieties of Nationalism," in Edward A. Tiryakian and Ronald Rogowski, eds., *New Nationalisms of the Developed West: Toward Explanation* (Boston: Allen & Unwin, 1985), pp. 87–108.

[8] E. J. Hobsbawm, *Nations and Nationalism since 1780* (Cambridge: Cambridge Univ. Press, 1990).

[9] See for example, Tom Nairn, *The Break-Up of Britain: Crisis and Neo-Nationalism* (London: New Left Books, 1977); and Terry Boswell and William J. Dixon, "Marx's Theory of Rebellion: A Cross-National Analysis of Class Exploitation, Economic Development, and Violent Revolt," *American Sociological Review* 58 (October 1993), pp. 681–702. For arguments that link income inequality to rebellion and violence, see Edward N. Muller and Mitchell A. Seligson, "Inequality and Insurgency," *American Political Science Review* 81:2 (June 1987), pp. 425–52.

[10] Michael Hechter, *Internal Colonialism: The Celtic Fringe in British National Development, 1536–1966* (London: Routledge, 1975). Hechter does focus on both the material conditions and expectations of regional elites; therefore, it is possible to consider his analysis in the second part of this chapter with orthodox critiques of objectivism where I discuss other models of perception and expectations. However, the primary force driving sovereignty movements in his model is negative economic conditions; therefore, I consider his work an example of an objectivist approach to the economy.

[11] Horowitz is primarily interested in explaining ethnic conflict as opposed to secession or sovereignty movements, but his extensive analysis does contain some discussion of separatism. Donald L. Horowitz, *Ethnic Groups in Conflict* (Berkeley: Univ. of California Press, 1985), p. 236. See also Horowitz, "Patterns of Ethnic Separatism," *Comparative Studies in Society and History* 23 (1981), pp. 165–95.

the international environment provide economic incentives that drive separatism.[12]

Orthodox Critiques of Objectivism

Purely objectivist approaches, but especially the subjective expected utility model, have been singled out for critique from a number of perspectives in recent years. However, rather than retreating from objectivism altogether, the dominant approach has been to consider ways in which objective understandings of economic conditions may be mediated.[13]

Research in American politics and comparative politics has empirically demonstrated the many gaps between economic conditions and the interests that supposedly flow from them. In 1977, Herbert Simon addressed the American Economic Association and argued that SEU by itself may be ill-equipped to handle choice processes.[14] Simon cited several empirical tests of economic decision-making that found that actual behavior did not match the subjective expected utility formulation. For example, Daniel Kahneman and Amos Tversky found that actors did not revise initial information when presented with subsequent information, and, in some cases, actors responded to the most recently received information without adequately considering prior information.[15] In addition, Howard Kunreuther showed that personal experience and subjective beliefs about facts were strongly

---

[12] See, for example, Alberto Alesina and Enrico Spolaore, "On the Number and Size of Nations," *Quarterly Journal of Economics* 112:4 (November 1997), pp. 1027–56; and Alberto Alesina, Enrico Spolaore, and Romain Wacziarg, "Economic Integration and Political Disintegration," *American Economic Review* 90:5 (December 2000), pp. 1276–96.

[13] In outlining critiques of objectivism, I use the terms *orthodox* and *heterodox* to refer to different positions toward objectivity. The orthodox critique recognizes problems with objectivity but remains largely oriented toward support of the concept of objectivity. The heterodox approaches also outline problems with objectivity but are less concerned with preserving the concept. These are, of course, ideal types, and in works cited there may be overlap in the orthodox and heterodox positions. The terms are consistent with Bourdieu's concept of habitus, which I discuss later. However, in the next chapter, I use the terms *orthodox* and *heterodox* to describe perestroika and its alternatives vis-à-vis the framework of habitus; hence, in Chapter 3, the terms describe a different phenomenon altogether (i.e., the understandings of Soviet power versus the concept of economic objectivity discussed in this chapter).

[14] Simon, 1978.

[15] Daniel Kahneman and Amos Tversky, "On the Psychology of Prediction," *Psychology Review* 80 (July 1973), pp. 237–51; also cited in Simon, 1978, p. 9. For an earlier treatment, see Ward Edwards, "Conservation in Human Information Processing," in Benjamin Kleinmuntz, ed., *Formal Representation of Human Judgement* (New York: Wiley, 1968), pp. 17–52.

related to actual decisions; in this regard, expected values for information about the world were inadequate to explain how economic choices were made.[16] The SEU formulation relies heavily on the quality of the information for rational decision-making; therefore, Simon's analysis of information and cognition went to the core of the SEU formulation.

Moreover, Simon went on to address the problem of *too much* information. Simon argued that the real problem, as indicated by empirical studies, is how to filter the mass of information and sort out what kind of information is necessary to solve a given problem. Turning the traditional search problem on its head, Simon argued that computational capacity of the human mind, as opposed to information, may be what is insufficiently available. Simon noted that "many of the central issues of our time are questions of how we use limited information and limited computational capacity to deal with enormous problems whose shape we barely grasp."[17] The fact that real problems are large and that human beings do nevertheless solve many of them, even with limited information and limited computational capacity, suggested serious problems with the SEU model. Simon went on to develop these issues more fully in the concept of *bounded rationality*, which has spawned generations of research.[18]

Orthodox Critiques of Objective Economic Interests

The theoretical problems with SEU and the development of the concept of bounded rationality corresponded with an abundance of empirical work that highlighted a lack of fit between macroeconomic conditions and stated individual-level economic interests.[19] This apparent disjuncture between aggregate and individual-level data was puzzling in itself, but it also

---

[16] Howard Kunreuther, *Disaster Insurance Protection: Public Policy Lessons* (New York: Wiley, 1978).

[17] Simon, 1978, p. 13.

[18] See Herbert A. Simon, *Models of Bounded Rationality*, 3 vols. (Cambridge, MA: MIT Press, 1982–1997). For a recent review of work related to bounded rationality, see Bryan D. Jones, "Bounded Rationality," *Annual Review of Political Science* 2 (June 1999), pp. 297–321. See also, James G. March, "Papers in Honor of Herbert A. Simon: Bounded Rationality, Ambiguity, and the Engineering of Choice," *The Bell Journal of Economics* 9:2 (Autumn 1978), pp. 587–608.

[19] Two broad ways of thinking about mediation of economic interests focus on *perceptions* and *interpretation*. The psychology literature and most of the orthodox critiques that I present in this section tend to focus on perceptions. Later, in the discussion of heterodox critiques I will address the issue of interpretation.

suggested a potentially deeper problem of economic interests' failure to correspond to economic conditions.

The objectivist position on the economy and political behavior in the American context had been established by work that has connected macroeconomic conditions with aggregate political behavior, namely voting and executive popularity.[20] However, alternative models of how economic conditions affect individual interests (e.g., "pocketbook" versus "sociotropic" models) suggested that the relationship between economic conditions and interests was not so simple.[21] And, the relationship among economic conditions, interests, and the rational-calculator model was challenged by individual-level survey evidence, which suggested that voters considered macroeconomic conditions over their own personal economic circumstances.[22] Moreover, individual-level surveys revealed that much of the voting public was unsophisticated, ignorant, and uninterested.[23]

This problem of economic interests possibly not corresponding to economic conditions was not limited to voting behavior. In comparative politics, a number of authors explicitly took up questions of why individuals or groups would choose to undertake action that seemed to go against

---

[20] See Gerald H. Kramer, "Short-Term Fluctuations in U.S. Voting Behavior, 1896–1964," *The American Political Science Review* 65:1 (March 1971), pp. 131–43. More recently, see Michael B. MacKuen, Robert S. Erikson, and James A. Stimson, "Peasants or Bankers? The American Electorate and the U.S. Economy," *The American Political Science Review* 86:3 (September 1992), pp. 597–611.

[21] The term *pocketbook* refers to the economic welfare of the individual, while *sociotropic* refers to the general welfare or the economic welfare of a society in which an individual is a member. In this sense, sociotropic considerations have an "altruistic" element. On "sociotropic" voting, see Donald R. Kinder and D. Roderick Kiewiet, "Economic Discontent and Political Behavior: The Role of Personal Grievances and Collective Economic Judgments in Congressional Voting," *American Journal of Political Science* 23:3 (August 1979), pp. 495–527; Donald R. Kinder and D. Roderick Kiewiet, "Sociotropic Politics: The American Case," *British Journal of Political Science* 11:2 (April 1981), pp. 129–61. On pocketbook voting, see Gerald H. Kramer, "The Ecological Fallacy Revisited: Aggregate versus Individual-level Findings on Economics and Elections, and Sociotropic Voting," *The American Political Science Review* 77:1 (March 1983), pp. 92–111.

[22] See Kinder and Kiewiet, 1979, 1981; and Morris P. Fiorina, *Retrospective Voting in American National Elections* (New Haven, CT: Yale Univ. Press, 1981).

[23] For an early statement, see Philip E. Converse, "The Nature of Belief Systems in Mass Publics," in David E. Apter, ed., *Ideology and Discontent*, (New York: Free Press, 1964), pp. 206–61. See also Donald R. Kinder, "Diversity and Complexity in American Public Opinion," in Ada W. Finifter, ed., *Political Science: The State of the Discipline* (Washington, DC: American Political Science Association, 1983), pp. 389–425; and W. Russell Neuman, *The Paradox of Mass Politics: Knowledge and Opinion in the American Electorate* (Cambridge, MA: Harvard Univ. Press, 1986).

individual interests, for example joining unions, given free-rider issues,[24] or mobilizing union activity, given low odds of success.[25] These examples illustrate that much of the work in the social sciences on political economy begins with the assumption of objectivist approaches to the economy but continues by questioning a simple reflective relationship and searching for solutions that make sense of the connections between economic conditions, economic interests, and political behavior.

Initially, some authors attributed the difference between aggregate and individual responses in American voting behavior to measurement error. Gerald Kramer, for example, argued that individual evaluations of the economy are "contaminated" by evaluations of personal financial situations, and that is why they don't correspond to macro-level economic conditions.[26] Thus, a widely accepted explanation for the inconsistency was "noise" or *random* variation in individual-level survey data.[27] The principal message of Benjamin Page and Robert Shapiro was that the public is "rational" in that attitudes basically correspond to interests, values, and economic conditions.

Later work, however, showed that the individual error term was not random but, rather, could reflect a range of systematic differences, for example in levels of information, which corresponded to other differences such as levels of media and elite influence or partisanship.[28] An optimistic reading of the problem of information provision argued that, with increasing information, policy preferences would become more rational.[29] Nevertheless, analyses of differential levels of information turn out to be just the tip of the iceberg in studies that increasingly problematized the relationship between economic conditions, interests, and behavior.

---

[24] Michael Wallerstein, "Union Organization in Advanced Industrial Democracies," *American Political Science Review* 83:2 (1989), pp. 481–501.

[25] Miriam Golden, *Heroic Defeats: The Politics of Job Loss* (New York: Cambridge Univ. Press, 1997).

[26] Kramer, 1983.

[27] Benjamin I. Page and Robert Y. Shapiro, *The Rational Public: Fifty Years of Trends in Americans' Policy Preferences* (Chicago: Univ. of Chicago Press, 1992).

[28] Marc J. Hetherington, "The Media's Role in Forming Voters' National Economic Evaluations in 1992," *American Journal of Political Science* 40:2 (May 1996), pp. 372–95; Larry M. Bartels, "Uninformed Votes: Information Effects in Presidential Elections," *American Journal of Political Science* 40:1 (February 1996), pp. 194–230; and Scott L. Althaus, "Information Effects in Collective Preferences," *The American Political Science Review* 92:3 (September 1998), pp. 545–58.

[29] Arthur Lupia and Mathew D. McCubbins, *The Democratic Dilemma: Can Citizens Learn What They Need to Know?* (New York: Cambridge Univ. Press, 1998).

The relevance of social context, power, and institutions in shaping economic interests has been pursued from a variety of angles. These approaches include arguments regarding elite and media influence, or even manipulation, in the shaping of citizens' attitudes.[30] Beyond active manipulation by elites or the media through the provision (or not) of information, the concept of "framing" suggests different ways of presenting or constructing issues and is one step closer to differential meaning of external reality and mediation of objective conditions.[31] Frames may be both cognitive structures and rhetorical devices,[32] and they can affect the salience of particular issues for individuals.[33] In addition, framing theory has been developed and applied very successfully outside of individualistic voting issues in the social movements literature.[34]

[30] For a general overview of elite manipulation and shaping of citizen attitudes, see Diana C. Mutz, Paul M. Sniderman, and Richard A. Brody, eds., *Political Persuasion and Attitude Change* (Ann Arbor: Univ. of Michigan Press, 1996). On "priming" and agenda setting, see Maxwell E. McCombs and Donald L. Shaw, "The Agenda-Setting Function of Mass Media," *Public Opinion Quarterly* 36:2 (Summer 1972), pp. 176–87; Shanto Iyengar and Donald R. Kinder, *News That Matters: Television and American Opinion* (Chicago: Univ. of Chicago Press, 1987); Jon A. Krosnick and Donald R. Kinder, "Altering the Foundations of Support for the President Through Priming," *The American Political Science Review* 84:2 (June 1990), pp. 497–512; and W. Lance Bennett and David L. Paletz, eds., *Taken by Storm: The Media, Public Opinion, and U.S. Foreign Policy in the Gulf War* (Chicago: Univ. of Chicago Press, 1994). On the role of elite discourse and categorization, see John R. Zaller, *The Nature and Origins of Mass Opinion* (New York: Cambridge Univ. Press, 1992); John W. Kingdon, *Agendas, Alternatives, and Public Policies*, 2nd ed. (New York: Harper Collins College Publishers, 1995); and William H. Riker, edited by Randall L. Calvert, John Mueller, and Rick K. Wilson, *The Strategy of Rhetoric: Campaigning for the American Constitution* (New Haven: Yale Univ. Press, 1996).

[31] On framing effects, see Thomas E. Nelson, Rosalee A. Clawson, and Zoe M. Oxley, "Media Framing of a Civil Liberties Conflict and Its Effect on Tolerance," *The American Political Science Review* 91:3 (September 1997), pp. 567–83; and James N. Druckman, "The Implications of Framing Effects for Citizen Competence," *Political Behavior* 23:3 (September 2001) pp. 225–56. On limitations of framing, see James N. Druckman, "On the Limits of Framing Effects: Who Can Frame?" *Journal of Politics* 63:4 (November 2001), pp. 1041–66.

[32] Thomas E. Nelson and Donald R. Kinder, "Issue Frames and Group-Centrism in American Public Opinion," *Journal of Politics* 58:4 (November 1996), pp. 1055–78.

[33] Bryan D. Jones, *Reconceiving Decision-Making in Democratic Politics: Attention, Choice, and Public Policy* (Chicago: Univ. of Chicago Press, 1994); and Dennis Chong, "Creating Common Frames of Reference on Political Issues," in Diana C. Mutz, Paul M. Sniderman, and Richard A. Brody, eds., *Political Persuasion and Attitude Change* (Ann Arbor: Univ. of Michigan Press, 1996), pp. 195–224.

[34] Two notable works in this large literature are Sidney Tarrow, *Power in Movement: Social Movements and Contentious Politics*, 2nd ed. (New York: Cambridge Univ. Press, 1998); and Taeku Lee, *Mobilizing Public Opinion: Black Insurgency and Racial Attitudes in the Civil Rights Era* (Chicago: Univ. of Chicago Press, 2002).

The concept of "heuristics" shares with the framing and elite influence models the attention it gives to the way in which interests are formed, but it takes into account the critiques of SEU and uses insights from the bounded rationality concept. Returning to the question of how citizens make decisions with limited computational capacity and limited information, heuristics can, to use Arthur Lupia's term, provide an "informational crutch." Adapting the *as if* assumption, Richard McKelvey and Peter Ordeshook argued that individuals might use heuristics to make choices *as if* they were informed.[35] Heuristics may be mechanisms for filtering information,[36] and they also may be "shortcuts," in the form of cues from trusted persons of shared values who enable individuals to get the information they need to make rational choices (although not everyone is convinced of the rationality of this process).[37] A heuristic could also be a personal experience (e.g., unemployment),[38] but the use of personal experience can vary with levels of political sophistication.[39] Similarly, rather than just providing information, heuristics may help individuals to develop their own

[35] Richard D. McKelvey and Peter C. Ordeshook, "Information, Electoral Equilibria, and the Democratic Ideal," *Journal of Politics* 48:4 (November 1986), pp. 909–37.

[36] Paul M. Sniderman, Richard A. Brody, and Philip E. Tetlock, with Henry E. Brady, *Reasoning and Choice: Explorations in Political Psychology* (New York: Cambridge Univ. Press, 1991); and Zaller, 1992.

[37] Edward G. Carmines and James H. Kuklinski, "Incentives, Opportunities, and the Logic of Public Opinion in American Political Representation," in John A. Ferejohn and James H. Kuklinski, eds., *Information and Democratic Processes* (Urbana: Univ. of Illinois Press, 1990), pp. 240–68; Samuel L. Popkin, *The Reasoning Voter: Communication and Persuasion in Presidential Campaigns* (Chicago: Univ. of Chicago Press, 1991); Arthur Lupia, "Busy Voters, Agenda Control, and the Power of Information," *The American Political Science Review* 86:2 (June 1992), pp. 390–403; Jeffery J. Mondak, "Source Cues and Policy Approval: The Cognitive Dynamics of Public Support for the Reagan Agenda," *American Journal of Political Science* 37:1 (February 1993), pp. 186–212; Arthur Lupia, "Shortcuts Versus Encyclopedias: Information and Voting Behavior in California Insurance Reform Elections," *The American Political Science Review* 88:1 (March 1994), pp. 63–76; and Lupia and McCubbins, 1998. However, not everyone agrees that heuristics entirely solve the problem of citizens' rationality: see Bartels, 1996, and James H. Kuklinski and Paul J. Quirk, "Reconsidering the Rational Public: Cognition, Heuristics, and Mass Opinion," in Arthur Lupia, Mathew D. McCubbins, and Samuel L. Popkin, eds., *Elements of Reason: Cognition, Choice, and the Bounds of Rationality* (New York: Cambridge Univ. Press, 2000), pp. 153–82.

[38] Carolyn L. Funk and Patricia A. Garcia-Monet, "The Relationship between Personal and National Concerns in Public Perceptions about the Economy," *Political Research Quarterly* 50:2 (June 1997), pp. 317–42.

[39] Pamela Johnston Conover, Stanley Feldman, and Kathleen Knight, "Judging Inflation and Unemployment: The Origins of Retrospective Evaluations," *Journal of Politics* 48:3 (August 1986), pp. 565–88.

preferences.[40] Heuristics may be institutional as well. For example, Paul Sniderman argues that political campaigns may constitute a mechanism that allows citizens to bridge gaps in information.[41]

Indeed, institutions and social context are background for many of these mechanisms, which mediate between external reality, interests, and behavior. In the American context, Gregory Markus found that partisan biases affect how individuals assess economic conditions, especially "pocketbook" concerns.[42] And, Diana Mutz argued that the views of others, via the results of mass surveys, influence individual judgments.[43] Finally, it should be recognized that these various mechanisms may be working together; that is, informational effects, elite influence, framing, heuristics, and institutional context may be operating simultaneously. For example, Raymond Duch, Harvey Palmer, and Christopher Anderson found that evaluations of the U.S. national economy varied according to four factors: information and media exposure, political attitudes, personal experiences, and socioeconomic characteristics.[44] In their words, "Our analysis provides fairly conclusive evidence that how people view economic performance is shaped by their political predispositions, personal financial experiences, socioeconomic situation, and level of understanding about the political economy."[45] Duch et al. specifically tested whether and under what circumstances views of the economy diverged from external reality; therefore, their findings

---

[40] Henry E. Brady and Paul M. Sniderman, "Attitude Attribution: A Group Basis for Political Reasoning," *The American Political Science Review* 79:4 (December 1985), pp. 1061–78; and Sniderman, Brody, and Tetlock, 1991.

[41] Paul M. Sniderman, "Taking Sides: A Fixed Choice Theory of Political Reasoning," in Arthur Lupia, Mathew D. McCubbins, and Samuel L. Popkin, eds., *Elements of Reason: Cognition, Choice, and the Bounds of Rationality* (New York: Cambridge Univ. Press, 2000), pp. 67–84. On this point, see also Donald A. Wittman, *The Myth of Democratic Failure: Why Political Institutions Are Efficient* (Chicago: Univ. of Chicago Press, 1995).

[42] Gregory B. Markus, "The Impact of Personal and National Economic Conditions on the Presidential Vote: A Pooled Cross-Sectional Analysis," *American Journal of Political Science* 32:1 (February 1988), pp. 137–54; and Christopher Wlezien, Mark Franklin, and Daniel Twiggs, "Economic Perceptions and Vote Choice: Disentangling the Endogeneity," *Political Behavior* 19:1 (March 1997), pp. 7–17. Similarly, Zaller found that new information is interpreted by reinforcing existing beliefs, which may be partisan in nature; Zaller, 1992.

[43] Diana C. Mutz, *Impersonal Influence: How Perceptions of Mass Collectives Affect Political Attitudes* (New York: Cambridge Univ. Press, 1998).

[44] Raymond M. Duch, Harvey D. Palmer, and Christopher J. Anderson, "Heterogeneity in Perceptions of National Economic Conditions," *American Journal of Political Science* 44:4 (October 2000), pp. 635–52.

[45] Duch et al., 2000, p. 649.

directly challenge the objective basis of economic understandings and interests. The critique of objectivism, however, does not stop with the establishment of heterogeneity of economic understandings. Rather, these findings highlight the question of the origin and mediation of alternative understandings and interests. One source of mediation, as discussed above, is institutions. Even for economists and adherents to the rational choice paradigm, institutions increasingly constitute an explanation for what might at first glance appear to be irrational behavior. For example, institutions are a way to incorporate "culture" into instrumental decision-making.[46] And, culture, via institutions, can be the mechanism for mediating between alternative choices.[47] In contrast to those who would like to extend rational-choice (and specifically economic) models to, in Gary Becker's words, "all human behavior,"[48] Debra Satz and John Ferejohn acknowledged the limitations of the rational choice paradigm. Instead, they considered the social and institutional context of choice and made the somewhat radical claim that "the theory of rational choice is most powerful in contexts where choice is limited." By limitations, they were referring to the social-structural environment in which choices are made. They argued,

We believe that rational-choice explanations are most plausible in settings in which individual action is severely constrained, and thus where the theory gets its explanatory power from structure-generated interests and not from actual individual

---

[46] For example, see Jon Elster, *The Cement of Society: A Study of Social Order* (New York: Cambridge Univ. Press, 1989); Avner Greif, "Cultural Beliefs and the Organization of Society," *Journal of Political Economy* 102:5 (1994), pp. 912–50; Robert H. Bates, Rui P. de Figueiredo, Jr., and Barry R. Weingast, "The Politics of Interpretation: Rationality, Culture, and Transition," *Politics and Society* 26:4 (1998), pp. 603–38; and Valerie Braithwaite and Margaret Levi, eds., *Trust and Governance* (New York: Russell Sage Foundation, 1998).

[47] For example, Ferejohn argues that "culturally shared understandings and meanings" are important for selecting among multiple equilibria (p. 285). John Ferejohn, "Rationality and Interpretation: Parliamentary Elections in Early Stuart England," in K. Monroe, ed., *The Economic Approach to Politics* (New York: Harper-Collins, 1991), pp. 279–305.

[48] Gary Becker, *The Economic Approach to Human Behavior* (Chicago: Univ. of Chicago Press, 1976), p. 8. Also, for a notable analysis that attempts to bring the rational choice framework (economic decision-making) to an explanation of values and norms, see Dennis Chong, *Rational Lives: Norms and Values in Politics and Society* (Chicago: Univ. of Chicago Press, 2000). For an overview of recent applications of economic analysis to human and social behavior, see Jeffrey Friedman, ed., *The Rational Choice Controversy: Economic Models of Politics Reconsidered* (New Haven, CT: Yale Univ. Press, 1996). This volume is a response to Donald P. Green and Ian Shapiro, *Pathologies of Rational Choice Theory: A Critique of Applications in Political Science* (New Haven, CT: Yale Univ. Press, 1994).

psychology. In the absence of strong environmental constraints, we believe that rational choice is a weak theory, with limited predictive power.[49]

Similarly, Arthur Denzau and Douglass North argued that institutions are crucial in supporting the development of "maximizing-style" economic decisions (which may have efficiency gains in resource allocation), and they also argued that understanding cognition will become increasingly important to explaining economic decision-making.[50]

These analyses suggest that the question of the origins of preferences cannot be dismissed simply by the inclusion of institutions as a mediating mechanism between economic reality and interests because the underlying cognitive model that supported the assertion of objectivity (i.e., the unmediated relationship between interests and the external environment) has also been increasingly undermined.[51]

Orthodox Critiques in Nationalism Studies

Most of the literature on the political economy of nationalism is characterized by orthodox critiques of objectivism. Rather than positing a strictly linear relationship between structural economic conditions and regionalist activism, the treatment of the economy in the literature on nationalism, regionalism, and separatism tends to consider mediating factors in the relationship between economic interests in sovereignty and objective economic conditions. Orthodox critiques of objectivity provide some insight into the mechanisms of mediation, which include changes in values, expectations and perceptions, and institutions. All these factors intervene between real economic conditions and group understandings, with an impact on both nationalist mobilization and the pursuit of greater sovereignty.

The concept of modernization or development occupies an important role in many of the most prominent theories of nationalism. Modernization was once thought to be the end of nationalism and particularism. The

---

[49] Debra Satz and John Ferejohn, "Rational Choice and Social Theory," *Journal of Philosophy* 91:2 (February 1994), p. 72.

[50] Arthur T. Denzau and Douglass C. North, "Shared Mental Models: Ideologies and Institutions," *Kyklos* 47 (1994), pp. 3–31; later republished in Arthur Lupia, Mathew D. McCubbins, Samuel L. Popkin, eds., *Elements of Reason: Cognition, Choice, and the Bounds of Rationality* (New York: Cambridge Univ. Press, 2000), pp. 23–46.

[51] For more on this point and an excellent review of the preference formation literature, see James N. Druckman and Arthur Lupia, "Preference Formation," *Annual Review of Political Science* 3 (June 2000), pp. 1–24.

process of development and its attendant changes in values, it was argued, would lead to a weakening of the salience of ethnicity and distinctive ethnic ties and would lead instead to universalist state-building, thereby reducing the probability of nationalism and separatism.[52] However, by the 1970s, regionalist and nationalist movements in some of the most industrialized countries in Europe appeared to challenge this argument.[53] It turned out that the same processes of state-building and economic development

[52] For an early statement linking modernization to social and political integration across ethnic communities, see Karl W. Deutsch, *Nationalism and Social Communication: An Inquiry into the Foundations of Nationality*, 2nd ed. (Cambridge, MA: MIT Press, 1966); and Karl W. Deutsch, Sidney A. Burrell, Robert A. Kahn, Maurice Lee, Martin Lichterman, Raymond E. Lindgren, Francis L. Loewenheim, and Richard W. Van Wagenen, *Political Community and the North Atlantic Area* (Princeton, NJ: Princeton Univ. Press, 1957). On the idea that modernity would reduce the salience of ethnicity, see Ernst B. Haas, "International Integration: The European and the Universal Process," *International Political Communities: An Anthology* (Garden City, NY: Anchor Books, 1966), pp. 93–129; Seymour M. Lipset and Stein Rokkan, "Cleavage Structures, Party Systems and Voter Alignments: An Introduction," in S. M. Lipset and S. Rokkan, eds., *Party Systems and Voter Alignments* (New York: Free Press, 1967), pp. 1–64; Edward Shils, *Center and Periphery: Essays in Macrosociology* (Chicago: Univ. of Chicago Press, 1975). On the Soviet Union, see Gregory Gleason, *Federalism and Nationalism: The Struggle for Republican Rights in the USSR* (Boulder, CO: Westview Press, 1990). For arguments against the claim that modernization or development would result in decreased regionalism or a weakening of the salience of ethnicity, see Anthony H. Birch, "Minority Nationalist Movements and Theories of Political Integration," *World Politics* 30 (April 1978), pp. 325–44; Walker Connor, "Nation Building or Nation Destroying?" *World Politics* 24 (April 1972), pp. 319–55; and Clifford Geertz, "The Integrative Revolution: Primordial Sentiments and Civil Politics in the New States," in Clifford Geertz, ed., *Old Societies and New States* (New York: Free Press, 1963), pp. 105–57.

[53] For analyses demonstrating the persistence of regionalism or nationalism in the face of modernization, see Thomas O. Hueglin, "Regionalism in Western Europe: Conceptual Problems of a New Political Perspective," *Comparative Politics* 18:4 (July 1986), pp. 439–58; Michael Keating, *State and Regional Nationalism: Territorial Politics and the European State* (New York: Harvester Wheatsheaf, 1988); Milton Esman, ed., *Ethnic Conflict in the Western World* (Ithaca, NY: Cornell Univ. Press, 1977); Sidney Tarrow, Peter J. Katzenstein, and Luigi Graziano, eds., *Territorial Politics in Industrial Nations* (New York: Praeger, 1978); Joseph Rudolph and Robert Thompson, "Ethnoterritorial Movements and the Policy Process: Accommodating Nationalist Demands in the Developed World," *Comparative Politics* 17 (April 1985), pp. 291–311; Laurence J. Sharpe, ed., *Decentralist Trends in Western Democracies* (London: Sage, 1979); Charles R. Foster, ed., *Nations without a State: Ethnic Minorities in Western Europe* (New York: Praeger, 1980); Jean Gottmann, ed., *Centre and Periphery* (Beverly Hills, CA: Sage, 1980); Per Torsvik, ed., *Mobilization: Center-Periphery Structures and Nation Building* (Bergen: Universitetsforlaget, 1981); Yves Meny and Vincent Wright, eds., *Centre-Periphery Relations in Western Europe* (London: Allen & Unwin, 1985); Stein Rokkan and Derek W. Urwin, eds., *The Politics of Territorial Identity* (London: Sage, 1982); and Edward A. Tiryakian and Ronald Rogowski, ed., *New Nationalisms of the Developed West: Toward Explanation* (Boston: Allen & Unwin, 1985).

associated with modernization could lead not only to the development of national-state consciousness and assimilation but also to within-state (or within-empire), group-based national consciousness, and hence to a greater level of internal nationalist or separatist movements.[54] Ernest Gellner notably argued, "The age of transition to industrialism was bound [to be] an age of nationalism."[55] The treatment of modernization and development as a crucial factor in the development of nationalism is now widely accepted, and it is generally consistent with the idea that economically advanced or developed areas will be most likely to advance nationalist or secessionist claims. However, the mechanism linking economic conditions and political action (either nationalist mobilization or assimilation) is essentially a change in values combined with economic and institutional resources, rather than just structural economic conditions alone.

An alternative mechanism for mediating between economic conditions and economic interests in greater sovereignty is relative expectations and perceptions. One of the earliest and most prominent statements on relative rather than real assessments of the economy, and indeed the origin of the term *relative deprivation*, comes from Ted Gurr's analysis of rebellion.[56] The concept of relative deprivation refers to the perceived, rather than real, disadvantage in the economic circumstances of oneself or one's group in comparison with others.[57] Relative deprivation provides a way of accounting for the variance in understandings of the economy and real economic conditions. A complementary thesis to relative deprivation is the idea that expectations about the economy, rather than existing economic conditions,

---

[54] Prominent analyses that focus on the role of modernization include Ernest Gellner, *Nations and Nationalism* (Ithaca, NY: Cornell Univ. Press, 1983); Miroslav Hroch, *Social Preconditions of National Revival in Europe* (Cambridge: Cambridge Univ. Press, 1985); and Benedict Anderson, *Imagined Communities: Reflections on the Origin and Spread of Nationalism*, rev. ed. (London: Verso, 1996). Anderson focuses more specifically on print capitalism. On the Soviet Union, see Philip G. Roeder, "Soviet Federalism and Ethnic Mobilization," *World Politics* 43:2 (January 1991), pp. 196–232.

[55] Gellner, 1983, p. 40.

[56] Ted Robert Gurr, *Why Men Rebel* (Princeton, NJ: Princeton Univ. Press, 1970). Also, for arguments that link regionalism with resentment at having to support poor or less developed neighbors, see John Agnew "Structural and Dialectical Theories of Political Regionalism," in A. Burnett and P. Taylor, eds., *Political Studies from Spatial Perspectives* (Chichester, UK: Wiley, 1981), pp. 275–89; and A. Mugham, "Modernization and Regional Relative Deprivation: Towards a Theory of Ethnic Conflict," in L. J. Sharpe, ed., *Decentralist Trends in Western Democracies* (London: Sage, 1979), pp. 279–312.

[57] On the gap between subjective perceptions and objective conditions, see Ralph Matthews, *The Creation of Regional Dependency* (Toronto: Univ. of Toronto Press, 1983).

may influence the development of regionalism.[58] Finally, another variation on this argument is that, particularly during periods of economic prosperity, disadvantaged ethnic groups, spurred on by the hope for greater economic opportunities and resources, will make regionalist claims.[59]

Relative deprivation, and the expectations that underlie the sense of deprivation, may be a function of actors' selection of comparative cases. The economic experience of Eastern European countries during the Cold War provides a good example: Under the postwar Soviet occupation, each country was better off economically in the 1980s than it had been following the end of World War II. However, the relevant comparison for Eastern European states was not their immediate postwar conditions but rather the economic conditions of their Western European neighbors. Therefore, in this case, the economic dissatisfaction was largely a function of the selection of comparative cases. Even so, these theories of relative deprivation and expectations tell us little about why groups choose the cases they do for comparison.

A final mechanism for mediation of economic conditions, which follows from orthodox critiques of economic objectivism, is found in institutions and the institutional resources of groups, including group skill sets and prospects for elite mobility. Particular institutions may make separatism less likely by appeasing autonomy demands (e.g., less taxes).[60] For example, building on the research agenda suggested by Charles Tiebout in 1956, several studies have attempted to work out the relationship between taxation policies and separatism.[61] James Buchanan and Roger Faith argue that central governments consider rich regions more likely to secede, but

---

[58] For example, Meadwell considers regionalism as a rational response to unfulfilled economic and political preferences. Hudson Meadwell, "A Rational Choice Approach to Political Regionalism," *Comparative Politics* 23:4 (1991), pp. 401–21.

[59] See Peter Gourevitch, "The Reemergence of Peripheral Nationalisms: Some Comparative Speculations on the Spatial Distribution of Political Leadership and Economic Growth," *Comparative Studies in Society and History* 21 (July 1979), pp. 303–22.

[60] For the argument that higher levels of institutional autonomy might appease separatist claims in the case of the Soviet Union, see Paul Brass, "Language and National Identity in the Soviet Union and India," in A. Motyl, ed., *Thinking Theoretically about Soviet Nationalities: History and Comparison in the Study of the USSR* (New York: Columbia Univ. Press, 1992) pp. 99–128.

[61] Charles Tiebout, "A Pure Theory of Local Expenditures," *Journal of Political Economy* 64 (October 1956), pp. 416–24. On the relationship between taxation and secession, see D. Andrew Austin, "Coordinated Action in Local Public Goods Models: The Case of Secession without Exclusion," *Journal of Public Economics* 58:2 (October 1995), pp. 235–57; and James Buchanan and Roger L. Faith, "Secession and the Limits of Taxation: Toward a Theory of Internal Exit," *American Economic Review* 77:5 (1987), pp. 1023–31.

because of this likelihood of secession, the demands of rich regions are more likely to be met, and secession is averted. In such models, separatism is a function of current institutional arrangements and regional economic endowment.

In addition to institutions that affect the region as a whole, institutions that affect group attributes and resources within the region may also mediate separatist demands. For example, in considering mobility prospects, David Laitin argued that if there were opportunities for economic advancement in the center, then regional elites would favor keeping ties with the center in order to retain privileges.[62] Similarly, others argued that separatism was more likely if mobility prospects in the center were blocked and breaking with the center bore greater opportunities for economic advancement.[63]

As we have already seen, Horowitz argued that the likeliest groups to seek separatism would be the "backward groups in backward regions."[64] He also argued that under certain institutional circumstances, "advanced groups" from "backward regions" might also support separatism even though their continued pursuit would be unlikely owing to their presumed preference to assimilate into the center where there were more economic opportunities. But, if their mobility prospects in the center were blocked and if they faced violence and severe discrimination, then advanced groups might support a separatist movement. Because discrimination and mobility prospects are almost always institutionalized, the relevant mechanism is not the economic position of groups within the region but rather the institutionalized differentiation of groups.

These arguments regarding the role of values, perceptions and expectations, and institutions all address, to some extent, why there might be variance in regionalism, given similar economic conditions. However, they

---

[62] David D. Laitin, "The Nationalist Uprisings in the Soviet Union," *World Politics* 44:1 (1991), pp. 139–77.

[63] For example, Mitra and Premdas both argue that blocked mobility and discrimination lead to secessionsist claims. Subrata K. Mitra, "The Rational Politics of Cultural Nationalism: Subnational Movements of South Asia in Comparative Perspective," *British Journal of Political Science* 25 (1995), pp. 57–78; and Ralph R. Premdas, S. W. R. de A. Samarasinghe, and Alan B. Anderson, eds., *Secessionist Movements in Comparative Perspective* (London: Pinter Publishers, 1990). Shastri merged insights from Hechter and Horowitz to argue that separatism was caused by the combination of blocked mobility prospects for advanced elites from backward regions and by the process of development of a "backward" region that would highlight economic potential. Amita Shastri, "The Material Basis for Separatism: The Tamil Eelam Movement in Sri Lanka," *Journal of Asian Studies* 49:1 (February 1990), pp. 56–77.

[64] Horowitz, 1985, p. 236.

all nonetheless posit an objective reality upon which institutions are based, and from which local perceptions may differ; in this sense, the economy itself remains real and objective. As I will discuss in the next section, accumulating evidence from a variety of disciplines makes this objective status of the economy difficult to sustain.

Heterodox Critiques: Constructivist Political Economy

Cognitive Bases of Constructivism: Schema Theory

Since the 1960s, but especially since the mid-1980s, research in cognitive science and psychology has increasingly questioned the classic view of cognition and has provided important scientific evidence against the mind-as-calculator model and its related presumption of objectivity. The development of connectionist neural models of cognition provided a major breakthrough in the conceptualization of mental processing of information, and social psychologists have expanded on and extended these insights in the field of social cognition.[65]

Schema theory is one area of research in this large and growing field that problematizes the objectivity of understanding and therefore provides a number of important insights for constructivist social science. *Schema*, as used in this study, refers to the interpretation of information about the outside world by using experience-derived patterns. Schemas are developed through interaction with material conditions and events and hence can be considered *products* of experience, but the act of *processing* information distinguishes schemas from being simply "pictures" in the mind. In other words, schemas are processors, developed through experience, used by individuals to understand information about the world. Robert Axelrod used schemas in a similar way, arguing that they describe "perceptual and cognitive processes."[66]

---

[65] For an excellent overview of the field, see Susan T. Fiske and Shelley E. Taylor, *Social Cognition*, 2nd ed. (New York: McGraw-Hill, 1991). For an overview of the large literature on social identity theory, see Henri Tajfel and John C. Turner, "An Integrative Theory of Intergroup Conflict" in M. Hogg and D. Abrams, eds., *Intergroup Relations: Essential Readings* (Philadelphia, PA: Psychology Press, 2001), pp. 94–109; and John C. Turner, "Some Current Issues in Research on Social Identity and Self-Categorization Theory" in N. Ellemers, R. Spears, and B. Doosje, eds., *Social Identity: Context, Commitment, Content* (Oxford, 1999), pp. 6–34.

[66] Robert Axelrod, "Schema Theory: An Informational Processing Model of Perception and Cognition," *American Political Science Review* 67 (1973), p. 1249. Axelrod used this model

By treating schemas as simultaneous products and processors of experience, schema theory addresses larger debates in social science regarding the distinction between subjectivity and empirical reality. Schema theory rejects objectivist readings of material conditions because it rejects the idea that subjectivity is a veil of cultural symbols masking the real external conditions. By making the claim that schemas are *processors of actual experience*, schemas cannot be reduced to mental representations separated from reality. And yet, experience is more than simply objective information, because similar experiences may be understood differently. In this way, schema theory does more than simply cast doubt on an overly materialist position. Through the conceptualization of an interactive relationship between the experience of material conditions and understanding, schema theory provides a middle ground in the debate between subjectivists and objectivists.

Roy D'Andrade, working in anthropology, but borrowing from cognitive science and psychology, has used schema theory in concert with social theory to render the concept of culture analytically more tractable. For example, D'Andrade has identified several implications of schema theory for the study of culture. First, culture is not reduced to simply symbolic representation; culture includes rules and propositions as well as patterns, and the learning of rules versus patterns has important consequences. Second, interaction with the physical environment (i.e., experience) is important to cultural learning and to the production of cultural representation. Third, the question of how culture can be both durable and changeable is theoretically resolvable. Fourth, epistemological issues regarding the relationship between subjective understandings and empirical reality are also theoretically resolvable. On this point, D'Andrade writes that "the notion that culture is a veil which continuously distorts what can be truly known of the external world changes from a plausible metaphor to an incomplete account of a much more complex process."[67]

Increasingly, advances in cognitive science have made their way into economics and the study of economic rationality.[68] Andy Clark, for example, argued that the critique of classical cognition speaks to recent work on

---

to dissect decision-making, via cognitive mapping, in order to classify the "preconceived notions" that are a crucial part of the decision-making process. He specifically uses schemas to describe information processing by individuals, rather than social groups or governments.

[67] D'Andrade, 1995, p. 149.

[68] For example, see Lupia et al., 2000.

"scaffolded choice" in economic decision-making.[69] He wrote: "One upshot of this recent explosion of work on bounded, real-time, embodied and environmentally embedded reason is a growing sense of discontent with the image of rational choice as maximizing reward relative to a complete and consistent ordering of preferences."[70] Similarly, Brian Arthur argued that the economy is traditionally thought of in physical terms with decision-making agents, but following theoretical contributions from psychology and cognitive science, the economy itself can be conceptualized as

a collection of beliefs, anticipations, expectations, and interpretations, with decision-making and strategizing and action-taking predicated upon these beliefs and expectations. Of course these two views are related. Activities follow from beliefs and expectations. And beliefs and expectations are mediated and sculpted by the physical economy they find themselves in.[71] _→ cognitive science and perception_

One of the central implications of the models of cognition outlined here is that economic rationality is not distinct from other types of rationality, and economic or material facts are not distinct from other aspects of the external environment. The discussion of these cognitive models suggests that decision-making models, which assume only rule-based serial calculation, are incomplete at best. Moreover, this research suggests a cognitive basis for constructivism and further support for the rejection of a single "true" or universal interpretation of economic conditions.

Constructivist Views of Economic Interests and the Economy

In my view, the defining characteristic of the many varieties of constructivism currently in use in social science research is the challenge they pose to essentialism and determinism.[72] Essentialist models, be they primordial,

---

[69] Andy Clark, "Economic Reason: The Interplay of Individual Learning and External Structure," in J. N. Drobak and J. V. C. Nye, eds., *The Frontiers of the New Institutional Economics* (New York: Academic Press, 1997), pp. 269–90. On scaffolded choice, he is mainly referring to Satz and Ferejohn, 1994, and Denzau and North, 1994 [2000]. For a discussion of economic action in contexts of uncertainty, see Jens Beckert, "What Is Sociological about Economic Sociology? Uncertainty and the Embeddedness of Economic Action," *Theory and Society* 25:6 (December 1996), pp. 803–40.

[70] Clark, 1997, p. 270.

[71] Brian Arthur, "Beyond Rational Expectations: Indeterminacy in Economic and Financial Markets," in Drobak and Nye, 1997, pp. 291–2.

[72] The distinction between orthodox and heterodox critiques is a matter of interpretation. I argue that the dividing criterion is the degree of essentialism in the treatment of political, social, or material conditions, but where one draws this line is a matter of debate. In a

77

materialist, or objectivist, posit a single correct interpretation of external reality, and deterministic models posit a privileged set of correct behaviors or processes that should follow from that reality. Orthodox critiques have recognized gaps in the understanding of reality, where individuals or groups don't seem to understand external conditions correctly, and they have recognized gaps in behavior where actions seem to diverge from what objective conditions would predict based on materialist (e.g., efficiency) or other essential interests (e.g., ethnic affiliation).

Constructivist theories are built upon these orthodox critiques of objectivity, but they are heterodox because they do not fundamentally recognize a single reality or a single correct path of action. As such, their purpose lies not in explaining away self-interest anomalies, but instead in recognizing these breaks with objective conditions as integral and constitutive elements of the processes under study. Constructivist approaches look beyond objective external conditions to the role of historical legacies, contingency,

footnote, Kathleen Thelen suggested a similar distinction for institutionalist analysis based on materialist approaches on the one hand and ideational approaches on the other, and she suggested that the materialist criterion cut across the rational choice/non-rational choice divide. See Kathleen Thelen, "Historical Institutionalism in Comparative Politics," *Annual Reviews of Political Science* 2 (1999), p. 380. In this framework, *materialist* work might include historical institutionalists such as Terry L. Karl, *The Paradox of Plenty: Oil Booms and Petro-States* (Berkeley: Univ. of California Press, 1997); Peter Swenson, *Fair Shares* (Ithaca, NY: Cornell Univ. Press, 1989); and Ellen M. Immergut, "The Theoretical Core of the New Institutionalism," *Politics and Society* 26:1 (1998), pp. 5–34; and rational choice scholars such as Jack Knight, *Institutions and Social Conflict* (New York: Cambridge Univ. Press, 1992); and George Tsebelis, *Nested Games: Rational Choice in Comparative Politics* (Berkeley: Univ. of California Press, 1990). Similarly, *ideational* work might include historical institutionalists such as Peter J. Katzenstein, ed., *The Culture of National Security: Norms and Identity in World Politics* (New York: Columbia Univ. Press, 1996a); Peter J. Katzenstein, *Cultural Norms and National Security: Police and Military in Postwar Japan* (Ithaca, NY: Cornell Univ. Press, 1996b); and Peter A. Hall, ed., *The Political Power of Economic Ideas: Keynesianism across Nations* (Princeton, NJ: Princeton Univ. Press, 1989); and rational choice scholars such as Douglass North *Institutions, Institutional Change and Economic Performance* (New York: Cambridge Univ. Press, 1990) and Margaret Levi, *Consent, Dissent and Patriotism* (New York: Cambridge Univ. Press, 1997). My approach to constructivism is consistent with Thelen's suggestion that rational choice is not the dividing criterion, but I extend the criterion beyond materialism/ideationalism to essentialism more broadly construed, as discussed later. This critique of essentialism has a long history. For example, in rejecting the modernity/tradition distinction, Rudolph and Rudolph presented one of the earliest challenges to the primordialist framework. They deprived culture of its essentialist cage and demonstrated how something as stable and traditional as caste had been reconceptualized and used in the construction of modernity in India. See Lloyd I. Rudolph and Susanne Hoeber Rudolph, *The Modernity of Tradition: Political Development in India* (Chicago: Univ. of Chicago Press, 1967).

human innovation, and experimentation in both the construction of reality and human interaction. It should be noted however that, as I will discuss later, constructivist political economy approaches are quite heterogeneous in their approaches to questions of agency and structure.

Max Weber's analysis of objectivity in the social sciences is one of the early works that addresses the foundation of constructivism through the questioning of the universal meaning of information.[73] Given the utter expansiveness of empirical knowledge, Weber argued not only that evaluative ideas are present in scientific analysis, but also that it is only through the use of evaluative ideas that scientists can make sense of empirical reality. Weber claimed that because even a mere description of the smallest bit of empirical reality "can never be exhaustive," and because there are an infinite number of causal explanations for any single event, an analysis "without presuppositions" (if it were even possible) could only result in "a chaos of 'existential judgments.'" This chaos is avoided both consciously and unconsciously through the use of evaluative ideas:

> Order is brought into this chaos only on the condition that in every case only a *part* of concrete reality is interesting and *significant* to us, because only it is related to the *cultural values* with which we approach reality. Only certain sides of the infinitely complex concrete phenomena, namely those to which we attribute a general *cultural significance* – are therefore worthwhile knowing.[74]

Weber's analysis suggests that values give external reality *meaning*. Furthermore, the claim that analysis is guided only by empirical reality, and that the facts can "speak for themselves," is, according to Weber, a result of "naive self-deception" on the part of the scientist.[75]

Moreover, Weber argued that science is incapable of "discovering" meaning in the world because meaning does not exist independently. In other words, understanding cannot come from the objective replication of unordered bits of empirical reality. Weber wrote:

> The fate of an epoch which has eaten of the tree of knowledge is that it must know that we cannot learn the *meaning* of the world from the results of its analysis, be it ever so perfect; it must rather be in a position to create this meaning itself. It must recognize that general views of life and the universe can never be the products of

---

[73] Max Weber, "'Objectivity' in Social Science," in Edward A. Shils and Henry A. Finch, trans. and eds., *The Methodology of the Social Sciences* (New York: The Free Press, 1949), pp. 50–112.
[74] Ibid., p. 78. Emphasis in original.
[75] Ibid., p. 82.

increasing empirical knowledge, and that the highest ideals, which move us most forcefully, are always formed only in the struggle with other ideals which are just as sacred to others as ours are to us.[76]

With this statement, Weber has turned about the relationship between scientific knowledge and specific values, ideas, and beliefs. Weber's analysis suggests the inescapable situatedness of knowledge and rejects the claim that ideas or beliefs inhibit the understanding of external reality, instead recognizing the necessary role of ideas in understanding external conditions.

Economic sociology extends this Weberian notion of situated knowledge by contextualizing the economy and calling into question the boundary between the social and the economic.[77] For example, in his work on socialist economies, János Kornai's *The Socialist System* outlined the *systemic* nature of the Soviet economy, as encompassing interactive social, political, and economic elements – an argument that also applies to capitalist systems.[78] Similarly, but in a more constructivist vein, Andrew Abbott critiqued the notion of "general linear reality."[79] Abbott considered demographic, sequential, and network perspectives and argued for the need to consider the timing and sequencing of factors, and the necessity of relaxing assumptions about the stability and the independence of entities or events in order to recognize how they can influence each other. Abbott also criticized the "univocal meaning" in variables, that is, the treatment of variables in models as having only one causal meaning. He noted for example that a single variable, such as "wealth" can have multiple meanings.[80] Recently, work in economic sociology has considered cultural understandings of the economy, including

[76] Ibid., p. 57.

[77] On contextualizing the economy, see Mark Granovetter and Richard Swedberg, eds., *The Sociology of Economic Life* (Boulder, CO: Westview Press, 1992). See also Arjun Appadurai, ed., *The Social Life of Things: Commodities in Cultural Perspective* (New York: Cambridge Univ. Press, 1986). For an encyclopedic review of economic sociology from a variety of perspectives, see Neil J. Smelser and Richard Swedberg, eds., *The Handbook of Economic Sociology* (Princeton, NJ: Princeton Univ. Press, 1994).

[78] János Kornai, *The Socialist System: The Political Economy of Communism* (Princeton, NJ: Princeton Univ. Press, 1992). Kornai also made the interesting argument that economic transitions (e.g., from socialism to capitalism) can be analyzed in a Kuhnian sense as encompassing paradigmatic shifts in understandings, rather than just changes in practices or material entities. János Kornai, "The System Paradigm," *Collegium Budapest Discussion Paper Series*, no. 58 (July 1999), pp. 1–27.

[79] Andrew Abbott, "Transcending General Linear Reality," *Sociological Theory* 6 (Fall 1988), pp. 169–86.

[80] Ibid., p. 175.

markets, as both a product and producer of culture, and the role of networks, gender, and social capital in the development of economic institutions and policy.[81]

The burgeoning field of historical institutionalism, and the empirical work that follows from it, has provided substantial support for the idea that politics and society shape economic institutions.[82] Among economists, institutional development has been divorced from purely functional or efficiency arguments to encompass the role of culture and informal institutions in formal institutional outcomes. For example, Douglass North argued that through the creation of particular incentive structures, culture and tradition influence informal institutions, which in turn influence the development of formal institutions. Together these processes affect efficiency outcomes and economic performance.[83] More recently, the varieties of capitalism literature has considered how certain institutions or policy choices raise returns for others.[84]

Many constructivists, rather than conceiving of political actors as separate from, or acting within, an exogenously given institutional context, emphasize the way that actors both create conditions – ideational, material, and institutional – and are shaped by those conditions. In this way, economic institutions are products of the mutually constituting interaction of actors and the social, political, and economic conditions in which they exist. For example, Gary Herrigel analyzed the development of alternative forms of capitalist organization in Germany (i.e., economic institutions) by disaggregating and denaturalizing the process of industrialization.[85] In

[81] See, for example, Mauro F. Guillén, Randall Collins, Paula England, and Marshall Meyer, eds., *The New Economic Sociology: Developments in an Emerging Field* (New York: Russell Sage, 2002).

[82] For a lucid discussion of three "types" of institutionalism (rational choice, historical, and sociological), see Peter A. Hall and Rosemary Taylor, "Political Science and the Three New Institutionalisms," *Political Studies* 44 (1996), pp. 936–57. Also, for an overview of the field, see Thelen, 1999, pp. 369–404.

[83] North, 1990. Similarly, Jack Knight was critical of approaches that considered institutions as necessarily efficiency-improving (evolutionary) and instead analyzed the role of distributional conflicts in institutional development. See Knight, 1992.

[84] Peter A. Hall and David Soskice, eds., *Varieties of Capitalism: The Institutional Foundations of Comparative Advantage* (New York: Oxford Univ. Press, 2001); and Steven K. Vogel, *Freer Markets, More Rules: Regulatory Reform in Advanced Industrial Countries* (Ithaca, NY: Cornell Univ. Press, 1996).

[85] Gary Herrigel, *Industrial Constructions: The Sources of German Industrial Power* (New York: Cambridge Univ. Press, 1996). See also Richard M. Locke, *Remaking the Italian Economy* (Ithaca, NY: Cornell Univ. Press, 1995); Bruce G. Carruthers, *City of Capital: Politics and*

a recent Russian example, David Woodruff analyzed the development (or lack thereof) of monetary consolidation, through an examination of how the meaning of money, that is, its value to local actors, varied (as a means of payment versus a medium of exchange).[86]

One mechanism for the interaction between actors and institutional development is the concept of networks. Networks are at once institutions, informal or sometimes formal, and are also actors. David Stark and László Bruszt analyzed the role of networks as deliberative institutions that functioned as alternatives to markets and hierarchies, and that were an important source of innovation in economic institutional development.[87] More recently, Gerald McDermott considered the role of industrial networks, in terms of associative ties, on the development of new economic institutions and economic reform (privatization and growth).[88]

In addition to emphasizing the interaction between actors and institutional development, constructivist approaches to the economy have also specifically focused on the role of norms, ideas, and ideology in shaping economic interests and institutions. For example, Peter Katzenstein demonstrated how norms affect the definition of interests and action in the form of appropriate conduct, and also how norms get institutionalized.[89] This work specifically critiqued the concept of economic interests as a direct reflection of economic conditions. Similarly, Mark Blyth provided a Polanyian account of the role of economic ideas in institutional change, emphasizing the mutual constitution of ideas and interests.[90] An example that speaks to the Soviet experience is Stephen Hanson's analysis of the role of Marxist and Leninist ideology in the development of Soviet economic institutions, in particular, conceptions of time – something that is often

---

Markets in the English Financial Revolution (Princeton, NJ: Princeton Univ. Press, 1996); Kathleen McNamara *The Currency of Ideas: Monetary Politics in the European Union* (Ithaca, NY, Cornell Univ. Press, 1998); and Adam Segal, *Digital Dragon: High-Technology Enterprises in China* (Ithaca, NY: Cornell Univ. Press, 2003). Segal explores regional understandings of economic development in China.

[86] David Woodruff, *Money Unmade: Barter and the Fate of Russian Capitalism* (Ithaca, NY: Cornell Univ. Press, 1999). See also Eric Helleiner, *The Making of National Money: Territorial Currencies in Historical Perspective* (Ithaca, NY: Cornell Univ. Press, 2003).

[87] David Stark and László Bruszt, *Postsocialist Pathways: Transforming Politics and Property in East Central Europe* (New York: Cambridge Univ. Press, 1998).

[88] Gerald A. McDermott, *Embedded Politics: Industrial Networks and Institutional Change in Postcommunism* (Ann Arbor, MI: Univ. of Michigan Press, 2002).

[89] Katzenstein, 1996b.

[90] Mark Blyth, *Great Transformations: Economic Ideas and Institutional Change in the Twentieth Century* (New York: Cambridge Univ. Press, 2002).

taken for granted as objective and outside the realm of ideology or social construction.[91]

A major area of research in constructivist political economy and historical institutionalism more generally has focused on the related issues of timing and interactions of political and social processes in shaping economic interests and institutions.[92] By demonstrating how timing matters to the construction of interests and policy outcomes, to paraphrase Paul Pierson, and "by embedding temporal processes in institutions," works that focus on path dependency and critical junctures further support the case against the objectivity of economic interests and external conditions.[93] Moreover, "feedback mechanisms," are another way of getting at the process by which actors, external conditions, and institutions are mutually constituting.[94]

By problematizing the formation of economic interests, constructivist political economy directly addresses the issue of the origins of preferences.[95]

---

[91] Stephen E. Hanson, *Time and Revolution: Marxism and the Design of Soviet Institutions* (Chapel Hill, NC: Univ. of North Carolina Press, 1997).

[92] For example, Rueschemeyer et al. argued that "causal analysis is inherently sequence analysis." Dietrich Rueschemeyer, Evelyne H. Stephens, and John D. Stephens, *Capitalist Development and Democracy* (Chicago: Univ. of Chicago Press, 1992), p. 4. Notable works that address the issue of timing include Sven Steinmo, *Taxation and Democracy: Swedish, British and American Approaches to Financing the Modern State* (New Haven, CT: Yale Univ. Press, 1993); Karen Orren and Stephen Skowronek, "Beyond the Iconography of Order: Notes for a 'New' Institutionalism," in L. C. Dodd and C. Jillson, eds., *The Dynamics of American Politics* (Boulder, CO: Westview, 1994), pp. 311–32; and Ira Katznelson, "Structure and Configuration in Comparative Politics," in M. I. Lichbach and A. S. Zuckerman, eds., *Comparative Politics: Rationality, Culture and Structure* (New York: Cambridge Univ. Press, 1997), pp. 81–112.

[93] Paul Pierson, "The Path to European Integration: A Historical Institutionalist Approach," *Comparative Political Studies* 29:2 (1996), p. 126. For a comprehensive review of path dependency, see Paul Pierson, "Path Dependence, Increasing Returns, and the Study of Politics," *American Political Science Review*, 94:2 (June 2000), pp. 251–67. On the legacies and reproduction of critical junctures, see Ruth B. Collier and David Collier, *Shaping the Political Arena* (Princeton, NJ: Princeton Univ. Press, 1991). Also see Ruth B. Collier, "Combining Alternative Perspectives: Internal Trajectories versus External Influences as Explanations of Latin American Politics in the 1940s," *Comparative Politics* 26:1 (1993), pp. 1–30; and Richard Locke and Kathleen Thelen, "Apples and Oranges Revisited: Contextualized Comparisons and the Study of Comparative Labor Politics," *Politics and Society* 23:3 (1995), pp. 337–67.

[94] For an analysis of how timing can affect power distribution via feedback mechanisms that are self-reinforcing, see Paul Pierson, "When Effect Becomes Cause: Policy Feedback and Political Change," *World Politics* 45:4 (1993), pp. 595–628.

[95] Thelen and Steinmo argued that one of the differences between rational choice approaches to institutions and historical institutionalism was the question of where preferences come from. In rational choice models, interests tend to be exogenous, whereas in historical

83

And, in contrast to external economic conditions, institutions are a primary source of the development of interests.[96] For example, John Zysman argued that "the definition of interests and objectives is created in institutional contexts and is not separable from them."[97] Similarly Theda Skocpol argued that institutions "affect the capabilities of various groups to achieve self-consciousness, organize, and make alliances."[98] Indeed, institutional contexts not only shape interests but also affect the constitution of particular groups themselves. For example, Gøsta Esping-Anderson analyzed the institutional context of the development of the working class in welfare states and in particular how the institutional context shaped groups' self-understandings and interests.[99] Others similarly argued that group interests are based on more than just objective material interests, being dependent as well on the institutional context that defines the identity and interests of the group.[100] Moreover, Margaret Weir found that in a particular institutional context, groups with similar objective economic conditions may have different interests.[101] In summarizing future directions for research in political economy, Peter Hall argued that "on many of the most important economic questions of the day, it cannot always be said that the interests of a group or individual are 'given' by their socio-economic position. On the contrary, those interests have to be derived via a process of

institutionalism, interests are endogenously arrived at the in the process of institutional development. See Kathleen Thelen and Sven Steinmo, "Historical Institutionalism in Comparative Politics," in S. Steinmo, K. Thelen, and F. Longstreth, eds., *Structuring Politics: Historical Institutionalism in Comparative Analysis* (New York: Cambridge Univ. Press, 1992), pp. 1–32. While this distinction generally holds, it is to some extent a matter of degree, especially with more current rational choice institutional work (e.g., Elster, 1989; North, 1990; Ferejohn, 1991; and Grief, 1994).

[96] For analyses that consider how institutions affect the development of interests, see Theda Skocpol, *Protecting Soldiers and Mothers: The Political Origins of Social Policy in the United States* (Cambridge: Belknap, 1992); Rueschemeyer et al., 1992; and Margaret Weir, *Politics and Jobs: The Boundaries of Employment Policy in the United States* (Princeton, NJ: Princeton Univ. Press, 1992).

[97] John Zysman, "How Institutions Create Historically Rooted Trajectories of Growth," *Industrial and Corporate Change* 3:1 (1994), p. 244.

[98] Skocpol, 1992, p. 47.

[99] Gøsta Esping-Anderson, *Three Worlds of Welfare Capitalism* (Princeton, NJ: Princeton Univ. Press, 1990).

[100] Weir, 1992; Peter A. Hall, "Policy Paradigms, Social Learning and the State," *Comparative Politics* 25:3 (April 1993), pp. 275–96; and G. Herrigel, "Identity and Institutions: The Social Construction of Trade Unions in Nineteenth-Century Germany and the United States," *Studies in American Political Development* 7 (Fall 1993), pp. 371–94.

[101] Weir, 1992.

interpretation."[102] As I will discuss later, constructivist approaches in the nationalism literature mirror these sentiments with regard to ethnicity and ethnic interests, but thus far have not incorporated constructivist understandings of the *economy* and *economic interests* into the study of nationalism, separatism, and regionalism.

Negotiating Economic Interests and Understandings of the Economy: Power, Social Context, and Habitus

Given the heterodox critiques of economic objectivity from cognitive science and psychology as well as constructivist views of economic interests and the economy (e.g., economic sociology and historical institutionalism), the question arises of how to understand why particular understandings of the economy and economic interests come to be held by different groups. Schema theory emphasizes the role of experience in the development of particular understandings, through associative links, but this conceptualization invites a discussion of how schema development occurs given an uneven distribution of power among groups and individuals in society. Institutional approaches have already, of course, suggested one source of particularistic interests and understandings, namely institutions, and some historical institutionalists have considered how power and legitimacy affect the way in which particular institutions develop and reproduce themselves.[103] However, within the constructivist literature there is some disagreement on questions of agency and structural constraints on institutional change.[104] To develop this aspect of constructivist political economy more fully, I argue that the role of power and social context – in other words, social theory – ought to be considered more explicitly.

---

[102] Peter A. Hall, "The Role of Interests, Institutions, and Ideas in the Comparative Political Economy of the Industrialized Nations," in M. I. Lichbach and A. S. Zuckerman, eds., *Comparative Politics: Rationality, Culture, and Structure* (Cambridge: Cambridge Univ. Press, 1997), p. 197.

[103] For example, Hall analyzed how policy paradigms change. Hall, 1993. In his work on norms, Katzenstein's discussion of political conflicts also brings in power relationships to some extent. Katzenstein, 1996b. And Stinchcombe considers the idea of legitimacy in explaining why certain norms or "scripts" are followed rather than others. Arthur Stinchcombe, "On the Virtues of the Old Institutionalism," *Annual Review of Sociology* 23 (1997), pp. 1–18.

[104] For a review of the structure/agency debates within the constructivist political economy literature, see Pepper D. Culpepper, *Creating Cooperation: How States Develop Human Capital in Europe* (Ithaca, NY: Cornell Univ. Press, 2003), Chapter 1, pp. 1–30.

Pierre Bourdieu's concept of *habitus* is particularly relevant in this regard. Consistent with the heterodox critiques of objectivity that I outlined earlier, Bourdieu rejects objectivist approaches to interests and action. Instead, he offers constructivists an insightful approach into the agency/structure problem, by conceiving it as a "dialectical relationship." As David Swartz writes, Bourdieu

argues against conceptualizing human action as a direct, unmediated response to external factors, whether they be identified as micro-structures of interactions or macro-level cultural, social, or economic factors. Nor does Bourdieu see action as the simple outgrowth from internal factors, such as conscious intentions and calculation, as posited by voluntarist and rational-actor models of human action.... Bourdieu wants to transcend this dichotomy by conceptualizing action so that micro and macro, voluntarist and determinist dimensions of human activity are integrated into a single conceptual movement rather than isolated as mutually exclusive forms of explanation. He thus proposes a structural theory of practice that connects action to culture, structure, and power. This theory undergrids his key concept, *habitus*.[105]

While this might seem like an impossible attempt to square the social science circle, I argue that the concept of habitus offers a relatively simple but productive way of conceptualizing how individuals and groups interact with each other and their environment, and how groups come to have particular understandings of politics, the economy, and their interests. The interplay of orthodox and heterodox conceptual categories in habitus provides the theoretical tools for understanding how a set of categories for understanding may reproduce itself through practice and may be both durable and subject to change. In this regard, the concept of habitus contributes a sense of the conceptual social arena in which possibilities are created and limited for particular understandings of the economy.

Bourdieu's notion of habitus consists of three related concepts: *doxa, orthodoxy*, and *heterodoxy*. Doxa refers to a set of socially stable categories functioning to create a system of meanings and values. The doxa, or set of understandings, appears not only as legitimate but also as natural or beyond

---

[105] David Swartz, *Culture and Power: The Sociology of Pierre Bourdieu* (Chicago, IL: Univ. of Chicago Press, 1997), pp. 8–9. Emphasis in original. In this volume, Swartz presents a lucid and concise overview of the secondary literature on Bourdieu and an analysis of Bourdieu's major contributions to social science. See also, Craig Calhoun, Edward Lipuma, and Moshe Postone, eds., *Bourdieu: Critical Perspectives* (Chicago, IL: Univ. of Chicago Press, 1993).

question. In fact, the most powerful aspect of doxa is the misrecognition of its constructedness, and this quality of naturalness is self-produced by the ordering process itself, thus giving order a self-perpetuating quality. Bourdieu outlined three ways in which the quality of naturalness is produced by the doxa. The first is through the quasi-perfect fit between experienced reality and the doxic processing of interpretations of reality.[106] Bourdieu writes:

Because the subjective necessity and self-evidence of the commonsense world are validated by the objective consensus on the sense of the world, what is essential *goes without saying because it comes without saying*.[107]

In other words, the fact that previously learned categories that are used to make sense of the world, seem to be consistent with new experiences, masks the constructed nature of those categories. Moreover, individuals may share the same categories with others in a society, thereby confirming and reinforcing an individual's sense of the naturalness of the categories. Bourdieu writes that a constructed ordering process may be reinforced through "institutions which constitute collective thought as much as they express it, such as language, myth, and art." Summarizing this point he notes that, "the self-evidence of the world is reduplicated by the instituted discourses about the world in which the whole group's adherence to that self-evidence is affirmed."[108] Status hierarchies illustrate this point. For example, in gender relations, the hierarchy of sex differentiation in occupational categories appears natural and is confirmed by reality: more women than men do stay home to raise children, suggesting that women prefer to stay home and are somehow better at it than men.

A second way in which doxa's apparent naturalness is self-produced is through the internalization of the limits of doxa. If a set of categories becomes so widely shared and unquestioned that it can be considered doxa, then the range of action that an individual can imagine as possible will be dependent upon the individual's understanding of previous experience. Where doxa is operating, the possibility for aspiring to actions that fall outside of the realm of previous understanding is severely limited because

---

[106] Pierre Bourdieu, *Outline of a Theory of Practice* (New York: Cambridge Univ. Press, 1977), p. 164.
[107] Ibid., p. 167. Emphasis in original.
[108] Ibid., p. 167.

aspirations may adjust to fit *uncritical* understandings. Bourdieu writes that when

> the established cosmological and political order is perceived not as arbitrary, i.e., as one possible order among others, but as a self-evident and natural order which goes without saying and therefore goes unquestioned, the agents' aspirations have the same limits as the objective conditions of which they are the product.[109]

Bourdieu writes that out of the dialectic between what is considered possible and what is desirable "arises the *sense of limits*, commonly called the *sense of reality*."[110] Thus, in addition to interpreting new experience according to previous categories, the doxic set of categories will also guide expectations of possibilities for future experiences. Yet future expectations will not be unlimited. Rather, expectations about future possibilities will reflect, and reinforce, previous understandings.

Finally, a third way that the natural quality of the doxa is self-produced is by the repeated use, and therefore reinforcement, of categories by those who are disadvantaged by the very same categories. For example, when women took jobs as nurses because medical school admission was closed to women, that is, by acting within the limits of the doxa, the naturalness of the hierarchy was reinforced. According to Bourdieu, members of

> social categories disadvantaged by the symbolic order, such as women and the young, cannot but recognize the legitimacy of the dominant classification in the very fact that their only chance of neutralizing those of its effects most contrary to their own interests lies in submitting to them in order to make use of them.[111]

While the discussion so far has concentrated on how doxa self-produces a quality of naturalness, absolute naturalness can only exist as an ideal or goal. Bourdieu does not explicitly reject absolute naturalness in his discussion of doxa, but his discussion of orthodoxy and heterodoxy implies this conclusion. Through Bourdieu's conception of orthodoxy and heterodoxy, we can access the second valuable insight of habitus, namely the theorization of change in ordered understandings.

Change in social understandings results from the interplay of orthodoxy and heterodoxy in the struggle over doxa especially during times of "objective crises," that is, when, for a variety of reasons, external events or factors call into question the naturalness of the doxa. As I discuss later,

---

[109] Ibid., p. 166.
[110] Ibid., p. 164. Emphasis in original.
[111] Ibid., pp. 164–5.

in this way, Bourdieu acknowledges the potential effect of external factors without reducing change wholly to those factors. Bourdieu writes that the attempt by the dominant classes to "defend the integrity of doxa" results in *orthodoxy* as "the necessarily imperfect substitute." Orthodoxy, therefore, "aims, without ever entirely succeeding, at restoring the primal state of innocence of doxa."[112] Orthodoxy can thus be understood as the practical imperfect approximation of doxa, that is, an attempt by certain groups to give a constructed set of interpretations a sense of naturalness. However, the orthodox formulation, in itself, reveals that the doxa is not beyond question, for if it were, there would be no need for a group to attempt to create a sense of naturalness. Bourdieu writes that orthodoxy implies "awareness and recognition of the possibility of different or antagonistic beliefs."[113] Moreover, in attempting to approximate the doxa, an orthodox formulation is contrasted against more radical alternatives, *heterodoxy*. Bourdieu argues that orthodoxy cannot exist without reference to heterodoxy. He writes that orthodoxy

exists only in the objective relationship which opposes it to heterodoxy, that is, by reference to the choice...made possible by the existence of *competing possibles* and to the explicit critique of the sum total of the alternatives not chosen that the established order implies.[114]

To summarize, the ideal doxa is a set of understandings that functions to create a system of meanings and values that appears beyond question. In practice, the orthodox formulation is the attempt by socially dominant groups to bring a set of understandings to the level of doxa. The heterodox formulation exists in tandem with the orthodox project, but the goal of heterodox groups is to reject the orthodox formulation in favor of an alternative set of understandings.

Heterodoxy can be understood as social change insofar as it is a disruption of the doxa. A crucial insight of Bourdieu's conception of habitus is that heterodoxy is produced by the orthodox attempt to reinforce the doxa. Given an external event or "objective crisis" that has called the doxa into question, there are two ways in which heterodoxy may come about: The first is by the process of selection. In the orthodox group's attempt to create a selective interpretation of experience that supports the doxa, certain interpretations are not selected. The selection process may serve

[112] Ibid., p. 169.
[113] Ibid., p. 164.
[114] Ibid., p. 169. Emphasis in original.

its intended purpose in strengthening the doxa, but it creates, by omitting certain understandings from its formulation, a space for heterodoxy should those unaccounted-for aspects of experience ever come to light.

A second way in which the orthodox project may produce heterodoxy is through the process of justification. Any attempt by the orthodox group to justify a particular interpretation, in an attempt to strengthen that interpretation, necessarily includes the possibility of exposing the arbitrary nature of the interpretation. For, if a widely shared set of categories were truly natural, there would be no need for its justification.

The process of justification is frequently a forced position. The orthodox group is forced to justify the doxa, usually because the constructed nature of the doxa has in some way come into question or been exposed, frequently as a result of some type of external crisis. Bourdieu notes that crisis may break the quasi-perfect fit between the accepted schemas and new experiences. He writes:

> The critique which brings the undiscussed into discussion, the unformulated into formulation, has as the condition of its possibility objective crisis, which, in breaking the immediate fit between the subjective structures and the objective structures, destroys self-evidence practically.[115]

However, it must be noted that, although a crisis may call the naturalness of the doxa into question, the orthodox group's attempt at justification may very well be successful, resulting in a strengthening of the doxa. Bourdieu states that "crisis is a necessary condition for a questioning of doxa but it is not in itself a sufficient condition for the production of a critical discourse."[116] In this formulation, Bourdieu gives a sense of how support for particular interpretations may simultaneously sow the seeds for new interpretation.

The concept of habitus is an attempt to explain how a particular set of understandings can take on a life of its own, such that it serves to structure subsequent understandings of experience. What is remarkable about the concept of habitus is that it not only addresses ordering processes but it also takes up the issue of how order creates the conditions and possibility of change.

In constructivist approaches to political economy, the role of contingency, human creativity, adaptability and experimentation are constant

---

[115] Ibid., pp. 168–9.
[116] Ibid., p. 169.

sources for change. However, by applying the concept of habitus to schema theory and constructivist sources for change, we can consider how a set of socially shared understandings can be institutionalized to work as a limiting force, while at the same time that set of understandings may serve as a basis for interpretive reformulation and novel ideational development because new understandings and interpretations may develop according to the categories of either an orthodox or heterodox project.

Although Bourdieu himself, in outlining the concept of habitus, did not emphasize the open-ended and contingent nature of interpretations of experience, we can adapt habitus to accommodate this process of change. In this way, there is no single path that interpretation must take, and each attempt to influence interpretation may or may not be successful. The discussion of habitus can therefore supplement the recognition by constructivists that the development of understandings is neither fixed nor pre-determined. And habitus brings to constructivist accounts of the economy an explicit recognition of the role of power and agency in the development of particular understandings.

Heterodox Critiques and Constructivism in Nationalism Studies

Constructivist approaches to ethnicity in the nationalism literature have by now become hegemonic in Western social science.[117] From Anderson to Gellner to Suny, the denaturalization of ethnicity and the nation has become almost "natural."[118] Even in rational choice explanations, ethnicity

---

[117] Interestingly, even though constructivist approaches to ethnicity dominate in North America and Europe, local actors in many parts of the world reject this approach and instead consider ethnicity to have a primordial quality. This is a curious disjuncture between the views of social scientists and the views of actors on the ground, which likely has implications for better understanding of the limits of constructivism.

[118] Anderson, 1996; Gellner, 1983; Ronald G. Suny, *The Revenge of the Past: Nationalism, Revolution, and the Collapse of the Soviet Union* (Stanford, CA: Stanford Univ. Press, 1993); and Rogers Brubaker, *Nationalism Reframed: Nationhood and the National Question in the New Europe* (Cambridge: Cambridge Univ. Press, 1996). These are examples of what is now an extremely large literature. Prominent works on the USSR and its successor states include Yitzhak M. Brudny, *Reinventing Russia: Russian Nationalism and the Soviet State, 1953–1991* (Cambridge, MA: Harvard Univ. Press, 1998); Rawi Abdelal, *National Purpose in the World Economy: Post-Soviet States in Comparative Perspective* (Ithaca, NY: Cornell Univ. Press, 2001); Mark R. Beissinger, *Nationalist Mobilization and the Collapse of the Soviet State* (New York: Cambridge Univ. Press, 2002); Ted Hopf, *Social Construction of International Politics: Identities & Foreign Policies, Moscow, 1955 and 1999* (Ithaca, NY: Cornell Univ. Press, 2002); Pauline Jones-Luong, *Institutional Change and Political Continuity in Post-Soviet Central*

has long ago been deconstructed. Going back to the 1970s, Robert Bates as well as Alvin Rabushka and Kenneth Shepsle pioneered the concept of ethnic entrepreneurs, arguing that apparently ethnic claims could actually be a function of economic interests rather than primordial ethnic interests.[119] More recently, David Laitin argued that even identity choices, may be driven by historic and future possibilities for economic opportunities.[120] A common element in all these arguments is that the treatment of national or ethnic interests fully appreciates constructivist, historical institutional approaches *in regard to ethnicity*.

Relatively few of the insights of social cognition, however, have worked their way into studies of nationalism. Donald Horowitz is the leading exception insofar as he has used social identity theory to explain ethnic conflict.[121] Yet, even though social identity theory, and in particular the minimal group thesis, provides a theoretical basis for non-essentialized, constructed ethnic difference, Horowitz tends not to take a constructivist approach to ethnicity.

Indeed, very little, if any, of the insights of social cognition or constructivist approaches to *the economy* have been appreciated in the constructivist nationalism literature. Prominent constructivist theorists such as Anderson and Gellner have treated the economy largely in terms of the orthodox critiques of objectivity, that is, focusing on institutions and/or other factors (e.g., value change) that mediate real external economic conditions.[122] Similarly, arguments regarding ethnic entrepreneurs and mobility prospects treat ethnicity as constructed, but the economy and economic interests as real, even if somewhat institutionally mediated.[123]

Asia: Power, Perceptions, and Pacts (New York: Cambridge Univ. Press, 2002); Dmitry Gorenburg, *Minority Ethnic Mobilization in the Russian Federation* (New York: Cambridge Univ. Press, 2003).

[119] Robert Bates, "Modernization, Ethnic Competion, and the Rationality of Politics in Contemporary Africa," in D. Rothchild and V. Olorunsola, eds., *State versus Ethnic Claims: African Policy Dilemmas* (Boulder, CO: Westview, 1983), pp. 152–71; and Alvin Rabushka and Kenneth A. Shepsle, *Politics in Plural Societies: A Theory of Democratic Instability* (Columbus, OH: Merrill, 1972).

[120] David D. Laitin, *Identity in Formation: The Russian-Speaking Populations in the Near Abroad* (Ithaca, NY: Cornell Univ. Press, 1998).

[121] Horowitz, 1985.

[122] See also Liah Greenfeld, *The Spirit of Capitalism: Nationalism and Economic Growth*, (Cambridge, MA: Harvard Univ. Press, 2001).

[123] Insofar as mobility prospects are institutionalized, mobility arguments are consistent with some historical institutionalist work discussed earlier, which considers the role of institutions in shaping both groups and interests, but in contrast to constructivist approaches,

In contrast, some research in the social movements literature has combined constructivist views of ethnicity with some insights from constructivist approaches to the economy. For example, the social movements literature has developed models that take into account the role of framing, institutional structures, opportunities, and resources, which go beyond formal institutions and structural economic or demographic factors.[124] For example, in his work on Eastern Europe, Grzegorz Ekiert went beyond formal political and economic factors in analyzing state practices, events, and collective memories in shaping the evolution of protests and the development of regimes in Eastern Europe.[125] More recently, Mark Beissinger has expertly and innovatively combined the insights of the social movements literature, which is based mainly on the American experience, with the nationalism literature to explain the "tides" of nationalist protests in the USSR.[126] However, while incorporating some of the heterodox critiques of objective economic interests, these works still do not take full advantage of the possibilities for thinking about the construction of economic interests provided by the heterodox critique.

The work that has come closest to combining an appreciation of the heterodox critiques of objectivity of the economy with the nationalism literature is Rawi Abdelal's analysis of the trade orientation of some of the states of the former Soviet Union after perestroika.[127] Abdelal argued that national identities best explain the choice of trade partners and the pattern of trade among former Soviet states. Although this important work addresses the construction of state economic interests, rather than problematizing

mobility arguments do not problematize the construction of economic interests and the economy in terms of mutually constituting actors and environments.

[124] See Doug McAdam, John D. McCarthy, and Mayer N. Zald, eds., *Comparative Perspectives on Social Movements: Political Opportunities, Mobilizing Structures, and Cultural Framings* (New York: Cambridge Univ. Press, 1996). In addition, for pioneering work in the development of the political-process model and the role of institutions, sense of efficacy, and opportunities in collective action (in particular the role of black churches, black colleges, and southern NAACP (National Association for the Advancement of Colored People) chapters in black protest movements), see Doug McAdam, *Political Process and the Development of Black Insurgency, 1930–1970* (Chicago: Univ. of Chicago Press, 1982).

[125] Grzegorz Ekiert, *The State against Society: Political Crises and Their Aftermath in East Central Europe* (Princeton, NJ: Princeton Univ. Press, 1996).

[126] Beissinger, 2002.

[127] Abdelal, 2001. Similarly, some work on ethnic networks considers the ethnicization of associative economic ties. See, for example, Ivan Light and Stavros Karageorgis, "The Ethnic Economy," in Neil J. Smelser and Richard Swedberg, eds., *The Handbook of Economic Sociology* (Princeton, NJ: Princeton Univ. Press, 1994), pp. 647–71.

the development of economic interests per se, in terms of the negotiation of multiple possible understandings of the economy, Abdelal considers the meaning and purposive goals of national identities in opposition to more straightforward economic interests which follow structural economic conditions.

Thus, while constructivist approaches to nationalism and social movements have made valuable contributions toward understanding those phenomena and toward a more nuanced understanding of the role of economics in nationalism, regionalism, and separatism, I argue that they nevertheless have, thus far, not fully appreciated the insights of heterodox approaches to the economy.

Imagined Economies

Given the evidence against the objectivity of economic interests in both orthodox and heterodox critiques, I argue that the nationalism literature, and in particular the understanding of the economic bases of nationalism and regionalism, could be significantly improved with greater integration of the insights of constructivist political economy, broadly conceived (i.e., social cognition and schema theory, economic sociology, historical institutionalism, and social theory).

In Table 2.1, I have summarized the state of the literature regarding approaches to the economy in the social sciences and studies of nationalism.[128] The left column identifies the position toward objectivity of the economy. The right column identifies approaches to the economy consistent with the position on objectivity, and also examples in studies of nationalism, separatism, and regionalism.

The contribution of the imagined economies framework is to bring previously established insights regarding the constructed nature of the economy and economic interests to the literature on movements for greater sovereignty including, nationalism, regionalism, and separatism. The argument is not that economic factors do not matter or that understandings of the economy are "unconnected to reality" but rather that the meaning of the economy is socially constructed by actors and their social and institutional contexts. Building on the work of constructivist political economy, the imagined economies framework suggests that (1) economic structural

---

[128] For concision, in this table I refer to nationalism, but I mean the term broadly to include studies of movements for greater sovereignty including regionalism and separatism.

Constructivist Political Economy and Nationalism

Table 2.1 *Summary of Approaches to the Economy and Examples in Studies of Nationalism, Separatism, and Regionalism*

Objectivism	General approach to the economy: • Based on the SEU model of economic rationality • Considers economic conditions and interests as unmediated and objective Examples in studies of nationalism, separatism, and regionalism: • Theories based on structural economic variables, regional endowment, underdevelopment, and the international trade environment
Orthodox Critiques of Objectivism	General approach to the economy: • Based on critiques of the SEU model and bounded rationality • Considers economic conditions and interests as mediated via a range of mechanisms, (e.g., elite influence, framing, heuristics, institutions, social context, and expectations) Examples in studies of nationalism, separatism, and regionalism: • Theories based on the process of modernization, relative deprivation, institutional appeasement, and mobility prospects
Heterodox Critiques: Constructivist Political Economy	General approach to the economy: • Based on constructivist political economy including schema theory, economic sociology, historical institutionalism, and social theory • Considers economic conditions and interests as intersubjectively socially constructed Examples in studies of nationalism, separatism, and regionalism: • Constructivist approaches to identity and nationalist mobilization • Constructivist approaches to the economy: **Imagined Economies Framework**

variables alone do not determine economic interests; (2) economic facts are subject to multiple understandings; and (3) interests and external conditions are mutually constituting. On the first point, there is some agreement with both heterodox and orthodox critiques of economic objectivity, but the second and third points are a departure from most orthodox critiques and are firmly in the constructivist camp.

Table 2.2 *Imagined Economies Framework*

Material "facts"; infinite bits of data		Cognition and interpretation via experiential processing of information about external conditions		Mediation of interpretations via habitus (interplay of doxa, orthodoxy, and heterodoxy) and institutional context		Development of intersubjective understandings of the economy		Development of specific economic and political interests (e.g., movements for greater sovereignty)
	→		→		→		→	

To be more specific, the imagined economies framework, as I will use it in this book, is outlined in Table 2.2. The starting point of the analysis is the infinity of bits of data that constitute external material reality. The cognitive and constructivist models that produce heterogeneous interpretations of the economy constitute the first part of the framework. The next part is the social and institutional context that mediates interpretations. This mediation is based on Bourdieu's concept of habitus, and its constituent elements of doxa, orthodoxy, and heterodoxy that together represent the concept of systemic, naturalized, power hierarchies that shape understandings in particular times and places. Through these cognitive, constructivist, and social processes, the result is a set of intersubjective understandings of the economy, part three. The interplay of these regional understandings of the economy in the institutional context of the time then produces economic interests in greater sovereignty, or the economic basis of sovereignty movements, which constitutes the final step in the analytical framework.

This chapter has outlined the theoretical basis for the first part of the framework. In the chapters that follow, I illustrate the remaining parts with empirical analysis. In Chapters 3 and 4, I use habitus to illustrate the field of possibility for regional understandings of the economy in the late Soviet period, and during the first Russian Republic. In Chapters 5 and 6, using content analysis, I detail local intersubjective understandings of the economy in Sverdlovsk and Samara and their connections to the movement for greater sovereignty in Sverdlovsk Oblast. And in Chapter 7, I illustrate the development of regional interest in greater sovereignty in Sverdlovsk through a narrative discussion that combines the particular institutional context and local understandings of the economy.

The imagined economies framework is a theoretical apparatus that can accommodate individual-level processing of information, while remaining attentive to the institutional context and the set of socially shared categories through which external reality is understood and interests are developed. I argue that objective economic conditions do not produce unmediated understanding, and like the nation, the economy is an imagined entity based on data that are subject to historical experience, institutional constraints, local interpretation, and power hierarchies. The analytical framework suggests a theoretical basis for how economic understandings might diverge from objective economic conditions, that is, a way to analyze heterogeneous interpretations of the economy, and therefore constitutes a novel contribution to the nationalism and political economy literatures.

3

Breaking the Soviet Doxa

PERESTROIKA, RASSTROIKA,
AND THE EVOLUTION
OF REGIONALISM

Do economic conditions determine people's interests? Most social science teaches us to presume so. Scholars, consequently, tend to account for the innumerable anomalous cases, which fail to conform to expectation, by resorting to arguments focused on informational deficiencies. Such explanations reinforce the presumption that a proper appraisal of economic conditions would produce the correct articulation of interests. The imagined economies framework offers a powerful and less presumptuous alternative to the traditional notion of how material conditions and articulated interests relate to each other, particularly in cases where there is, objectively, significant difference between them. What people think about the economy, however far-fetched it may seem vis-à-vis measured economic data, can be more important than what we might otherwise consider the statistical truth about their conditions. The originality and usefulness of the framework lie in its explanation of the articulation of interests not in the usual materially measurable terms but in terms of local experience, local categories of analysis, and local intersubjective notions of what economic conditions *mean*.

Regionalism in the Russian Federation, or nationalism in the USSR, poses two questions for which we still do not have satisfactory answers: First, why do economic interests in greater sovereignty develop beginning in the late 1980s and not before? Clearly, economic conditions had been comparably woeful before 1989. And, second, given the pattern of regionalism, how did a centralized system produce such differentiated understandings of the regional economies – in other words, how did different regions that share a Soviet history, but especially those that share a common language, ethnicity, and even economic structure, come to interpret similar economic events differently. To understand the arrival of economically based appeals for regional sovereignty, let us begin by turning our attention to the conceptual landscape of perestroika.

The profound ideological and institutional disruption of the Gorbachev era (1985–91) and the tumultuous start of the first Russian republic (1991–3) created a new basis for regionalized political and economic interests. Bourdieu proves especially useful in analyzing the institutional changes of the widely remembered but poorly understood period of 1985–93. In Bourdieu's terms, the period represents a struggle between orthodox and heterodox projects that effectively created new categories for thinking about regional politics and economics. I argue in this chapter that perestroika can be fruitfully examined, using Bourdieu's concept of habitus, as an orthodox project aimed at propping up the crisis-ridden doxa of centralized Soviet political and economic power. Gorbachev's perestroika, literally "restructuring,"[1] produced a heterodox reaction that I term *rasstroika*, literally de-structuring.[2] Rasstroika represents the struggle against Gorbachev's perestroika by nationalists and other anti-Soviet actors, a confrontation made possible only by the emergence of perestroika itself. Whereas Gorbachev was attempting to restructure the boundaries of political and economic organization in order to rebuild and revive central Soviet power, those who opposed central Soviet power took advantage of the perestroika-stimulated possibility of rethinking Soviet political and economic boundaries. Nationalists and other anti-USSR actors not only went further than Gorbachev had foreseen but also had entirely opposite motivations, at first haphazardly shifting and muddling the boundaries of political and economic organization, and later aiming in a more focused effort to decentralize, diminish, and destroy Soviet power.

The definition of an orthodox versus a heterodox action depends on the goals, rather than the consequence of the action. Those actions – even radical attempts at reform that failed – that were nevertheless meant to

---

[1] According to Archie Brown, the term *perestroika* was an "inspired" choice. It carried no connotations of past political reforms or attempts at dissent and, therefore, could be embraced by everyone, from the most conservative (e.g., Yurii Afanas'ev) to the most liberal (e.g., Andrei Sakharov). See Archie Brown, *The Gorbachev Factor* (New York: Oxford Univ. Press, 1996), p. 124.

[2] According to the Oxford Russian Dictionary and Igor Yatskovich, "the prefix 'raz-' denotes 1) division into parts (*raskroshit'*); 2) distribution, direction of action in different directions (*raz"ekhat'sia*); 3) action in reverse (*razminirovat'*); 4) termination of action or state (*razliubit'*); 5) intensification of action (*raspliasat'sia*)." See Igor Iatskovich, "Some Ways of Translating English Phrasal Verbs into Russian," *Translation Journal* 3:3 (July 1999). Available at *http://accurapid.com/journal/09russ.htm* (12 May 2004).

strengthen Soviet power belong to the orthodox, whereas those actions that oppose the orthodox actions and that, even if only modestly at first, attempt to chip away or diminish Soviet power belong to the heterodox. Rasstroika, like perestroika, operates within the confines of the doxa of Soviet central power, remaining within, rather than transcending Soviet conceptualizations of power and interests. In other words, both orthodox and heterodox projects share the organizing category of Soviet power. Therefore, when the doxa of the Soviet Union ended in 1991, so too did the orthodox and heterodox movements.

Broadly speaking, perestroika unitentionally, but effectively, diminished the power of the Communist Party of the Soviet Union (CPSU) and, by introducing heterogeneity in frameworks for thinking about politics and economics at the regional level, it caused the breakup of the USSR.[3] These events produced throughout the USSR the agitation of political and economic organization that allowed for the conceptualization of territorialized, national, and regional difference, and ultimately regionalism within the Russian Federation. In particular, the heterodox response of rasstroika was an explosion of previously held ways of making sense of the world – radical doubt about who or what was involved, responsible, and important – which led to different ways of thinking about economy and about the political institutions necessary for regional, as well as national and federal, governance.

The interplay of perestroika and rasstroika provoked a clash of alternative political and economic organizational structures. It was a revolutionary conceptual event as much as an institutional struggle; consequently, territorial units of the USSR emerged from the period with markedly heterogeneous political and economic understandings. Indeed, the perestroika-rasstroika dialectic provided the foundation for the development of divergent,

---

[3] Depending on one's point of view, this is perhaps a radical statement. For analysis that supports this view, see Steven Kotkin, "1991 and the Russian Revolution: Sources, Conceptual Categories, Analytical Frameworks," *The Journal of Modern History* 70:2 (June 1998), pp. 384–425. On the role of ideological context in explaining the Soviet collapse as well as the endurance of the Russian Federation, see Stephen E. Hanson, "Ideology, Interests, and Identity: Comparing the Soviet and Russian Secession Crises," in Mikhail Alexseev, ed., *Center-Periphery Conflict in Post-Soviet Russia: A Federation Imperiled* (New York: St. Martin's Press, 1999), pp. 15–46. For discussion of other factors that led to the breakup of the USSR, see Brown, 1996; Jerry F. Hough, *Democratization and Revolution in the U.S.S.R., 1985–1991* (Washington, DC: Brookings, 1997); Michael McFaul, *Russia's Unfinished Revolution: Political Change from Gorbachev to Putin* (Ithaca, NY: Cornell Univ. Press, 2001); and Steven L. Solnick, *Stealing the State: Control and Collapse in Soviet Institutions* (Cambridge, MA: Harvard Univ. Press, 1997).

regionally specific understandings of the economy as well as the development of novel political institutional solutions, including the movements for greater sovereignty. It is these divergent, intersubjective local understandings of the economy that I term *imagined economies*.

The orthodox and heterodox projects of perestroika and rasstroika litter the discourse of institutional change between 1985 and 1993. By analyzing the arena of political and economic governance during this period, I will demonstrate that the conceptualization of political and economic categories by Russian actors underwent a radical transformation from a doxic position of central homogeneous control to one of heterogeneous open-ended possibility.

In order to outline the context of competing orthodox and heterodox projects and their effects on regional political and economic categories, this chapter first briefly outlines the doxic conception of Soviet economic and political power and the challenges to the doxa presented by the stagnation of the late Brezhnev era. It then chronologically traces the events between 1985 and 1991, showing how the orthodox operations of Gorbachev's perestroika, aimed at strengthening the Soviet system, unintentionally inspired and provoked the heterodox actions of others aimed against the Soviet system.

The Soviet Doxa

Four elements of the Soviet system are of particular significance in mapping the context of later imagined economies. The first is the Soviet conception of Marxist-Leninist ideology. Second is the system of political authority or the paths to power. The third is the conceptualization and institutional structure of nations and regions in the USSR. And finally, the fourth element is the Soviet conceptualization of economic interests, which of course overlaps with the idea of class.

Soviet Marxist-Leninist ideology was fundamentally based on the idea that society was moving toward communism. Soviet ideologues, and particularly Lenin, formulated a more specific relationship between political institutions and economic outcomes.[4] Above all, there was a necessarily "leading role" for the Communist Party in the political and economic

---

[4] For an excellent treatment of Leninist ideology, see Ken Jowitt, *New World Disorder: The Leninist Extinction* (Berkeley: Univ. of California Press, 1992). Also see Mojmir Križan, "The Ideological Impasse of Gorbachev's Perestroika," *Studies in Soviet Thought* 40 (1990),

revolutionary transformation of society, based in large part on the Party's scientific knowledge of Marxism. Central state planning would be required for social ownership of property (the means of production) and the mobilization of society toward industrialization. This ideological basis for political and economic relations formed the foundation of Soviet elites' political education. That Marxist-Leninist ideology was not uniformly accepted, or even that it might have been superficially dismissed by segments of the population, does not detract from the fact that it was still the official discourse of the regime and that it nonetheless deeply structured debate about the relationship between power, the political system, and the economy of the USSR. Marxist-Lenninst ideology was therefore the necessary reference point for Gorbachev's later attempts to reform the system.

Paths to Power

The second important facet of the doxa of the Soviet system was the institutionalized system of political and economic authority: the paths to power. The main categories by which the CPSU structured economic and political power, the system of socialist institutions, were interwoven into the hierarchy of the Communist Party.

Since the 1930s, a centralized party bureaucracy allowed political elites radiating from Moscow to decide the most significant political and economic questions facing each regional level of the USSR.[5] These questions

pp. 113–35; and Tom Casier, "The Shattered Horizon: How Ideology Mattered to Soviet Politics," *Studies in East European Thought* 51:1 (1989), pp. 35–59.

[5] This is not to suggest that there was not interaction and tension between regional party elites and central authorities; however, the source of regional political authority was the central apparatus of the CPSU. For arguments on the circular nature of appointments in the Soviet system, see Robert V. Daniels, "The Secretariat and the Local Organizations in the Russian Communist Party, 1921–1923," *American Slavic and East European Review* 1 (1957), pp. 32–49; and more recently, Graeme Gill, *Origins of the Stalinist Political System* (Cambridge: Cambridge Univ. Press, 1990), pp. 315–16. For arguments that are critical of the traditional view of central authority, see Stephen F. Cohen, *Bukharin and the Bolshevik Revolution: A Political Biography, 1888–1938* (New York: Knopf, 1973), p. 327; J. Arch Getty, *Origins of the Great Purges: The Soviet Communist Party Reconsidered, 1933–1938* (Cambridge: Cambridge Univ. Press, 1988), p. 198; Lynne Viola, "The Campaign to Eliminate the Kulak as a Class, Winter 1929–1930: A Reevaluation of the Legislation," *Slavic Review* 3 (1986), pp. 650–72; and Tamas Gabor Rittersporn, *Stalinist Simplifications and Soviet Complications: Social Tensions and Political Conflicts in the USSR, 1933–1953* (Chur, Switzerland: Harwood, 1991), p. 20. On regional influence in the post-Stalin period, see George W. Breslauer, "Regional Party Leaders' Demand Articulation and the Nature of Center-Periphery Relations in the USSR," *Slavic Review* 45:4 (Winter 1986), pp. 650–72; Jerry F. Hough, *The Soviet Prefects: The Local*

included, for example, the redistribution of resources among regions. The self-evidence and propriety of centralized political and economic categories were achieved, substantially, by orthodox efforts to establish systematic mis-recognition of the arbitrariness of central Soviet rule as an organizing prin-ciple and by major legitimizing events, such as the victory over Germany in World War II and the early successes of Soviet industrialization and modernization.

The Communist Party drew its stability and strength from the *nomen-klatura* system, the set of rules that determined the political position of ac-tors within the hierarchy of power and organizations. Its central feature was the primacy of Communist Party organizations over all other organizations. The nomenklatura system consisted of several rungs, divided into three main levels of appointed positions, followed by CPSU Central Committee-approved positions.[6] The first rank included the General Secretary of the CPSU Central Committee, members of the Politburo, candidates for mem-bership in the Politburo, and secretaries of the Central Committee. The second level included the nomenklatura of the Politburo, that is, those positions appointed at Politburo sessions including: first and sometimes second secretaries of republican-level central committees; first secretaries of regional party committees and municipal committees of large cities; union ministers; high-level military officers; ambassadors of all socialist and G-7 countries; directors of the largest factories of the military-industrial complex; directors of artistic and literary societies; and editors-in-chief of central party publications. The third level included the nomenklatura of the secretariat of the Central Committee, that is, those positions appointed at CPSU Central Committee Secretariat sessions, including deputy ministers;

Party Organizations in Industrial Decision-Making (Cambridge, MA: Harvard Univ. Press, 1969), pp. 256–71; and Donna Bahry, *Outside Moscow: Power Politics and Budgetary Policy in the Soviet Republics* (New York: Columbia Univ. Press, 1987), pp. 158–64.

[6] On the structural organization of political power in the Soviet Union, see Raymond A. Bauer, Alex Inkeles, and Clyde Kluckhohn, *How the Soviet System Works: Cultural, Psycho-logical, and Social Themes* (Cambridge, MA: Harvard Univ. Press, 1956); Hough, 1969; Jerry F. Hough and Merle Fainsod, *How the Soviet Union Is Governed* (Cambridge, MA: Harvard Univ. Press, 1979); and Philip G. Roeder, *Red Sunset* (Princeton, NJ: Princeton Univ. Press, 1993). On the nomenklatura system in particular, see Stephen Kotkin, "In Search of the Nomenklatura: Yesterday's USSR, Today's Russia," *East European Constitutional Review* 6:4 (Fall 1997), pp. 104–20; and Michael Voslensky, *Nomenklatura* (Garden City, NJ: Dou-bleday, 1984). On changes in the nomenklatura during perestroika, see Ronald J. Hill and John Löwenhardt, "Nomenklatura and Perestroika," *Government and Opposition* 26:2 (Spring 1991), pp. 229–43; and Olga V. Kryshtanovskaia, "Transformation of the Old Nomenklatura into a New Russian Elite," *Russian Social Science Review* 37 (July–August 1996), pp. 18–40.

second secretaries of regional party committees; and first secretaries of regional soviet executive committees. These three levels were followed by positions requiring the consent of the departments of the Central Committee (i.e., positions where appointments were approved but not initiated). Finally there were positions in regional committees, municipal committees, district committees, and lower-level party organizations.[7]

The set hierarchy and the fact that all positions in political, economic, and even cultural organizations had to be approved by known organizational levels of the CPSU meant that there was a unified understanding with regard to the basis of political and economic power. Individuals could be removed from their positions, and there was a degree of uncertainty in appointments, but the party leadership, and hence the political leadership, was relatively stable.

Nations and Regions

The institutionalized stability of the CPSU was, until perestroika, the source of the stability of the Soviet state. The *Union* of Soviet Socialist Republics was, after all, institutionally a federal state.[8] Indeed, the Soviet Union's centralization came via the CPSU and central ministries, not through the institutional state structure.[9] The basic unit of the system of state political institutions in the USSR was the "soviet" of people's deputies. The soviet was a legislative council that existed at every level of the USSR's territorial hierarchy. And every soviet, at every level, had a complementary party organization that held the real power. Central control was also imposed through union-level branch or sectoral central ministries. The overlap of party and state organizations in the Soviet Union was not problematic in terms of understandings of authority because everyone understood that the CPSU was in charge.

At the very top of the state's institutional hierarchy was the USSR Supreme Soviet of People's Deputies. For this body, as in the case of the lower-level soviets, all nominations (and hence elections) were subject to the nomenklatura system of appointments. However, the USSR, rather than

[7] Kryshtanovskaia, 1996, p. 20.
[8] On federalism in the Soviet Union, see Chapter 3, "Soviet 'Federalism'" in Jeffery Kahn, *Federalism, Democratization, and the Rule of Law in Russia* (New York: Oxford Univ. Press, 2002), pp. 69–82.
[9] This fact turned out to be very important to the breakup of the Soviet Union after the destruction of the Party during perestroika.

consisting of a series of centralized state political institutions, was instead a federation of 15 territorial units (union republics), each with separate political institutions (soviets of people's deputies). The Russian republic was not just a constituent union republic; it was a federation as well, and, mirroring the structure of the USSR it contained a variety of constituent territorial units, each containing smaller-scale territorial units and complementary political institutions. However, an important institutional feature was that the RSFSR, unlike other union republics, lacked the highest level of party and state institutions (e.g., a republican party first secretary). Instead Russian regional and republican elites reported to union-level institutions.

All of the union republics (as well as the sub-union republics within republics) had an ethnic character. Each republic was named after a particular ethnic group, and each one supposedly represented some level of national self-determination of the titular ethnic group. In practice, as is well-known, ethnic groups of all types in the Soviet Union were subject to the dictates of Soviet nationalities policy, which was aimed at promoting Soviet power rather than the interests of ethnic groups.[10] However, as the late 1980s would show, the construction of national or ethnic identities and interests was also a major, if unintended, consequence of Soviet nationalities policy.[11]

That the construction of national identities and interests was mostly ignored by scholars until the late 1980s is not just an academic oversight. Rather it is indicative of the relative power of national groups and ethnic-territorial units versus party organizations during the Soviet period. In other words, although Soviet nationalities policy created the administrative

---

[10] For an early analysis of ethnic groups in the Soviet Union that treats identity as fixed and focuses on the use of force against ethnic groups, see Richard Pipes, *The Formation of the Soviet Union* (Cambridge, MA: Harvard Univ. Press, 1964).

[11] An early constructivist approach to the USSR is Gerhard Simon, *Nationalismus und Nationalitätenpolitik in der Sowjetunion: von der totalitären Diktatur zur nachstalinschen Gesellschaft* (Baden-Baden: Nomos, 1986). Amongst the many other works on the goals and consequences of Soviet nationalities policy, see Kotkin, 1998, pp. 384–425; George Liber, *Soviet Nationality Policy, Urban Growth, and Identity Change in the Ukrainian SSR, 1923–34* (Cambridge: Cambridge Univ. Press, 1992); Terry Martin, *The Affirmative Action Empire: Nations and Nationalism in the Soviet Union, 1923–1939* (Ithaca, NY: Cornell Univ. Press, 2001); Yuri Slezkine, "The USSR as a Communal Apartment, or How a Socialist State Promoted Ethnic Particularlism," *Slavic Review* 53:2 (Summer 1994), pp. 414–52; Rogers Brubaker, *Nationalism Reframed: Nationhood and the National Question in the New Europe* (Cambridge, MA: Cambridge Univ. Press, 1996), pp. 23–54; and Ronald Grigor Suny, *The Revenge of the Past: Nationalism, Revolution, and the Collapse of the Soviet Union* (Stanford, CA: Stanford Univ. Press, 1993).

units that would later produce nationalist interests, there was, until the breakdown in the Communist Party during perestroika, limited room for articulation, let alone full-scale pursuit, of national and territorial interests. It is consequently not surprising that scholars focused their attention on the Party and the hierarchical collection of state institutions in which the Party governed the country.

Within each union republic, there was a series of smaller-scale regional units (e.g., autonomous republics, oblasts, krais, autonomous okrugs, and autonomous oblasts), and each of these units had smaller-scale soviets (e.g., republican soviets, oblast soviets, and krai soviets). Within the territorial units, villages, cities, and districts also each had soviets. In total, at varying territorial levels, the USSR in 1985 contained 52,074 soviets of people's deputies.[12] Among them were 129 oblast-level soviets, 2,137 city soviets, 645 city district soviets, 3,828 urban soviets, and 42,176 village soviets. In all cases, at every level, the soviet (legislative council) had an executive committee, and each soviet and executive committee was subordinate to the next higher level in the hierarchy.

A discussion of the manner in which regional political organizations were composed will demonstrate the effects of the party and nomenklatura system on state institutions at the regional level.[13] Deputies to local soviets (municipal and regional legislatures) were non-competitively "elected" and at their first session, they elected an executive committee (*ispolnitel'nyi komitet soveta* or ispolkom). After this first session, the soviet hardly met. The chairman of the regional ispolkom was appointed by the Central Committee secretariat.

In addition to a regional soviet, each oblast contained an oblast-level party organization (*oblastnoi komitet* or obkom), whose first secretary controlled appointments and recruitment of party membership and positions in the region. This first secretary was himself appointed by the CPSU Politburo. The most important elite positions in the regions were the first secretary of the CPSU, the ispolkom chairman, and the CPSU second secretary. In addition, certain managers of collective farms or enterprise directors, who also were likely to be nomenklatura appointees, might form part of the regional elite. A typical regional political elite career pattern was

---

[12] Richard Sakwa, *Soviet Politics* (London: Routledge, 1990), p. 152.
[13] For a rich and detailed discussion of the dynamic relationship between party and state institutions during the entire Soviet period at the local level, see Timothy J. Colton, *Moscow: Governing the Socialist Metropolis* (Cambridge, MA: Harvard Univ. Press, 1995).

to start out as second secretary, then become ispolkom chairman, and then first secretary.[14]

Nominations for the oblast and city soviets were made at workplaces by the workplace party committee's secretary, who was also appointed by the obkom. Thus, the CPSU through the Politburo, then through the obkom, and finally through workplace party committee secretaries, controlled the composition of elections to the oblast and city soviets, and therefore the composition of the ispolkoms, which were the regional government organizations. The composition of the soviets could be broad including party and non-party members, but the ispolkom was entirely composed of party members, usually high-ranking members.[15] The nomenklatura system of appointments exerted a similar effect on all state organizations at all levels of government.

While acknowledging the primacy and importance of the CPSU as an institution in governing the USSR, one would nevertheless not want to overstate the actual level of control by the center over the regions. Several contemporary studies, even of the Stalin period, call into question the idea of totally centralized political and economic power and instead suggest a level of decentralized decision-making and dissent.[16]

The historical record shows that relationships between regional authorities and central ministries were always somewhat rocky and varied over time and place.[17] During the revolution, the Russian state was obviously weakened, and it took some years for the Soviet state to secure authority over all its territory. In addition, even the Communist Party organizations in the regions were sometimes divided. For example, in early 1918, there was an attempt to form a Urals "autonomous soviet republic."[18] And in 1922, as the civil war was coming to an end, V. M. Molotov at the Eleventh

---

[14] Kimitaka Matsuzato, "Local Elites Under Transition: County and City Politics in Russia 1985–1996," *Europe-Asia Studies* 51:8 (1999), p. 1368.

[15] Jeffrey W. Hahn, "The Development of Local Legislatures in Russia: The Case of Yaroslavl," in J. Hahn, ed., *Democratization in Russia: The Development of Legislative Institutions* (Armonk, NY: M. E. Sharpe, 1996), p. 164.

[16] See for example, Sarah Davies, *Popular Opinion in Stalin's Russia: Terror, Propaganda and Dissent, 1934–1941* (Cambridge: Cambridge Univ. Press, 1997); and James R. Harris, *The Great Urals: Regionalism and the Evolution of the Soviet System* (Ithaca, NY: Cornell Univ. Press, 1999). Also see works cited in footnote 5 in this chapter.

[17] For further discussion of the issue of the branch ministries versus the territories, see "Traditional Soviet Regional Policy," Chapter 2 in Peter Kirkow, *Russia's Provinces: Authoritarian Transformation versus Local Autonomy?* (New York: St. Martin's Press, 1998), pp. 23–45.

[18] N. Lisovskii, *1917 god na Urale* (Cheliabinsk: Iuzhno-ural'skoe knizhnoe izdatel'stro, 1967), p. 514; cited in Harris, 1999, p. 40, footnote 8.

Party Congress singled out seven regions as having the most serious internal party divisions: Samara, Simbirsk, Donbass, Petrograd, Briansk, Tula, and Nizhegorod. The Samara leadership apparently went so far as to arrest its fellow party rivals.[19]

During the civil war, the control of the economy was somewhat centralized in the departments of the Supreme Economic Council (*Vysshii sovet narodnogo khoziaistva* or *VSNKh*), otherwise known as *glavki*. After the war, these agencies were accused of "bureaucratism," and in the early 1920s, Soviet authorities granted regional enterprises greater control.[20] But central authorities soon accused regional officials of excessive "localism" (*mestnichestva*).[21] In the late 1920s, some regional elites initially supported Stalin because they thought he would favor greater and faster industrialization and, in particular, more investment for the regions.[22]

The State Committee for Planning (*Gosudarstvennyi planovyi komitet* or Gosplan) and central agencies generally, found themselves frequently at odds with regional elites owing to the regions' failure to meet the fantastic targets of the five-year plans. But, with the German invasion in 1941, the regions were given greater responsibility because of the need to evacuate both government and industry, which entailed limitations on the capacity of the center. Following the war, the balance of power shifted back to the central ministries (formerly commissariats).[23]

After Stalin's death, Nikita Khrushchev used the disgruntlement of regional officials toward the central ministries and Gosplan to his advantage in his power struggles with his rivals. Some of his rivals, like Georgii Malenkov, had supported the central ministries and Gosplan. Khrushchev, understanding that regional officials constituted the largest group in the Central Committee, suggested a series of reforms that instituted regional economic councils (*Sovet narodnogo khoziaistva* or Sovnarkhoz) and promised more power to the territories at the expense of the central ministries.[24]

---

[19] *Odinnadtsatyis" ezd RKP(b) mart-aprel' 1922 goda: stenograficheskii otchet* (Moscow: Gosudarstvenoe izdatel'stvo politicheskoi literatury, 1961), p. 55; cited in Harris, 1999, pp. 41–2, footnote 14.

[20] Edward H. Carr, *The Bolshevik Revolution, 1917–1923* (London: Macmillan, 1950–3), vol. 2, pp. 180–2.

[21] Harris, 1999, p. 47.

[22] For more on the regional support for and rise of Stalin in the late 1920s, see Harris, 1999, Chapter 3, pp. 70–104.

[23] Harris, 1999, Chapter 7, pp. 191–208.

[24] For more on 1950s economic competition amongst regions, see Bahry, 1987. On the sovnarkhoz reforms, see Hough, 1969.

Khrushchev then engineered his rivals' defeat via the Central Committee, where he carried the strong support of regional leaders. Regions did not waste time taking advantage of their new power. Sverdlovsk, for example, suggested reuniting the pre-1934 oblasts into a Urals Economic Zone. But Khrushchev was only interested in regional autonomy so long as it helped him defeat his rivals. After that contest ended in 1957, Khrushchev attempted to reign in regional authority.[25] His subsequent turn *against* the regions led their leaders to shift their support in the Central Committee. This time, it was Khrushchev's rivals who rallied the regions. He was dismissed in 1964.

Under Leonid Brezhnev, the Sovnarkhoz reforms were suspended, and some power was restored to the ministries, but the regions and ministries continued to vie for greater authority. The power of local entities did not go unnoticed in the center. Studies of local government in the late Soviet period concede the presence of regional influence in Soviet policy-making through the efforts of local-level soviets and party officials.[26] Yet, a bit of de jure autonomy for union republics, or lobbying by the union republics or regions, never called into question the authority structure or chain of command or the Party's supremacy. It always remained clear and uncontested where the lobbying had to be directed.

Regional party leaders had a definite sense of where they and their organizations fit in the power hierarchy in relation to other regional elites and union or republican leaders. The idea of a separatist movement of any kind under this type of institutional framework was literally unimaginable because any expression by political or economic elites of regional goals that contradicted the discourse of central party power was proscribed by the circular nature of CPSU appointments. A declaration of sovereignty could hardly have been the result of a regional organizational agenda since the CPSU was the dominant political organization at all territorial levels of the USSR. Moreover, such a move by anyone in a particular territorial unit would have quickly resulted in a dismissal of that

---

[25] For discussion of Khrushchev's reforms, see Barbara Ann Chotiner, *Krushchev's Party Reform: Coalition Building and Organizational Innovation* (Westport, CT: Greenwood Press, 1984); and William J. Conyngham, *Industrial Management in the Soviet Union: The Role of the CPSU in Industrial Decision-Making, 1917–1970* (Stanford, CA: Hoover Institution Press, 1973).

[26] See Jeffrey W. Hahn, *Soviet Grassroots: Citizen Participation in Local Soviet Government* (Princeton, NJ: Princeton Univ. Press, 1988); Bahry, 1987; and Blair Ruble, *Leningrad: Shaping a Soviet City* (Berkeley, CA: Univ. of California Press, 1990).

person as well as the territorial-level party elites who would have been held responsible. → CPSU → tight control on regional elites

Class and Economic Interests

Four aspects of Soviet economics are especially relevant to understanding the changes of the perestroika era.[27] First, Soviet economic policy was derived from scientific Marxist principles, which suggested that societies move from feudalism to capitalism to socialism, via both industrialization and the eventual victory of the working classes, the proletariat, over capitalists. This Marxist trajectory meant that the Soviet Union was committed to industrialization. Second, for Marxists the economy is primary. Interests are an unproblematic reflection of an individual's economic position, and those who share economic positions constitute classes. The reduction of interests to strictly economic conditions and the assumption of shared economic conditions thus negated the possibility of individual interests.

Third, by abolishing private property and replacing it with social ownership of the means of production, the Party, as the vanguard of the proletariat, claimed to have removed the economic basis for non-proletarian interests. The extreme emphasis on the social left no room for individual economic advancement (let alone wealth accumulation), and class replaced the individual (as well as the region) as the unit of analysis in understanding politics, society, and the economy.

Fourth, as follows from the preceding points, socialism fundamentally rejects markets as the means of distributing resources in a society. Instead, mirroring its central control of the political system, the Party directed central control of the economy through its dominance of state institutions, planned all types of production, and set all prices and wages.[28] To meet

---

[27] For a comprehensive discussion of the Soviet economic system that details the relationship between ideas, politics, and the economy, see János Kornai, *The Socialist System: The Political Economy of Communism* (Princeton, NJ: Princeton Univ. Press, 1992). Also, for a detailed treatment of Soviet economic history, see Alec Nove, *An Economic History of the U.S.S.R.*, 3rd ed. (New York: Penguin, 1992).

[28] A related point is that value was defined in terms of productive contribution; therefore, prices were set centrally, and many indicators of the economy were calculated in terms of physical volume, thus eliminating the possibility of market prices or profit margins as conveyors of information about the economy. However, the idea of "profit" and "prices" did bear some relation to market forces in the 1920s. At that time, because regions kept a good amount of the profit from their territories' industrial enterprises, there were incentives to produce efficiently, in the sense of "at a profit." The center was also interested in efficiency,

plan targets, central planners controlled labor mobility union-wide, ordering workers and directing resources to particular places at particular times. The needs of central planners necessarily trumped region-based planning. Understandably, central planning did not come about overnight. For much of the 1920s, Gosplan did not have the organizational capacity to know the productive capacity of regions or enterprises, and central planners had to depend on regions to submit information about their own capacities. In the 1930s, and especially with the shift from the first to the second five-year plans, the Soviet state and the institutions of the "planned-administrative economy" were increasingly consolidated.[29] From the 1930s on, Gosplan and the center relied less on regions for planning; instead, central institutions were used to force regions to meet plan targets.

These Soviet economic practices and principles contain several important implications for the development of regional understandings of the economy. First, on a practical level, central planning in the Soviet system set out specific redistributive schemes for regions that were based on central goals of industrialization and homogenization of economic conditions across the union. In general, this meant that there was union-level provision of union-level public goods (e.g., defense) and local provision of local public goods. Sub-union units had very little discretion in taxation or expenditure, but the amount of tax revenue they were allotted by the center generally matched their obligations.[30] Moreover, this practice of state, rather than market, distribution of the nation's resources shaped regional understandings of both the obligations of the center to the regions and the relationship among regions. There had certainly always been competition among regions of the USSR for industrial resources and investment. However, throughout the Soviet period, regions looked to the center as the source of territorial economic growth, and they relied on the center for investment and key inputs including labor.[31]

Second, given the emphasis on class and the derivation of interests from material conditions, there is extremely limited room in the official Soviet

---

but the notion of efficiency in the 1930s came to mean reducing central investment and increasing regional production to such an extreme that production targets were beyond the capacity of the inputs, and therefore impossible to achieve.

[29] Harris, 1999, p. 123.

[30] Philip Hanson, *Regions, Local Power and Economic Change in Russia* (London: Royal Institute of International Affairs, 1994), p. 24.

[31] Harris documents the issue of regional labor supply in his discussion of the expansion of the Gulag system. See Chapter 4, "The Gulag," Harris, 1999, pp. 105–22.

paradigm for the development of territorial, rather than class-based interests. As in the case of national identities and interests, this condition does not suggest that such interests did not exist; rather, it implies that their full articulation was impossible within the Soviet system.

Decline of Soviet Doxa

Despite the necessarily incomplete character of central control over the regions and despite shortcomings in the actuality of Soviet doxa, center-controlled Soviet discourse remained relentless in its insistence on class interests over regional interests. Even so, the strength of Soviet doxa had been in gradual decline since Khrushchev, and its background assumptions and naturalized categories of analysis were ever more challenged by a series of crises including the train of criticisms of the Stalin period and a number of internatonal actions in the 1960s that challenged Soviet power.

Under Brezhnev's leadership, the Soviet system faced further domestic and international challenges. First and foremost, the economy that had grown so rapidly (at great human cost) in the early decades of Soviet power had come to a near standstill. The Kosygin economic reforms of the 1960s could not address the fundamental problems inherent in the Soviet economy, such as the lack of incentives and information necessary for effective planning. Thus the imbalanced and costly focus on defense and heavy industry at the expense of technology and consumer goods continued unabated. The expansion of Soviet oil exports and rising world oil prices in the 1970s masked, for much of the Brezhnev era, what would otherwise have been a stark indication of the failings of central Soviet economic leadership. However, not everything was hidden. Shortages, which always existed to some degree during the Soviet period, had become almost a way of life. In 1981, standing in line for retail goods was estimated to take up 190 hours per adult per year.[32] Thus, public satisfaction and trust in the system rapidly deteriorated and the quality of naturalness in the conception of central Soviet political and economic power was being steadily chipped away by the increasing contradiction between reality and the Soviet ideal.

Soviet citizens' confidence continued to erode as the ideology of the Soviet Union faced challenges both at home and abroad. For example, dissidents, such as Aleksandr Solzhenitsyn, were internationally recognized (and in Solzhenitsyn's case, awarded the Nobel Prize for literature in 1970)

---

[32] Hans Aage, "Popular Attitudes and Perestroika," *Soviet Studies* 43:1 (1991), p. 8.

but then deported or put on trial. Soviet military intervention in Afghanistan in 1979 met very strong international criticism including the embarrassing boycott by the United States and a number other countries of the 1980 Olympic Games in Moscow. And, in the 1980s, staunchly anticommunist Western leaders such as Ronald Reagan and Margaret Thatcher took strong stands against the Soviet Union.

In the face of these domestic and international challenges, the Soviet leadership was at its weakest. Brezhnev had led the Party since Khrushchev's removal in 1964, but in his later years Brezhnev infirmly presided over almost open corruption and embezzlement of public resources for private gain. In 1982, Brezhnev finally died and was replaced by Yurii Andropov, who attempted to rein in corruption and initiated a purge of party officials. But Andropov died in 1984 and was replaced by the elderly Konstantin Chernenko who also died in office in 1985 and was then replaced by Mikhail Gorbachev.

As Gorbachev entered office, every aspect of the Soviet system was subject to question: Soviet ideology, the CPSU and system of authority, the socialist economy, and Soviet foreign policy were all showing signs of dysfunction. Yet it must be noted that despite all these problems, there were still no serious movements for nationalism or regionalism in 1985. The cracks in the Soviet doxa had created some opportunities for questioning by the mid-1980s, but the framework for thinking about regional interests remained a Soviet one; that is, space for the imagination of regional interests had not yet opened up. Though there were indeed a range of grievances against the system, these remained rather disorganized and confined by Soviet categories of thinking.

The Orthodoxy-Heterodoxy Dialectic: Perestroika-Rasstroika, 1985–1991

Regional and national demands and appeals for sovereignty began to develop into articulated interests during – and indeed because of – the ideological and institutional struggles over the Soviet doxa initiated by Gorbachev's rule. In brief, the struggle between perestroika, Gorbachev's orthodox movement to strengthen Soviet power, and rasstroika, the resultant heterodox movement against Soviet power, eventually led to the breakdown of Soviet doxa and the possibility of conceiving of and expressing regional demands and the consequent construction of regional interests. As we shall see, each of perestroika's orthodox attempts to strengthen the conception of the Soviet doxa tended, instead, to open two doors, one toward strengthened doxa and one toward space for heterodoxy. That is, opportunities for the heterodox project, which would in the end radically upset Soviet political and economic power, were made possible by the orthodox project itself.

Ideological Foundations

When Mikhail Gorbachev became general secretary of the CPSU in 1985, he inherited a host of problems, but, as general secretary, he also had a tremendous amount of power to impose the kind of solutions that he deemed necessary. Examining Gorbachev's own understanding of the crisis facing the Soviet Union yields the inescapable conclusion that the intention behind perestroika all along, up to and even beyond the end of the Soviet Union, was the revival and strengthening of the Soviet system via the orthodox buttressing of the traditional Soviet doxa.[33]

Early on, Gorbachev argued that the problems in the Soviet Union went beyond shortcomings in production or economic performance. Instead, he recognized that there had been "a gradual erosion of ideological and moral values."[34] Gorbachev saw that economic crises combined with ideological and moral decay exposed the gap between the doxic conception of Soviet political and economic power and experienced reality. He wrote:

The presentation of a "problem-free" reality backfired: a breach had formed between word and deed, which bred public passivity and disbelief in the slogans being proclaimed. It was only natural that this situation resulted in a credibility gap: everything that was proclaimed from the rostrums and printed in newspapers and textbooks was put in question. Decay began in public morals; the great feeling of solidarity with each other that was forged during the heroic times of the Revolution, the first five-year plans, the Great Patriotic War and postwar rehabilitation was weakening; alcoholism, drug addiction and crime were growing; and the penetration of the stereotypes of mass culture alien to us, which bred vulgarity and low tastes and brought about ideological barrenness, increased.[35]

---

[33] For the most comprehensive analysis of Gorbachev's ideas and actions, see Brown, 1996. On ideational change introduced by Gorbachev, and its Leninist inspiration, see, in particular, Chapter 4, "The Power of Ideas and the Power of Appointment," pp. 89–129. For additional analysis by one of Gorbachev's closest aides, see A. S. Cherniaev, *Shest' let s Gorbachevym: po dnevnikovym zapisiam* (Moscow: progress, kul'tura, 1993), also published in English as *My Six Years with Gorbachev* (University Park, PA: Pennsylvania State Univ. Press, 2000).

[34] Mikhail S. Gorbachev, *Perestroika i novoe myshlenie dlia nashei strany i dlia vsego mira* (Moscow: politicheskoi literatury, 1987), p. 16.

[35] Gorbachev, 1987, pp. 16–17.

Therefore, rather than continuing to entertain limited types of reform programs, such as had been considered under Brezhnev, Andropov, and Chernenko, Gorbachev and others in the leadership of the CPSU decided to pursue a radically more comprehensive set of reforms.[36] What distinguished Gorbachev from his predecessors was not his willingness to attempt economic reform – limited economic reforms had been discussed at various points in the postwar Soviet period – but, rather, his attempt to reform the economy through ideological and political changes to the centralized Soviet system.

Gorbachev's radical plan to strengthen Soviet power was worked out in the form of glasnost and perestroika. Glasnost, which was in essence a policy of "openness" or liberalization of debate in order to allow for the Party to have access to better information, in fact marked a crucial first step in the interrogation of Soviet frameworks of understanding. Perestroika, which was primarily a program to restructure power from the Party to state institutions (the soviets), followed on the heels of glasnost conceptually and chronologically in pushing Soviet doxic reconsidering toward the rethinking of Soviet institutions of power and authority.

In a speech to the Twenty-Seventh Congress of the CPSU in February 1986, Gorbachev was very critical of the stagnation (*zastoi*) of the Brezhnev era. He justified the need for glasnost by saying that "Truth is the main issue. Lenin said: More light! The Party should know everything!" Here and at many other points Gorbachev made clear that the intended goal of glasnost was strengthening the Party, not liberalization or some level of democratization.[37] Moreover, a reminder of the untoward reality of a closed society came almost as soon as glasnost was launched. In April, an accident occurred that caused a fire at the now infamous Chernobyl nuclear power plant in Ukraine. Large amounts of radiation were released over Ukraine, Belarus, and Russia, yet people in the most severely affected areas (as well as others in Europe and the world), as well as the hundreds of volunteers who ultimately gave their lives to put out the fires, were not protected or told immediately about the health dangers they faced. In the

---

[36] For a discussion of various economic reform plans, see Vladimir Mau, "The Road to Perestroika: Economics in the USSR and the Problems of Reforming the Soviet Economic Order," *Europe-Asia Studies* 48:2 (March 1996), pp. 207–24; and Mau, *The Political History of Economic Reform in Russia, 1985–1994* (London: Centre for Research into Communist Economies, 1996).

[37] For more discussion of glasnost and the relationship between information, scientific knowledge, and the Party, see Križan, 1990, p. 133, footnote 19.

end, however, the Chernobyl accident became a catalyst for a widening of glasnost.

The debate over wage reform in 1986 also nicely highlights the way in which Gorbachev's proposals for strengthening the system unintentionally opened up space for questioning some of the principles on which the system had been built.[38] Gorbachev wanted to address the problem of getting people to work harder; this brought up the question of incentives and, naturally, of wage differentials (i.e., paying people to work harder). But, according to traditional Soviet ideology, wage differentials should have gradually declined over time through the building of socialism; in other words, there was to be what was called "wage leveling" (*uravnilovka*). The move away from wage leveling and toward differentiation implied that the concept of social justice (*sotsial'naia spravedlivost'*), which was something repeatedly emphasized by Gorbachev, had to be reconfigured to mean equality of opportunity rather than equality of compensation.[39] In addition, at first, wage differentials were not meant to address labor supply and mobility issues, such as getting people to work in one region rather than another, or work in one industry or firm rather than another. But Soviet economists and sociologists, such as Tatiana Zaslavskaia, argued that compensation for productive contribution that takes quality and quantity into account (in other words wage differentials) could be used to address the "acuteness of the labor shortage."[40] In the end, a major wage reform program, which called for increases of 20–25% in wages, supposedly contingent on improved enterprise productivity, was approved on 17 September 1986.[41] Although the reform

---

[38] For an analysis of the discourse of new understandings of the economy under perestroika, see Aage, 1991, pp. 3–25. This article details plans for reform in five areas of economic activity: wage inequality, prices, state expenditure, unemployment, and private activity. In each of these areas, the author compares Gorbachev's views, views of other elites, and views of society.

[39] See, for example, Peter Hauslohner, "Gorbachev's Social Contract," *Soviet Economy*, 3:1 (January–March 1987), pp. 61–2, 68, 84; Janet G. Chapman, "Income Distribution and Social Justice in the Soviet Union," *Comparative Economic Studies* 31:1 (Spring 1989), pp. 14–15, 27–41; Alec Nove, "'Radical Reform,' Problems and Prospects," *Soviet Studies* 39:3 (July 1987), p. 460; Aaron Trehub, *Radio Liberty Research*, RL 84/86 (February 1986) and 361/87 (September 1987); and Vladimir Shlapendokh, *Soviet Public Opinion and Ideology* (New York: Praeger, 1986).

[40] Tatiana I. Zaslavskaia, "Chelovecheskii faktor i sotsial'naia spravedlivost'," *Sovetskaia kultura*, no. 10, 23 January 1986, p. 3.

[41] *Sotsialisticheskii trud*, no. 1 (January 1987), pp. 74–81; Stanislav S. Shatalin, "Sotsial'noe razvitie i ekonomicheskii rost," *Kommunist* 63:14 (September 1986), p. 63; and Chapman, 1989, p. 14.

[handwritten annotation: "3 ways increase incentives"]

program did not succeed in getting rid of wage leveling, it did bring about wage increases, and it did open the door to reconsideration of important Soviet economic principles, including the broad question of incentives and the basis for material compensation.

Perestroika reforms accelerated in 1987. In a speech to the Central Committee on 27 January 1987, Gorbachev reaffirmed the Party's "leading role" and said that perestroika was "the reestablishment and development of Leninist principles of democratic centralism in the management of the national economy."[42] And, in his book, he wrote that perestroika was "a direct continuation of the great achievements, upon which our Leninist Party embarked in the October days of the year 1917."[43] In this sense, perestroika was continuing the revolution, and like the revolution, it contained demands for ideological, as well as political and economic, institutional changes.[44]

The evidence that Gorbachev was sincere in his return to Lenin is abundant and persuasive.[45] Gorbachev frequently spoke of returning to Lenin's true ideas and intentions as the guiding principles for perestroika. He wrote that "the works of Lenin and his ideals of socialism remain for us an

---

[42] Mikhail S. Gorbachev, "Doklad general'nogo sekretaria TsK KPSS M. S. Gorbacheva na plenume TsK KPSS 27 ianvaria 1987 goda," *Izvestiia*, no. 28, 28 January 1987b, pp. 1–5.

[43] Gorbachev, 1987, p. 47.

[44] For additional analysis of redefining socialism and ideology under Gorbachev, see Brown, 1996; Casier, 1999; Jeff Checkel, "Ideas, Institutions, and the Gorbachev Foreign Policy Revolution," *World Politics* 45:2 (January 1993), pp. 271–300; John Gooding, "Perestroika and the Russian Revolution of 1991," *Slavonic and East European Review* 71:2 (April 1993), pp. 234–56; Christopher Smart, "Gorbachev's Lenin: The Myth in Service to Perestroika," *Studies in Comparative Communism* 23:1 (1990), pp. 5–22; Elizabeth Teague, "Redefining Socialism in the USSR," in John E. Tedstrom, ed., *Socialism, Perestroika, and the Dilemmas of Soviet Economic Reform* (Boulder, CO: Westview Press, 1990), pp. 22–39; Adam B. Ulam, "Perestroika and Ideology," in Ellen F. Paul, ed., *Totalitarianism at the Crossroads* (New Brunswick, NJ: Transaction Books, 1990), pp. 31–49; and Sylvia Woodby, "Ideology and Perestroika," in Sylvia Woodby, ed., *Gorbachev and the Decline of Ideology in Soviet Foreign Policy* (Boulder, CO: Westview Press, 1989), pp. 5–13.

[45] For discussion of the role of Lenin in Gorbachev's thinking, see Brown, 1996, Chapter 4. In addition, as Brown discusses, popular support for Lenin at the end of the 1980s was quite high. For example, a survey in December 1989 by the All-Union Center for the Study of Public Opinion (*Vsesoiuznyi tsentr izucheniia obshchestvennogo mneniia* or VTsIOM) noted that 72% of respondents considered Lenin, out of a list of 18 people including Einstein, Darwin, and Newton, "the most outstanding scholar/scientist of all." Respondents could name more than one person, and following Lenin were Mendeleev (53.5%) and Marx (51.4%). See VTsIOM, *Obshchestvennoe mnenie v tsifrakh*, 3:10 (January 1990), p. 7, cited in Brown, 1996, p. 338, footnote 1.

inexhaustible source of dialectical creative thought, theoretical wealth, and political sagacity."[46] In addition, Gorbachev claimed that it is from Lenin that one learns that democracy is an essential part of socialism. Gorbachev wrote that "the essence of Perestroika lies in the fact that *it unites socialism with democracy* and revives the Leninist concept of socialist construction both in theory and in practice."[47]

Thus, rather than using perestroika to criticize Marxism-Leninism, perestroika was a return and a reinterpretation meant to reveal the true Marxism-Leninism.[48] In other words, Gorbachev's reaction to contemporary problems was one of interpreting them not as indicators of problems with socialism but rather as indicators that the Soviet system was not truly socialist. Gorbachev was far from alone in this thinking. The economist and deputy prime minister Leonid Abalkin, for example, argued that the Soviet system, such as it stood in the late 1980s, did not actually meet the economic and social criteria for socialism.[49]

Yet sometimes the attempts to reinterpret Marxism-Leninism were tripped up in contradictions. In a well-known article in *Novyi mir* in 1987, Nikolai Shmelev argued that, "according to Leninism, profit is a basic principle of economic accountability."[50] Redefining profit as consistent with Leninism, when the state has not yet even embraced the concept of market prices, leaves the observer to wonder what is meant by Leninist profit (i.e., is it the difference between somewhat arbitrary centrally set prices for inputs and output?). Statements such as Shmelev's exemplify the idea that orthodox actions unintentionally provided opportunities for alternative interpretation.

The critique of the present, in the name of the authentic path obscured by history, required a revision of Soviet history, including open-ended reinterpretations and reevaluations of the past. In February of 1987, Gorbachev told journalists and writers at a meeting in Moscow that "the truth must be complete." Further, referring to the victims of the Soviet regime and the traditional lack of discussion, he noted that "we must not forget names, and

---

[46] Gorbachev, 1987, p. 20.
[47] Gorbachev, 1987, p. 31. Emphasis in original.
[48] For additional analysis of the idea that Gorbachev's vision and perestroika were not a fundamental ideological shift from Soviet socialism, see Križan, 1990.
[49] L. Abalkin, *Financial Times*, 13 December 1988; cited in Teague, 1990, p. 23.
[50] Nikolai Shmelev, "Avansy i dolgi," *Novyi mir*, no. 6 (June 1987), p. 152.

it is all the more immoral to forget or pass over in silence large periods in the life of the people. History must be seen for what it is."[51]

These invitations to reconsider Soviet history raised questions as to the goals of perestroika. Through reinterpretations of Lenin's writings and criticisms of Stalinist excess, Gorbachev had appropriated the concepts of "socialism" and "democracy" as part of the perestroika-defined system of Soviet power. Moreover, by casting perestroika in terms of *strengthening* socialism, Gorbachev was able to refute criticisms that his orthodox program of perestroika could be weakening rather than enhancing Soviet political and economic power. He wrote:

> To put an end to all the rumors and speculations that abound in the West about this [the question of giving up on socialism], I would like to point out once again that we are conducting all our reforms in accordance with the socialist choice. We are looking within socialism, rather than outside it, for the answers to all the questions that arise. We assess our successes and errors alike by socialist standards. Those who hope that we shall move away from the socialist path will be greatly disappointed. Every part of our program of perestroika – and the program as a whole, for that matter – is fully based on the principle of more socialism and more democracy.[52]

Gorbachev did not portray perestroika as merely one option for reinvigorating the Soviet system; rather, he posited perestroika as the only means of saving the Soviet system. In discussing the pace of perestroika and the alternatives, he wrote:

> When asked if we are not pushing it too hard, we reply: no we are not. There is no reasonable alternative to a dynamic, revolutionary perestroika. Its alternative is continued stagnation. Upon the success of perestroika depends the future of socialism and the future of peace. The stakes are too high. Time dictates to us a revolutionary choice and we have made it. We will not retreat from perestroika but will carry it through.[53]

Economic Reforms

Gorbachev undertook serious economic policy revision beginning in 1987 with several measures designed to cut back bureaucracy and stimulate individual initiative. Two crucial laws, the Law on State Enterprise and the

---

[51] "Ubezhdennost' – opora perestroiki. Vstrecha v TsK KPSS," *Izvestiia*, no. 46, 15 February 1987, pp. 1–2.

[52] Gorbachev, 1987, p. 32.

[53] Ibid., p. 55.

Law on Cooperatives were passed, and debate over many economic issues continued throughout the year. Under perestroika, individual enterprises and their directors were supposed to be given more responsibility for organizing the economy, while CPSU oversight departments and central ministries would have less authority. The idea behind these new measures was to promote individual initiative, which would revive the socialist economy. Another perestroika program for stimulating individual entrepreneurial activity, meant to enhance restructuring of central economic policy, was the concept of *cooperatives*. The Law on Cooperatives was passed in 1987, and the rate of participation in cooperatives grew rapidly.

The setting up of cooperatives by enterprises was directly related to the Law on State Enterprise, which gave enterprises control over the possession, use, and administration of assets, including the right to transfer assets. By forming cooperatives, state enterprises, which were under the control of industrial ministries, could transfer activities and the necessary assets to subsidiary cooperatives, which they had themselves set up and which were not subject to ministerial control. The enterprise would then sell these subsidiary cooperatives raw materials and buy back products needed to meet the industrial ministry targets; meanwhile, the subsidiary cooperative would profit from the sales back to the enterprise as well as through sales on the open market.[54] Initially, the formation of cooperatives was one of the few ways that enterprises could escape ministerial control. The struggle between the central ministries and individual enterprises was a historical rift that symbolized the clash between centralized power and regional assertions. The 1987 laws concretely supported enterprise directors, and therefore regional as opposed to central control over resources. However, at the regional level, the laws and the retreat of the center intensified struggles between regional governments and enterprises over resources.[55]

These new laws, which would create the conditions for later spontaneous privatization, were enacted in a context of intense debate over a number of issues including wages, unemployment, prices, and even the role of the state in the economy. Interestingly, Gorbachev and those around

---

[54] Simon Clarke, "Privatisation: The Politics of Capital and Labour," in Stephen White, Alex Pravda, and Zvi Gitelman, eds., *Developments in Russian and Soviet Politics* (Durham, NC: Duke Univ. Press, 1994), p. 169.

[55] David Woodruff, *Money Unmade: Barter and the Fate of Russian Capitalism* (Ithaca, NY: Cornell Univ. Press, 1996), pp. 70–1.

him saw past practices and traditional Soviet thinking as the problem for perestroika. Rather than appreciating either the inflationary consequences of rising wages or foreseeing the potential for massive inequality (which turned out to be the future), Soviet economists in 1987 pointed back to wage leveling as a serious problem. In *Sotsialistichekii trud*, one economist argued in January 1987 that "today wage leveling has become one of the chief braking mechanisms in our economy."[56] Similarly, in describing the challenges facing perestroika, Gorbachev noted that "the tendency towards wage leveling has stubbornly continued to gain ground."[57]

In 1987, most Soviet economists were in favor of prices that would improve incentives, but like Soviet consumers they still shared the belief that certain necessary goods and services should remain available to the population. There was a general understanding that if prices reflected supply and demand, then deficits would *appear* to go away because the prices of goods in short supply would go up, and therefore demand would decrease, leaving more goods on the shelf. But some argued that this sort of logic did not increase the actual supply of goods, and therefore there would actually still be a deficit in the household, if not in the store. For example, an article in *Literaturnaia gazeta* noted that "increasing retail prices and removing subsidies does not in itself provide more meat or milk."[58]

Moreover, summarizing the views of readers, *Literaturnaia gazeta* editors argued:

Provided people are not starving, half-empty shelves in the stores are less aggravating than flourishing stalls in what it is the custom to call *kolkhoz* markets, where the apparent abundance is due to unduly high prices. Apart from this, it should not be forgotten that people here have for decades been imbued with the ideals of socialist justice.[59]

Similarly, other economists claimed:

We should not provide an abundance of various types of food if the majority of the population cannot afford them. But it is precisely this that is inherent in the proposal to eliminate food shortages by sharply reducing the group of people consuming the

---

[56] I. I. Gladkii, "Vazhneishee sotsial'no-eknomicheskoe meropriiatie piatiletki," *Sotsialistich-eskii trud*, no. 1 (January 1987), p. 10.

[57] Mikhail S. Gorbachev, "O zadachakh partii: po korennoi perestroike upravleniia ekono-mikoi," *Pravda*, no. 177, 26 June 1987c, p. 1.

[58] R. Grinberg and A. Rubinstein, "Skol'ko platit' za produkty?" *Literaturnaia gazeta*, no. 33, 12 August 1987, p. 12.

[59] M. Aleksandrova, "Chego ia boius'," *Literaturnaia gazeta*, no. 33, 12 August 1987, p. 12.

foodstuffs. . . . We think this method of overcoming shortages is absolutely unacceptable in our society."[60]

The attitudes of the population by and large reflected a specific, Soviet, understanding of demand. First, the idea of *relative demand*, or demand that is a function of prices or how much in terms of resources (money, time, etc.) someone is willing to devote to a particular good is not recognized. Instead, demand is viewed in absolute terms, that is, how much of a particular good a person objectively needs. Aage writes that "the distinction between shortages resulting from excess demand created by low prices and true scarcity in relation to an absolute standard of need is not recognized. Therefore, low prices are often regarded as a criterion of consumer well-being, on the principle that 'prices are low, so everybody can afford to buy the goods.'"[61] In this context, even though economists and government elites agreed that some type of price reform was necessary, they also agreed that it was a step that could not be taken very soon. Instead, in a July 1987 resolution, Gorbachev postponed price reform until 1990–1 but made some general points about increasing flexibility and decentralization of prices.[62]

The contradictory discourse of the debates over wage and price reform, in which individual incentives were to be offered simultaneously along with measures to preserve social justice and social support, was reflected as well in the discussion of unemployment. Some people including Gorbachev were simply against unemployment. Since 1930 unemployment did not exist officially in the USSR, and full employment was constitutionally guaranteed. Gorbachev reacted to Nikolai Shmelev's 1987 plan in which Shmelev suggested deliberately increasing unemployment, by saying "he apparently proposes . . . that there be unemployment. That is not for us."[63]

The question of transferring workers also naturally arose during discussion of unemployment and layoffs. Some experts were in favor of leaving it to workers to find new jobs on their own. However, given that full employment was in the Constitution, there were no unemployment benefits or other types of support for joblessness. Perhaps this explains why both Zaslavskaia and Shmelev, for example, thought there should be centralized planning for placement of workers and an obligation on the part of workers

[60] Grinberg and Rubinstein, 12 August 1987, p. 12.
[61] Aage, 1991, p. 9.
[62] Aage, 1991, p. 7.
[63] Interview with Mikhail S. Gorbachev, "Vstrecha na izbratel'nom uchastke," *Pravda*, no. 173, 22 June 1987, p. 1.

to work where sent. However, there was debate about how this should be done; for example, should workers be moved across regions, or industries, or from skilled to unskilled jobs, if skilled jobs were not available? The 1987 economic reforms, which included the two crucial laws (on State Enterprise and Cooperatives) and the continuing price, wage, and unemployment debates, all fundamentally addressed the question of the role of the state in the economy, and in doing so they also provoked further debate over the question of distribution of resources in the USSR. Although regionalized economic interests were not yet being articulated, the 1987 debates suggest opportunities for their consideration because all of the economic reform issues had a potential regional component (e.g., regional or territorial control of resources, wage and price differentials across territories, and labor mobility).

Political Discussion and Dissent

One way in which we see perestroika's orthodox intentions spawning unanticipated heterodoxy lies in the self-reinventions of leading political and economic actors. The strongest opponents of the Soviet system turned out to be the most powerful and those who most owed their careers to the system. The reality that only those in such positions of power would have been powerful enough to criticize the system publicly explains the apparent irony. Insiders thus became outsiders because no one but an insider would be permitted near the edge.[64]

On the economic side one can see this quite directly in early joint-venture and cooperative participation. Who but the most trustworthy members of the Party could have been permitted to dabble in capitalist entrepreneurship and interaction with the West? All the early joint ventures had links to the CPSU either in charter capital or through organizational affiliation or both. There was a list of "authorized organizations" that could form joint ventures, as well as a list of organizations that secretly participated in joint ventures. All these authorized organizations were headed by CPSU nomenklatura.[65] On the political side, there were a number of examples of powerful CPSU members who began as staunch proponents of perestroika

---

[64] For further analysis of the idea that it was insiders who destroyed the system from within, see Steven L. Solnick, *Stealing the State: Control and Collapse in Soviet Institutions* (Cambridge, MA: Harvard Univ. Press, 1997); and David M. Kotz and Fred Weir, *Revolution from Above: The Demise of the Soviet System* (New York: Routledge, 1997).

[65] Kryshtanovskaia, 1996, pp. 28–31.

and ended up as leaders of the opposition, or rasstroika (e.g., Boris Yeltsin, Aleksandr Yakovlev, and Eduard Shevardnadze). The year 1987 was a time of elite zigzagging between various positions on politics, society, culture, and the economy, all supposedly in support of perestroika. However, in trying to hammer out the real perestroika, the real socialism, the real Leninism, and the real supporters of orthodox (Soviet doxic) reform, each of these elite squabbles created more and more room for reinterpretation of the Soviet system. The culture and literature debates in *Sovetskaia kul'tura* during the summer of 1987 provide an interesting illustration of this process.[66] Egor Ligachev, a conservative Politburo member and second secretary of the CPSU, issued a prominent critique of cultural politics under perestroika.[67] Ligachev criticized the demands for "greater self-determination" at the congresses of the creative unions and instead called for greater control over culture by the Party and state.[68] One of Ligachev's main opponents in the debate over cultural politics was another (recently promoted) Politburo member, Aleksandr Yakovlev.[69] Gorbachev responded to this debate by saying that perestroika is "not only negation, and if it is negation, it is dialectical negation," and "we would be very disturbed if suddenly, instead of the consolidation of our creative intelligentsia, there should take place, so to speak, a squabble." Moreover, while

---

[66] On cultural politics under perestroika, see Yitzhak M. Brudny, *Reinventing Russia: Russian Nationalism and the Soviet State, 1953–1991* (Cambridge, MA: Harvard Univ. Press, 1998); Riitta Pittman, "Perestroika and Soviet Cultural Politics: The Case of the Major Literary Journals," *Soviet Studies* 42:1 (January 1990), pp. 111–32; and Patrick O'Meara, "Glasnost, Soviet Culture and the Debate on History," in R. J. Hill and J. A. Dellenbrant, eds., *Gorbachev and Europe: Toward a New Socialism?* (Hants, UK: Edward Elgar Publishing, 1990), pp. 111–36. Also, on the leadership struggles in the main cultural institutions of cinematography, theatre, and literature, see John Dunlop, "Soviet Cultural Politics," *Problems of Communism* 36:5 (1987), pp. 34–53.

[67] About Ligachev, Iivonen wrote "[he is] a typical representative of the Gorbachev era, who supports and actively encourages all measures which aim to develop and strengthen the Soviet system. In this context he is prepared to give his approval even to far-reaching reforms. On the other hand, his behavior... indicates that he sets very strictly defined limits to the scope of permitted criticism." Jyrki Iivonen, *Uuden Neuvostojohdon muotokuvat* (Espoo, Finland: WeilintGöös, 1986), p. 63, cited in Pittman, 1990, p. 115.

[68] Egor Ligachev, "Razdvigat' ramki deiatel'nosti, okhvatyvat' vse uchastki kul'turnogo stroitel'stva: perestroika v sfere kul'tury i mesto v etoi rabote gazety 'Sovetskaia kul'tura'" *Sovetskaia kul'tura*, no. 81, 7 July 1987, p. 2.

[69] Yakovlev had become a secretary of the Central Committee in January 1987 and a member of the Politburo in June 1987. For an animated analysis of the ideas and personalities behind both traditional Soviet thinking and perestroika, see Robert English, *Russia and the Idea of the West* (New York: Columbia Univ. Press, 2000). Also, besides Gorbachev's own writings, another notable insider account is Cherniaev, 1993.

124

acknowledging "extreme acts (*krainosti*)" Gorbachev claimed that they were taking place within "a struggle for socialism."[70]

In general, criticism during perestroika began with safe subjects such as protecting the environment, or preserving historical monuments; it then moved on to more questionable, but still established, material, such as denunciations of the Stalin period as deviations from true socialism. But, as the general issue of self-determination among cultural organizations spilled over into debates over greater autonomy for other groups, and as the protection of historical monuments turned to national historic monuments, and as Stalin's excesses were expanded to include Soviet nationalities policy, the concept of national differences and even grievances against the Soviet regime, in the name of "cultural activism," were starting to take shape. In response to "cultural activists," Gorbachev replied that "we are a state that unites a unique friendly family of peoples! That is Lenin's testament!"[71] The following week, also in *Sovetskaia kul'tura*, Aleksandr Yakovlev – who in 1973 had been fired as Acting Head of the Central Committee's Science and Cultural Department (and sent to Canada as ambassador) due to an article in *Literaturnaia gazeta* in which he had criticized certain journalists for having nationalist leanings – argued that identity group-based politics, including nationalism and promotion of religion, represented a serious threat to society in the Soviet Union.[72] By naming nationalism, Yakovlev had acknowledged and legitimated it as a force to be reckoned with.

Beyond the culture debate, a second major public dispute among elites in 1987 concerned the so-called *Yeltsin affair*. Boris Nikolaevich Yeltsin was born in Sverdlovsk Oblast in 1931. He became first secretary of the Sverdlovsk Party Committee in 1976 and was brought to Moscow by Gorbachev in 1985, as secretary of the Central Committee for Construction, and then in the same year promoted to first secretary of the Moscow City Party Committee. In the beginning of perestroika, Yeltsin's credentials as a party member and ally of Gorbachev and his reform program were impeccable, and in 1986 he became a candidate member of the Politburo. However, like perestroika itself, Yeltsin, in the name of saving and improving the system, soon demanded more than the system could handle.

---

[70] Mikhail S. Gorbachev, "Prakticheskimi delami uglubliat' perestroiku," *Sovetskaia kul'tura*, no. 85, 16 July 1987, pp 1–2.

[71] Ibid.

[72] Aleksandr Yakovlev, "Perestroika i nravstvennost'," *Sovetskaia kul'tura*, no. 87, 21 July 1987, p. 2. For discussion of Yakovlev's dismissal from *Literaturnaia gazeta*, see Pittman, 1990, p. 113.

At the Central Committee plenum on 21 October 1987, Gorbachev delivered a preview of the speech that he was to present at the seventieth anniversary of the revolution in November.[73] The speech was an unprecedented and radical denunciation of Stalin and a call for reevaluation of the past. After listening to Gorbachev's speech, Boris Yeltsin went to the podium and said that he agreed with Gorbachev but went on to claim that, in essence, perestroika had not gone far enough, and Yeltsin then suggested that a new "cult of personality" was forming around Gorbachev.[74] A range of speakers then took the floor to denounce Yeltsin. Shortly thereafter, on November 11, the Moscow City Party Committee met, with Gorbachev and a very ill Yeltsin in attendance, and removed Yeltsin from his position as first secretary. He was also later dismissed from the Politburo and demoted to the post of first deputy chairman of the State Construction Committee. The Yeltsin affair is an example of how perestroika heralded opportunities for heterodoxy, which could hardly have been imagined five years earlier.

While some scholars, as well as the Soviet leadership at the time, have analyzed events in 1987 by describing the players as either supporters or opponents of perestroika, the Yeltsin affair demonstrates the limitations of such categories. The orthodoxy-heterodoxy (perestroika-rasstroika) dialectic is better able to capture the complexity of the situation because the crucial distinction is between those who are trying to strengthen the Soviet system (perestroika), however incompetently, and those who, thanks to the opportunities provided by perestroika, come to oppose the Soviet system (rasstroika). Actors such as Yeltsin started out in favor of perestroika and the system but became anti-system thanks to conceptual opportunities opened up by the orthodox movement itself. Gorbachev, as leader of the orthodoxy, was pro-perestroika and also pro-system. Those such as Ligachev because they were pro-system, had no choice but to go along with Gorbachev and reluctantly support perestroika. In other words, in contrast to the emerging

---

[73] A full transcript of the 21 October 1987 Central Committee Plenum was published in *Izvestiia TsK KPSS*, no. 2 (February 1989), pp. 209–87.

[74] For discussion of the "Yeltsin affair," see the 21 October 1987 Central Committee Plenum transcript, ibid., as well as the Moscow City Committee Plenum of 11 November 1987 (where Yeltsin was removed as first secretary) and speeches at the Nineteenth Party Conference in June and July 1988 available in *XIX Vsesoiuznaia konferentsiia Kommunisticheskoi partii Sovetskogo Soiuza, 28 iiunia – 1 iiulia 1988 goda: stenograficheskii otchet v dvuk tomakh* (Moscow: politicheskoi literatury, 1988). For a summary of the events, see Brown, 1996, pp. 169–72.

heterodox movement, Gorbachev and Ligachev shared the same goal – the strengthening of Soviet power.

Despite the accumulating evidence that the greatest threat to the Soviet Union and to perestroika would come not from the conservatives such as Ligachev but from a diverse group of heterodox actors who would take advantage of perestroika's political and economic opportunities, Gorbachev pressed on even further with perestroika and with attacks against conservatism. For example, apparently unmoved by the potential for nationalism and radical reconsideration (or even rejection) of Soviet territorial power that had been foreshadowed in the debates over culture and national autonomy, Gorbachev suggested reworking the boundaries of Soviet power.[75] First, Gorbachev rhetorically argued that he wanted to change Russia's place in Europe. He claimed that Russia had always been part of Europe, and he flatly stated in his book *Perestroika*, "we are Europeans."[76] Moreover, he rejected Soviet autarky and the argument for Soviet political and economic specificity by arguing that "Europe 'from the Atlantic to the Urals' is a cultural-historical entity united by the common heritage of the Renaissance and the Enlightenment, of the great philosophical and social teachings of the nineteenth and twentieth centuries."[77] Gorbachev followed this rhetoric with substantive action; throughout 1987, Gorbachev led negotiations on the elimination of intermediate-range nuclear forces (INF), first in Europe and then globally (culminating with the signing of the INF Treaty on 8 December 1987). And, a second major component of Gorbachev's revision of Soviet foreign policy in 1987 was the consideration of the withdrawal of Soviet troops from Afghanistan (a process that led to the eventual pullout beginning in October 1988 and ending in February 1989).

But Gorbachev's domestic battles continued. In November of 1987 on the seventieth anniversary of the revolution, Gorbachev gave detailed figures of the purges under Stalin and claimed that any progress in socialism

---

[75] On reconceptualizing the relationship between Europe and Russia during perestroika, see Neil Malcolm, "New Thinking and After: Debate in Moscow about Europe," in Neil Malcolm, ed., *Russia & Europe: An End to Confrontation?* (New York: Pinter Publishers, 1994), pp. 151–81; Daniel Nelson, "The Soviet Union and Europe," *Telos* 84 (1990), pp. 142–54; and Timo Vihavainen, "Russia and Europe: The Historiographic Aspect," in Vilho Harle and Jyrki Iivonen eds., *Gorbachev and Europe* (London: Pinter Publishers, 1990), pp. 1–21. On historical conceptualizations of the relationship between Europe and Russia, see Mark Bassin, "Russia Between Europe and Asia," *Slavic Review* 50:1 (1991), pp. 1–17.

[76] Gorbachev, 1987, p. 200.

[77] Ibid., p. 207.

made under Stalin was made despite him, rather than because of him.[78] In addition, along this path of reevaluating the past, many banned books and films, like *Dr. Zhivago* and Anatolii Rubakov's *Children of the Arbat*, a story about life under Stalin, were published. And popular journals such as *Ogonek* published discussions between readers and controversial authors such as Rubakov about their work.[79] Even films such as *Repentance*, a Georgian film that issued a scathing and horrifying critique of Soviet society and Stalinism, were widely distributed. Hundreds of political prisoners were also released, highlighting the fact that their arrests by Soviet authorities had been unjust.

In a report to the Central Committee in February 1988 published in *Pravda*, Gorbachev stated that, besides alcohol and oil, there had been no growth in the USSR for the last twenty years. The reason, he argued, was a departure from Leninist principles. He said:

Throughout the last 70 years our party and people have been inspired by the ideas of socialism and have been building it. But by virtue of both external and internal factors, we were unable to realize sufficiently fully the Leninist principles of the new social system. This was seriously hampered by the personality cult, the administrative decree system of management which grew up in the thirties, bureaucratic, dogmatic and voluntarist distortions, tyranny, and in the late seventies and early eighties a lack of initiative and retarding phenomena leading to stagnation.[80]

Similarly, Georgii Razumovskii, an early supporter of Gorbachev and recently promoted by him to candidate member of the Politburo, gave a speech on Lenin's birthday in 1988 wherein he argued that perestroika "has brought us closer to Lenin, and Lenin to us." Moreover, he said Lenin's ideas were the "starting point" of perestroika.[81]

But not everyone was convinced by perestroika's reinterpretation of Soviet ideology. In an article in *Literaturnaia Rossiia*, on 27 March 1987, Petr Proskurin, who was at the time a secretary of the RSFSR and USSR writers' unions criticized *Pravda*, *Literaturnaia gazeta*, *Ogonek*, and *Moskovskie novosti* for ignoring the fact that "the word 'communist' has disappeared from the

[78] See the full transcript of the 21 October 1987 Central Committee Plenum in *Izvestiia TsK KPSS*, no. 2 (February 1989), pp. 209–87.
[79] "Deti arbata," *Ogonek*, no. 27, 4–11 July 1987, pp. 4–5.
[80] Mikhail S. Gorbachev, "Rech General'nogo sekretaria TsK KPSS M.S. Gorbacheva na Plenume TsK KPSS 18 fevralia 1988 goda," *Pravda*, no. 50, 19 February 1988, p. 1.
[81] G. Razumovskii, "Za obnovlenie sotsializma, za leninizm. Doklad tovarishcha Razumovskogo G. P. na torzhestvennom sobranii, posviashchennom 118-i godovshchine so dnia rozhdenia V. I. Lenina," *Pravda*, no. 114, 23 April 1988, pp. 1–2.

vocabulary of several generations of Soviet writers."[82] Moreover, Ligachev, who was clearly a supporter of the Soviet system, but nevertheless deeply disturbed by what he thought were risky, potentially anti-Soviet, elements in perestroika, secretly attempted to reorient the orthodoxy.[83] Ligachev supported, if not masterminded, the publication in 1988 of a letter by Nina Andreeva, a pro-Stalinist high school chemistry teacher. The Andreeva letter was published in *Sovetskaia Rossiia* and was entitled "I Cannot Betray My Principles." In it, Andreeva defended Stalinism and charged that "left wing liberal intellectuals" were betraying socialism.[84] On 5 April 1988, *Pravda* replied to Andreeva's letter with a full-page editorial, attributed to Aleksandr Yakovlev.[85] And soon after, *Sovetskaia Rossiia* declared in an editorial that the "publication of Andreeva's letter had been a mistake."[86] Nevertheless, the Andreeva letter had become an anti-perestroika, pro-Soviet manifesto. The letter was important for the rasstroika movement, because the publication of the letter could only mean that either the Party was going to reverse course, or that powerful members of the Party were not in agreement. In this way, it functioned as a very open and public example of officially sanctioned dissent. This pattern whereby perestroika, or pro-system events, created opportunities for rasstroika, or anti-system opposition, would be repeated over and over throughout the rest of the perestroika era.

Gorbachev called the Nineteenth Party Conference of the CPSU in June 1988 in order to shore up union-wide support for perestroika. The last party conference had been in 1941. Now 5,000 delegates from across the Soviet Union were to meet to vote on a new set of reforms. The conference represented one of the first signs of serious formal institutional change because Gorbachev's proposals included explicit attempts to separate the functions of the CPSU and state bodies by upgrading state institutions and replacing the nomenklatura system of appointments with multicandidate elections to legislatures. Such changes implied not only removing key

---

[82] Dunlop, 1987, p. 47, citing *Literaturnaia Rossiia*, 27 March 1987.

[83] Ligachev was really quite limited in what he could do. As someone committed to the Soviet system, he had to support the CPSU command structure and Gorbachev. For a similar argument on nomenklatura acquiescence, see Kotkin, 1997.

[84] N. Andreeva, "Ne mogu postupitsia s printsipami," *Sovetskaia Rossiia*, no. 60, 13 March 1988, p. 3. For further discussion of this event, see Brown, 1996, pp. 172–5; and Andrei Grachev, *Kremlevskaia khronika* (Moscow: EKSMO, 1994).

[85] "Printsipy perestroiki: revoliutsionnost' myshleniia i deistvii," *Pravda*, no. 96, 5 April, 1988, p. 2. This was reprinted in *Sovetskaia Rossiia*, no. 79, 6 April 1988, p. 2.

[86] "Partiia idet vo glave perestroiki," *Sovetskaia Rossiia*, no. 87, 15 April 1988, p. 3.

functions and tasks from the CPSU but also radically restructuring the CPSU itself.[87]

The conference engendered a range of heterodox reactions including large street protests in Moscow calling for elections and criticizing the CPSU.[88] These demonstrations illustrate the difficulty of the task faced by perestroika as an orthodox movement. While such demonstrations may seem pro-perestroika by their support of reforms, the calls that emerged for multiparty elections clearly infringed on the power of the CPSU as an organizing force in the Soviet Union and hence belong not to Gorbachev's project of perestroika but to rasstroika.

Similarly, although the 1988 CPSU reforms were conceived by Gorbachev and other pro-perestroika actors as a way to strengthen Soviet power, the restructuring of the CPSU marked a major step in diminishing Soviet power by shifting the bases of power in federal and territorial relations throughout the USSR. Following earlier public recognition of splits in the Party[89] and the debates of the Nineteenth Party Conference, serious restructuring of the CPSU began in July 1988 at the plenum of the CPSU Central Committee.[90] In August, Gorbachev suggested eliminating all branch economic departments of the CPSU Central Committee, each of which had overseen several ministries.[91] The recommendations of the summer were enacted by October, when all the economic departments were abolished, thereby reducing the number of Central Committee

[87] See speeches of the Nineteenth Party Conference cited in note 74. Also for additional discussion, see Brown, 1996, pp. 175–9.

[88] On public protests and rallies in Moscow, see Colton, 1995, pp. 589–92; and for discussion of the development of "informal" groups, see Valerii Fadeev, *Pokhozhdeniia neformala: Ocherk 88 goda*, vol. 1 (Moscow: Russkoe slovo, 1992), p. 37.

[89] For example, as early as 1985, Aleksandr Yakovlev had suggested splitting the party in two. Other prominent reformers including Stanislav Shatalin and Fedor Burlatskii had also made suggestions. Similarly, Tatiana Zaslavskaia wrote in June 1988 of the difficulties facing perestroika. The main one she claimed was that there were a number of different "interests" that opposed perestroika. She outlined the attitudes of ten social groups, rating them on an eight-point scale from "initiators" to "reactionaries." See T. Zaslavskaia, "O strategii sotsial'nogo upravleniia perestroika," in N. Afanas'ev, ed., *Inogo ne dano* (Moscow: progress, 1988), pp. 11, 39. Zaslavskaia was the reputed author of the "Novosibirsk Report" (published as "The Novosibirsk Report," *Survey* 28:1 (Spring 1984), pp. 88–108), which was presented in a closed conference in 1983 and was an early, if muted, indication of heterogeneous interests in the USSR. That report was then revised and presented in more detail in her 1988 article.

[90] For a summary of these changes, see Brown, 1996, pp. 184–6; and Roeder, 1993, pp. 226–8.

[91] Mikhail S. Gorbachev, "Postanovlenie Politbiuro TsK KPSS 8 sentiabria 1988 g.," *Izvestiia TsK KPSS*, no. 1 (January 1989), pp. 81–6.

departments from twenty to nine.[92] These changes were supposed to limit party repetition of state functions (i.e., state ministries were freer from party control and instead were eventually supposed to be under the oversight of the new Congress of People's Deputies).[93]

Of those subunits of the CPSU that remained, the most important were restructured, and in ways that stoked regional initiative. Most importantly, the secretariat of the Central Committee was replaced by six Central Committee commissions, which led to the eventual elimination of the staff of the CPSU and a decrease in secretariat meetings. Thus, by the end of 1988, the party secretariat's union-wide supervisory role had effectively ended. And the 1988 CPSU reform had important regional implications.[94] Because the pre-perestroika governance institutions of the USSR were essentially federal, what made the USSR a centralized state was the CPSU. Removing CPSU oversight allowed all the federal units (especially union republics) to begin behaving as independent states.

Each orthodox move by Gorbachev seemed to create opportunities for the heterodox project of rasstroika. In a now ironic statement, Gorbachev, in speaking about the necessity of perestroika, criticized the earlier leadership of the Soviet Union for not recognizing the consequences of its policies. He wrote: "we only thought that we were in the saddle, while the actual situation that was arising was one that Lenin warned against: the automobile was not going where the one at the steering wheel thought it was going."[95]

Heterodox reactions to perestroika were not confined to political activity. On the economic side, the 1988 CPSU reforms reinforced the effects of the earlier Laws on State Enterprise and Cooperatives by allowing economic actors, mainly enterprise directors, tremendous latitude to make decisions without regard to central planning.

By December 1988, cooperatives employed 787,000 people (and by the end of 1991 that number would rise to 11 million out of a total work

---

[92] The only departments left related to the economy were a socioeconomic department and an agriculture department. In addition to changes affecting the economic departments, the Department of Relations with Communist and Workers' Parties of Socialist Countries was incorporated into the International Department.

[93] However, change was not limited only to the Central Committee: From 1986 to 1990, four state committees were eliminated (from 23 to 19), and 18 ministerial posts were eliminated, bringing the number from 55 to 37, and the staff of the ministries was cut by one third. See Roeder, 1993, p. 227.

[94] For more on this point, see Kotkin, 1997.

[95] Gorbachev, 1987, p. 18.

force of 135 million).[96] However, cooperatives hardly represented private entrepreneurial initiative: 85% of cooperatives were set up by state enterprises, where such enterprises were the cooperatives' main suppliers or customers.[97] Moreover, cooperatives were widely viewed by the public as speculative operations where goods that should have been sold at state stores, but were unavailable, were resold at 50–100% higher prices.[98] *Moskovskie novosti* claimed that cooperatives brought "almost nothing but high prices," and that they were "a social evil, a malignant tumor."[99] Even Gorbachev admitted some problems with cooperatives. In *Pravda* he wrote: "Clearly we need honest work initiative, but not of the sort displayed by some cooperatives, which exploit shortages to the degree of outright greed. I can say that to this end, they will be subject to progressive taxation. I think that would be fair."[100]

Maintaining a coherent argument in support for cooperatives and increasing wage differentials was not easy. Gorbachev tried to make a distinction between those who make more money through "honest labor" and those who earn money through speculation, corruption, and private renting of apartments.[101] Similarly the economist and deputy prime minister Leonid Abalkin said that "under socialism, the question can only be posed like this: not 'much' or 'little,' but 'earned' or 'unearned.'"[102] And, Ruslan Khasbulatov, who would later become speaker of the RSFSR Supreme Soviet, stated that "We must not be afraid that some people may earn too much. What is important is this: that every ruble is genuinely earned, and then it will have a direct effect on increasing our national wealth and raising people's living standards."[103]

---

[96] Peter Rutland, "The Economy: The Rocky Road from Plan to Market," in Stephen White, Alex Pravda, and Zvi Gitelman, eds., *Developments in Russian and Post-Soviet Politics* (Durham, NC: Duke Univ. Press, 1994), p. 141.

[97] Clarke, 1994, p. 167.

[98] A. Jones and W. Moskoff, "New Cooperatives in the USSR," *Problems of Communism* 37:6 (November–December 1989), p. 32.

[99] V. Loshak, "Ogon' iz vsekh kalibrov," *Moskovskie novosti*, no. 33, 13 August 1989, p. 7; and Loshak, "Nastuplenie na kooperativy ...," *Moskovskie novosti*, no. 39, 24 September 1989, p. 5.

[100] Mikhail S. Gorbachev, "Slovo rabochei Moskvy. Vstrecha M. S. Gorbacheva c kollektivom Pervogo Gosudarstvennogo podshipnikovogo zavoda," *Pravda*, no. 68, 8 March 1988, p. 2.

[101] "Doklad General'nogo sekretaria TsK KPSS tovarishcha Gorbacheva M.S. 25 fevralia 1986 goda," *Ekonomicheskaia gazeta*, no. 10, March 1986, p. 9.

[102] L. Abalkin, "Sterzhen ekonomicheskoi zhizni," *EKO*, no. 9 (September 1986), p. 9.

[103] R. Khasbulatov, "Chto vidno v zerkale tseny," *Pravda*, no. 166, 15 June 1986, p. 2.

But the problem was, what did this distinction between "earned" and "unearned" mean in practice? Some economists like Stanislav Shatalin were arguing that the country needed to get over the "fear of so-called excessive incomes."[104] There were also those who thought that there should be maximum incomes, and that there should be no "Soviet millionaires."[105] Aage illustrates well the conceptual dilemma over prices and wages that faced those trying to support perestroika. He writes:

Wage differentials could not be considered purely as an incentive without regard to fairness, and a price offer is not neutral but subject to a moral standard, even if everybody is free to take it or leave it. A high price at the kolkhoz market is not a welfare-augmenting increase in the range of options, but an insult. The concepts of "unearned income," "illegal income" and "*spekuliatsiia*" as distinct from "market clearing" derive their existence from these cultural values.[106]

Further muddling the conceptual boundaries was the attempt by orthodox actors to blame current problems, which seemed to the public to have been created by perestroika, on past policies and anti-perestroika reactionaries.[107] Moreover, some pro-perestroika actors took the criticism of the past even further and blamed not just misinterpretations of Lenin or Stalinist excesses, but Marxism itself. For example, Alexander Tsipko, a Central Committee member and consultant to Gorbachev argued that the problem is "not just with the mustaches but with the beards."[108] Tsipko's comment illustrates the way in which even those who thought they were supporting the system by supporting perestroika and criticizing Stalin, were opening up space for further heterodox critique leading to criticism of Lenin and Marx as well.

As perestroika pushed on, 1989 saw further weakening of Soviet authority, in the form of the CPSU, and greater variety in terms of organizational power, including increased decentralization. In March and April of 1989, semi-free elections were held for 2,250 seats in the USSR Congress of

[104] S. S. Shatalin, "Aktivnaia, sil'naia sotsial'naia politika," *Ekonomicheskaia gazeta*, no. 20, May 1986, p. 6.

[105] V. Rogovin, "Sotsial'naia spravedlivost' i sotsialisticheskoe raspredelenie zhiznennykh blag," *Voprosy filosofii*, no. 9 (September 1986), pp. 15, 20.

[106] Aage, 1991, p. 14.

[107] For example, Zaslavskaia blamed shortages on anti-perestroika forces. See Zaslavskaia, 1988, p. 26.

[108] A. Tsipko, "Istoki stalinizma," *Nauka i zhizn'*, [in four parts] nos. 11, 12 (1988), and nos. 1, 2 (1989); and Aleksandr Tsipko "Chelovek ne mozhet izmenit' svoei prirode," *Politicheskoe obrazovanie*, no. 4 (1989), pp. 67–78.

People's Deputies. These elections were likely intended by Gorbachev to shore up pro-perestroika forces. Although the elections were marked by CPSU organizational dominance, they still resulted in some significant shocks to the CPSU and the system of Soviet authority, which was not Gorbachev's intention. For example, Boris Yeltsin, who had scandalously resigned from the Party in the fall, defeated the conservative CPSU-backed Evgenii Brakov. In addition, Yurii Solovev, the first secretary of the Leningrad Oblast Committee of the CPSU and candidate member of the Politburo of the CPSU Central Committee, ran for election and was defeated. That a member of the first rank of the nomenklatura could be defeated in an election was a significant signal that the system of nomenklatura appointments, which had always structured organization and power in the Soviet Union, was changing.

Another sign of change was the unprecedented mass retiring at the April 1989 plenum of the CPSU Central Committee of seventy-four members and twenty-four candidates for membership.[109] And soon after, official factions within the CPSU, such as the Interregional Group of Deputies, would be formed.[110] The loss of power by the CPSU was not, however, replaced by an equally stable system of political authority. Instead, the transition to elections was accompanied by a great deal of uncertainty, not only about electoral outcomes but also about which institutions and organizations would even be relevant in the future.

Elections, and the new state (rather than party) institutions that they empowered, affected power relations not only in the center but at other territorial levels as well. For example, the USSR Congress of People's Deputies elected from among its members a new USSR Supreme Soviet with Gorbachev as chairman. Similarly, in Russia (the RSFSR) a *Russian* Congress of People's Deputies was formed which then elected an upper body, the *Russian* Supreme Soviet, which was composed of two chambers, a Council for the Republic and a Council for Nationalities, each with 126 members. The first session of the Russian Congress of People's Deputies

---

[109] Kryshtanovskaia, 1996, p. 22. Gorbachev's purge of the Party was not without precedent; there were similar (though smaller-scale) purges in the 1930s.

[110] For more on the development of informal groups and social organizations, see Vyacheslav Igrunov, "Public Movements: From Protest to Political Self-Consciousness," in Brad Roberts and Nina Belyaeva, eds., *After Perestroika: Democracy in the Soviet Union* (Washington, DC: The Center for Strategic and International Studies, 1991), pp. 14–31; and Fadeev, 1992.

was held in May–June 1990, and Boris Yeltsin was elected Chairman of the Russian Supreme Soviet.[111]

A key characteristic of these state organizations was that their members were elected, but they also contained new suborganizations relevant to regional governance, such as the Council for the Republic and the Council for Nationalities. The Russian Congress of People's Deputies represented a crucial break with the doxa of central Soviet power because it was a territorially defined political institution operating in opposition to central institutions, namely the USSR Congress of People's Deputies and USSR Supreme Soviet. Moreover, the election of Yeltsin, who had become by 1990 one of Gorbachev's strongest critics, as chairman of the Russian Supreme Soviet symbolized a victory for the heterodox project of rasstroika. The legitimate ascendance of the once-disgraced Yeltsin demonstrated that the location of political and economic power in the Soviet Union was in a process of transformation.

The development of specifically Russian state institutions was not unique. Throughout the broader sphere of Soviet power, including both the USSR and Eastern Europe, perestroika and the decline of the CPSU corresponded with increasingly territorialized, anti-Soviet demands. As one after another of the Eastern European countries rejected Soviet power in 1989, union republics pressed republican political and economic demands. In August, nationalists in Moldova reinstated Romanian as the official language of the republic, leading Russians and Ukrainians to demand autonomy. In September, the Ukrainian Popular Movement for Perestroika (*Rukh*) held its founding congress. By December, the Lithuanian Communist Party had left the CPSU and the Latvian parliament deleted references to the Communist Party's "leading role" from its Constitution.

Formal recognition of the progressive weakening of the CPSU vis-à-vis state institutions came in March 1990 when, following the CPSU Central Committee's February approval, the USSR Congress of People's Deputies officially removed from the Constitution Articles 6 and 7, which had guaranteed the dominance of the CPSU in political and economic life. In addition, the phrase, "the leading role of the Communist Party – the vanguard of all the people" was deleted from the preamble to the Constitution,

---

[111] Jeffrey W. Hahn, "Introduction: Analyzing Parliamentary Development in Russia," in J. Hahn, ed., *Democratization in Russia: The Development of Legislative Institutions* (Armonk, NY: M. E. Sharpe, 1996), p. 15.

and other parties were legalized.[112] Equally important, the institution of the presidency was founded. The establishment of the office of the presidency, responsible to the Constitution rather than the CPSU, was in essence another nullification of the preeminent role of the CPSU.[113] However, as it turned out, rather than democratic elections entirely replacing the nomenklatura system of appointments, a haphazard system of elections plus appointments and rule by executive decree came into place. This institutional shift was characterized by the development of unchecked executive authority and rule by decree at both the union and republican levels.

The destruction of the CPSU introduced a historic transformation of the categories used to understand political and economic power; this process forced regional leaders, among others, to rethink strategies for political and economic organization since the well-worn paths to Soviet political and economic power were increasingly closed out. Using perestroika-empowered republican state institutions, heterodox alternatives to Soviet power gained momentum throughout 1990. Several union republics began passing laws that contradicted USSR laws. Then in March 1990, the newly elected Lithuanian parliament declared independence from the USSR, and the Estonian parliament declared a transition to independence. By May, the Latvian parliament voted to declare independence. Even more detrimental to the USSR and the Soviet doxa, in June 1990 even Russia, along with Uzbekistan and Moldova, issued a declaration of sovereignty. And by October, most of the other union republics followed suit.

These sovereignty declarations were a major sign that state institutions were no longer under the control of either the CPSU or the central government of the USSR. However, they also represented the new regionalization of politics in the USSR. And, this process was happening not only at the USSR level but within republics such as Russia as well. Throughout 1990, several legislative alliances and parties were formed, as were various factions within the Congress of People's Deputies.[114] Within the Russian

---

112 "Ob uchrezhdenii posta prezidenta SSSR i vnecenii izmenenii i dopolnenii v konstitutsiiu (osnovoi zakon) SSSR," *Izvestiia*, no. 75, 16 March 1990, pp. 2–3.

113 G. Ovcharenko and Y. Ursov, "Za obnovlenie sotsializma, za leninism," *Pravda*, no. 59, 28 February 1990, p. 1.

114 For example, in preparation for the March 1990 elections to the Russian Congress of People's Deputies, the Democratic Russia bloc was founded. In May 1990, the Democratic Party of Russia was founded, and the founding of the RSFSR Communist Party followed in June 1990.

Congress of People's Deputies there were three bases of factions: (1) territorial, either by region or groups of regions such the Far North or the Urals; (2) occupational, for example, educators, medical workers, or the KGB; and (3) political, in the sense of ideas rather than institutional interests.[115] Although for various complex reasons these factions did not develop into really effective parties, they nevertheless represented a new organization of regional interests.[116]

The new parties and factions in the union and in the Russian Congress of People's Deputies vastly expanded the character of regional interests in political organizations. In a break from both the doxic conception of central Soviet power and the orthodox program of perestroika, regional interests, for the first time, could be expressed in openly territorial or national terms. Through elections and participation in new political bodies, regions could attempt to articulate their own interests. This heterodox institutional framework was very different from the nomenklatura system of appointments where regional interests were totally subordinated to the agenda of the CPSU.

The articulation of regional interests was also evident in movements for greater sovereignty within the RSFSR itself. By 1990 most regions had a plan for self-administration (*samoupravlenie*).[117] Out of 73 regions (republics, oblasts, krais, and AOs) in the RSFSR, 17 declared sovereignty before June 1991, 16 declared themselves Free Economic Zones, and 40 did neither.[118] At the same time that regional movements within the RSFSR were organizing, the central authority of the union was increasingly threatened. Gorbachev tried to take decisive action by getting the USSR Supreme Soviet to allow him to rule by decree in September 1990. In

[115] Jerry F. Hough, "The Structure of the Russian Legislature and Its Impact on Party Development," in J. Hahn, ed., *Democratization in Russia: The Development of Legislative Institutions* (Armonk, NY: M. E. Sharpe, 1996), pp. 87–8.

[116] See ibid. for a discussion of why factions did not develop into parties.

[117] For regional plans, see *Pervyi s"ezd narodnykh deputatov SSSR, 25 maia–9 iiunia 1989 g.: stenograficheskii otchet* (Moscow: Verkhounogo Soveta SSSR, 1989), vol. 2, pp. 47, 66, 152–3, 298–9; Woodruff, 1999, p. 75; and James Hughes, "Regionalism in Russia: The Rise and Fall of the Siberian Agreement," *Europe-Asia Studies* 46:7 (1994), pp. 1133–61. On the "Urals Association," see B. Khorev, " 'Libo vedomstvennost', libo kompleksnost'," *Voprosy ekonomiki*, no. 4 (April 1989), p. 65.

[118] On sovereignty declarations by oblasts and free economic zone declarations, see Beth Mitchneck, "An Assessment of the Growing Local Economic Development Function of Local Authorities in Russia," *Economic Geography* 71:2 (April 1995), pp. 150–70. On declarations of sovereignty, see also Chapter 5, "The Process of Federal Transition" in Kahn, 2002, pp. 102–41.

November 1990, Gorbachev proposed a new draft union treaty, but it was doomed to failure from the start. The treaty did not mention the republics' right to secede, though many had already announced independence. It kept USSR laws as primary, though many republics had passed laws that contradicted USSR laws. The treaty made Russian the state language, while republics had already declared titular languages as state languages. And finally, on economic issues, the treaty gave republics limited authority over certain enterprises, while the Laws on State Enterprise and Cooperatives and the diminishment of the CPSU had already allowed enterprises to ignore central authority. Thus, it was not surprising that the Baltics, Armenia, Georgia, and Moldova refused even to participate in discussions over the treaty. Another draft with the right to secession was introduced, but the remaining nine union republics demanded more negotiation of the treaty.[119]

After believing for years that the threat to the USSR and perestroika was coming from old-thinkers (or "anti-perestroika reactionaries"), and therefore pushing harder for perestroika against such imagined forces, Gorbachev finally in the fall of 1990 stopped blaming conservatives and realized that it was the heterodox elites, such as Yeltsin and other elected republican leaders, who posed the greatest danger to the union. Gorbachev therefore turned to conservatives in a desperate attempt to save the Soviet system. He made a last-ditch effort in January 1991 to use force to crack down on Lithuanian and Latvian independence movements and in December brought in conservatives such as Boris Pugo, Gennadii Ianaev, and Valentin Pavlov, who would eventually plot the coup to overthrow Gorbachev, ostensibly to save the union.

It is impossible to understand how Gorbachev could be so obtuse, except with the insight that for Gorbachev, perestroika was an orthodox pro-Soviet project. Gorbachev apparently believed that those who took up the banner of perestroika were like him, sharing the goal of a strengthened Soviet system. And he believed that people would voluntarily make the "socialist choice." But he was wrong. The perestroika/anti-perestroika dichotomy did not capture the real divide, which was between those who were for Soviet power (orthodox) and those who were against it (heterodox). Understanding perestroika as fundamentally intended to strengthen Soviet power renders Gorbachev's reactions sensible: To this day he cannot acknowledge that perestroika was responsible for the destruction of the Soviet Union, and

---

[119] For more on this process, see Kotkin, 1997.

he feels betrayed. Because the heterodox movement was a function of the opportunities presented by Gorbachev and the orthodoxy of perestroika, Gorbachev, in a sense, is right that he was betrayed. But it was his own doxic myopia, rather than the actions and signals of actors at the time, that prevented him for so long from understanding that heterodox actors did not share his goals. _) Reason for fall of USSR

As 1991 began, central Soviet authority continued to weaken while republican and regional authority increased. The rise in Yeltsin's power, like that of other union republican leaders, directly coincided with waning support for perestroika and the rising unpopularity of Gorbachev as president of the USSR. In February, the Baltic countries held plebiscites to demonstrate the will of their citizens to secede from Soviet Union. In March, in an attempt to shore up popular support across the union, a referendum was held on preservation of Soviet Union. Even though 76.4 % of participants voted to remain in the union, the referendum, like so many perestroika actions, created heterodox opportunities. Six union republics (Armenia, Georgia, Moldova, Lithuania, Latvia, and Estonia) boycotted the referendum all together, and Kazakhstan changed the wording of the question, while both Ukraine and Russia added their own questions to the ballots.[120] In Russia, against Gorbachev's wishes, a question on the creation of a Russian presidency was added. This question passed and allowed Yeltsin to be elected president of the Russian Republic in June.

Amidst all this political turmoil, economic conditions continued to deteriorate and authority over economic resources, as in politics, was increasingly regionalized and subject to intense conflict.[121] A crucial component in the restructuring of the CPSU was that the elimination of central ministries and centrally appointed party bureaucrats created a space for enterprise directors and other regionally located elites to assume the former governance functions of the CPSU. The significance of CPSU downsizing was not a revolution in actual personnel but rather a revolution in the source of personnel appointment. Regionally located elites increasingly became independent of central oversight, and regional political and economic organizations increasingly took on region-specific responsibilities.

The 1990 Law on Property had allowed even greater freedom of the regional enterprises' own activities in that it allowed state enterprises to convert themselves into joint stock companies, with shares bought by other

---

[120] McFaul, 2001, pp. 96, 103.
[121] See, for example, Woodruff, 1999, p. 74.

state firms. By January 1991, there were 1,200 joint stock companies. The transformation of state enterprises into private enterprises by the state itself continued throughout 1990 and was not limited to factories. In the banking sector, state banks (from the system of industrial-construction and housing-welfare banks) turned into over 2,000 "commercial" banks mainly doing inter-enterprise lending using state credits.[122] In several of these new commercial banks, the buildings, equipment, personnel, and directorate stayed the same.[123] In general, those who had been in management positions before perestroika used the perestroika reforms to solidify their control over resources. This assertion of control over resources by enterprise directors and other nomenklatura managers represented a de facto regional division of resources. There was no formal plan within perestroika to give control of resources to regionally located economic elites, but that was one of the effects of nomenklatura-directed privatization.

However, this appropriation of resources by the nomenklatura did not entirely favor the regions. In Russia, for example, the old central ministries also tried to join in the process of privatization. Through amendments to the Law on State Enterprises in 1989, ministries were transformed into holding companies in the form of interbranch state associations (*mezhotraslevoe gosudarstvennoe ob"edinenie* or MGO), concerns, and state associations. It is estimated that 50% of ministries had privatized themselves in this way by mid-1991, while the rest followed suit after 1991.[124] In this process, the property under the control of ministries became the property of the ministry leadership (although there were some battles between the ministries and individual enterprises). Similarly, stock market structures (the Russian Commodities and Raw Materials Exchange, the Moscow Commodities Exchange, and the Moscow Investment Exchange) developed out of Gossnab (*Gosudarstvennyi komitet po material'no-tekhnicheskomu snabzheniiu* or State Committee for Material and Technical Supply) and were headed by Komsomols (members of the *Vsesoiuznyi Leninskii Kommunisticheskii soiuz molodezhi*, VLKSM, or All-Union Lenin Communist Youth League) and former Gossnab specialists.[125] Privatization of the ministries

[122] Rutland, 1994, pp. 147–8. For further discussion of the transformation of the banking system, see Juliet Johnson, "Banking in Russia," *Problems of Post-Communism* 43:3 (May–June 1996), pp. 49–60; and Juliet Johnson, *A Fistful of Rubles: The Rise and Fall of the Russian Banking System* (Ithaca, NY: Cornell Univ. Press, 2000).

[123] Kryshtanovskaia, 1996, p. 28.

[124] Clarke, 1994, p. 169.

[125] Kryshtanovskaia, 1996, p. 28.

and other federal economic organizations also supported the development of Moscow-based financial-industrial groups.

However, aside from the regional elites' takeover of resources located in the respective regions, there was little further regional distribution of ministerial resources. Instead, those resources were concentrated in Moscow-based organizations. The conceptual association of Moscow with the central government meant that privatization of ministerial resources did not support any inter-regional conflict over privatized property. Instead, privatization supported the distinction between territorial regions on the one hand and Moscow and the central government on the other. Moreover, the regionalization of economic understanding was not just occurring at the union level; within the Russian Federation, for example, sub-national regions were increasingly left without economic direction from either the Russian federal or the USSR central government, and in this chaotic time regions were facing food and other goods shortages, as well as rising inter-enterprise debts.

By the summer of 1991, the political chaos in the union was coming to a head. Negotiations over the union treaty had begun in April, and by July a new draft treaty was agreed upon by Gorbachev and most of the union republics. The treaty in many ways marked the end of the USSR. It did not use the word *socialist*, and it eliminated central institutions such as the USSR Supreme Soviet. It also made republican laws primary and gave union republics the right to secede as well as authority over most government functions.

The signing of the treaty was set for August 20, but it never occurred because on August 19 the State Committee for the State of Emergency (*Gosudarstvennyi komitet po chrezvychainomu polozheniiu* or GKChP), a group of eight top Soviet government officials, many of whom were Gorbachev's recent appointees, announced a state of emergency, removing Gorbachev from power, in order to save the Soviet state and economy. Yeltsin led protests outside the Russian parliament building, famously standing atop a tank, and the coup, lacking support in both the population and the military, failed after three days.

The attempted coup was the culmination of the struggle between orthodox attempts to save the USSR and the forces supporting rasstroika. The coup was a desperate effort to save the USSR, but ultimately it was the failure of the attempted coup that finally delegitimized and shattered the doxa of Soviet central power. In the aftermath of the coup, it was clear to almost everyone, except Gorbachev, that Yeltsin and other rasstroika "reformers" at all territorial levels of the union had effectively won. Gorbachev tried and failed to win support of the republics for the new union treaty in October. Instead, throughout the fall, the remaining union republics that had not already done so declared independence. The Belovezhskaia accords were signed in secret by Yeltsin and the leaders of Belarus (Stanislav Shushkevich) and Ukraine (Leonid Kravchuk) on December 7, proclaiming the foundation of the Commonwealth of Independent States. Gorbachev resigned as president of the USSR and announced that at year's end all central government structures would cease to exist. This was the formal end of the Soviet Union and of Soviet doxa.

4

To Each His Own

THE DEVELOPMENT OF HETEROGENEOUS REGIONAL UNDERSTANDINGS AND INTERESTS IN RUSSIA

The first Russian Republic, which began in the fall of 1991 and lasted until December 1993, was outside the organizing framework of the Soviet doxa. Instead, this was a period of contestation over power and the system of authority that would structure political and economic relations in the Russian Federation. Politically, it was a game of musical chairs: All the rules and paths to power had been upset, and no one knew which institution would turn out to be the relevant one. The Federation Treaty and the Constitution were works-in-progress, and there were many organizational choices facing political actors including multiple seats of authority in the region. But, who knew which chair would be left when the music stopped – would it be the executive or the legislature, the center or the regions? On the economic side, the de facto decentralization of economic resources that began under perestroika and accelerated with the decline of the CPSU represented the transformation from Soviet principles of redistribution to a Hobbesian every-region-for-itself state of anarchy that exacerbated regional inequality. During this period, regions came to appreciate the new opportunities that had opened up to them and the urgency of making choices; consequently, at this time they developed a sense of *post-Soviet* regional economic interests.

In this chapter, I analyze the post-doxa period of the first Russian Republic from the late fall of 1991 to December 1993 as a space for the development of new, differentiated, regional understandings, that is, heterogeneous conceptualizations and solutions to problems. The lack of an established conceptual structure allowed for the emergence of novel categories of regional political and economic thinking, as well as the formation of regional interests which, as I demonstrate in later chapters, provided crucial support for movements for greater sovereignty.

Regions and Political Authority

One of the effects of the breakup of the USSR was that, in the process of the union republics' (including the RSFSR's) struggles for independence from the USSR, political leaders encouraged independence movements by sub-union republics. For example, both Gorbachev and Yeltsin at various points encouraged Russian regional sovereignty movements in order to weaken each other's position. Gorbachev courted separatism amongst republics located within the RSFSR in order to weaken Yeltsin's position as leader of the RSFSR, while Yeltsin supported separatism and movements for sovereignty amongst all republics (both at the union level, and at the sub-union level within the RSFSR) in order to weaken the union government and hence Gorbachev's position. This background of the Yeltsin-led RSFSR struggle against the USSR is essential to the context of separatism within Russia, in that regions within Russia received mixed signals about the locus of power in the RSFSR and the consequences of engaging in separatism.

In the final years of perestroika, as power was shifting to the union republics, the Congress of People's Deputies (CPD) of the RSFSR established a Constitutional Commission in June 1990, consisting of more than one hundred Supreme Soviet deputies. This Commission then established a Working Group, headed by Oleg Rumiantsev which would be critical to drafting the Russian Constitution.[1] Rumiantsev's Working Group prepared an initial draft in November 1991 and then a revised version of the first draft, which was rejected by the CPD in early 1991. A second draft was submitted on 10 October 1991, but it was also rejected.

Part of the trouble with the draft constitution was that the primary constituent units of the Russian Federation had not been agreed upon. When the Russian Federation was established in December 1991, it consisted of 16 republics, 5 autonomous oblasts, 10 autonomous okrugs, 49 oblasts, and

---

[1] For a list of all constitutional drafts see Jeffrey Kahn, *Federalism Democratization, and the Rule of Law in Russia* (New York: Oxford Univ. Press, 2002), p. 133. For the actual constitutional drafts, see Konstitutsionnaia komissiia, Rossiiskoi Federatsii, *Konstitutsionnyi vestnik*, no. 1–16 (Moscow: komissiia, October 1990–May 1993); and *Konstitutsionnoe soveshchanie: stenogrammy, materialy, dokumenty: 29 aprelia–10 noiabria 1993 g.* (Moscow: iuridicheskaia literatura, 1995–6). For commentary on the constitutional drafts, see I. G. Shablinskii, *Predely vlasti: borba za Rossiiskuiu konstitutsionnuiu reformu: 1989–1995 gg.* (Moscow: tsentr konstitutsionnykh issledovanii Moskovskogo obshchestvennogo nauch. fonda, 1997); Suren A. Avakian, *Konstitutsiia Rossii: priroda, evoliustiia, sovremennost'* (Moscow: Rossiiskii iuridicheskii izdatel'skii dom, 1997), especially Chapter 3; and a series of articles from 1992 to 1994 in *East European Constitutional Review*.

6 krais. Within the first few months of 1992, 4 of the 5 autonomous oblasts became republics, and also in 1992 Chechnia and Ingushetia were officially separated, bringing the number of republics to 21 by the end of the year. A Federation Treaty was signed on 31 March 1992 by all territorial units of the Russian Federation except Chechnia and Tatarstan. The Treaty contained different types of powers for four different types of units: (1) the federal government; (2) the 21 republics; (3) the 10 autonomous okrugs and 1 autonomous oblast; and (4) the 49 oblasts, 6 krais, and 2 federal cities.

In the Treaty, the republics alone were given special rights. They had their own constitutions (which had to be consistent with the federal constitution), and they got control of territorial natural resources as well as the right to conduct their own foreign and trade policies. In the Soviet period, autonomous okrugs had been subordinated to a "host" krai or oblast. But the 1992 Federation Treaty gave them direct representation in federal institutions.[2] The specifics of the rights of republics and AOs were to be worked out with further joint federal-republic legislation, and the demands for secession were to be resolved by the federal government.[3] But many republican constitutions violated the federal one, and many republics simply asserted control over resources without joint federal legislation.[4] For oblasts and krais, according to the Treaty, the oblast or krai and the central government were supposed to develop budget and tax systems "on the basis of common principles."[5] In practice, this meant that each oblast or krai was supposed to draft a charter (a type of regional constitution) outlining a variety of regional laws and regulations. The charter would then be subject to approval by the Russian Supreme Soviet. From its inception, the Federation Treaty was riddled with ad hoc amendments and hidden informal agreements. Consequently, tensions and conflicting claims about

---

[2] On the Khanty Mansiisk case, see Gary Wilson, "'Matryoshka Federalism' and the Case of the Khanty Mansiysk Autonomous Okrug," *Post-Soviet Affairs* 17:2 (2001), pp. 167–94.

[3] The 1993 Constitution made AOs both equal-status subjects of the Federation and, at the same time, subjects under the jurisdiction of host regions. However, the laws regulating relations between AOs and host regions were, by 2001, still not worked out.

[4] This vagueness in rules governing center-regional relations was by no means new. Harris detailed how even during the 1930s there was a marked lack of specificity in central directives, and regions used this wiggle room to adapt central directives to their own interests. See James Harris, *The Great Urals: Regionalism and the Evolution of the Soviet System* (Ithaca, NY: Cornell Univ. Press, 1999), p. 122.

[5] R. G. Abdulatipov and L. F. Boltenkova, eds., *Federativnyi dogovor: dokumenty, kommentarii* (Moscow: respublika, 1992).

inter-regional and center-region responsibilities proliferated throughout 1992.

In April 1992 at the CPD's Sixth Congress, a third official constitutional draft, crafted by Rumiantsev's Working Group, which included the Federation Treaty (in section 3), was discussed. In that draft, the two main items of disagreement were sections 4 and 5, which dealt with the federative structure and executive-legislative relations, respectively.[6] Two additional alternative versions of the official draft were also submitted for discussion: one from St. Petersburg Mayor Anatolii Sobchak and the Movement for Democratic Reform, which gave more power to the legislature and a range of rights to ethnic groups; and a second, revised version from Yeltsin's former legal advisor, Sergei Shakhrai, which was balanced in favor of the executive. Both the alternative versions were rejected by the CPD.[7] Regions, and especially republics, made use of the lack of a federal constitution to formulate their own responses. For example, on 6 November 1992, the Supreme Soviet of the Republic of Tatarstan adopted a new Constitution declaring Tatarstan a sovereign state, a move that was rejected as unconstitutional by Rumianstev's Constitutional Commission.[8]

Institutional uncertainty was not restricted to the federal level. The same power struggles, including the shift from CPSU to state institutions and battles among state institutional actors (executive versus legislative), that resulted in multiple authorities at the union level was played out in the regions.[9] And, just as the demise of the CPSU and state institutional fluidity had made the paths to power uncertain at the union level, it was also unclear to regional elites in Russia where authority would finally be located. Initially, just as at the union level, there was a shift in the regions from party to state institutions. However, after the 1990 elections to local soviets, at Gorbachev's request, many important regional political positions were held

---

[6] "Constitution Watch," *East European Constitutional Review* 1:1 (Spring 1992), p. 6.

[7] "Constitution Watch," *East European Constitutional Review* 1:2 (Summer 1992), p. 6.

[8] "Constitution Watch," *East European Constitutional Review* 1:3 (Fall 1992), p. 9.

[9] Kimitaka Matsuzato, "Local Elites Under Transition: County and City Politics in Russia 1985–1996," *Europe-Asia Studies* 51:8 (1999), pp. 1367–1400. This article details changes in regional and sub-regional (county and city) political-administrative power, mainly in Samara and Tambov. On the redefinition of power relations in Russia from perestroika to 1993, see Adrian Campbell, "Local Government Policymaking and Management in Russia: The Case of St. Petersburg (Leningrad)," *Policy Studies Journal* 21:1 (Spring 1993), pp. 133–42. This article details the shift from party organizations to soviets and from soviets to regional executives, using St. Petersburg as a case.

concurrently: For example, the same person could be local first party secretary and local soviet chairman. And in 1991, the chairmanship of both the local soviet and the executive committee of the soviet (*ispolnitel'nyi komitet soveta* or ispolkom) could be held concurrently.

From the fall of 1991, Yeltsin worked to fortify federal executive authority by constructing an institutional framework in which positions of political and economic leadership would be based on the will of the executive as opposed to elections or the former system of CPSU appointments.[10] The organizational development that followed was basically an extension of the office of the presidency vertically down to the level of municipalities and across all regions of the Federation. In an open attempt to strengthen his position by weakening his opponents in regional soviets, Yeltsin created a system of regional executive institutions in which there was an initial one-year moratorium on elections, during which his administration appointed all heads of administration (who later would be named governors), mayors, and presidential representatives in the regions.

The significance of the creation of presidential representatives and heads of administration is that these posts were totally unaccountable to regional (elected) legislatures. Previously, the ispolkom (the executive committee of the regional soviet, which was elected from within the soviet) functioned as the nominal regional executive (since the party first secretary had functioned as the real executive). Yeltsin intended to replace the ispolkoms with these appointed heads of administration. Regional soviets could nominate candidates for the post of head of the administration, but for the first year Yeltsin would have the final say. The Russian Congress of People's Deputies initially agreed to only a one-year moratorium on elections to regional executive positions, but in 1992 the decision on when to hold elections was postponed for another year.[11] As it turned out, some regions held their first gubernatorial elections as late as 1996.

In addition to regional executives, Yeltsin also created a system of presidential representatives, who were to be the president's "eyes and ears" in the regions. These executive regional organizations contradicted the system of elections and exposed the inconsistency of regional representation in

---

[10] For more on the changing structure of regional administration after the 1991 coup, see Richard Sakwa, *Russian Politics and Society* (London: Routledge, 1993), pp. 197–200.

[11] Jeffrey W. Hahn, "Introduction: Analyzing Parliamentary Development in Russia," in J. Hahn, ed., *Democratization in Russia: The Development of Legislative Institutions* (Armonk, NY: M. E. Sharpe, 1996), pp. 18–19.

political institutions. However, the result was not a clear dominance of federal executive authority in the regions. Although the creation of centrally controlled regional executives (heads of administration and presidential representatives) was intended to strengthen central control, the regional soviets still had some ability to block executive initiatives, and many heads of administration turned out to be loyal to local networks of regional interests rather than to the federal government.[12]

In the fall of 1992, Yeltsin also created a Council of Heads of Republics, by presidential decree on October 16, which allowed the president to meet with republican leaders directly. In response, non-republican regional elites (oblasts and krais) demanded a Council of the Federation with full regional representation.[13] In 1992, it was still not obvious which of all these newly created regional political institutions would turn out to be most important, and it was also no longer the case that regional elites shared the same career patterns. Up until 1991, the position of local first secretary of the Party had been an important stepping stone for other regional executive positions (ispolkom chair or head of administration); this was similar to Gorbachev's or even Yeltsin's trajectory of moving from the Party into state legislative and then executive positions. An important post-1991 difference was that there were many opportunities for political career revival of regional elites after being removed from or quitting the CPSU. And in some regions, new local leaders without elite CPSU experience appeared after the democratic elections in the spring of 1990 and remained in power up to the appointment of heads of administration in 1991. Finally, some heads of administration were selected who had neither CPSU elite experience nor the experience of winning office in the spring 1990 elections. Moreover, not all regions of a similar institutional type (republic, oblast, krai, AO) had the same set of local political institutions.[14] In short, there was a great deal of political

---

[12] For more on this point, see Josephine Andrews and Kathryn Stoner-Weiss, "Regionalism and Reform in Provincial Russia," *Post-Soviet Affairs* 11:4 (October–December 1995), pp. 384–406.

[13] Edward Walker, "The Neglected Dimension: Russian Federalism and Its Implications for Constitution-making," *East European Constitutional Review* 2:2 (Spring 1993), pp. 26–7.

[14] On the fluidity of legal-territorial boundaries, the Republic of Sakha sought in the early 1990s to extend territorial rights to aboriginal groups by recreating *obshchinas*, a pre-twentieth-century socioeconomic unit of land ownership and government. They also considered creating "ethno-cultural" reserves or "national townships." G. Fondahl, O. Lazebnik, and G. Poelzer, "Aboriginal Territorial Rights and the Sovereignty of the Sakha Republic," *Post-Soviet Geography and Economics* 41:6 (2000), pp. 401–17.

institutional flexibility both in relations among regions, and in the constitution of political authority within the region.[15]

By 1993, each region had at least five authorities: the chairmen of the regional and municipal soviets, the heads of the regional and municipal administrations, and the presidential representative. But even individually, these institutions were not so clear. Some of the regional soviets were too large to actually govern effectively; the St. Petersburg soviet, for example, had four hundred deputies.[16] And given that elections had occurred at different times and with different outcomes in mind – consider that the 1990 elections that produced elected soviets were still operating within the CPSU and Soviet system – the appointed regional executives were often at odds with the communist-dominated soviets. In addition, in some cases the local executive committee (ispolkom), whose members were appointed by the local soviets, also competed either with the soviet chairmen or the heads of administration.[17] Rather than serving as checks and balances on each other, these overlapping regional authorities competed for authority in the same areas. And, just as the situation at the federal level was uncertain, in 1993 it was also still not clear which of these regional political institutions would ultimately win out.

Thus, the institutional framework, or rules, which would prescribe the type of organizational development and corresponding set of opportunities available for regions within the Federation, were not fixed. Throughout 1992–3, real possibilities for fundamentally reworking federal relations and regional institutions existed. The battle between the executive and legislative branches represented a struggle between competing understandings of the bases of political and economic power. Executive appointments and decrees and the resulting organizations contravened the principle introduced in the early years of perestroika that power was to be located in elected organizations. At the regional level, this institutional conflict left a slew of organizations in a condition of uncertainty about the sources of legitimate power and the possibilities for pursuing regional interests. This flexibility in

---

[15] For an analysis of heterogeneous reactions by regional elites in the early post-Soviet period, see Mary McAuley, *Russia's Politics of Uncertainty* (New York: Cambridge Univ. Press, 1997).

[16] This was a legacy from the Soviet past, when the party institutions were the primary governance bodies and the state institutions did not need to actually govern.

[17] For an extended discussion of regional political authority during this period, see Oleg Pchelintsev, "Regional Hierarchy Under Threat: A Spatial Dimension of the Socio-Economic Crisis in the Former Soviet Union and Russia," *International Regional Science Review* 15:3 (1993), pp. 267–79.

the institutional framework of the Federation provided space for imagining novel political and economic institutions and was essential for the creative development of regionally specific understandings of the political situation facing the region and the regional economy.

End of Soviet Redistributive Principles

As in the political sphere, the institutional framework for federal and regional economic relations in 1992 was unstable and did not demarcate the parameters of regional economic autonomy within the Federation. On top of this regional dimension was the simultaneous reworking of the entire economic institutional framework in general, from Soviet central planning to a market economy. With respect to understandings of the economy, there was a reworking of the *principles* of allocation as well as the *actual* allocation of federal and regional resources.[18]

The perestroika-era laws, as discussed previously, de facto had transferred a great deal of control over resources to enterprise directors and other nomenklatura economic elites. However, after the breakup of the USSR, this de facto control became increasingly legitimized and legal. In July 1991, the All-Union Law on Destatization and Privatization allowed for the conversion of state enterprises to different forms of property including leased, collective, cooperative, joint stock, and private.[19] Although enterprise directors continued to seek greater juridical rights of control over their enterprises, there were no laws on the implementation of the Law on Destatization and Privatization. Consequently, at the beginning of 1992, although there were over three thousand leased enterprises and almost one thousand non-state enterprises, state-owned enterprises still accounted for 96% of production.[20]

After much debate, in July 1992 a privatization program was offered whereby enterprises, through their labor collectives, were allowed to choose

---

[18] For an analysis of the lack of consistent understanding about the economy, see David M. Woodruff, *Money Unmade: Barter and the Fate of Russian Capitalism* (Ithaca, NY: Cornell Univ. Press, 1999). Woodruff analyzes the proliferation of uses and values of money in the post-Soviet period, as well as attempts by the federal government to impose meanings on money.

[19] Simon Clarke, "Privatisation: The Politics of Capital and Labour," in Stephen White, Alex Pravda, and Zvi Gitelman, eds., *Developments in Russian and Soviet Politics* (Durham, NC: Duke Univ. Press, 1994), p. 170. For a detailed discussion of privatization, see Hilary Appel, *A New Capitalist Order: Privatization and Ideology in Russia and Eastern Europe* (Pittsburgh, PA: Univ. of Pittsburgh Press, 2004).

[20] Ibid., p. 171.

one of three options of privatization. The consequence, if not intention, of this program was to give a legal basis to the regional elite appropriation of within-region resources. Of the three options, the most popular was the second, whereby the workers would receive 51% of the shares for almost nothing, and the remaining 49% would be sold at auction; these shares were usually bought up by management. Because privatization was mainly carried out by regional and municipal property committees, and because most, though not all, managers were regional actors, insider privatization had the effect of regionalizing economic resources.

In addition, regional governments were also scrambling to appropriate what resources they could. A survey of industrial enterprises by Irina Boeva et al. claimed that in the late summer of 1991, regional governments had appropriated between 10% and 15% of regional output.[21] These resources were then used by the regional governments in barter operations.[22] An additional sign of the chaos of the time was that there were a number of reports of regionally imposed trade barriers in 1991 and early 1992. Philip Hanson cited reports of such controls in Karelia, Stavropol', Vologda, Krasnoiarsk, Nizhnii Novgorod, and the city of Moscow, but many others were also reported in the press.[23] Similarly, in discussing conditions in 1992, Oleg Pchelintsev argued:

Republican and local level authorities have taken the place of enterprises as basic economic units. They appropriate a significant portion of key commodities (such as fuel, raw materials, foods, and consumer goods) under the pretext of needing to maintain regional commodity inventories. Local officials use these inventories in inter-governmental barter to provide the community with commodities not locally produced.[24]

In general, despite fears of appropriation by Moscow, there turned out to be very little territorial-based reshuffling of regional resources.[25] In most

---

[21] Irina Boeva, Tatiana Dolgopiatova, and Viacheslav Shironin, *Gosudarstvennye predpriiatiia v 1991–1992 gg.: ekonomicheskie problemy i povedenie* (Moscow: institut ekonomicheskoi politiki, 1992), cited in Philip Hanson, "Local Power and Market Reform in Russia," *Communist Economies & Economic Transformation* 5:1 (1993), p. 49.

[22] This type of appropriation of resources, i.e., in-kind taxation, largely declined after price liberalization in 1992. See Woodruff, 1999, p. 87.

[23] Hanson, 1993, p. 49.

[24] Pchelintsev, 1993, p. 276. Pchelintsev presents a prescient analysis of the problems with decentralization due to the lack of political and economic infrastructure in the regions.

[25] An example of this fear is that in Cheliabinsk, the regional soviet passed an ordinance banning voucher privatization on the grounds that it would lead to the sale of regional enterprises to Moscow-based actors.

cases – aside from a small number of the largest enterprises that the federal government retained control over in order to privatize later (through corrupt auctions) – resources were appropriated to private organizations of within-territorial affiliation; that is, regional nomenklatura acquired the resources located within the region. In the relatively few cases of territorial disputes over privatization, nearly all were disputes between regional actors and Moscow-based actors, rather than inter-regional disputes. Not insignificantly, this meant that there was no pattern of one region or group of regions systematically appropriating resources that had been previously used or managed by other regions. In addition, there was no ethnic or religious pattern in the appropriation of resources. Thus, broadly speaking, territorial units neither gained additional resources nor lost control of the resources located within their territorial space through the privatization process. Rather, they got what they happened to have. From this perspective, privatization heralded the future of heterogeneous regional economic conditions.[26]

In addition to privatization, fiscal responsibility was another area where regionalization of the economy prevailed over central Soviet understandings. In the Soviet model, central planning implied that the allocation of resources and direction of economic development were to be carried out by the CPSU-controlled government. The basic understanding that went along with central planning under the Soviet system was that regions were not at liberty to claim regional resources as their own, nor were they responsible for solving regional economic problems without the help of the central government. Rather, regions and municipalities were given a set of obligations and also a certain amount of resources to meet those obligations.

After the end of the USSR, regional governments became responsible for a range of new social services beyond their previous obligations, and there were new plans for tax collection and redistribution, but there was no new *principled* formula for regional redistribution. Instead, regions' revenues in 1992–3 were based on their inherited tax base and to a large degree on ad hoc negotiations with the center.[27] Regions did not set their own tax rates or

---

[26] This heterogeneity is consistent with the later observed regional differences in privatization. For data on rates of privatization in 1993 and 1994 for large and small enterprises, see Darrell Slider, "Privatization in Russia's Regions," *Post-Soviet Affairs* 10:4 (1994), pp. 367–96.

[27] For example, in November 1991, enterprise directors from Sverdlovsk sent a letter to Yeltsin complaining about the breakdown in inter-regional trade and claiming that other regions were taking advantage of Sverdlovsk's products while not sending supplies,

bases; instead, they were given some percentage of a value-added tax (VAT) collected in the region, with the rest going to Moscow. This redistributive scheme for taxes not only no longer matched local obligations but no longer even had that goal.[28] The lack of a central concept for redistribution was keenly appreciated in the regions. For example, experts from the History Institute of the Siberian branch of the Russian Academy of Sciences issued a report arguing that "the federal leadership does not have its own concept of regional socioeconomic development and national-state structure and this kind of position has no future and is historically doomed."[29]

The destruction of the doxa and the idea of central redistribution necessarily entailed the disordering of the background sense of regional hierarchy, that is, the status framework of regions vis-à-vis other regions as components of the state. During the Soviet period, distribution of resources to regions was based on the particular place that the region occupied in the Soviet economy; this applied to human capital as well as to goods and services.[30] For example, the northern territories were "overpopulated" in Soviet times because people were sent there to work on Soviet projects and paid several times the average wage. They would work for about ten years and return to the central or southern regions. But as perestroika progressed and the Soviet system was dismantled, major works projects declined and inflation lowered the values of what wages were paid, which led to massive out-migration.[31]

Ideally, Soviet central planning should have been replaced by market mechanisms. But while rasstroika was anti-Soviet, it was not necessarily pro-market. The result was the replacement of the Soviet regional and municipal administrative hierarchy by an ad hoc system of confused regional

---

especially food, to Sverdlovsk. "Sverdlovsk Appeals to Yeltsin for Economic Aid," *FBIS Daily Report – Soviet Union* 91:215, 6 November 1991, p. 59 [from Nadezhda Potapova, *TASS*, 2 November 1991, Moscow]; and *Ural'skii rabochii*, 5 November 1991, cited in Gerald M. Easter, "Redefining Centre-Regional Relations in the Russian Federation: Sverdlovsk Oblast'," *Europe-Asia Studies* 49:4 (1997), p. 621.

[28] Philip Hanson, *Regions, Local Power and Economic Change in Russia* (London: Royal Institute of International Affairs, 1994), p. 24.

[29] "Regional Negative Attitude to Center Cited," *FBIS Daily Report – Soviet Union* 92:59, 26 March 1992, p. 54 [from *Postfactum*, 25 March 1992, Moscow].

[30] Even within regions, the distribution of resources according to Soviet ideology affected more than just industrial production. Patterns of urbanization and migration were also ideological: suburbs, single-family homes, and cars were rejected as too individualistic. Instead, large urban centers with massive apartment buildings and public transportation were established. Pchelintsev, 1993, p. 278.

[31] Ibid., pp. 278–9.

authorities, half-hearted attempts at organization by the center, and the venality of short time horizons. The decline of the Soviet system, writes Oleg Pchelintsev,

destroyed the system of priorities, which for many decades determined the predominance of cities and regions with heavy industries (mining, metallurgy, engineering, chemistry) and defense industries. In the former Soviet Union, industrial location was determined by the decisions of central industrial ministries. Now there is chaos that is the result of bureaucratic decision-making by independent regional and local authorities and enterprises operating without a coordinating mechanism such as would be provided by a well developed market.[32]

The 1992 freeing of prices and soaring inflation only exacerbated regional difficulties. As help from the federal government appeared increasingly less likely, regions attempted to solve their own problems.[33] The basic characteristic of the institutional framework for the allocation of resources in the Russian Federation in 1992 was that regions had to literally and conceptually fend for themselves. There could be no reliance on promises of real material assistance from the federal government, and regions could hardly continue to conceive of the economy in terms of Soviet planning.

In October of 1992, Yeltsin attended a meeting of heads of regional administrations and acknowledged that economic reforms were largely being determined by the regions rather than the center. In this context, he agreed to a tax plan more advantageous to the regions.[34] However, by the end of 1992, it was apparent that economic agreements were increasingly easy to come by; the problem was that there were constantly new sets of agreements, which contradicted or negated the progress of earlier agreements. This happened even at the highest levels. For example, Egor Gaidar had been serving as prime minister informally and presiding over economic

---

[32] Ibid., p. 277.

[33] For example, in the context of rapid inflation which led to cash shortages, in Sverdlovsk Oblast from December 1991 to March 1992, the deficit increased by a factor of almost 3,000 (from 700,000 to 2 billion rubles). Sverdlovsk Oblast resolved this situation through "various barter operations," including a special agreement with the Goznak money-printing factory in Perm' Oblast. Nevertheless, even with such agreements, by June 1992 the cash deficit in Sverdlovsk Oblast was estimated at 5.5 billion rubles. "Regional Negative Attitude to Center Cited," *FBIS Daily Report – Soviet Union* 92:59, 26 March 1992, p. 54 [from *Postfactum*, 25 March 1992, Moscow]. For analysis of barter in Russia during this period, see Woodruff, 1999).

[34] Sergei Khrushchev, "The Political Economy of Russia's Regional Fragmentation," in Douglas W. Blum, ed., *Russia's Future: Consolidation or Disintegration* (Boulder, CO: Westview Press, 1994), p. 100.

reform since the fall of 1991. He was formally appointed by Yeltsin in June 1992 but was never confirmed by the Supreme Soviet. In December, in the face of parliamentary opposition to Gaidar's reforms, Yeltsin replaced Gaidar with Viktor Chernomyrdin. Similarly, the Federation Treaty, and the steady stream of paperwork, extraordinary meetings, special agreements, and the selective endorsement of articles that followed the signing of the Treaty, had done little to support clarity in the economic policies directed toward Russian regions. A January 1993 report by *Izvestiia* claimed that "governmental reform programs may appear acceptable on paper, but it is unclear who is prepared to carry them out. As a result, the crisis has become more severe and the regions are shedding their old assumptions of central responsibility."[35]

The inability to count on agreements with the center only increased throughout 1993. Despite the passage of the law "On the Principles of Budgetary Rights and Rights to Form and Use Non-Budget Funds by Representative and Executive Institutions of the State Power," intended to create a stable basis for the formation of regional budgets, the Ministry of Finance, in summarizing the results of 1993, reported that *every* subject of the Federation had made a special agreement for its budget which differed from the initial federal budget.[36] The way in which agreements were worked out, that is on an ad hoc basis, and the lack of clear institutional structure for implementing those agreements continued to obfuscate the meaning of particular agreements.[37] Thus, throughout 1992, contradictory understandings of inter-regional and center-region economic relations proliferated.

In early 1993, Vladimir Shumeiko, first vice-premier of the Russian Government, delivered the results of a report on the achievements and mistakes of the government's socioeconomic program for 1992.[38] He noted

---

[35] "O finansovo-ekonomicheskoi politike Rossii v 1993 godu," *Izvestiia*, no. 15, 26 January 1993, p. 5.

[36] Ministerstvo Finansov Rossiiskoi Federatsii, "Rossiiskie finansy v 1993 godu," *Voprosy ekonomiki*, no. 1 (1994), pp. 39–41. For further discussion of this point, see Hanson, 1994, p. 24.

[37] For example, throughout 1992, instead of supporting the consolidation of economic institutions, Yeltsin made a habit of personally promising to handle all sorts of economic problems in the regions. See, for example, "Meets with Sverdlovsk Officials," *FBIS Daily Report – Soviet Union* 92:110, 8 June 1992, p. 40 [from Mayak Radio Network, 7 June 1992, Moscow]; and "Conversion Issues Discussed," *FBIS Daily Report – Soviet Union* 92:111, 9 June 1992, p. 63 [from *Interfax*, 8 June 1992, Moscow].

[38] Vladimir Shumeiko, "Kak my zhili v 1992 godu, i kak budem zhit' v 1993 godu," *Rossiiskie vesti*, no. 31, 16 February 1993, pp. 2–3.

that, at the beginning of the implementation of the reform program, there were significant differences across regions in terms of social and economic development and potential. He listed statistics for output, income, and prices across regions. In addition, he noted that, beyond the terms of the Federation Treaty, there were forty separate agreements in 1992 between the central government and particular subjects of the Federation granting special additional economic and social benefits and rights. These special agreements amounted to over a trillion rubles. Yet, Shumeiko argued,

The government's greatest political and indeed economic mistake on this issue was the unsystematic distribution of subsidies, credits, and benefits, the lack of a full range of specific interconnected regional development programs elaborated jointly with the subjects of the Federation, and the lack of coordination on this question with the Supreme Soviet, which also allocated around 8 billion rubles to individual regions from its reserve fund.

As a result, he added, "by the end of 1992 the existing distortions in the socioeconomic development of individual regions had not only not been eliminated but in a number of cases had even intensified."[39]

The evidence of rising regional inequality during 1991–3 is irrefutable, and regional inequality was fundamental to the construction of the understandings of regional difference. Leonid Fedorov surveyed the literature on regional inequality and argued that, by any possible measure, regional inequality rose dramatically starting in 1991 (and leveled off only in 1996).[40] From 1990 to 1993, Gini coefficients for both regional incomes and expenditures radically increased as shown in Table 4.1.

Likewise, in Russia as a whole, a World Bank report on inequality showed a rise in the Gini coefficient from 0.26 in the period 1987–90 to 0.48 in the period of 1992–4.[41] This was higher than any Eastern European country and among the highest among former Soviet Union (FSU) states. Table 4.2 shows a rare estimate, for this period, of regional standards of living based on combining regional price differences and wages.

As the concept of real income suggests, inequality across regions was related to price differences. A survey by Vladimir Shprygin reported

---

[39] Ibid., p. 3.
[40] Leonid Fedorov, "Regional Inequality and Regional Polarization in Russia, 1990–1999," *World Development* 30:3 (2002), pp. 443–56.
[41] World Bank, *Making Transition Work for Everyone: Poverty and Inequality in Europe and Central Asia* (New York: World Bank, 2000), p. 140.

Table 4.1 *Russian Regional Gini Coefficients, 1990–1997[a]*

Year	Regional Income Gini Coefficients	Regional Expenditure Gini Coefficients
1990	0.11	0.13
1991	0.11	0.12
1992	0.19	0.17
1993	0.21	0.29
1997	0.29	0.37

[a] Derived from data from Leonid Fedorov, "Regional Inequality and Regional Polarization in Russia 1990–1999," *World Development* 30:3 (2002), p. 448. The Gini coefficient ranges from 0 to 1, where 0 represents perfect equality and 1 is total inequality. For comparison with coefficients for countries as a whole, most communist countries had been around 0.2, whereas European countries were around 0.3, and the United States was higher, around 0.4. Most Latin American countries were above 0.45, with some like Mexico, Guatemala, and Honduras around 0.6.

Table 4.2 *Standard of Living in Russian Regions' per capita, March 1993[a]*

Region	Standard of Living
Russian Federation Average	100.0
North	126.9
North-West	60.4
Central	74.0
Volga-Viatka	83.3
Central-Black Earth	100.4
Volga	126.4
North Caucasus	86.6
Urals	109.8
West Siberia	154.1
East Siberia	113.4
Far East	112.5

[a] L. Nemova, "Rynok truda," *EKO*, no. 10 (1993), p. 38.

differences in prices (in multiples) for a range of consumer goods across regions. For example, regional car prices varied by 1.5 times, TVs by 2.5 times, radios by 2.7 times, fruit and vegetables by 11 times, meat by 4 times, and bread by 5 times.[42] In addition, a Goskomstat survey of

[42] Vladimir Shprygin, "Regional'nyi oblik rynka," *Ekonomika i zhizn'*, no. 21, May 1992, p. 7.

Table 4.3 *Variance in Regional Food Consumption:*
Percent of Regions within 10% of Russian Average
Consumption Rate[a]

Food Products	1990	1993	% Change 1990–1993
Meat	56	52	−7%
Vegetables	43	35	−19%
Sugar	69	51	−26%
Milk	71	39	−45%

[a] Derived from Lavrovskii, 1999.

132 cities on 1 September 1993, claimed that bread prices were controlled in 40% of surveyed cities, sugar in 11%, and milk in 26%.[43]

Inflation and differences in prices across regions were so pronounced that it remains very difficult to understand values denominated in current rubles for the early 1990s. Moreover, this issue of price data itself produced imaginative space for alternative understandings of the economy because regional actors at the time had information about their own wages and prices but only minimal data about other regions (the systematic comparative data on local prices and real incomes is largely a post-1995 phenomenon). Thus it would have been very difficult at the time to evaluate objectively how one region compared with another.

Another indicator of post-1991 regional inequality is the *variance* among regions in the consumption of food products. Boris Lavrovskii considered how many regions were within 10% of the all-Russia average consumption for a range of food products during 1990 and 1993 (see Table 4.3).[44] Higher numbers in the 1990 and 1993 columns in Table 4.3 indicated less variance in consumption, and hence less inequality, because they suggest greater numbers of regions that are close to the Russian average. Similarly, lower numbers indicate greater inequality. For some products such as milk, the regional variance in consumption from 1990 to 1993 increased substantially. Whereas 71% of regions were within 10% of the average consumption of milk in 1990, only 39% were within 10% of the average by 1993, suggesting that the number of regions in the extremes (either very high or very low consumption) had gone up by 45%.

[43] Goskomstat Rossii, "Rekordnye tempy," *Delovoi mir*, no. 179, 18 September 1993, p. 5.
[44] Boris L. Lavrovskii, "Izmerenie regional'noi asimmetrii na primere Rossii," *Voprosy ekonomiki*, no. 3 (1999), pp. 42–52.

Understandings of regional economies and their place in the Federation were upset by this raft of new economic and political relations between regions: increasing regional inequality; the privatization process, which legally validated the control of territorially located resources by regional actors; the lack of a coherent proposal for central redistribution of resources on the basis of economic need or territorial or other cultural (ethnic, religious, or historical) considerations; and the serious economic crisis that generally decreased the ability of the Russian federal government to meet the needs of regions and the society as a whole.

This combination of factors allowed the concept of current "endowment" to replace the previous conception of a centrally determined policy of regional redistribution according to "need" (albeit "need" defined in terms of the objectives of the central planners of the Soviet state). Current endowment meant that rich regions were going to have lots of resources to control, while poor regions would be left poor – in other words, regions would be increasingly different, and they would be on their own. This appreciation of difference and the need for each region to find its own solution constituted a major step toward the development of differential regional conceptualizations of the sources of economic and political responsibility.

Constitutional Debate and Uncertain Federal Authority

As 1992 wore on, the power struggle between Boris Yeltsin and the parliament, which had held political and economic reform in a chaotic stalemate, continued to worsen. Each side attempted to take decisive action. The seventh Congress of People's Deputies was held in December 1992, and in early 1993 Yeltsin created a Constituent Assembly outside of the CPD to draft the constitution. At that time, Yeltsin was considering the creation of a Federation Council (*Sovet Federatsii*) with all subjects of the Federation represented, and in his April 1993 draft constitution the Federation Council, rather than the CDP, was to control all ministerial appointments.[45] This point is indicative of the relevance of the federal executive-legislative power struggle on region-center relations. The Federation Council was suggested by the president as an alternative to the Parliament, but the consequence of that move would have been greater rights for the regions.

[45] For analysis of the creation of the presidency, the duma electoral law, and the Federation Council, see Michael McFaul, "Institutional Design, Uncertainty, and Path Dependency during Transitions: Cases from Russia," *Constitutional Political Economy* 10:1 (March 1999), pp. 27–52.

159

As had become clear from the constitutional debates, the status of different types of subjects of the Russian Federation (republics, oblasts, krais, and AOs) was not equal. Throughout 1993, regional relations in Russia reflected not only differences between federal and regional-level organizations, but regional interests were increasingly expressed in terms of oblasts and krais on the one hand, and republics on the other.[46] In early 1993 the two groups of regional leaders met separately on a number of occasions with both Yeltsin and his government as well as with Ruslan Khasbulatov, chairman of the Supreme Soviet.[47] The leaders of the oblasts and krais wanted greater political and economic rights in the new constitution, while republican leaders wanted to preserve the special status of republics within the Federation.

President Yeltsin and the Russian Supreme Soviet continued their struggle over the economic and political direction of the country in early 1993 by challenging each other to referendums in order to use the popular mandate as a means of shoring up institutional legitimacy. An eighth CPD was held on 10 March 1993, and a ninth one took place on 26 March 1993.[48] After a great deal of maneuvering reminiscent of the spring 1991 referendum and showdown between Gorbachev and Yeltsin, a referendum was hastily called for 25 April 1993, which asked Russian citizens to vote on four questions related to support for Yeltsin versus the Congress. The first two concerned confidence in the president and his economic policy, and the second two asked for approval for early elections of the president and the parliament.[49]

---

[46] Interestingly, AOs (the autonomous okrugs and the one autonomous oblast) do not seem to have been solidly placed on either side of this debate. For a demand by oblast Soviet chairmen for federal budget amendments, see "Biudzhet-93: Regiony ugrozhaint nepouinoveniem," *Rossiiskaia gazeta*, no. 21, 2 February 1993, p. 3.

[47] For example: On a prominent meeting between republican leaders and Yeltsin, see Radik Batyrshin, "Glavy eks-avtonomii snova vstrechaiutsia s El'tsinym," *Nezavisimaia gazeta*, no. 24, 9 February 1993, p. 1; on a meeting between Prime Minister Victor Chernomyrdin and heads of oblasts and krais, see Vol'demar Koreshkov, "Glava pravitel'stva–za sil'nuiu regional'nuiu politiku," *Rossiiskaia gazeta*, no. 31, 16 February 1993, pp. 1–2; on a speech by Khasbulatov to regional leaders in Novosibirsk, see "Vystuplenie Ruslana Khasbulatova v Novosibirske," *Rossiiskaia gazeta*, no. 35, 20 February 1993, p. 1, 4; and on a meeting between oblast and krai leaders and Deputy Prime Minister Sergei Shakhrai, see Aleksandr Koretskii, "Kraia i oblasti poluchat pravo na sobstvennye zakony," *Kommersant'-Daily*, no. 32, 23 February 1993, p. 1.

[48] For a detailed report of the events of February–March 1993 leading up to the April referendum, see "Special Reports: Crisis in Russia," *East European Constitutional Review* 2:2 (Spring 1993), pp. 15–23.

[49] The questions were: (1) Do you trust Russian President Yeltsin? (2) Do you approve of the socioeconomic policy conducted by the Russian president and by the Russian government

This opportunity was not missed by regional leaders who recalled how union republics had used the 1991 referendum to push their own sovereignty claims by not participating, by not cooperating in organizing the vote, or by adding their own questions and making political or economic demands. Initially several republics were against participating in the referendum, but after Yeltsin presented his draft constitution to the Council of Heads of Republics, most republics agreed to participate in the referendum. But the republics were not the only regions making demands. On March 27–28 in Khabarovsk, a Siberian Congress of People's Deputies met and called for "decolonization" of Siberia.[50] In the end, three oblasts and two republics added supplementary questions to the referendum ballot, and in one republic, Tatarstan, the vote was invalidated by low turnout.[51] Yet overall, the referendum turned out to be a major success for Yeltsin.[52]

Following his victory in the April referendum, Yeltsin convened an ad hoc Constitutional Conference to be held in the Kremlin beginning on June 5. Yeltsin asked that the Council of Heads of Republics comment on the constitution and that each republic send two delegates to the Constitutional Conference.[53] Later, Yeltsin expanded the constitutional debate to other regions; in the end, he invited seven hundred regional and republican officials as well as other politicians (although ignoring the Supreme Soviet) to the Constitutional Conference.[54] All 88 regions (except Chechnia) participated. Ten days were allotted to the delegates to make changes and come up with a final draft constitution.

Various parties supposed that the numerous governance disputes – between different branches of government, as well as between different levels of government, which had plagued Russia since its foundation following

since 1992? (3) Should the new presidential election be conducted earlier than scheduled? (4) Should the new parliamentary election be conducted earlier than scheduled?

[50] Walker, 1993, p. 26.

[51] "Special Reports: Crisis in Russia," *East European Constitutional Review* 2:2 (Spring 1993), p. 21.

[52] On the first two questions of trust in Yeltsin and support for economic reform, the results were 58.7% and 53.0% in favor, respectively. On the last two questions regarding early elections, 49.5% wanted early presidential elections, whereas 67.2% wanted early parliamentary elections. Neither of the last two questions received the necessary 50% of voter participation to make them binding. See Michael McFaul, *Russia's Unfinished Revolution: Political Change from Gorbachev to Putin* (Ithaca, NY: Cornell Univ. Press, 2001) for more discussion of this referendum.

[53] Walker, 1993, p. 27

[54] Dwight Semler, "Special Reports," *East European Constitutional Review* 2:3 (Summer 1993), pp. 20–1.

the breakup of the USSR – would be addressed and to some degree resolved by a new Russian constitution. All sides considered the possibility that they might win some concessions in the form of constitutionally specified rights and responsibilities. Both the stakes and expectations were high, and for this reason the Constitutional Conference was an important event for the development of sovereignty movements.[55]

However, the federal question was not resolved at the conference. The Russian regions (oblasts and krais) disagreed with the republics, and Yeltsin's attempts to win republican support only exacerbated the dissatisfaction of the Russian regions. For example, before the convention, several regions such as Sverdlovsk Oblast, Vologda Oblast, Primorski Krai, and Chita Oblast were considering changing their status to *republic* in order to get the political and economic rights promised to republics. Moreover, oblast and krai officials were meeting separately to discuss the draft constitution. On June 16, there was still no agreement, and a ten-day recess was called. Meanwhile, a sixty-member Conciliatory Commission was established by Yeltsin to work out the differences, but after ten days, there was still no agreement. In the draft constitution, only republics were called "sovereign," and it stipulated that half of the seats in the Federation Council would be held by republican representatives, even though republics represented only 18.5% of the population of the country.[56] It was no surprise then that on June 26, when the full seven hundred-member body reconvened, there was still no agreement on the draft constitution, though they did agree to hold another meeting in July.

The Constitutional Conference reconvened on July 12 to consider the Conciliatory Commission's draft. The draft was very different from the initial June version; it combined some of the CPD's drafts as well as the president's and added five hundred amendments. The regional issue remained unresolved, but Russian regions were given the right to have *charters* (as opposed to republican *constitutions*) and to pass some laws (but not on taxes), and all regions were given the right to negotiate bilateral treaties

---

[55] I discuss the role of the conference in sovereignty movements in greater detail, specifically in reference to the Sverdlovsk case, in Chapter 7. For additional analysis of this point, see Lilia Shevtsova, *Yeltsin's Russia: Myths and Reality* (Washington, DC: Carnegie Endowment for International Peace, 1999), pp. 126–7. Shevtsova argues that the Constitutional Conference was a key event for the formulation of later sovereignty claims. She notes, for example, that at this event leaders of Irkutsk Oblast suggested merging with Krasnoiarsk Krai to create a republic in Eastern Siberia.

[56] Semler, Summer 1993, p. 20.

with the center, a right that was initially reserved for Tatarstan. But this was not enough for some regions.

As I discuss in Chapter 7, Sverdlovsk voted to change its status to *republic* right after the Constitutional Conference, and on July 15 several Siberian regions also called for full economic sovereignty. Nevertheless, the draft was approved by 433 out of 585 voting participants, but only 5 republics supported it. It was then sent to all regions for review. Even though the July 12 draft had combined the president's and CPD's drafts, it still favored the president and therefore had almost no chance of being approved by the Supreme Soviet. The Supreme Soviet moved quickly (on July 16) to pass a law that ensured (by making the requirements of a referendum so difficult to meet) that only the Supreme Soviet would be able to adopt a new constitution.[57]

As these constitutional debates make clear, in 1993 the perceived division between the republics and other subjects (oblasts and krais) of the Russian Federation intensified. Throughout the year, republics and oblasts traded accusations of who was paying more or less to the federal budget, while the federal government claimed that no one was paying.[58] For example, *Nezavisimaia gazeta* reported on 1 September 1993 that "according to experts' calculations, more than 30 of the 88 federation subjects have unilaterally reduced their tribute to the Kremlin."[59] *Nezavisimaia gazeta* also reported that even the "primordial Russian lands," which had earlier supported the central government, in contrast to the national republics, had made claims that "the Russian Finance Ministry is not returning the agreed upon part of their tribute." Therefore, the newspaper claimed, certain regions had themselves calculated how much should be paid to the federal government by subtracting the amount that should be returned in subsidies from the amount they were to pay. In this way, regions hoped to avoid having to haggle or beg for their own money back. Similarly, *Rossiiskie vesti* reported that increasing numbers of oblasts, krais, and republics had unilaterally reduced or halted payments to the federal budget, citing local budget needs and a lack of federal funding. In addition, the state tax service reported that

---

[57] Ibid., p. 21.
[58] See, for example, V. Petrovskii, "My poidem drugim putem," *Rossiiskaia gazeta*, no. 127, 6 July 1993, p. 2; V. Petrovskii, "Respubliki suvernny, no tak zhe bespravny," *Rossiiskaia gazeta*, no. 129, 8 July 1993, p. 2
[59] P. Batyrshin, "Nalogovaia voina tsentra i regionov," *Nezavisimaia gazeta*, no. 165, 1 September 1993, p. 3.

for the first half of 1993, at least one trillion rubles was not sent to the federal budget.[60] Current analysis suggests that despite regional claims and numerous Russian newspaper articles (as well as assertions by several scholars of post-Soviet politics), Moscow's assertion that regions actually withheld taxes from the center is questionable.[61] Similarly, the reports of regional trade barriers may or may not have been true. Sometimes measures that were announced never materialized, or sometimes the measures were very short-lived. Nevertheless, the fact that claims of tax-withholding and regional trade barriers received so much attention and were believed to be true, whether or not they actually occurred, had an impact on the way citizens across the Federation understood the regionalization of the Russian economy.

As the summer progressed, the dual political stalemates between the federal executive and legislature, and between the regions and the center, came to a boiling point. Yeltsin and his government, despite the earlier referendum success, met with increasing resistance from the Supreme Soviet. Yeltsin attempted to convene the Federation Council at various points late in the summer, but there was too much opposition from regional and republican elites, which postponed the meeting several times. The Federation Council finally met on 18–19 September 1993, but it refused to approve Yeltsin's constitution or to replace the Supreme Soviet as the upper parliamentary body, as Yeltsin had wanted. At the time, it was not clear whether the executive or the legislature was going to win out, and regions were apparently not ready to choose Yeltsin at that moment.[62]

In the midst of regional machinations, the tension in Moscow between Yeltsin and the Parliament finally erupted into an all-out power struggle in late September. After the Supreme Soviet's attempts to remove Yeltsin from office in the spring and summer had failed, and after months of

---

[60] *FBIS Daily Report – Soviet Union* 93:187, 29 September 1993, p. 20 [from A. Diordiyenko, "Tax Arrears Total 1 Trillion Rubles," *Rossiiskie vesti*, 22 September 1993, p. 1].

[61] Aleksei Lavrov, regional specialist in the Presidential Administration, argued that during 1991–3 only four regions – Chechnia, Tatarstan, Bashkortostan, and Sakha – actually withheld taxes. The debate centers on the technical ability, as opposed to intention, of regions to keep taxes from going to the center. Aleksei M. Lavrov, "Pochemu dotatsionnye regiony golosuiut za kommunistov, ili mify Rossiskogo federalizma," *Politicheskaia sreda*, 10 April 1996, p. 3.

[62] Dwight Semler, "Focus: Crisis in Russia," *East European Constitutional Review* 2:4 (Fall 1993), pp. 108–9.

government deadlock, Yeltsin reacted decisively on 21 September 1993 by dissolving the Russian Supreme Soviet and Congress of People's Deputies with Decree 1400, and by calling for new parliamentary elections to be held on December 11 and 12.[63] Some Supreme Soviet deputies followed the decree and left the "White House," the building that housed the parliament, but others stayed in the building in defiance of Yeltsin's decree. Those deputies who stayed, barricaded themselves in the White House and responded to Yeltsin's decree by impeaching Yelstin, electing Alexander Rutskoi president, and forming a new government.

During this time, small crowds of protesters supporting the parliamentarians lined the perimeter of the White House.[64] Also, in order to protest Yeltsin's decree, representatives from 62 regions and republics, including 14 regional administrators who had been appointed by Yeltsin, met in Moscow.[65] And the Novosibirsk legislature offered to host the CPD after Yeltsin's decree.[66] Nevertheless, tanks surrounded the parliament building, and the deputies were ordered to leave.

The standoff in Moscow turned violent on the weekend of October 3 and 4 when Khasbulatov and Rutskoi encouraged paramilitary forces to take over the Moscow mayor's offices and the Ostankino television tower in an attempt to spur a popular rebellion in favor of the Supreme Soviet. This was a terrible miscalculation on the part of the deputies, and Yeltsin used their attempt to incite the population to violence as the basis for giving the order to bomb the parliament building. With the recalcitrant deputies still inside, the White House was heavily shelled and nearly destroyed. Eventually Khasbulatov, Rutskoi, and other deputies were arrested.

Shortly afterward, a smaller-scale but nonviolent version of this executive-legislative battle was played out at the regional level. On October 6, Yeltsin made a televised appeal for regional and local soviets to voluntarily close. Few accepted this request, and so on October 9 and 26 he issued additional decrees dissolving *all* elected soviets, and the powers of regional soviets were transferred to the regional heads of administration until new elections for regional legislatures could be held in December 1993.

---

[63] For extended discussion of this process, see McFaul, 2001.
[64] Ironically, during the attempted coup in 1991, the White House had been the site of courageous demonstrations by both Yeltsin and Khasbulatov, among other Moscovites, against the coup plotters.
[65] Semler, Fall 1993, p. 111.
[66] "Constitution Watch," *East European Constitutional Review* 2:4 (Fall 1993), p. 17.

The dissolution of the soviets and the promulgation of Decree 1400 were extremely consequential for Russian political institutional development. At the federal level, the Federation Council was to be the upper house of the new bicameral Russian legislature; the lower house was to be called the *Duma*, which replaced the Supreme Soviet and Congress of People's Deputies. Duma elections were slated for December 12. The Federation Council was to be composed of two members from each of the 89 subjects of the Federation and was designed to provide greater regional representation in central government institutions. Earlier, the Federation Council was supposed to be composed of the heads of administration as well as the leaders of the soviets. But, with the soviets gone, half the seats were open, and elections to fill the Federation Council were also called for December.[67]

Finally, there was also a national referendum to approve a new constitution. The new Russian Constitution put to a vote in the December 12 referendum turned out to be substantially different from the draft constitution distributed to regional leaders in June. It still substantially increased the power of the president, but whereas the June draft preserved significant political and economic distinctions according to named regional statuses (i.e., republics, oblasts, krais, autonomous okrugs, and autonomous oblasts), the new Constitution contained a crucial legal provision that stated that at least de jure, all 89 subjects of the Federation were equal.[68] Although the implementation of the Constitution remains a serious issue, the changes to the Constitution effectively took the wind out of the sails of any movement aiming to achieve *constitutional* equality.

Conclusion

The first Russian Republic was a period of heterogeneous regional understandings. Keen uncertainties proliferated as a result of the constant flux in the rules setting the place of regions within the Federation. The absence of any allocation scheme for federal and regional resources was another

---

[67] Semler, Fall 1993, p. 113.

[68] Equality of all subjects of the Russian Federation is guaranteed in Article 5 of the Constitution. The exact wording is: "in interrelationships with federal institutions [organs] of state power all subjects of the Russian Federation possess equal rights." Article 5, *Konstitutsiia Rossiiskoi Federatsii*, 1993. For additional discussion of the powers accorded to regions in the December 1993 Russian Constitution, see Edward W. Walker, "Special Reports: Designing Center-Region Relations in the New Russia," *East European Constitutional Review* 4:1 (Winter 1995), pp. 54–60.

aggravating factor. The year 1993 represented a crescendo in the lack of specification of the economic rights and responsibilities of federal and regional authorities, and this fluidity in political and economic categories was an essential context for the development of specific regional understandings of the economy, which precipitated the construction of particular political and economic interests in greater sovereignty.

5

Imagined Economies in Samara and Sverdlovsk

DIFFERENCES IN REGIONAL UNDERSTANDINGS OF THE ECONOMY

Now let us turn our attention directly to the two regions that are the specific focus of this study, Samara and Sverdlovsk Oblasts, in order to investigate the relationship between "objective" economic conditions and regional understandings of the economy.[1] Local economic discourse is one way of accessing regional understandings of the economy during the 1990–3 period, and regionally produced newspapers and publications offer an invaluable trove of local discourse. Using quantitative and qualitative content analysis of 579 regional articles, I document interpretations in Samara and Sverdlovsk in four economic issues areas: fiscal policy, production, prices, and trade; and I compare those understandings with objective accounts. This systematic analysis demonstrates that differences in regional understandings of the economy are not predicted well by objective accounts of economic conditions. In particular, differences between Samara and Sverdlovsk in regional assessments of the benefits of particular economic events in the region are far greater than would be expected given the objective economic similarity of the two regions. Moreover, as I will discuss later in greater detail, while Samara and Sverdlovsk are quite similar in terms of economic conditions, there was little regional activism in Samara (activism score of 0 out of 9, see Chapter 1), while there was a great deal of activism in Sverdlovsk (activism score of 8).

In order to situate the comparison of economic understandings in the two regions, I first briefly outline historical, geographic, and political conditions in the regions to demonstrate that there are no overarching, non-economic

[1] Throughout this chapter, by "objective" I am referring to the type of economic information that is agreed upon by outside analysts and that is generally available in traditional quantitative data sets.

168

differences that might compromise the suitability of the economic comparison. Next, I discuss the objective economic conditions of the regions, and I outline what one would expect in terms of economic understandings based on those differences. I begin the content analysis section with a brief explanation of the procedures for coding regional understandings of the economy, and finally I present the results of the content analysis.

Samara and Sverdlovsk

My choice of Samara and Sverdlovsk Oblasts was based on an analysis of a number of factors. Above all, I looked for regions that were economically similar. However, to make the economic comparison, I also had to consider other non-economic factors including historical relations, physical geographic characteristics, and political conditions. Both Samara and Sverdlovsk share a history of peaceful relations with the Russian state and have no experience of independent statehood. The ethnic composition of both regions is strongly Russian, 83% in Samara and 89% in Sverdlovsk.[2] Because of the potential relationship between population size and regional activism (as evident from the analysis in Chapter 1), it was necessary to choose regions with relatively large populations. Samara and Sverdlovsk have populations of 3.3 million and 4.7 million, respectively, both far above the Russian regional average (oblasts and krais) of 1.9 million and among the most populous regions in the Russian Federation.[3]

The capital city of Sverdlovsk is Ekaterinburg (see Map 2). With a population of 1.6 million, it is the fourth largest city in Russia. Samara is distinguished from other regions of Russia in that it has two major cities, Samara and Tol'iatti, which are only seventy kilometers apart (see Map 3). Their populations are 1.3 million and 700,000, respectively.

Samara and Sverdlovsk are also similar in terms of their relative distance from Moscow and territorial size.[4] Samara is located on the Volga River and is part of the Volga macro-region. The Volga region borders, but is distinct from, the Urals. Sverdlovsk is located in the center of the Ural

[2] Valerii A. Tishkov, ed., *Narody Rossii entsiklopedia* (Moscow: nauchnoe izdatel'stvo, Bol'shaia Rossiiskaia entsiklopedia, 1994), pp. 439–40.

[3] Among all 89 subjects, Sverdlovsk was the fifth most populous (as of 1993), and Samara was ranked eleventh. Among the oblasts and krais, Sverdlovsk is third, and Samara is seventh.

[4] Sverdlovsk is 1,667 kilometers from Moscow and 194,800 square kilometers in size. Samara is 1,098 kilometers from Moscow and 53,600 square kilometers in size. While Sverdlovsk might seem much larger in territorial size than Samara, given the variance in size of all regions of the federation, they are relatively similar.

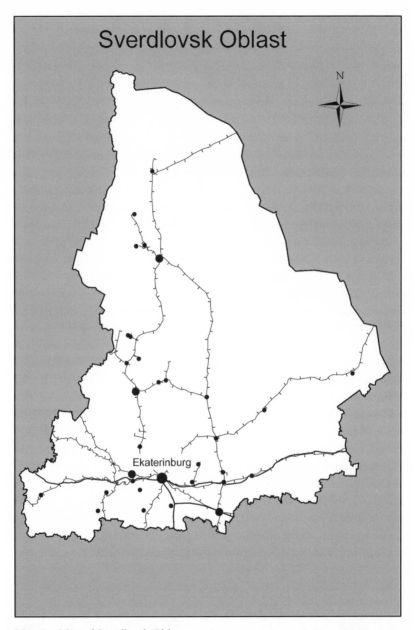

Map 2 Map of Sverdlovsk Oblast
Map created by Y. M. Herrera using *ESRI Data & Maps*, 2000, and *World Complete GfK Macon*, 2003.

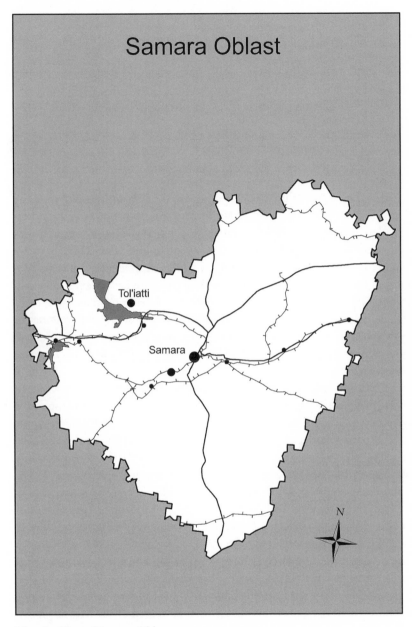

Map 3 Map of Samara Oblast
Map created by Y. M. Herrera using *ESRI Data & Maps*, 2000, and *World Complete GfK Macon*, 2003.

mountains, which is of course the historic (imagined) border between Europe and Asia. It is important that Samara and Sverdlovsk are not part of the same macro-region because some regional movements for greater sovereignty were expressed in terms of the macro-regions. For example, the movement for greater sovereignty in Sverdlovsk Oblast was expressed as a movement for the creation of a Urals Republic, which included other oblasts in the Urals.

History and Political Climate in Samara

Samara became part of the Russian empire in the sixteenth century, and the city of Samara was founded in 1586. Samara was known during the Soviet period as Kuibyshev (1935–91). During World War II, the central Soviet administrative and diplomatic institutions (including Stalin's bunker) were relocated from Moscow to Samara. In addition, evacuated military production was relocated to Samara, forming the core of Samara's industrial development. Samara thus became a center of defense production, specifically Soviet aircraft and rocket production, and was also a training center for cosmonauts. Because of military research and defense production, Samara was a high-prestige region of the USSR, and the city of Samara was a "closed city" until 1991.

The regional executive in Samara during the 1990s was Konstantin Titov. Before being elected governor in 1996 (and again in 2000), he was appointed by Yeltsin as head of the Samara Administration in 1991 (*Glav Administratsii*). Titov is regarded as a centrist, pragmatic "manager" and has played an active role in national politics. Titov was born in 1944 in Moscow and graduated from the Kuibyshev Aviation Institute in Samara.[5] He worked at the Kuibyshev aerospace plant and was a member of the Komsomol in the late 1960s, but from 1970–3 served in the Komsomol City Committee. He then went on to the Kuibyshev Institute of Planning and then to the Informatika research center. In 1990, Titov was elected to the Samara City Soviet, which he chaired from 1990 to 1991. As such, he was also a bureau member of the Samara City Committee of the CPSU. Titov quit the Party and resigned from the Samara City Committee in August 1991, and he became one of the founders of a local branch of the Movement for

---

[5] For more detail on Titov's career, see Pavel Romanov and Irina Tartakovskaya, "Samara *Oblast*': A Governor and His Guberniya," *Communist Economies & Economic Transformation* 10:3 (1998), pp. 351–2.

Democratic Reforms. On 21 August 1991, the acting chairman of the oblast soviet Viktor A. Tarkhov was removed by Yeltsin, and Titov was appointed Head of Administration on August 31. Titov did not initially have the support of the oblast soviet, but he brought with him to the oblast level many of his colleagues from the city soviet. There was some tension between Titov and the mayor of the city of Samara, Oleg Sysuev, but it was not particularly serious. Sysuev had been a party member and was also appointed by Yeltsin in December 1991.

In a study of sub-regional city politics from 1985 to 1996, Kimitaka Matsuzato concluded that Samara represents a case of "*caciquismo*," or rural boss-type one-party dominance.[6] This institutional structure, according to Matsuzato, is the result of a number of factors: the persistence of old nomenklatura elites such as Communist Party first secretaries and chairmen of the executive committees of the Soviets (*ispolnitel'nyi komitet soveta* or ispolkom), a "pragmatic" political culture, and the assistance of central regional administration in the consolidation of local elite executive power. Although Titov personally does not fit this pattern, Matsuzato argued that the pattern of elite transition in Samara was characterized by the movement of CPSU first secretaries and ispolkom chairmen into the soviets and then into appointed executive positions (mayors or heads of administration). Matsuzato claimed that, of the appointed sub-regional executives in Samara, 34% were former first secretaries and 40% were former ispolkom chairmen. However, Matsuzato found a different pattern in Sverdlovsk where a significant number of appointed executives had not been party first secretaries or ispolkom chairs, but instead entered politics through the 1990 local soviet elections. In Samara, only 6% of appointed executives followed this pattern. The remaining 20% of appointed executives in Samara were neither party first secretaries, ispolkom chairmen, nor elected deputies from the 1990 elections.[7]

Samara was a fairly strong supporter of Boris Yeltsin in 1991 and 1993.[8] However, support for Yeltsin does not necessarily correspond to support for or against movements for greater sovereignty because a lack of support for Yeltsin might have signaled strong support for communists or the legislature (Supreme Soviet) rather than support for greater sovereignty.

---

[6] Kimitaka Matsuzato, "Local Elites Under Transition: County and City Politics in Russia 1985–1996," *Europe-Asia Studies* 51:8 (1999), pp. 1367–1400.
[7] Ibid., p. 1369.
[8] The regional vote for Yeltsin in June 1991 was 68%, and in 1993 it was 60.9%.

In explaining Samara's political disposition, Matsuzato argued that Samara has a "pragmatic" political culture. He wrote: "The Samara electorate does not pay attention to the political or moral consistency of the leaders, as long as they are good managers." Moreover, in describing Samara he wrote that "votes are cast not for programs or ideas but for concrete interests or personal confidence in leaders."[9]

History and Political Climate in Sverdlovsk

Ekaterinburg, the capital of Sverdlovsk Oblast, was founded in 1723 and was named after Peter the Great's wife Ekaterina I. In the Soviet period, the city of Ekaterinburg and the oblast were renamed Sverdlovsk. The Urals area in the eighteenth century was found to have a wealth of coal, iron, gemstones, and other minerals, but metallurgy quickly became the most important industry in the region. By the end of the eighteenth century, there were 176 metallurgical plants in the Urals, and at the beginning of the nineteenth century, the Urals produced 75% of Russia's iron.[10] However, after technical advances led to the use of coal rather than wood fuel for blast furnaces, the Urals fell behind technologically by the 1860s. At the end of the nineteenth century, when Russia began a massive railway construction program under Sergei Witte, southern Ukraine, abundant in coal, was chosen over the Urals for state metallurgical investment. In the 1920s, southern Ukrainian production of iron rose steeply compared to the Urals, and the coal-based process was increasingly more efficient. As technology advanced, it became clear that only with massive central state investment could the Urals transform its metallurgical industry from wood to coal-based processing.

In the late 1920s, Urals political and economic elites lobbied the center for more investment and massive projects such as the Uralmash and Magnitnogorsk giganto-factories. These investment plans culminated with the Great Urals Plan of 1930. The plan envisioned the Urals as the USSR's main site of heavy industry. It was monumental in scope and entailed the doubling of capital investment as well as increases in production by several times. However, although it was the basis for massive investment, the

[9] Matsuzato, 1999, pp. 1395, 1396.

[10] S. G. Strumilin, *Ocherki ekonomicheskoi istorii Rossii i SSSR* (Moscow: nauka, 1966), p. 321. For more on Urals history, see James R. Harris, *The Great Urals: Regionalism and the Evolution of the Soviet System* (Ithaca, NY: Cornell Univ. Press, 1999), especially Chapter 1.

Great Urals Plan never delivered on its productive promise. This failure can be attributed to a number of reasons, including lack of skilled labor, lack of cokeable coal, general incompetence, disorganization, and mismanagement, as well as the purges of political and economic elites during the Terror of the 1930s.[11] Sverdlovsk industry recovered, however, with World War II. Like Samara, Sverdlovsk was a major site of relocation for defense industries during World War II, when over one thousand factories were moved to the region. And because of the military orientation of its industry, Sverdlovsk, like Samara, was a closed city during the Soviet period. After the 1991 coup attempt, the city was "opened," and the historical name of the city of Ekaterinburg was restored; the oblast, however, retains the Soviet name.

The regional executive in Sverdlovsk, Eduard Rossel, was elected in 1995 (and again in 1999) but has led the region since 1990.[12] Rossel, the son of German peasants, was born near Kirov in 1937. His father and grandfather were killed in 1937 in Stalin's purges, and his mother was sent to a labor camp in 1941, forcing Rossel to live in an orphanage for six years.[13] Rossel holds a degree from the State Mining Institute in Sverdlovsk and was head of the Main Directorate of Construction for the Central Urals (*Sreduralstroi*), which was the largest construction company in the USSR.[14] He was elected chairman of the oblast soviet and the ispolkom (executive committee of the Soviet) in 1990. After the 1991 coup attempt, Rossel, as well as Sverdlovsk citizens generally, supported Yeltsin strongly and publicly against the coup plotters, and he was later appointed head of administration by Yeltsin.[15]

Interestingly, the Urals was the home of many prominent Moscow politicians, including, of course, Boris Yeltsin. Soviet Prime Minister Nikokai Ryzhkov was also from the Urals and had been a former director of the gargantuan Uralmash machine-building factory. Rossel knew Boris Yeltsin from the time he worked at *Sreduralstroi* because Yeltsin at that time was working for the Party, in charge of construction in Sverdlovsk. When Yeltsin left Moscow in disgrace in the fall of 1989, he returned to Sverdlovsk, and

---

[11] See Harris, 1999, for an extended discussion of the Great Urals Plan.

[12] For more on Rossel, especially in the post-1994 era, see Yaroslav Startsev, "Gubernatorial Politics in Sverdlovsk *Oblast*'," *Post-Soviet Affairs* 15:4 (1999), pp. 336–61.

[13] " 'Ivan Ivanovich' Rossel',"*Argumenty i fakty*, no. 42, October 1995, p. 3.

[14] "9 krugov: Eduarda Rosselia," *Ogonek*, no. 35, August 1995, p. 21.

[15] *Vechernii Sverdlovsk*, 21 August 1993, p. 1; and *Ural'skii rabochii*, 25 October 1991, p. 1. Also cited in Gerald M. Easter, "Redefining Centre-Regional Relations in the Russian Federation: Sverdlovsk *oblast*'," *Europe-Asia Studies* 49:4 (1997), p. 621.

Rossel helped him organize meetings with citizens. Rossel later campaigned for Yeltsin in the 1991 elections for the presidency of the RSFSR.[16] Sverdlovsk, like Samara, was the site of relatively early support for democracy in Russia.[17] In 1989, a branch of the Movement for Democratic Choice was founded in Sverdlovsk, and the region later became a stronghold of the Democratic Russia movement.[18] In the 1990 elections, 54% of the Movement for Democratic Choice candidates won local soviet seats, and they won sixty out of the two hundred seats in the Sverdlovsk City Soviet.[19] Also in those 1990 elections, Rossel became chair of the Sverdlovsk Oblast Soviet. Sverdlovsk was also a very strong supporter of Yeltsin in 1991 and 1993.[20] Political culture in Sverdlovsk was marked by relatively strong consensus between the executive and the legislature, although as in Samara, there was some tension between the Ekaterinburg city government headed by Arkadii Chernetskii and the oblast government. In considering regional elites during the 1990s, Yaroslav Startsev argued that the shared sense of regional ideology was striking. He wrote: "What is largely missing from politics in Sverdlovsk are ideological differences among representatives of the various parties and movements and among political competitors."[21]

Economic Conditions in Samara and Sverdlovsk

Both Samara and Sverdlovsk had highly educated populations, including a high concentration of scientists and engineers. In the 1990s, industry in Samara was based on defense, aerospace, automobiles, and petrochemicals.

[16] "9 Krugov: Eduarda Rosselia," *Ogonek*, no. 35, August 1995, p. 21; and *Vechernii Sverdlovsk*, 8 August 1991, p. 2, cited in Easter, 1997, p. 621.

[17] On early party development in Sverdlovsk, see Vladimir Gel'man and Grigorii Golosov, "Regional Party System Formation in Russia: The Deviant Case of Sverdlovsk Oblast," *The Journal of Communist Studies and Transition Politics* 14:1–2 (March–June 1998), p. 33; and M. Steven Fish, *Democracy from Scratch: Opposition and Regime in the New Russian Revolution* (Princeton, NJ: Princeton Univ. Press, 1995), pp. 139–42, 148–56.

[18] For a discussion of the history of the Democratic Russia movement throughout the country, see Yitzhak M. Brudny, "The Dynamics of 'Democratic Russia' 1990–93," *Post-Soviet Affairs* 9:2 (1993), pp. 141–70.

[19] See Gel'man and Golosov, 1998, p. 33; and Sergei Ryzhenkov and Galina Liukhterkhandt-Mikhaleva [sic], with Aleksei Kuz'min, eds., *Politika i kul'tura v rossiiskoi provintsii: Novgorodskaia, Voronezhskaia, Saratovskaia, Sverdlovskaia Oblasti* (Moscow: Letniisad, 2001) pp. 150–208.

[20] The regional vote for Yeltsin in June 1991 was 84.8%, and in 1993 it was 84.4%.

[21] Startsev, 1999, p. 357.

The Volga Automobile Factory (*Vozhskii avtomobil'nyi zavod* or VAZ) is located in Tol'iatti; it was built in the 1970s and manufactures the Lada (as well as the Niva and Samara) cars. The main industries in Sverdlovsk were metallurgy, machine building, and defense, but forestry and chemicals were also important to the region's economy.[22]

Both Samara and Sverdlovsk, like the rest of Russia, were hit hard by the economic decline of the perestroika era and the cuts to the defense industry in particular. Production in the early 1990s in both regions plummeted. However, both regions turned out to be among the economically strongest subjects in the entire Russian Federation. A range of indices have ranked regions' relative economic strength and/or potential: Both Samara and Sverdlovsk consistently appeared on these lists together among the top regions in the Federation. For example, in an impressive analysis of the federal Fund for Financial Support of Regions (*Fond finansovoi podderzhki (regionov) sub"ektov Rossiiskoi Federatsii* or FFSR), which was created in 1994, Shinichiro Tabata calculated the FFSR share in regional budget revenues (i.e., how much of a region's revenue comes from the center) for 1994, 1996, and 1997.[23] For all three years, both Samara and Sverdlovsk did not receive FFSR resources, placing them among the nine "donor subjects" of the Federation (among these nine donors there were only four oblasts).[24] Similary, Samara and Sverdlovsk were also both among Aleksei Lavrov's somewhat less scientific, but widely cited, ten to twelve "donor regions," which contributed more in taxes to the federal budget than they received back in subsidies.[25] Another acknowledgment of Samara and Sverdlovsk's relative economic strength was Philip Hanson's list of the seven regions in 1996 which contributed over one half of the entire budget revenue of the Russian Federation. Hanson claimed that both Samara and Sverdlovsk contributed between 3% and 4% of the total Federation revenue.[26] And

---

[22] For an assessment of sub-regional economic conditions within Sverdlovsk, see E. Kozakov and A. Shelomentsev, "Otsenka sotsial'no-ekonomicheskogo sostoianiia depressivnykh regionov," *Ekonomist*, no. 11 (1999), pp. 75–81.

[23] Shinichiro Tabata, "Transfers from Federal to Regional Budgets in Russia: A Statistical Analysis," *Post-Soviet Geography and Economics* 39:8 (1998), p. 458.

[24] Other donors are Moscow city, Lipetsk Oblast, the Republic of Tatarstan, the Republic of Bashkortostan, Khanty-Mansiisk AO, Iamalo-Nenets AO, and Krasnoiarsk Krai.

[25] Aleksei Lavrov, *Mify i rify Rossiiskogo biudzhetnogo federalizma* (Moscow, 1997).

[26] *Gubernskii vestnik* (Samara), 30 August 1996, p. 7, cited in Philip Hanson, "Samara: A Preliminary Profile of a Russian Region and Its Adaptation to the Market," *Europe-Asia Studies* 49:3 (1997), p. 411. The other regions were Moscow city 26%, Khanty-Mansiisk 9%, and Nizhnii Novgorod and St. Petersburg both 3–4%.

Hanson placed both Samara and Sverdlovsk among his list of "survivor regions"; that is, those regions that had, by 1997, a high inflow of foreign currency per capita and, therefore, according to his analysis, higher per capita real income.[27] The basic conclusion of these various analyses is that, in terms of economic strength, both Samara and Sverdlovsk ranked among the highest in the Federation by several different measures.

Table 5.1 shows how Samara and Sverdlovsk compare to the other 55 oblasts and krais of the Russian Federation in terms of four economic issue areas: fiscal relations, production, prices, and trade. The first column of the table lists the specific indicators for each issue and the period covered. These economic issue areas were selected for comparison because they were important topics in the discourse of the regional economy, that is, there were many articles on these topics, and the discourse of these issues will be analyzed in the content analysis section later in this chapter. Most of these variables have been described in the analysis in Chapter 1, with the exception of trade values, which are related to retail trade rather than exports, as in Chapter 1. Retail trade indicators have been added here because retail trade constituted a significant portion of the discourse of the regional economy.

In order to compare Samara and Sverdlovsk, the second and third columns in Table 5.1 list the average values for the two regions for each of the indicators. The fourth column lists the mean values for all 55 oblasts and krais. The italicized numbers indicate which values are "better" than the oblast and krai mean, in the sense of higher production or value, or lower costs. In every one of these indicators, except nominal income in Sverdlovsk where the value is slightly below average, both Samara and Sverdlovsk out-perform the mean. This is consistent with the analysis of donor regions and the finding that both Samara and Sverdlovsk are among the economically better off regions of the Federation. One additional point worth considering is that even though on a per capita basis Samara is slightly ahead of Sverdlovsk, in terms of the region as a whole, given its large population and industrial capacity, Sverdlovsk is often ahead of Samara in regional comparisons (as is evident in the industrial production and total retail trade turnover values).

In addition to regional average values and comparisons to the mean, the second type of information conveyed in Table 5.1 is the variance in the indicator values of all oblasts and krais and the relative difference between

---

[27] Hanson, 1997, pp. 407–29.

Table 5.1 Comparison of Samara and Sverdlovsk in Four Economic Issue Areas with the 55 Oblasts and Krais of the Russian Federation

	Samara Average Values[a]	Sverdlovsk Average Values[a]	Mean Values for All Oblasts and Krais	Standard Deviation	Sam.-Sver. Difference	% of Std. Dev.[b]
Fiscal Relations						
Per capita net tax payments, 1992 (1000s of rubles)	24.30	11.72	7.53	9.18	12.58	137.0%
Per capita net tax payments, 1992 as % of Russian average (all 89 subjects)	772.7%	372.7%	240.0%	291.9%	400.0%	137.0%
Production						
Region's industrial production as % of Russian total, 1990–3 (all 89 subjects)	3.2%	4.3%	1.3%	1.0%	1.1%	106.5%
Region's per capita industrial production as % of Russian average, 1991–3 (all 89 subjects)	155.2%	136.7%	95.2%	39.1%	18.5%	**47.3%**
Prices						
Average monthly income in the region as % of Russian average, 1990–3 (all 89 subjects)	100.0%	97.8%	98.3%	31.5%	2.2%	**6.9%**
Cost of 19 basic food products as % of income, 1992–3	29.0%	33.5%	38.0%	7.7%	4.5%	**58.3%**
Cost of 19 basic food products as % of Russian average, 1992–3 (all 89 subjects)	74.7%	86.3%	97.9%	19.9%	11.6%	**58.3%**
Trade						
Retail trade turnover as % of Russian total, 1990–3 (all 89 subjects)	2.3%	3.1%	1.2%	0.8%	0.8%	104.8%
Per capita retail trade turnover values % of Russian average, 1990–3 (all 89 subjects)	104.3%	98.1%	93.3%	17.2%	6.3%	**36.4%**

[a] Italicized numbers indicate values that are "better" than mean.
[b] Bolded values are less than one standard deviation difference.

values for Samara and Sverdlovsk. The point of this information is to situate the differences between Samara and Sverdlovsk vis-à-vis the overall variance in the indicators in order to be able to assess the relative similarity in values for Samara and Sverdlovsk. Toward this goal, the fifth column lists the standard deviation (square root of the variance) for each indicator. The sixth column lists the absolute difference between Samara and Sverdlovsk, while the final column lists this difference as a percentage of the standard deviation. In other words, the final column shows how much of a standard deviation the difference between the two regions constitutes. All the bolded values in the final column indicate that the difference between the two regions is less than one standard deviation. The difference between Samara and Sverdlovsk in net tax payments is, however, relatively large, and this is noteworthy given the significance of net tax payments in the quantitative analysis in Chapter 1. Besides net tax payments, the two indicators whose differences in value are above one standard deviation (% of total Russian production, and retail trade turnover) are both indicators that represent a percentage of the Russian total value, rather than a per capita value, and the difference is largely a function of population (the difference is greatly reduced in the per capita values). Nevertheless, the differences are still only a small amount more than one standard deviation (106.5% and 104.8%, respectively).

There are three conclusions to be drawn from Table 5.1. First, both Samara and Sverdlovsk are above-average regions in these four issue areas (net taxes, production, prices, and trade); and, second, the differences between Samara and Sverdlovsk are in most cases quite small, relative to the variance in the values of the indicators. Third, the one exception in this pattern is net tax payments, where Samara pays significantly more into the federal budget per capita than Sverdlovsk.

Given these indicators of regional economic conditions derived from traditional data sets, we can outline what the expected interpretations of the regional economy would be, if they were based on "objective" economic conditions. These expectations and the reasons behind them are summarized in Table 5.2. Overall, except in fiscal relations (the issue of net tax payments to the center), there should be few differences in interpretations of economic conditions between Samara and Sverdlovsk.

In considering political and economic conditions in Samara and Sverdlovsk, a review of economic conditions from traditional sources, as well as political, historical, and geographical factors, does not suggest there should be very great differences in interpretations of the regional economy.

Table 5.2 *Comparison of Samara and Sverdlovsk: Expected Interpretations in Four Economic Issue Areas, Based on Objective Economic Conditions*

Economic Issues	Expected Regional Interpretation	Reason
All issue areas	Minimal difference between regions	Overall the regions are economically very similar.
Fiscal relations	Samara should be more negative than Sverdlovsk	Samara contributes much more to the federal budget (1.82 std. dev. above average). Sverdlovsk contributes less than Samara to the federal budget, but still more than other regions (0.45 std. dev. above average).
Production	Minimal difference between regions	Only 0.47 std. dev. difference for per capita indicators between regions. Both regions are well above the Russian average.
Prices	Minimal difference between regions	Only 0.58 std. dev. difference for price indicators, and less for nominal income, 0.07. Samara is greater than the Russian average on all three indicators. Sverdlovsk may be slightly more negative because prices are higher than in Samara (although still less than the Russian average) and wages are lower.
Trade	Minimal difference between regions	Only 0.36 std. dev. difference for per capita indicator. Both regions are greater than the Russian average.

The one exception is net tax payments, where interpretation of fiscal relations should be more negative in Samara. We can now turn to the content analysis of regional economic discourse in order to evaluate regional understandings of the economy.

Content Analysis of Regional Understandings of the Economy

Beginning with glasnost and continuing into the early 1990s, Russian regional newspapers underwent a significant transformation. Soviet central censorship was nearly eliminated in its overt forms, and regional papers were increasingly able to give voice to local concerns and issues, including criticism of the central government. The number of newspapers had risen exponentially by 1993, although many newspapers were short-lived. This was a golden moment for the press – most papers were still funded by the state and therefore did not have to meet market constraints, such as profitability, yet state control over content had largely disappeared.[28] For these reasons, local newspapers in the early 1990s are an excellent source for accessing local discourse or the ways in which local actors understood the world. I collected nearly two thousand articles related to economic events in Samara and Sverdlovsk covering the period 1990–3. I tried to capture some of the dynamism of this period by focusing not only on traditionally high-subscription papers but also by looking at newer papers. The articles come from fourteen newspapers distributed and published in Sverdlovsk Oblast and nineteen newspapers distributed and published in Samara Oblast.[29]

The analysis of the articles is based on systematic coding of each article.[30] The content of the articles was divided into five attributes: (1) action or topic of the article; (2) source of action; (3) source location; (4) affected actors; and (5) affected location. And the content was also evaluated along a "benefit" dimension.[31] The attribute called *action or topic of the article* represented a short, but precise, summary of the action discussed in the article. The attribute called *source of action* represented the name, specified or implied in the article, of the actors or act that was the motivating source of the action in the article topic. The *source location* represented the location of the actors or act that was the motivating source of the action in the topic. The *affected actors* was similar to the source actor, except that this criterion represented who was receiving, rather than motivating, the consequences of the action in the topic. Likewise, the *affected location* represented the location, specified or implied in the article, of the actors who were receiving the consequences of

---

[28] As it turns out, this situation did not last long. In the mid to late 1990s, with both encroaching market demands and increasing state or oligarchic control, the number of papers and the breadth of content were sharply reduced.

[29] My selection of articles was based on two methods. In the first, I went through the regional newspaper subject indices in local libraries. My second method was to select major newspapers in each region and read through each issue of selected newspapers covering the entire 1990–3 period. In Sverdlovsk, the daily newspapers that I used most were *Ural'skii rabochii* (Urals Worker), *Vechernii Sverdlovsk/Ekaterinburg* (Evening Sverdlovsk/Ekaterinburg), *Za vlast' sovetov* (Power to the Soviets), and *Oblastnaia gazeta* (Oblast Newspaper). In Samara, the main papers I used were *Volzhskaia kommuna* (Volga Commune), *Samarskie izvestiia* (Samara News), *Delo* (Business), and *Volzhskaia zaria* (Volga Dawn).

[30] In analyzing the articles, I worked with four research assistants to code the articles for content. I reviewed all the coded articles, and 5% of the articles were recoded by different assistants to check the consistency of the coding.

[31] The articles were initially coded along three evaluative dimensions: *organization, equity,* and *benefit,* but the differences in these dimensions did not turn out to be significant, and, hence, only *benefit* was used.

the action in the article topic. The *benefit* dimension refers to the normative consequences of an action on affected actors and is represented as "positive" or "negative." For example, in an article about production in the region, if the article said that production at a local Samara factory decreased because Moscow authorities failed to follow through on promises to send necessary inputs, the topic of the article would be "production decrease"; the source of action would be "lack of supplies"; the source location would be "Moscow"; the affected actors would be Samara citizens; and the affected location would be Samara. The benefit dimension would be coded as "negative."

In the end, 1,441 articles related to economic subjects were coded.[32] Of these, there were 1,276 in which at least some part of Sverdlovsk Oblast or Samara Oblast was the *affected location*.[33] My analysis focuses on this group, since at issue is understandings of economic issues in Samara and Sverdlovsk Oblasts. I also excluded articles for which it was not possible to evaluate the benefit dimension, which brought the total number down to 1,251. Finally, in order to compare regional understandings of the economy with objective economic conditions as discussed earlier, I also excluded articles unrelated to the four economic issue areas of fiscal policy, production, prices, and trade, which further reduced the total number of articles to 579 (193 for Samara and 386 for Sverdlovsk). Table 5.3 lists the article topics that were included in each of the four economic issue areas.

I will present my analysis of regional understandings of the economy through a discussion of six tables that illustrate regional differences in interpretations of economic events. The first two tables contain information on all economic issue areas, and subsequent tables report findings for each issue area. The point of these comparisons is to demonstrate the relationship between regional location and the evaluation of benefit to the region for a range of economic topics.

Table 5.4 lists the overall difference in benefit evaluations between Samara and Sverdlovsk for all the economic issue areas, among all source locations. Table 5.4 compares the attributes of *affected location* with the *benefit* dimension. Affected location refers to whether the action in the article affected either Samara Oblast (or a city in Samara Oblast), listed in the second column, or Sverdlovsk Oblast (or a city in Sverdlovsk Oblast), listed in

[32] Of the remaining articles, some were coded under the movement for greater sovereignty category and will be discussed in other chapters; others turned out to be on non-economic topics.

[33] In the remaining 165 articles, the *affected location* was the entire Russian Federation, the Soviet Union, or some other non-Sverdlovsk or non-Samara location.

Table 5.3 *Article Topics in Economic Issue Areas*

Economic Issue Areas	Article Topics	Number of Articles
Fiscal relations	• State and regional budget formation • Division of economic responsibility between center and other levels of government • Regional and city "khozraschet" (self-financing) • Regional contributions and subsidies to the federal budget • Taxes, including regional, city, enterprise, individual, and sales taxes	104
Production	• Restructuring of production including conversion • Firms adjusting to market conditions • Production shortfalls • Production of defective/substandard products • Industrial policy	211
Prices	• Price increases in food and other goods and services • Control of price increases • Wages and changes in standard of living • Inflation • Nonpayments problem; lack of physical currency • Monetary issues; credit or check issues; other cash substitution strategies	113
Trade	• Retail trade; shortages and rationing of products at retail outlets • Lines for products at retail outlets • Auctioning of retail products; resale of used products • Coordination of supplies by government and enterprise • Inter-enterprise supply agreements and contracts; supply shortages	151
Total number of articles		579

the third column. The benefit evaluations, negative and positive, are listed in the rows as numbers of articles as well as percentages of the total articles. The last column and row in each of the tables lists the total number of articles, by region and evaluation. The chi-squared score is also listed at the bottom left of each table.[34]

---

[34] This chi-squared test evaluates whether the observed distribution is significantly different from what we might expect by chance, if there were no regional differences in benefit

Table 5.4 *Regional Understandings of the Economy: Content Analysis of All Four Economic Issue Areas*

Benefit Evaluation	Affected Location		Total
	Samara	Sverdlovsk	
Negative	103	272	375
	53%	70%	65%
Positive	90	114	204
	47%	30%	35%
TOTAL	193	386	579
	100%	100%	100%

Pearson chi^2(1) = 16.4845, Pr = 0.000.

Table 5.4 shows overall that in Sverdlovsk the interpretation of the benefit to the region of a range of economic issues is far more negative than in Samara. Indeed for the same types of economic issues, the number of negative articles in Sverdlovsk was 32% higher than in Samara.[35] A further refinement of this analysis divided the regional articles by source location, that is, to see whether the attribution for a given action to a regional source, as opposed to an outside source, makes a difference in the evaluation of the benefit of the action to the region. The expectation is that regional interpretations of economic events are more likely to be negative when an outside source is the cause of the action. Table 5.5 repeats the analysis in Table 5.4 but divides the regional entries by source location. The column headings of "Samara Source" and "Sverdlovsk Source" mean that Samara or Sverdlovsk was the source location. The column heading of "Moscow Source" means that Moscow was specified or directly implied as the source location.[36]

In Table 5.5, we see that as expected, in both regions, when Moscow is the source of an action, the assessment of benefit to the region is more negative. However, once again, interpretations of economic issues are more negative in Sverdlovsk than in Samara. This negativity is quite extreme in Sverdlovsk

evaluations, given the distribution of regional entries. Following convention, a p-score of less than 0.10 is considered significant (i.e., there is less than a 10% likelihood that the observed distribution occurred by chance).

[35] Separate tables for all four economic issue areas with combined source locations are listed in the appendix, Tables A6–A9. Tables with disaggregated source locations follow in the text.

[36] Moscow as a source was implied if the source actor was the federal government of Russia.

185

Table 5.5 *Regional Understandings of the Economy: Content Analysis of All Four Economic Issue Areas, by Source Location*

Benefit Evaluation	Affected Location Is Samara		Affected Location Is Sverdlovsk		
	Samara Source	Moscow Source	Sverdlovsk Source	Moscow Source	Total
Negative	45	58	147	125	375
	45%	63%	63%	81%	65%
Positive	56	34	85	29	204
	55%	37%	37%	19%	35%
TOTAL	101	92	232	154	579
	100%	100%	100%	100%	100%

Pearson chi^2(3) = 36.5582, Pr = 0.000.

Table 5.6 *Regional Understandings of the Economy: Content Analysis of Fiscal Relations*

Benefit Evaluation	Affected Location Is Samara		Affected Location Is Sverdlovsk		
	Samara Source	Moscow Source	Sverdlovsk Source	Moscow Source	Total
Negative	5	28	10	27	70
	26%	74%	67%	84%	67%
Positive	14	10	5	5	34
	74%	26%	33%	16%	33%
TOTAL	19	38	15	32	104
	100%	100%	100%	100%	100%

Pearson chi^2(3) = 19.4502, Pr = 0.000.

when Moscow is the source of action: 81% of events were evaluated as being of negative benefit to the region.

The next step in the analysis was to divide the evaluations of articles by is-sue area. This allowed for a more fine-grained comparison between regional understandings of the economy and objective economic conditions, since the articles were directly comparable to the objective indicators. Table 5.6 represents a subset of the analysis in Table 5.5, including only those articles related to fiscal policy.

186

Here again, while both regions evaluate Moscow-sourced action more negatively, the evaluations in Sverdlovsk are more negative than in Samara. This finding is particularly significant because the objective economic conditions suggest that Samara, as one of the largest net tax payers in the Federation, should have much more reason than Sverdlovsk for complaint. The greater negativity in Sverdlovsk, in contrast to expectations based on objective economic conditions, is suggestive of the mediated nature of regional economic understandings.

To better appreciate these mediated understandings, some examples from the texts of the articles will help illustrate the surprising divergence in interpretations of fiscal policy. In the summer of 1993, the head of the Sverdlovsk administration, Eduard Rossel, complained about the lack of central government funding. In an interview he said:

Look, what is this for a system? We remit federal taxes. And after that Moscow sends this money to support federal institutions, situated in the oblast. We pay Russia, let's say, in support of higher education institutions (we have 17 institutes), but afterwards our faculty don't receive monthly salaries. However, we are amongst the accused in this case.[37]

Moreover he framed the difficult economic situation facing Sverdlovsk Oblast in terms of how much Sverdlovsk paid into the federal budget and regional inequality, especially in comparison with republics. Rossel continued,

Winter is approaching. For winter we are not preparing. We're buying neither oil, nor coal, nor coke. We're not renovating the boilers. We calculated that we need, for all these necessities, 260 billion rubles in credits. But this money isn't there. However, permit me to say, we pay, and pay conscientiously, federal taxes. What? Should we behave like Tatarstan, which doesn't remit these taxes? Lower them [taxes], like them [Tatarstan]?[38]

It was the case that Sverdlovsk was paying more than some republics, like Tatarstan, into the federal budget, but the interesting thing is that so were other regions like Samara. Indeed, given the discourse of inequality in fiscal relations in Sverdlovsk, we would expect even more complaints in Samara, which paid more than twice Sverdlovsk's amount per capita. However, as

[37] Interview with E. Rossel, "V Moskvu za rzhavym gvozdem," *Ural'skii rabochii*, no. 151, 13 August 1993, p. 2.
[38] Ibid.

187

Difference Between the Sum of Federal Taxes and the Sum of Federal Subsidies for the Volga Region, (in millions of rubles)					
	Payments in federal taxes	Subsidies from the federation	Difference	Population at the beginning of 1992 (in 1000s)	Per capita difference (in 1000s of rubles)
Samara	94,834	9,257	−85,577	3,296	−25.96
Nizhnii Novgorod	81,554	14,333	−67,221	3,704	−18.15
Ul'ianovsk	27,174	5,676	−21,498	1,444	−14.89
Saratov	33,279	7,215	−26,064	2,711	−9.61
Penza	14,696	5,072	−9,624	1,514	−6.36
Chuvashiia	13,326	7,167	−6,159	1,363	−4.55
Astrakhan	8,356	4,986	−3,370	1,010	−3.34
Mordoviia	8,433	7,514	−919	964	−0.96
Marii El	5,567	6,353	+786	762	+1.03
Kalmykiia	1,777	4,000	+2,223	327	+6.8
Tatarstan	93	38,036	+37,943	3,696	+10.27

Figure 5.1 Front page article in Samara. *Komsomol'skaia pravda v Samare*, 17 July 1993, p. 1 (originally in Russian, translated by author)

the content analysis of articles related to fiscal policy showed, there was much less negativity in Samara.

Given the difficulty until 1994 (as discussed in Chapter 1) of regions actually knowing how much they paid into the federal budget and how much they received, it might be argued that elites and citizens in Samara were unaware that their region was paying so much into the federal budget. Yet there is evidence that Samara officials and citizens did have information suggesting that their region was paying more than other regions into the federal budget. Figure 5.1 reprints a front page article (translated into English) from a Samara newspaper in the summer of 1993.

The article consisted of a table listing how much each of the regions in the Volga area paid in federal taxes and how much they received in subsidies. This information was also broken down per capita. It is quite clear that Samara not only paid more than every other region in the Volga area but that Samara paid over 350% more per capita than Tatarstan. In the rest of the newspaper for that day, there was no comment on these figures. In

Table 5.7 *Regional Understandings of the Economy: Content Analysis of Production Issues*

	Affected Location Is Samara		Affected Location Is Sverdlovsk		
Benefit Evaluation	Samara Source	Moscow Source	Sverdlovsk Source	Moscow Source	Total
Negative	13	16	41	42	112
	37%	47%	47%	78%	53%
Positive	22	18	47	12	99
	63%	53%	53%	22%	47%
TOTAL	35	34	88	54	211
	100%	100%	100%	100%	100%

Pearson chi^2(3) = 18.7780, Pr = 0.000.

contrast, such an article in Sverdlovsk would likely have been followed by strong complaints of Sverdlovsk's excessive contribution.

Moreover, as is consistent with the content analysis, the comments of the head of the Samara administration, Konstantin Titov, are suggestive of the difference from Sverdlovsk in interpretation of the economic crisis facing the region. In an interview in the summer of 1993, Titov stated that, after discussing production statistics over the last three years, he concluded, "All negative indicators are lower than the Russian average." Moreover, he continued, "Of course there is a recession. But I personally don't consider this a big disaster. Normal structural reorganization is proceeding." In the interview, Titov made efforts to frame the problem facing the regions as a general problem in the Federation, rather than, as in Sverdlovsk, as a consequence of regional inequality. He said, "As you see, not all is so very bad. It would have been desirable to more quickly be able to stand on our feet, to begin advances on all fronts. But there are not enough resources or credits. This is a disease of the whole state."[39]

In addition to fiscal policy, I also conducted content analysis on articles related to production, prices, and trade. The results of these analyses are presented in Tables 5.7, 5.8, and 5.9, respectively. As shown in Table 5.7, in the interpretation of production in the regions, a majority of evaluations in Samara are positive given both source locations. In Sverdlovsk, the evaluations are, in general, again more negative than in Samara, but a majority

[39] Interview with K. Titov, "Ne zhdat' milostei ot pravitel'stva," *Volzhskaia zaria*, no. 113, 27 July 1993, p. 2.

189

of evaluations are positive when Sverdlovsk is the source location. And the largest difference in positive and negative evaluations, and the most negativity in Sverdlovsk, comes about when Sverdlovsk is affected and Moscow is the source location (column 4). Some examples from Sverdlovsk articles will help illustrate the sense of grievance picked up by these negative codings.

One issue that became clear after 1991 was that many industrial regions lacked the infrastructure to produce consumer goods, yet they could no longer rely on the center or other regions to meet the needs of their citizens. For example, one journalist noted: "The oblast until perestroika worked according to the necessities of the economy of the former USSR. This is shown in the structure of its industry, patently not oriented to the needs of the population."[40] Another article is suggestive of the extremely negative tone toward Soviet central industrialization policy that was occasionally represented in Sverdlovsk:

Under the dictatorship, the Urals was a colony. Bolshevik Moscow sucked dry the juices of the outlying areas, tightening around itself material and intellectual resources and leaving us harmful manufacturing with radiation and artificial, choleric bacteria. Offense here is huge. Debt unpaid. And it is understandably the wish of the outlying areas now to straighten themselves out.[41]

This negative interpretation of Soviet industrialization policies, I argue, affected the way regional actors in Sverdlovsk evaluated the economic conditions of the 1990s, and in particular declining production. In other words, these interpretations, subject to larger historical and social understandings, mediated the role of economic "facts" in political action.

On the issue of prices, because most of the articles were about price increases, it is understandable that most of the articles evaluated the impact on the region as negative. The results for this issue area are presented in Table 5.8. It is interesting that in this case, Sverdlovsk is actually slightly less negative than Samara when Sverdlovsk actors are the source of action. But Sverdlovsk is more negative than Samara when Moscow is the source. However, in this case, the differences between Samara and Sverdlovsk are not particularly stark.

Finally, on regional trade issues, Table 5.9 presents a regional comparison of interpretations and again shows much higher negativity in Sverdlovsk. As in the case of production, Samara had more positive than negative

---

[40] Galina Karelova, "Pervyi shag k svobode," *Oblast'naia gazeta*, no. 100, 3 September 1993, p. 2.
[41] Ol'ga Shcherbinina, "Zachem raschleniat' Rossiiu," *Na smenu!*, no. 124, 7 July 1993, p. 1.

Economic Understandings in Samara and Sverdlovsk

Table 5.8 *Regional Understandings of the Economy: Content Analysis of Price Issues*

Benefit Evaluation	Affected Location Is Samara		Affected Location Is Sverdlovsk		Total
	Samara Source	Moscow Source	Sverdlovsk Source	Moscow Source	
Negative	14	7	37	32	90
	74%	88%	71%	94%	80%
Positive	5	1	15	2	23
	26%	12%	29%	6%	20%
TOTAL	19	8	52	34	113
	100%	100%	100%	100%	100%

Fisher's Exact[a] = 0.042.
[a] In this case, and subsequently all others where some of the cell entries contained were less than 3 observations, instead of the chi-squared test, I used Fisher's Exact Test. The p-value of 0.042 is within the commonly accepted significance range.

Table 5.9 *Regional Understandings of the Economy: Content Analysis of Trade Issues*

Benefit Evaluation	Affected Location Is Samara		Affected Location Is Sverdlovsk		Total
	Samara Source	Moscow Source	Sverdlovsk Source	Moscow Source	
Negative	13	7	59	24	103
	46%	58%	77%	71%	68%
Positive	15	5	18	10	48
	54%	42%	23%	29%	32%
TOTAL	28	12	77	34	151
	100%	100%	100%	100%	100%

Pearson chi^2(3) = 9.2686, Pr = 0.026.

evaluations when Samara actors were the source. Interestingly, Sverdlovsk is more negative when Sverdlovsk actors are the source than when Moscow actors are the source.

Overall, the content analysis suggests that regional understandings of the economy are more negative in Sverdlovsk compared to Samara. In both regions, assessments of benefit to the region are more negative when Moscow is the source location (except in regional trade in Sverdlovsk), but in *all cases* (regardless of source location) assessments in Sverdlovsk are more negative than in Samara.

Table 5.10 *Comparison of Samara and Sverdlovsk: Expected and Observed Interpretations in Four Economic Issue Areas*

	Expected Regional Interpretation Based on Objective Economic Conditions	Observed Interpretation Based on Content Analysis of Regional Newspapers[a]
All issue areas	Minimal difference between regions	Sverdlovsk articles were 32% more negative (Tables 5.4 and 5.5)
Fiscal relations	Samara will be more negative than Sverdlovsk	Sverdlovsk articles were 36% more negative (Table 5.6 and Appendix Table A6)
Production	Minimal difference between regions	Sverdlovsk articles were 38% more negative (Table 5.7 and Appendix Table A7)
Prices	Minimal difference between regions	Differences were not very great: articles were 3% more negative in Sverdlovsk (Table 5.8 and Appendix Table A8)
Trade	Minimal difference between regions	Sverdlovsk articles were 50% more negative (Table 5.9 and Appendix Table A9)

[a] In this column, the negativity rating is the combined rating for all source locations.

Besides greater negativity in Sverdlovsk, an important finding of this content analysis is that there are significant differences between the two regions in interpretations of economic events that go beyond what would be predicted by the conditions in the regions contained in traditional data sets. In Table 5.10, a summary of the findings from the content analysis of the newspaper articles regarding differences in understandings of the economy in the two regions is compared with the data on economic conditions listed in Table 5.2.

The expected and observed interpretations do not converge, except in the assessments of price issues, where interpretations in the two regions did not strongly differ. Thus, on the basis of the content analysis and comparison with the analysis of economic conditions from traditional sources, I argue that although "objective" accounts predict some level of regional under-standings of the economy, the observed variance in regional understand-ings of the economy, and in particular the greater negativity in Sverdlovsk compared to Samara Oblast, is not well predicted by objective economic conditions. In other words, objective accounts of economic conditions are underdetermining of regional interpretations of the economy.

This finding of territorialized divergence between objective conditions and regional understandings suggests that differences in regional understandings of the economy can be considered a possible source of explanation as to how similar economic conditions can lead to different political outcomes, such as the movement for greater sovereignty in Sverdlovsk versus the absence of such a movement in Samara. That is, returning to the puzzle of the inconclusive quantitative analysis in Chapter 1, the concept of regional understandings of the economy takes us closer to explaining the role of economic factors in political movements. Rather than rejecting the economic basis of sovereignty movements, the concept of imagined economies or region-specific understandings of the economy allows us to see how the same set of objective economic conditions can be interpreted in different ways, leading to divergent political outcomes.

In the next chapter, through further content analysis, I will develop the point that the negativity in Sverdlovsk's economic assessments deserves our attention. I will accomplish this by presenting a detailed analysis of how the claims in support of the movement for a Urals Republic were directly related to the perceptions, identified in the content analysis in this chapter, of negative treatment of the region by the center. In other words, I will demonstrate the relationship between particular understandings of the economy and movements for greater sovereignty.

6

Regional Understandings of the Economy and Sovereignty

THE ECONOMIC BASIS OF THE MOVEMENT FOR A URALS REPUBLIC

The findings of Chapter 5 compel us to ask, how then are regional understandings of the economy related to movements for greater sovereignty? I argue that content analysis of Sverdlovsk newspaper articles related to the sovereignty movement will demonstrate that the movement for a Urals Republic was driven by concerns over inequality, both economic and constitutional. In other words, the movement was based on regional actors' belief that Sverdlovsk Oblast was treated unfairly in the Federation by the existing institutional structure, and that greater economic and political autonomy in the form of upgraded political status – to *republic* – was the solution to the inequality and adverse economic circumstances facing Sverdlovsk.

The analysis of regional actors' arguments for and against the movement for a Urals Republic also provides evidence that economic and constitutional inequality were not merely concepts strategically invented by regional elites in Sverdlovsk. By analyzing the arguments made by Sverdlovsk actors against the movement for a Urals Republics, I show that these anti-Urals Republic arguments did not dispute the claims of economic and constitutional inequality but instead focused mainly on the threat to the unity and continued existence of the Russian Federation and on claims of the illegality of the sovereignty movement.

Finally, by contrasting the arguments presented by Sverdlovsk and non-Sverdlovsk actors regarding the causes of the movement for a Urals Republic, the content analysis in this chapter also provides evidence of a particularly *regional* understanding of the economy, in the sense that Sverdlovsk actors share particular beliefs; for example, the issue of inequality is salient among Sverdlovsk actors only. Nearly all Sverdlovsk actors referenced economic and constitutional inequality as the cause of the movement, regardless of their position on the movement, while non-Sverdlovsk actors largely attributed other causes to the movement. In this sense, location was a significant predictor of the understanding of the basis for the sovereignty movement.

Content Analysis Overview

In analyzing the arguments for and against the Urals Republic, I considered 56 articles from eight major newspapers published in Sverdlovsk Oblast, each of which contained specific arguments for or against the Urals Republic.[1] Among the articles, 37 contained arguments in favor of the formation of a Urals Republic, and 19 advanced arguments against the Urals Republic.

For each of the articles, I also coded the location of the author or actor making the argument. Actors were coded as being located in Sverdlovsk if their biographical description in the article noted that they were either living or were working in Sverdlovsk.[2] The actors coded as being located in Moscow were mainly federal government officials stationed in Moscow, while the actors coded as being located in the Russian Federation were individuals who represented national organizations, such as political parties or economic organizations located across regions of the Federation.[3]

Table 6.1 shows the relationship between the location of the actor and the actor's position toward the movement for a Urals Republic. Of the 37 articles that argued for the Urals Republic, 33 were by actors located in Sverdlovsk, and the remaining 4 articles represented arguments by Russian Federation actors. There were no arguments made by Moscow actors in favor of the movement for a Urals Republic. In contrast, of the 19 articles that advanced arguments against the movement for a Urals Republic, 10 contained arguments by Sverdlovsk actors, 8 by Moscow actors, and 1 by a

---

[1] In total, I collected over one hundred articles whose content was related to the movement for a Urals Republic, but the fifty-six articles that I selected for consideration in this chapter were chosen because they each contained an explicit argument either for or against the movement.

[2] For example, reporters for Sverdlovsk papers, managers of Sverdlovsk enterprises, and Sverdlovsk government officials were all coded as being located in Sverdlovsk.

[3] The one exception to these guidelines was that the presidential representative in Sverdlovsk, a federal government official working in Sverdlovsk, was coded as being located in Moscow because his job was to be President Yeltsin's "eyes and ears" in the region, and he therefore occupied a particular "outsider" status among government officials in Sverdlovsk. However, individuals who worked in Sverdlovsk divisions or departments of national organizations were coded as being located in Sverdlovsk because such individuals represented Sverdlovsk in national organizations as opposed to representing national organizations in Sverdlovsk.

Table 6.1 *All Articles Containing Arguments Favoring or Opposing the Urals Republic:*
Relationship Between Actors' Locations and Positions on the Urals Republic

	Location of the Actor Whose Argument Is Reported in the Article			
Position Toward the Urals Republic	Sverdlovsk Oblast	Russian Federation	Moscow	All Locations
Against	10	1	8	19
	23%	20%	100%	34%
In favor	33	4	0	37
	77%	80%	0%	66%
All positions	43	5	8	56
	100%	100%	100%	100%

Fisher's exact test = 0.000.

Russian Federation actor. These data suggest that arguments in favor of the movement for a Urals Republic advanced by actors located in Sverdlovsk and the Russian Federation significantly outnumbered arguments against the movement, while arguments advanced by Moscow actors were unanimously against the movement for a Urals Republic.[4] In itself this finding suggests a difference between Sverdlovsk and non-Sverdlovsk actors regarding the Urals Republic: In particular, Moscow actors were much more likely to oppose the Urals Republic. This is an expected finding, but it is only the tip of the iceberg.

Arguments in Favor of the Movement for a Urals Republic

In order to consider the claim that the movement for a Urals Republic was based on the idea that Sverdlovsk Oblast was subject to constitutional and economic inequality, I analyze in detail the arguments made in support of the Urals Republic. Table 6.2 presents a subset of Table 6.1, namely the articles containing arguments in favor of the movement for a Urals

---

[4] It is perhaps worth repeating that the data in this chapter are drawn only from Sverdlovsk newspapers, and thus they represent the presentation of arguments within Sverdlovsk Oblast. Many more arguments regarding the Urals Republic were published elsewhere (such as Moscow-based newspapers), but data from those articles are not included here because it was prohibitively difficult to systematically collect articles on the Urals Republic published outside the region (owing mainly to a lack of electronic or other reliable indexing). Hence, the claims in this chapter are consequently based on and limited to articles published in Sverdlovsk.

Table 6.2 *Articles Containing Arguments in Favor of the Urals Republic:*
Relationship Between Actors' Locations and Reasons for Supporting the Urals Republic

Primary Reason for the Supporting Urals Republic	Location of the Actor Whose Argument Is Reported in the Article[a]		
	Sverdlovsk Oblast	Russian Federation	All Locations
Constitutional inequality	13	2	15
	39%	50%	41%
Economic inequality	18	0	18
	55%	0%	49%
New federalism	2	2	4
	6%	50%	11%
All positions	33	4	37
	100%	100%	100%

Fisher's exact test = 0.012.
[a] There were no articles containing arguments by Moscow actors in favor of the Urals Republic.

Republic according to the primary reason for supporting the movement and the location of the actor making the argument.[5]

Constitutional inequality and economic inequality were closely linked at this time because economic autonomy and regional economic policy were a function of a region's legal status. And the ongoing reconfiguration of the economic principles of federal relations concerned both current regional economic policy and the debate over the formation of a new Russian constitution that would regulate future regional economic policy. However, in order to appreciate the economic-based claims of inequality in their distinction from the constitutional arguments, I divided the concept of "inequality" into "economic" and "constitutional" categories.

The row entitled "Constitutional inequality" contains articles in which the range of political rights assigned to oblasts in the Russian constitution was cited as the primary reason for forming a Urals Republic. The second row contains articles in which "Economic inequality" was cited as the primary reason for supporting the Urals Republic. As I mentioned earlier, equality of economic rights was to some degree addressed by arguments regarding constitutional inequality. However, the articles in this row focus on specifically economic as opposed to political rights.

The third row among the primary reasons for supporting the movement for a Urals Republic, entitled "New federalism," contains articles in which

[5] These articles are listed in row 2 of Table 6.1.

the primary reason for support was to build a new type of decentralized federation based on administrative units, which would contain multiple ethnic groups. This is close to an argument for "multiculturalism" or ethnic diversity. There was some overlap between categories in that articles which argued against inequality also sought to restructure federal relations. However, in contrast to the articles in the inequality categories, arguments in the new federalism category were more focused on positive future opportunities (for creating more democratic and harmonious ethnic relations throughout the Russian Federation) than on resolving current problems in Sverdlovsk Oblast.

The data in Table 6.2 indicate that almost all of the arguments in support of the Urals Republic made by Sverdlovsk actors reference some kind of inequality. Only 2 out of 33 claim new federalism as the primary reason for support of the Urals Republic rather than inequality. Of the 4 arguments advanced by actors located in the Russian Federation, 2 claim constitutional inequality as the primary reason for support, and 2 claimed new federalism as the primary reason. These aggregate numbers of articles give some sense of arguments in favor of the Urals Republic, but more detailed discussion of the actual arguments will illustrate what was meant by "inequality" and will demonstrate how it is related to the negative understandings of the economy outlined in Chapter 5.

In Favor of the Urals Republic: Constitutional Inequality

Explicit arguments in favor of a Urals Republic started to appear only in 1993, and as I discussed in Chapter 4, the summer Constitutional Conference of 1993 was a crucial event in the development of sovereignty movements. Just days after that conference, the tenth session of the Sverdlovsk Oblast Soviet was held in July 1993. At this session, during which the soviet was set to vote on changing the status of Sverdlovsk from *oblast* to *republic*, Eduard Rossel, then head of the administration of Sverdlovsk Oblast, gave a speech in favor of the change. He stated that after the signing of the Federal Treaty in March 1992, "a number of sharp problems and vitally important contradictions arose."[6] Rossel listed three such sets of problems: First, regions which signed the Treaty turned out to have unequal status and the "different constitutional-legal status of regions defined them [regions]

---

[6] Eduard Rossel, "Stat' polnotsennym sub'ektom federatsii," *Oblastnaia gazeta*, no. 75, 6 July 1993, p. 1.

unequally in economic, political and judicial rights."[7] Second, Rossel argued that the problems and contradictions of the Federal Treaty resulted in un-equal rights among citizens of the Russian Federation. And third, he claimed that the sovereignty of republics was "in conflict with the sovereignty of Russia."[8] Rossel concluded that "all these facts brought the administration [of Sverdlovsk Oblast] to look for the path of equalizing the status of the territory. It is our firm belief, that all subjects of the Federation should be equal in political, economic, and social rights."[9]

At the same oblast soviet session, Anatolii Grebenkin, chairman of the oblast soviet, also gave a speech in which he argued that "today, the struc-ture of the Russian Federation – is a model of an asymmetrical federation, consisting of three types of subjects: republics; oblasts, krais and federal cities; [and] autonomous okrugs. This structure is unique in the world; in fact there are no such federations in which subjects of a federation are un-equal."[10] Grebenkin went on to explain how the formation of the Urals Republic would solve the problem of federal inequality. He said:

In our variant, strong republics will herald a new, unified, integrated Russian Feder-ation, based on symmetrically formed subjects, where all subjects of the Federation are equal. This equality secures the equality of the rights of citizens; it secures the equal rights of subjects in the use of resources, ownership and disposal of property entering the international arena.[11]

After voting to change officially the status of Sverdlovsk Oblast to re-public, the Sverdlovsk Oblast Soviet issued an official explanation in which the deputies outlined the seven reasons for changing the status of the oblast. These included: (1) strengthening Russian statehood on the basis of the formation of a federation of subjects having equal rights; (2) secur-ing equal rights of Russian citizens; (3) working out the division of power between the Federation and its subjects; (4) creating the conditions for the proper fulfillment by institutions of the Russian Federation and its

---

[7] Ibid. This same exact phrase was repeated by several different Sverdlovsk officials through-out 1993. See also, for example, Aleksei Vorob'ev, "Put' k ustoichivoi federatsii," *Oblastnaia gazeta*, no. 96, 25 July 1993, p. 2.

[8] Rossel, 6 July 1993, p. 1.

[9] Ibid.

[10] Anatolii V. Grebenkin, "My budem reshitel'ny," *Oblastnaia gazeta*, no. 75, 6 July 1993, p. 1. Of course, this is not true; there are asymmetrical federations (e.g., the United States, if one considers the status of Washington, DC, Puerto Rico, and Native American reservations), but the reality of other states was not a relevant point for Grebenkin.

[11] Ibid.

subjects of their functions; (5) restoring the health of relations between subjects of the Russian Federation; (6) effectively carrying out economic reform; and (7) advancing the positive growth of the constitutional process in the Russian Federation.[12] Following the vote by the Sverdlovsk Oblast Soviet, Sverdlovsk leaders held numerous press conferences and gave interviews to explain why it was necessary to change Sverdlovsk's status. Anatolii Grebenkin, for example, stated in an interview that "it is necessary to explain both to the people of the Urals and to the people of Moscow that we are not fighting for the breakup of Russia, but for equal rights of all subjects of the Federation."[13]

The idea that the formation of the Urals Republic was necessary owing to constitutional inequality was not confined only to Sverdlovsk political elites such as Rossel and Grebenkin. V. Basmanov, a graduate student from Sverdlovsk, wrote an article to express his support for the initiative of the Sverdlovsk Oblast Soviet. He argued that "one must consider the declaration of a Urals Republic as a first step on the path to building a state based on new principles – on the principle of the priorities of the interests of territories and equal rights of all territories forming the state."[14]

The idea of constitutional inequality was also expressed by Valerii Trushnikov. Trushnikov had served as first vice-chairman of the Sverdlovsk Soviet Executive Committee (*ispolnitel'nyi komitet soveta* or ispolkom), and later as first vice-head of the Sverdlovsk Administration and chairman of the Government of the Urals Republic. However, after Rossel was fired as head of the oblast administration for his involvement in the movement for a Urals Republic, Trushnikov was appointed by Yeltsin as head of the Sverdlovsk administration.[15] Following his appointment, Trushnikov gave his views on the movement for a Urals Republic in an interview:

It is absurd to accuse people of the Urals of separatism or striving towards isolation – we wanted to be of equal rights with all other krais, oblasts, [and] republics entering the Russian Federation. If in the past projects of the Constitution of the Russian

---

[12] "O statuse Sverdlovskoi Oblasti v sostave Rossiiskoi Federatsii," *Ural'skii rabochii*, no. 123, 7 July 1993, p. 1.

[13] "Glavnoe, chtoby nas poniali," *Vechernii Ekaterinburg*, no. 135, 21 July 1993, p. 1.

[14] V. Basmanov, "Ural'skaia Respublika – start v budushchee Rossii," *Na smenu!*, no. 133, 20 July 1993, p. 1.

[15] Trushnikov was not the ideal choice for central authorities because he had actively participated in the movement for the Urals Republic, but central authorities were limited in their choice by the fact that there were not many officials in Sverdlovsk who had not been involved in and supportive of the Urals Republic.

Federation these equal rights had been provided for – there would have been no need to work on the organization of a Urals Republic.[16]

One of the ways in which Sverdlovsk actors portrayed constitutional inequality was by articulating and underscoring the differences between republics on the one hand and oblasts and krais on the other. Aleksei Vorob'ev, director of the Office of the Head of Administration of Sverdlovsk Oblast and one of the principal writers of the Constitution of the Urals Republic, wrote in an article that "in contrast to krais and oblasts, sovereign republics received the right to determine independently the system of institutions of power and administration, budget and tax policies, [and] the activities of federal institutions located in the republican administrative-territorial units."[17]

In addition to calling for rights equal to republics, some Sverdlovsk actors also openly questioned the legitimacy of any type of distinction between administrative-territorial units on the basis of ethnicity or nationality. For example, Aleksandr Levin, the press secretary of Eduard Rossel, wrote: "Why do we need to become a republic? In order to receive economic, legal, and political independence."[18] He then claimed that "it is necessary to find new (and all new – it's good to forget about the old) approaches to the formation of the state." In particular, Levin was arguing against the principle of rights being accorded to specific ethnic groups and in particular, the "titular" groups of the republics (i.e., Tatars in Tatarstan). In arguing against special privileges for republics, Levin disparaged the idea that republics even represent national groups. He wrote that

in Sverdlovsk Oblast live people of 120 nationalities. What – are we supposed to choose a titular nation? It's no secret that in a number of republics, in handing out the passport, the question [regarding nationality] is put point-blank: either you fill in "titular", or you'll be fined. Understandably, there are few who want to be fined.[19]

Here Levin is referring to the process of filling in the nationality question on the passport and suggesting that political and economic pressure was put on citizens to declare themselves part of the titular group, presumably

---

[16] "Zhizn' prodolzhaetsia. Trudnaia zhizn'...," *Oblastnaia gazeta*, no. 131, 16 November 1993, p. 1.
[17] Vorob'ev, 25 July 1993, p. 2.
[18] Aleksandr Levin, "Desiat' dnei v noiabre," *Oblastnaia gazeta*, no. 137, 1 December 1993, p. 3.
[19] Ibid.

in order to increase the political and economic power of the group and, via the titular group, the power of the republic as well.

Rossel similarly criticized the idea of nationality-based rights and un-equal rights among the territories of the Federation. In an interview fol-lowing the adoption of the Urals Constitution and the formal declaration of the Urals Republic, Rossel explained that "with our decision, we say 'no' to a federation based on a union of sovereign states. With our decision we say 'no' to a federation on the basis of self-determined nations. We also say 'no' to a federation of unequal subjects."[20]

Among the articles that I considered, two Russian Federation actors who argued in favor of the Urals Republic also cited constitutional in-equality as the primary reason for support. Georgii Satarov, director of the Center for Applied Political Research (*Tsentr prikladnykh politicheskikh issledovanii* (*informatika dlia demokratii*) or INDEM), stated in an interview that "in voting for the Urals Republic, the leadership of Sverdlovsk made it clear that Russian krais and oblasts no longer intend to be calmly recon-ciled to the existence of more privileged subjects of the Federation, such as in the case of republics."[21] Similarly, an expert from the Russian Con-stitutional Conference, Viacheslav Nikonov called the declaration of the Urals Republic "a natural reaction to the inequality of the subjects of the Federation."[22]

In Favor of the Urals Republic: Economic Inequality and Autonomy

Articles citing constitutional or economic inequality were often related be-cause constitutional equality was supposed to lead to economic equality, and economic inequality was considered a reason for seeking constitutional equality. In some cases, the same actors made arguments based on assertions of both constitutional inequality and economic inequality.

One sign of the relationship between economic and constitutional claims appears in an article that reported on an opinion poll taken in August 1993. The poll was based on the answers of 163 randomly selected residents of Sverdlovsk Oblast (including 61 residents of Ekaterinburg). Besides show-ing support for the oblast soviet's decision to change the status of Sverdlovsk

---

[20] Eduard Rossel, "K zhiteliam Ural'skoi Respubliki: obrashchenie E. E. Rosselia," *Vechernii Ekaterinburg*, no. 212, 5 November 1993, p. 2.
[21] "Torg budet neumesten," *Ural'skii rabochii*, no. 124, 8 July 1993, p. 1.
[22] "Lish' by ne separatisty," *Ural'skii rabochii*, no. 124, 8 July 1993, p. 1. The Constitutional Conference was set up in 1993 to draft a new Russian constitution.

Oblast (55% of respondents – up from 40% in July), the poll also reported that 46% of respondents "were hoping that the vote for the Urals Republic [by the oblast soviet on July 2, 1993] would change the economic position of the oblast for the better," and 23% hoped that the vote would "secure equality of all subjects of the Russian Federation." The poll also found that, among those who voted "yes" to the referendum on 25 April 1993, 72% supported the July decision of the oblast soviet.[23] While the numbers in the poll are not especially remarkable, the fact that the questions regarding support for the Urals Republic focused on the economic position of the oblast and equality of subjects of the Federation provides evidence that those issues were both salient factors in support for the Urals Republic.

Yet, in some cases, a sense of particularly *economic* grievance is clear from a close reading of the arguments. For example, one of the arguments for why Sverdlovsk's economy would improve with the creation of a Urals Republic relied on the assumption that Sverdlovsk was truly a wealthy region and that under regional as opposed to Moscow-based governance of the economy, Sverdlovsk would be able realize its full economic capacity. For example, in an article explaining why the status of the oblast needed to be raised to that of republic, Rossel reasoned that because of "the economic potential of Sverdlovsk Oblast" the territory would prosper if Sverdlovsk authorities were given more responsibility in the form of higher status in the Federation. Rossel argued that "raising the status [of Sverdlovsk Oblast] would allow the [oblast] soviet to more urgently decide questions of financial independence by leaving to it [the oblast soviet] the same level of authority over spending of oblast revenue as is held by such republics as Bashkortostan and Tatarstan."[24]

Rossel's statement makes clear that a central aspect of economic responsibility concerned control over taxation. In an interview in late July 1993, Rossel declared that "my basic argument of its advantage [the founding of a Urals Republic] – is the necessity of economic equal rights of regions. Tax assessment of the territories should be equal. Nothing else is worth the idea of the Urals Republic."[25] Also, an article reporting on the press conference

---

[23] "Storonnikov vse bol'she," *Oblastnaia gazeta*, no. 97, 27 August 1993, p. 2. The referendum asked residents whether they agreed that Sverdlovsk should have the same rights as republics. I discuss the referendum in greater detail in Chapter 7.

[24] "My ne soshli c konstitutsionnogo polia," *Na smenu!*, no. 124, 7 July 1993, p. 1.

[25] Eduard Rossel, "Zhizn' u nas segodnia takaia, chto bez politiki nikak nel'zia . . . ," *Ural'skaia gazeta*, no. 23, July 1993, pp. 2–3.

given by Rossel and Grebenkin following the vote by the Sverdlovsk Oblast Soviet to change the status of the oblast, explained that the "basic goal of the creation of the Urals Republic is a sharp increase in the tempo of reform of the local economy, since currently the legal basis of the Russian Federation lags behind the demands of life."[26] The article also noted that Sverdlovsk was paying 1.2 trillion rubles into the federal budget and that "naturally, republican status provides the possibility for leaving in 'our treasury' considerably more resources for solving internal problems."[27] Another article on the press conference elaborated on this point in greater detail. The reporter wrote:

But we cannot, in particular, allow that the oblast collected taxes in the sum of 1.2 trillion rubles, but left us – 360 billion. To where and for what goes our money, we don't know. And the main point of disagreement is not in order to grab more to eat. We after all are ready to help the weak, the backward. But we should know about this [aid] in detail: where, to whom, and how much. And what kind of return? And what will we (oblast or Urals Republic) get out of it (either today or in the future)?[28]

A third article on the press conference noted that the change in status of Sverdlovsk Oblast was necessary "first of all in order to protect our economic interests." The reporter followed this statement with the warning, "we don't want to be second-class people in our own country."[29]

The issue of equal taxation was largely directed against the republics, which, it was argued, paid less in taxes and received more subsidies as well as political autonomy than oblasts. One reporter wrote:

And, let's honestly say: Well, what are today's sovereign republics? They are getting the chance to form independently not only a system of institutions of power and administration on their territory (which is tempting enough), but also to define budget and tax policies, to engage in independent foreign trade, to have their own private property, real estate, and above all – to control the work of federal organizations, and yes still also to receive from our pie a large slice for their own table (subsidies) – who would freely refuse such a gift? And that is why, in protection of their privileges, the national card is raised. But many republics have among them

---

[26] S. Riabov, "Dva mneniia ob Ural'skoi Respublike: za," *Ural'skaia gazeta*, no. 22, July 1993, p. 1.
[27] Ibid.
[28] B. Timofeev, "Za ruku ne kusai kormiashchuiu," *Ural'skii rabochii*, no. 122, 6 July 1993, p. 1.
[29] L. Minina, "Khotim okhladit' goriachie golovy, – zaiavliaiut 'roditeli' Ural'skoi Respubliki," *Vechernii Ekaterinburg*, no. 125, 7 July 1993, p. 1.

only a small percent, as we say, of the titular nation. That is why in many cases over the fence of sovereignty stick up the hairy ears of economic interests.[30]

Although the movement for a Urals Republic was aimed at turning Sverdlovsk Oblast into a republic, leaders in Sverdlovsk repeatedly emphasized that by republican status they mainly sought economic as opposed to cultural autonomy or full political independence. In an interview in August 1993, Eduard Rossel attempted to clarify the goals of the movement for a Urals Republic. He said, "we don't need sovereignty, nor our own passport, flag, crest, hymn, [or] borders. We recognize citizenship and the superiority of the laws of Russia. But, we really need economic and legal independence. This would give us the possibility to more quickly and less painfully reform the economy."[31]

In this same interview, Rossel highlighted another theme of the debate over economic equality and autonomy, namely, the idea that Sverdlovsk, because of its particular industrial organization, was more negatively affected by central economic policies than other regions of Russia. Rossel stated that Sverdlovsk is "in general the single, stable, uninterrupted working oblast." In explaining current conditions, he continued, "yes, industrial production fell. But after all, this was all military orders. Now demand for the output of 'defense industries' [oboronki] gradually is increasing, [and] production is growing."[32] This statement nicely combines bits of economic reality agreed upon by outside sources with specific regional interpretations. Indeed, central defense orders were cut, and production declined in Sverdlovsk, but Sverdlovsk was not, according to non-Sverdlovsk accounts, the "single, stable uninterrupted working oblast."

The idea that Sverdlovsk's economy was a victim of central economic policy was repeated in several articles regarding the issue of economic inequality and the movement for a Urals Republic. In support of the movement for a Urals Republic, B. Karpov, chairman of the governing board of the Urals Department of the All-Russia Culture Fund, wrote that, in regard to economic policy, "in the Urals they always put in the minimum, and took out the maximum – that's how it always was."[33] Karpov also made an

---

[30] B. Timofeev, "Ch'i ushi za suverennym zaborom," Ural'skii rabochii, no. 121, 3 July 1993, p. 1.

[31] Eduard Rossel, "Nam ne nuzhen suverenitet, no ochen' nuzhna ekonomicheskaia i zakonodatel'naia samostoiatel'nost'," Na smenu!, no. 144, 4 August 1993, p. 2.

[32] Ibid.

[33] B. Karpov, "Podumaite sperva, ne otvergaite srazu," Vechernii Ekaterinburg, no. 132, 16 July 1993, p. 2.

argument about the why the Urals region was suffering under the current economic policy. He wrote:

The primary and most important wealth of the Urals – is factories. Metallurgy, machine building, complex technology, qualified workers with unique specializations. Today our Urals wealth is under threat "thanks" to the out of control policies of the central Moscow leadership. The dubious state economic experiment, called conversion, deprived Russia of the traditional market for the sale of armaments. These markets today are made up of aggressive competitors, but Urals factories and the Russian treasury are deprived of millions of dollars. Why is it that in this difficult time free Tatarstan, by unknown means, receives (and controls in contrast to Sverdlovsk Oblast) the right to specially export armaments abroad.[34]

Similarly, in an article entitled, "Our Rights We Take Ourselves," which was published following the decision of the Sverdlovsk Oblast Soviet to change its status to republic, a Sverdlovsk reporter stated that, in the Federation, which divides subjects into "three unequal grades," Sverdlovsk is "again given the role of supplier of food and means for the well-to-do existence of others."[35] The reporter further stated that "in the last few years we, it seems, became peculiar hostages of the new powers: Sverdlovsk Oblast supports the president and his policies almost totally, independent of how people are living under them – while there, on top, evidently, they decided to give us back nothing." Here the author is likely referring to the extraordinarily high level of support by Sverdlovsk elites and citizens alike for Yeltsin during 1991–3, despite Yeltsin's lack of support for the equal rights of oblasts and republics and his lack of specific economic support for Sverdlovsk. In explaining how it is possible that such a situation could exist, the reporter wrote that "we are just like in the old anecdote, remember: The Urals – that's the place where they still work."[36]

The idea that Sverdlovsk was faring worse than other regions despite the hard work of its population and despite its support of central policies was also articulated in an article by Galina Karelova, a vice-chairman of the oblast soviet. In her article, entitled "First Step to Freedom," Karelova explained why Sverdlovsk was currently in a particularly bad economic position. Karelova noted that Soviet planning had oriented the economy of Sverdlovsk toward industry rather than consumer goods. She also claimed

[34] Ibid.
[35] Natal'ia Ponomareva, "Svoi prava voz'mem sebe sami," *Oblastnaia gazeta*, no. 75, 6 July 1993, p. 1.
[36] Ibid.

that with the breakup of Soviet economic relations, the lack of state orders for industrial goods, and the extreme weakening of investment, Sverdlovsk became a supplier of raw materials, metals, and machines. But Karelova argued that in a time of crisis other regions could "hold out" without these goods; however, she explained, "from [other regions], we need those goods which are demanded by people today – grain, sugar, butter, meat, etc." In characterizing current relations between regions in the Russian Federation, Karelova wrote that "from any point of view, any analysis of the change in economic relations [since the Soviet period] would show that they [economic relations] currently do not favor oblasts." In order to improve this situation, Karelova said that "time and a great amount of money" are necessary for restructuring, and it is for that reason that Sverdlovsk Oblast has raised the question of aid to republics. She wrote that "all aid should be built only on an equal basis, and not on the basis of old ideological and political stereotypes." Thus, Karelova argued that the decision of the Oblast Soviet was a move toward "protection of the interests of the population of the oblast" and, she contended, "the issue is not ambition by [regional] powers, but the socioeconomic position of Sverdlovsk Oblast."[37]

In a less generous interpretation of central economic policy toward Sverdlovsk, Dr. Vladimir Kuznetsov wrote an article affirming that the Urals Republic would be a means of saving the resources of Sverdlovsk from Moscow bureaucrats and foreigners. Kuznetsov wrote that "the creation of republics among regions of Russia deprives central bureaucrats of the possibility of giving away without any control the wealth of Russia to countries of the near and far abroad." He went on to declare that

If the whole country were created according to the example of the Urals Republic, that is, regional republics, then nine out of every ten Moscow bureaucrats would lose their lucrative position and be forced to earn bread by their own labor. The creation of the Urals Republic appears as the first step in the freeing of the country from the putrid venom of these bureaucrats.[38]

Although not all arguments regarding the Urals Republic were as vivid as Kuznetsov's, the preceding discussion of articles suggests the significant

---

[37] Galina Karelova, "Pervyi shag k svobode," *Oblastnaia gazeta*, no. 100, 3 September 1993, p. 2.
[38] Vladimir Kuznetsov, "Luchshe zhit' svoim umom," *Oblastnaia gazeta*, no. 98, 31 August 1993, p. 2.

role of the idea of economic inequality and autonomy in support for the Urals Republic.

In Favor of the Urals Republic: New Federalism

In contrast to the arguments about inequality and autonomy, the articles containing arguments in the category of *new federalism* considered the Urals Republic as an opportunity for novel institutional development, as opposed to a measure aimed at correcting festering injustices. One such line of argument was that territorial structures like the Urals Republic could serve as new, more cooperative, and harmonious multinational units. One article, entitled "Urals Republic – The Most Multinational in the World," reported on the International Congress of Finno-Ugric Culture held in Khanty-Mansiisk in July 1993.[39] Several scholars at the conference expressed support for the Urals Republic as a model of a multinational territorial formation that would unite various ethnic groups with their "Russian brothers." One specialist even proposed that the Mansi people should join the Urals Republic, with the Urals Republic including several oblasts in the greater Urals region.

A second type of article in the new federalism category concerned democratization. For example, representatives from various small parties and organizations in Sverdlovsk published an article in which they stated: "we support the creation of a republic, since we see in it the natural result of the on-going growth in our society of democratic processes." These representatives considered decentralized power to be more democratic and responsive to local needs. The representatives wrote that with the creation of a republic "the regional government will be more protective of the interests of the residents of the region and considerate of their opinions as opposed to [government] departments which are thousands of kilometers away."[40]

The new federalism articles made up a relatively small minority of the total number of articles in support of the Urals Republic, yet they witness the fluidity of political and economic categories during the period of the movement for the Urals Republic. That is, the Urals Republic represented a novel approach to the organization of politics and economics.

---

[39] D. Agurov, "Ural'skaia Respublika – samaia mnogonatsional'naia v mire," *Na smenu!*, no. 129, 14 July 1993, p. 2.

[40] D. Nedobeiko, V. Tolstenko, and B. Guseltov, et al., "Ural'skaia Respublika – tozhe sub"ekt," *Na smenu!*, no. 168, 8 September 1993, p. 2.

Table 6.3 *Articles Containing Arguments Against the Urals Republic:*
Relationship Between Actors' Locations and Reasons for Opposing the Urals Republic

	Location of the Actor Whose Argument Is Reported in the Article			
Primary Reason for Opposing the Urals Republic	Sverdlovsk Oblast	Russian Federation	Moscow	All Locations
Illegal/Unconstitutional	2	0	4	6
	20%	0%	50%	32%
Threat to Russian statehood	8	0	3	11
	80%	0%	38%	58%
Nothing to disagree on	0	0	1	1
	0%	0%	12%	5%
Need for economic connections	0	1	0	1
	0%	100%	0%	5%
All positions	10	1	8	19
	100%	100%	100%	100%

Fisher's exact test = 0.033.

Arguments Against the Movement for a Urals Republic

Now let us turn our attention to the arguments against the movement. By analyzing negative arguments both in terms of the *reasons for opposing* the movement as well as the *acknowledged causes* of the movement, the sense of shared regional understandings becomes visible. The reasons for opposition may or may not correspond to the acknowledged cause of the movement. However, to the extent that actors from similar locations share beliefs about the underlying causes of the movement, it suggests similar understandings of local political and economic conditions, even if solutions differ.

As a first step in this analysis, Table 6.3 presents a subset of Table 6.1, containing the 19 articles opposing the Urals Republic, showing the relationship between the actor's location and the primary reason for opposition.[41] In Table 6.3 the first row, entitled "Illegal/Unconstitutional," contains articles whose primary argument against the Urals Republic was that its formation went against the Russian Constitution or other laws of the Russian Federation, including presidential decrees. The second row among the reasons for opposition, entitled "Threat to Russian statehood," contains articles in which the primary argument against the Urals Republic

---

[41] These articles are listed in row 1 of Table 6.1. Table 6.3 is similar to the presentation of data in Table 6.2 but contains the articles opposing rather than supporting the Urals Republic.

was that it would weaken the unity, or even cause the disintegration, of the Russian state, similar to the fate of the USSR. The row entitled "Nothing to disagree on" contains an article in which the reason for opposing the Urals Republic is that the actor does not see any reason for Sverdlovsk to be dissatisfied with the status quo. Finally, the row entitled "Need for economic connections" contains an article in which an actor argues that the creation of a Urals Republic would work against strengthening inter-regional economic relationships and therefore make the economy as a whole in Russia worse off.

For all actors, the most frequently cited reasons for opposition (17 out of 19) were that the movement was illegal or unconstitutional, or that it was a threat to Russian statehood. For Sverdlovsk actors, the majority of articles opposed to the Urals Republic cited the threat to Russian statehood as the primary reason for opposition (8 of 10 articles). Even though Table 6.3 suggests that location has some effect on the reason for opposing the Urals Republic movement, the difference is not large.

In contrast to the arguments favoring the Urals Republic where the causes of the movement and reasons for support were largely identical, in the case of the arguments against the Urals Republic, the reason for opposition was almost always different from the acknowledged causes. Thus, the next step in the analysis is to consider the acknowledged causes of the Urals Republic movement. If pro-Urals Republic supporters were making up claims about the basis for the movement, we would expect anti-Urals Republic arguments to debunk the claims of supporters because, presumably, those who opposed the Urals Republic would not have had incentives to construct explanations of the causes of the movement that were similar to the explanations offered by proponents.

Table 6.4 takes the same 19 opposition articles from Table 6.3 but illustrates the relationship between actor location and acknowledged cause of the Urals Republic movement. As in Table 6.2, the rows headed by "Constitutional inequality" and "Economic inequality" in Table 6.4 contain articles with arguments in which both constitutional and economic inequality were referenced as a motivation for the movement to create a Urals Republic. But, in addition to constitutional and economic inequality, Table 6.4 also contains two additional acknowledged causes of the Urals Republic: the row headed by "Increase in power of regional elites" contains articles in which it was argued that the movement for the Urals Republic was simply an attempt by Sverdlovsk political elites to gain more power, and the row headed by "Misunderstandings of economics" contains an article in which

Table 6.4 *Articles Containing Arguments Against the Urals Republic:*
Relationship Between Actors' Locations and Acknowledged Causes of the Urals Republic

	Location of the Actor Whose Argument Is Reported in the Article			
Acknowledged Cause of the Urals Republic	Sverdlovsk Oblast	Russian Federation	Moscow	All Locations
Constitutional inequality	4	0	1	5
	40%	0%	12%	26%
Economic inequality	6	0	0	6
	60%	0%	0%	32%
Increase power of regional elites	0	0	3	3
	0%	0%	38%	16%
Misunderstanding of economics	0	1	0	1
	0%	100%	0%	5%
No cause given	0	0	4	4
	0%	0%	50%	21%
All acknowledged causes	10	1	8	19
	100%	100%	100%	100%

Fisher's exact test $= 0.000$.

an actor argues that the movement for the Urals Republic was caused by a lack of proper understanding of economics by Sverdlovsk elites. Finally, the row headed "No cause given" contains articles in which no cause for the Urals Republic was acknowledged.

In this case, the results are starker. An actor's location is strongly correlated with the acknowledged cause of the Urals Republic movement. All Sverdlovsk actors who opposed the Urals Republic cited either constitutional or economic inequality as an acknowledged cause of the movement, despite the actor's opposition to the movement. In contrast, only one Moscow actor and no Russian Federation actor acknowledged constitutional or economic inequality as the basis for the Urals Republic movement.

The significance of this finding is that it supports the claim that inequality was not a concept merely invented by elites who stood to gain from the creation of a Urals Republic. If that were the case, we would expect the arguments of political opponents of the Urals Republic to have exposed the spuriousness of the claim of inequality put forth by proponents of the Urals Republic. More detailed analysis of the actual arguments of actors from different locations will further illustrate this claim.

Table 6.5 *Articles Containing Arguments by Sverdlovsk Actors Against the Urals Republic Movement:*
Acknowledged Causes of the Movement and Reasons for Opposition

Acknowledged Cause of the Movement for a Urals Republic	Primary Reason for Opposing the Urals Republic		
	Illegal/Unconstitutional	Threat to Russian Statehood	All Reasons
Constitutional inequality	0	4	4
Economic inequality	2	4	6
All acknowledged causes	2	8	10

Arguments by Sverdlovsk Actors Against the Urals Republic

In focusing on arguments against the Urals Republic by Sverdlovsk actors only, Table 6.5 combines the first columns from Tables 6.3 and 6.4, presenting the arguments according to reason for opposition and acknowledged causes of the movement.[42] In Table 6.5, the columns list the reasons for opposing the Urals Republic, while the rows list the acknowledged causes of the movement.

As noted in Table 6.4, in *all* articles in which Sverdlovsk actors opposed the Urals Republic, either constitutional or economic inequality was acknowledged as a cause of the movement, despite the actor's opposition to the movement. Remarkably, Sverdlovsk actors arguing against the Urals Republic did not dispute the pro-Urals Republics claims of economic and constitutional inequality. Instead, they focused mainly on the illegality (or lack of constitutional basis) of the Urals Republic and on the threat to the integrity of the Russian Federation. The majority of articles opposed to the Urals Republic cited the threat to Russian statehood as the primary reason for opposition.

Sverdlovsk Opposition: The Urals Republic Is Illegal/Unconstitutional

One of the principal arguments of deputies who voted against the change in status of Sverdlovsk Oblast to republic was that the results of the referendum of April 1993 spoke only to economic issues, and that without a specific referendum on changing Sverdlovsk's political status, any move

---

[42] The data in this table also appear in the top left cell of Table 6.1.

to do so would be unconstitutional. For example, in a public declaration, four deputies who voted against the change wrote that "voters did not vote for the creation of a Urals state, but only for the support of the idea of raising the economic status of the oblast."[43] This statement suggests that the deputies acknowledged economic inequality and the need for greater economic autonomy in Sverdlovsk, but they considered the creation of a Urals Republic unconstitutional. In similar fashion, V. Ivanov, a metal worker from Ekaterinburg, wrote a letter to the editor of the newspaper *Na smenu!* disagreeing with the oblast soviet's vote to change the status of Sverdlovsk. Mr. Ivanov argued that Sverdlovsk's movement for "economic independence" was illegally widened to include political independence.[44] In his article, Mr. Ivanov did not deny the economic basis of the movement for the Urals Republic, but he argued that the movement was not proceeding according to the Constitution.

Sverdlovsk Opposition: The Urals Republic Threatens Russian Statehood

Although the lack of constitutional basis or the illegality was important to some Sverdlovsk actors, the majority of Sverdlovsk actors who opposed the Urals Republic did so because of the threat posed by the Urals Republic to the statehood of the Russian Federation; in other words, they feared the disintegration of Russia, similar to the breakup of the Soviet Union. In an official announcement, the deputies who voted against the change of status to republic outlined why they opposed the change. The dissenting deputies wrote: "we consider, that the given decision is not conducive to the setting up of genuine equal rights, but brings further tension to internal relations in Russia and threatens the unity of the country."[45] In the statement, the deputies made clear that they supported the establishment of equal rights, but they opposed the vote for changing the status of Sverdlovsk on the grounds that it threatened the integrity of the state as a whole.

Similarly, in an article explaining his opposition to the Urals Republic, Iurii Samarin, the chairman of the Ekaterinburg City Soviet, wrote, "I, of course, am for socioeconomic equality. But in a civilized way. The center

---

[43] Iu. V. Lipatnikov et al., "Zaiavlenie: protiv," *Ural'skaia gazeta*, no. 22, July 1993, p. 1.
[44] V. Ivanov, "Ural – opornyi krai respublik," *Na smenu!*, no. 136, 23 July 1993, p. 1.
[45] "Zaiavlenie," *Oblastnaia gazeta*, no. 76, 7 July 1993, p. 1.

should finally determine the needs for the maintenance of the state as a whole and agree on normative deductions [of tax obligations] with subjects of the Federation."[46] However, although Samarin acknowledged that a fair regional policy was needed, he then admitted, "in the referendum I said 'No' to equal rights for Sverdlovsk Oblast with republics. And it is not because these rights somehow bother me. Something else bothers me. What bothers me is anxiety, based on the fact that now, similar declarations can split Russia. And after that there will be no talk about equal rights." Samarin's argument was that although he was for equal rights for Sverdlovsk in principle, the reality of the chaos that would follow the breakup of Russia, which itself would be the result of declarations of greater sovereignty by oblasts such as Sverdlovsk, would leave the oblast with fewer rights than the current situation of unequal rights with republics.

Another example of this argument, which acknowledged inequality but opposed the Urals Republic as a threat to the integrity of Russia, can be found in an article that chronicled the meeting between Vladimir Isakov, a prominent legislative deputy in the Supreme Soviet of the Russian Federation from Sverdlovsk, who headed the Committee of the Supreme Soviet for Constitutional Legislation, and deputies of the Sverdlovsk Oblast Soviet. When Isakov was asked to explain his position toward the Urals Republic, he began his remarks by saying that the most pressing problem facing Russia was the issue of unity because "the same processes of disintegration, which had at one time brought about the breakup of the USSR, were at work in Russia." Isakov later acknowledged that there were "deformities" in the rights of oblasts and krais as compared to republics, and he stated that the Constitutional Committee had suggested giving to oblasts and krais "those rights which republics have in the economic sphere." However, Isakov ultimately believed in the possibility of working out any inequities through discussions over the new constitution, and he was opposed to the Urals Republic because he considered that it would lead to the "destruction of Russia."[47]

The idea that the creation of the Urals Republic was a threat to Russia and therefore not the proper solution to inequality was held not only by democrats such as Samarin and Isakov but also by Russian nationalists. The

[46] Iurii Samarin, "Ura, respublika!" *Na smenu!*, no. 159, 26 August 1993, p. 1.
[47] Natal'ia Ponomareva, "A my poidem svoim putem," *Oblastnaia gazeta*, no. 103, 14 September 1993, p. 2.

Sverdlovsk chairman of the *Rodina* (Motherland) movement and central committee member of the Liberal Democratic Party of Russia (*Liberal'no-demokraticheskaia partiia Rossii* or LDPR), V. Sen'ko, opposed the movement for a Urals Republic.[48] He wrote, "the creation of the Urals Republic – it is an instinctual, biological, live response to the pressure of federal power and national republics."[49] Sen'ko also added that "Russia truly needs a regionalization of politics, politics which will strengthen the rights and possibilities of distinct Russian lands." However, he cautioned, "politics should be carried out with appropriate means and in the framework of a single Power [*edinoi Derzhavy*], not by the path of artificial cultivation of new states on her territory."[50]

Like the LDPR, the party activists of the Ekaterinburg Organization of the Communist Party of the Russian Federation opposed the vote by the oblast soviet as posing a danger to Russian unity. It was reported that the activists claimed that "political and short-term economic advantages can turn out to have too high a cost for Russia."[51] However, the communists, in contrast to the LDPR, acknowledged economic inequality in particular as the motivating source of the Urals Republic movement. The communist activists "agreed that in the Federation there should be neither privileged nor socially-economically pinched subjects. No one should live on the expense of another." Echoing this sentiment, a deputy in the Ekaterinburg City Soviet and chairman of the Glasnost Committee, Stanislav Iachevskii, said in an interview, "I do not deny itself the idea of more economic independence of the region." However, Iachevskii argued that "the step by the oblast soviet is of a provocative character. Following behind it will be an escalation of tensions within Russia."[52]

A parliamentary correspondent, B. Iarkov, who opposed the decision of the Sverdlovsk Oblast Soviet was even more dire in his prediction of the consequences of Sverdlovsk's decision. He wrote that "the decision of the session of the Sverdlovsk Oblast Soviet probably will serve as a detonator, as incitement for other oblasts. We really stand as an example, as a nasty

---

[48] The Liberal Democratic Party of Russia is, despite its name, neither liberal nor democratic. The party is led by Vladimir Zhirinovskii, a xenophobic Russian nationalist.
[49] V. Sen'ko, "Opyt drevnei gretsii – na sluzhby gosmuzham," *Ural'skii rabochii*, no. 127, 13 July 1993, p. 2.
[50] Ibid.
[51] G. Shteinberg, "Ne toi dorogoi," *Ural'skii rabochii*, no. 126, 10 July 1993, p. 1.
[52] "Respublika rezoniruet," *Na smenu!*, no. 124, 7 July 1993, p. 1.

example, for imitation." Regarding the solution to the crisis facing Russia, Iarkov wrote that "the exit is not in the political leveling of statuses of subjects of the Federation, but in economics."[53]

In general, arguments against the Urals Republic put forth by Sverdlovsk actors demonstrate that those Sverdlovsk actors who opposed the creation of the Urals Republic did so because they considered it either a threat to Russia or unconstitutional, but they did not deny that Sverdlovsk was being treated unfairly in economic policy and in the Constitution. This finding suggests that economic and constitutional inequality was not merely a concept strategically invented by regional elites in Sverdlovsk. Moreover, these articles are further evidence that the narrative of inequality and negative treatment of the region by Moscow, as suggested by the discussion of the economy in Chapter 5, played a critical role in the movement for the Urals Republic.

Arguments by Moscow and Russian Federation Actors Against the Movement for a Urals Republic

The principal difference in the arguments made by Sverdlovsk and non-Sverdlovsk actors against the Urals Republic is that actors in Moscow and the Russian Federation almost never cited constitutional and economic inequality as a cause of the movement for the Urals Republic. Table 6.6 contains arguments by Moscow and Russian Federation actors who opposed the Urals Republic. Similar to Table 6.5, Table 6.6 presents articles according to the primary reason for opposing the movement as well as the acknowledged cause of the movement. In comparison with Table 6.5 (which contained arguments by Sverdlovsk actors), there are both more types of reasons for opposing the Urals Republic and more types of causes attributed to the movement.

From Table 6.6, we see that 8 out of the 9 articles by Moscow and Russian Federation actors do not acknowledge economic or constitutional inequality as a cause of the movement for a Urals Republic. This is in sharp contrast to Table 6.5 in which all Sverdlovsk actors acknowledged some kind of inequality as a cause of the Urals Republic. In addition, it is notable that only Moscow actors make the argument that the Urals Republic is an attempt by regional elites to gain more power. Discussion of the actual

---

[53] B. Iarkov, "Deputatskaia publika i Ural'skaia Respublika," *Na smenu!*, no. 123, 6 July 1993, p. 1.

Table 6.6 *Articles Containing Arguments by Moscow and Russian Federation Actors Against the Urals Republic Movement:*
Acknowledged Causes of the Movement and Reasons for Opposition

Acknowledged Cause of the Movement for a Urals Republic	Primary Reason for Opposing the Urals Republic				
	Illegal/ Unconstitutional	Threat to Russian Statehood	Nothing to Disagree on	Need for Economic Connections	All Reasons
Constitutional & economic inequality	0	1	0	0	1
Increase power of regional elites	1	2	0	0	3
Misunderstanding of economics	0	0	0	1[a]	1
No cause given	3	0	1	0	4
All acknowledged causes	4	3	1	1	9

[a] Russian Federation actor.

arguments by non-Sverdlovsk actors against the Urals Republic will further illustrate how the Moscow and Russian Federation actors understood the movement for a Urals Republic.

Moscow Opposition: The Urals Republic Is Illegal/Unconstitutional

One of the two main arguments against the Urals Republic was that it was illegal and unconstitutional. Although some Sverdlovsk actors agreed with this position, their view of the basis of the movement was quite different from Moscow actors. The comments of Nikolai Medvedev, the chairman of the Russian Federation Commission for the Nationalities-Federation System and Inter-ethnic Relations, exemplifies the very negative view of the actions and motives of Sverdlovsk elites. On the same day as the adoption of the Constitution of the Urals Republic (27 October 1993), Medvedev issued a response in which he strongly criticized the actions of the Sverdlovsk Oblast Soviet. Medvedev said that the decision "has once again vividly proved the irresponsibility of these obsolescent power bodies, their political ambitiousness and lack of any prospect for them." Medvedev said that the adoption of the Urals Republic Constitution "can be qualified as

217

non-compliance with known decrees of the President regarding the steps towards constitutional reform." Moreover, he stated:

Subjects of the Federation have clear-cut functions. Even if there were no decrees from the president, under the present constitution, oblast soviets do not have the right to decide questions of national-territorial structure. This decision complies neither with the existing constitution, nor even with the draft of a new constitution to be discussed today by the Constitutional Conference. A region can have only a charter, not a constitution.

Medvedev declared that by its actions the Sverdlovsk Oblast Soviet had "exceeded its powers clearly set in the Federation Treaty and the Russian Constitution." At the end of the interview, Medvedev restated his view of the cause of the movement for a Urals Republic by ominously suggesting that "one of the possible variants of resolving the situation – is to call to account the irresponsible leadership of the [Sverdlovsk Oblast] Soviet. It is fully realistic that the soviet can be disbanded, but the officials in such an event should be held personally responsible."[54]

In contrast to Medvedev's accusation of the role of Sverdlovsk elites in the movement for the Urals Republic, other articles in which the Urals Republic was denounced as illegal or unconstitutional did not explicitly offer an explanation of the cause the Urals Republic. For example, after the vote by the Sverdlovsk Oblast Soviet to change the status of Sverdlovsk Oblast to a republic, Yeltsin's press secretary, Viacheslav Kostikov declared that "the leveling of constitutional status cannot occur according to the wish of one or a few subjects of the Federation. Such activities affect all levels of the state structure of Russia."[55] Kostikov did not claim that Sverdlovsk elites were trying to increase their own power, but he also explicitly rejected their claims of inequality. Similarly, the head of the Administration of the President of the Russian Federation, Sergei Filatov, said that "the proclamation by the Sverdlovsk Oblast Soviet of a Urals Republic appears to be a serious blow to constitutional reform and is not conducive to the acceptance of the Basic Law of Russia."[56] But like Kostikov, Filatov offered no explanation for the movement for a Urals Republic. Finally, when Yeltsin issued a decree disbanding the Sverdlovsk Oblast Soviet and removing Rossel from his post as head of the administration because of his activity related to creating a

---

[54] N. Medvedev, "Oblastnoi sovet prevysil polnomochiia," *Ural'skii rabochii*, no. 206, 29 October 1993, p. 1.

[55] "El'tsin – protiv?" *Ural'skii rabochii*, no. 124, 8 July 1993, p. 1.

[56] "Pogrozili pal'chikom. Poka," *Ural'skii rabochii*, no. 122, 6 July 1993, p. 1.

Urals Republic, Yeltsin also offered no acknowledgment of what had caused the Urals Republic. According to the president's press service, the decree which halted the activities of the Sverdlovsk Oblast Soviet on 9 November 1993 was simply the result of "the repeated breach by the [Sverdlovsk Oblast] Soviet of the Constitution of Russia and Russian laws."[57]

Moscow Opposition: The Urals Republic Threatens Russian Statehood

As in the case of Sverdlovsk actors, non-Sverdlovsk actors' other primary reason for opposing the Urals Republic was that it threatened Russian statehood. One article by a Moscow journalist, although not singling out Sverdlovsk in particular, mildly acknowledged some inequality among the rights of oblasts and krais but argued that the movement for a Urals Republic was disruptive of the ongoing process of state-building, including constitutional reform in Russia.[58] In contrast, most other Moscow actors cited the threat to Russian statehood as a reason for opposing the Urals Republic without acknowledging any kind of inequality as a basis of the Urals Republic.[59] Instead, they followed the reasoning of Nikolai Medvedev in accusing Sverdlovsk elites of being interested in increasing their own political power. For example, Vitalii Mashkov, the Representative of the President in Sverdlovsk Oblast, gave an interview in which he stated that there was no premise for the creation of the Urals Republic except that it was "in the interests of elite groups in the power structure." Mashkov also called the movement "a political game by the leadership of Sverdlovsk." He stated that although there was a need for regional policy, "there is one path – from the center." He stated that "everything should be done by the center administering the process, in that way we would not have had the splash of separatism by regions and we would have been able to guarantee the preservation of the integrity of Russia."[60]

---

[57] "Prezident uprazdniaet Ural'skuiu Respubliku," *Ural'skii rabochii*, no. 214, 11 November 1993, p. 1.

[58] L. Tsukanova, "Sverdlovskaia oblast' ili Ural'skaia Respublika?" *Vechernii Ekaterinburg*, no. 212, 5 November 1993, p. 2.

[59] Interestingly, on the basis of central newspapers, Steven Solnick, "Will Russia Survive? Center and Periphery in the Russian Federation," in Barnett Rubin and Jack Snyder, eds. *Post-Soviet Political Order: Conflict and State Building* (New York: Routledge, 1998), pp. 72–5, paints a very negative picture of the Urals Republic and the reaction to it from other regions. This negative view is consistent with my analysis of the arguments of non-Sverdlovsk actors.

[60] V. V. Mashkov, "Ob Ural'skoi Respublike – vser'ez," *Doverie*, no. 42–3, 1993, p. 9b.

Moscow Opposition: Nothing to Disagree on

Yeltsin was out of the country at the time the Sverdlovsk Oblast Soviet voted to change the status of the oblast, but when he returned to Russia, his response was that he did not understand what need there was for Sverdlovsk to become a republic. He said:

In agreement with the new Constitution, republics, oblasts and krais in economic spheres have full equal rights. Among them there may be some kinds of questions, [or] grudges towards the current work of the government. All right, let's discuss these issues. But first, let's consider them in the framework of the constitutional process. In the project of the new Constitution, there is no talk of economic privilege. So, then what's the argument about? About which "special rights"? What? Do the people of the Urals really, for example, want to set up for themselves some kind of "state" language besides Russian?[61]

This was the only article I found in which the opposition to the Urals Republic was based on the idea that there was no reason for Sverdlovsk to be dissatisfied with its status as an oblast.[62] President Yeltsin's comment on the equality of all subjects in the Constitution stands in sharp contrast to the existing drafts of the Constitution at that time (July 1993) and to the statements by Sverdlovsk actors. In commenting on the Urals Republic, Yeltsin denied inequality toward Sverdlovsk but also did not attribute other negative motives to the leadership of Sverdlovsk in pursuing the movement for a Urals Republic.[63] In addition, Yeltsin also did not indicate whether he considered the Urals Republic unconstitutional or a threat to Russian statehood.

Russian Federation Opposition: Need for Economic Connections

A final reason put forth by a Russian Federation actor opposed to the movement for a Urals Republic concerned the preservation of economic

---

[61] B. Yeltsin, "Tak o chem zhe spor?" *Ural'skii rabochii*, no 128, 17 July 1993, p. 1.

[62] It should be noted, however, that some arguments against the Urals Republic did not explicitly state any cause for the movement; that is, they only stated their own reasons for opposition.

[63] Yeltsin is himself a native of Sverdlovsk, and many commentators within the region interpreted his silence on the Urals Republic as a sign of his tacit support. Even when the Urals Republic Constitution was declared illegal and the Sverdlovsk Oblast Soviet disbanded, several Sverdlovsk actors claimed that there were certain people within Yeltsin's inner circle, namely Nikolai Medvedev rather than the president himself, who were opposed to the Urals Republic.

relations. Mark Massarskii, an entrepreneur and president of the International Association Directors of Enterprises, gave an interview in which he discussed regional movements in Russia. Massarskii argued against all movements for greater sovereignty including the movement for a Urals Republic because he believed that it was necessary to establish economic connections rather than new boundaries. He stated that "fugitives turn out to be bankrupt very quickly. The path of economic autarky lacks perspective." In explaining why regions nonetheless persist in pushing for sovereignty and what in particular explains the Urals Republic, Massarskii said that "the illusion of economic independence is characteristic of all subjects of the Russian Federation – all of them without exception."[64]

Massarskii's argument comes closest to that offered by many Western scholars regarding the economic basis of the Urals Republic. While Massarskii may have been right that a movement for greater sovereignty, such as the Urals Republic, would lead to a breakdown in economic relations, hence worsening economic conditions, my findings suggest that his view was not shared by any significant number of Sverdlovsk actors. I found no articles in which any Sverdlovsk actors, either proponents or opponents of the Urals Republic, considered the Urals Republic to be based on a misunderstanding of the economic consequences of independence.

The analysis of the arguments by Moscow and Russian Federation actors demonstrates the dissimilarity of the views of Sverdlovsk and non-Sverdlovsk actors toward the Urals Republic. In particular, the idea that Sverdlovsk was subject to inequality was not evident among non-Sverdlovsk actors. Although this finding seems intuitively obvious, it underscores the claim that the movement for the Urals Republic was related to a particular understanding of inequality, especially regarding the regional economy, which had developed in Sverdlovsk, and which was not shared by those outside the region, especially Moscow actors.

Conclusion

In this chapter, I examined the arguments for and against the Urals Republic to demonstrate that the idea that Sverdlovsk suffered constitutional and economic inequality was at the heart of the movement for the Urals Republic. The presentation of arguments in favor of the Urals Republic

---

[64] M. Massarskii, "'Begletsy' neizbezhno stanut bankrotami," *Ural'skii rabochii*, no. 140, 29 July 1993, p. 2.

demonstrated that among Sverdlovsk actors there was a widely shared idea of inequality toward Sverdlovsk in comparison with other regions in the Russian Federation. And the presentation of arguments against the Urals Republic also suggested that the idea of inequality seemed to be particular to Sverdlovsk actors.

These findings are consistent with the evidence presented in Chapter 5 regarding the more negative understandings of the economy in Sverdlovsk compared to Samara. The data in this chapter suggest that, in attempting to create a Urals Republic, Sverdlovsk actors were voicing their demand that there should be economic and political equality among all subjects in the Federation, and that greater economic autonomy was the solution to the economic crisis facing the region.

7

Regional Understandings, Institutional Context, and the Development of the Movement for a Urals Republic

Social and institutional contexts affect the development and mediation of local understandings of the economy, as well as the transformation of those understandings into political and economic interests. The perestroika era, and in particular the interplay of orthodox and heterodox attempts at reinterpretation, which eventually destroyed the Soviet doxa, opened the conceptual space for new understandings of the economy and for regional relations in the Federation. That heterogeneous understandings of the economy existed and that they were connected to movements for greater sovereignty has been demonstrated in Chapters 5 and 6. In Sverdlovsk in particular, there was a great deal of negativity in understandings of the economy, and these negative interpretations of economic conditions were linked to the arguments regarding the formation of a Urals Republic. But, in order to complete the story of the formation of economic and political interests and the economic basis of movements for greater sovereignty – that is, to understand the transformation of economic understandings into political interests – we must return to the specific institutional context of the first Russian Republic, 1991–3, outlined in Chapter 4, and consider how the events and institutional configuration of that period affected the construction of political and economic interests in greater sovereignty.

There was no set of fixed economic interests (either corresponding or not corresponding to objective accounts), which, when presented with an institutional opportunity, resulted in the movement for the Urals Republic. Rather, I suggest that the existence of wide possibilities for rethinking political and economic categories and the activation of the idea of inequality through the experience of attempting constitutional reform *created* "economic interests" in support of the Urals Republic. In this sense, there was no constant interest in a movement for greater sovereignty, which turned into

223

action as soon as exogenous events lowered the costs of such action. Instead, I argue that there was dynamic interaction between institutional context, events, and interpretations of the economy in which particular understandings were activated and developed in response to certain experiences, and those understandings themselves became the fuel for subsequent action.

In the case of Sverdlovsk, the rewriting of the oblast charter and the federal Constitution ignited the debate over inequality toward the region. This debate resonated with the already existing negative understandings of the economy held by actors in the region, and the negative understandings of the economy further exacerbated the sense of unacceptable constitutional and economic inequality toward the region. Moreover, the particular institutional context of fluid political and economic categories made some alternatives for action seem necessary and others impossible. In short, there was no a priori fixed interest in sovereignty or republican status in Sverdlovsk; rather, the movement for the Urals Republic can be explained by the institutional context of perestroika, which produced negative understandings of the economy, and then the transformation of those understandings in the context of the institutional events of 1992–3.

In contrast, in the case of Samara, although the idea of regional inequality did present itself, especially when Samara leaders were forced to comment on the actions and arguments of Sverdlovsk officials, the idea of regional inequality did not become as salient a force supporting a movement for greater sovereignty in Samara as it had in Sverdlovsk because the set of negative understandings of the economy, which would have served as seedlings from which the idea of regional inequality could be cultivated into an interest in greater sovereignty, were less prevalent in Samara than in Sverdlovsk. In other words, the difference between outcomes in Sverdlovsk and Samara regarding movements for greater sovereignty ultimately was that, in comparison to Sverdlovsk, in Samara there were less negative understandings of the economy. Hence, in Samara there was only weak development of economic-based interests supporting a movement for greater sovereignty.

It is within the context of extreme institutional uncertainty, the "musical chairs" period of the first Russian Republic, that we must analyze the development of the movement for the Urals Republic in Sverdlovsk Oblast and the lack of a sovereignty movement in Samara Oblast. Three key institutional events are especially important to Russian regional sovereignty movements: the Federation Treaty and the 1993 referendum, the Constitutional Conference, and the September-October crisis between the federal executive and legislature.

The Federation Treaty and the 1993 Referendum

Although most Russian regions had been in economic crisis for several years, and heterogeneous understandings of the economy had arisen at various times especially during perestroika, the idea of changing the status of Sverdlovsk Oblast in order to eliminate political and economic inequities truly came to life during the discussions over the formation of the Sverdlovsk Oblast Charter in early 1993, a process that had its roots in the 1992 Federal Treaty. One reporter stated the relationship between the movement for a Urals Republic and the formation of the oblast charter directly: "the cause of the future change in status came up in the course of working on the charter of the oblast: to be precise, it was when they discussed the limitation of rights (and more to the point, responsibilities) of the oblast in comparison with republics in the Russian Federation."[1]

However, the Sverdlovsk Oblast Soviet first attempted to solve the question of the equality of rights of the subjects of the Federation by working within the rules of the 1992 Federal Treaty. The Sverdlovsk Oblast Soviet prepared a charter in early 1993 and sent it to the Russian Supreme Soviet. Unfortunately, the first copy of the charter was apparently "lost," and so another copy was sent, but Sverdlovsk never received a response.[2] Regarding this lack of response, a newspaper reporter commented that "from Moscow they don't always (to put it lightly) see our problems, concerns, [and] specifics."[3] The Press Center of the Oblast Soviet was less generous; it noted that instead of the cooperation stipulated by the 1992 Federal Treaty in outlining budgetary and tax laws that affect the region, as of 1993 "the oblast is being totally pushed out of the process."[4]

When the all-Russia referendum was announced in early April, the deputies of the Sverdlovsk Oblast Soviet decided to use the opportunity to bring attention to their demands regarding constitutional and economic equality. The deputies voted to add a fifth question regarding the status of Sverdlovsk Oblast to the referendum ballots distributed in Sverdlovsk Oblast. The exact question of the referendum was: "Do you agree that Sverdlovsk Oblast in its authority should have rights equal to republics of

---

[1] Iurii Bozhenko, "Korotkii vek," *Ural'skii rabochii*, no. 215, 12 November 1993, p. 1.
[2] A. Levin, "Desiat' dnei v noiabre," *Oblastnaia gazeta*, no. 137, 1 December 1993, p. 3.
[3] B. Timofeev, "My sprosim, a otvet v Moskvu unosim," *Ural'skii rabochii*, no. 72, 17 April 1993, p. 1.
[4] Press-tsentr oblsoveta, "Gde khoziain – tam poriadok," *Ural'skii rabochii*, no. 76, 23 April 1993, p. 1.

the Russian Federation?"[5] Since the Sverdlovsk Oblast Soviet's initiative had not been formally approved, the question regarding equal status with republics was not officially called a referendum question but a "poll."[6]

In explaining why the oblast needed to add a question to the referendum, Eduard Rossel, head of the Administration of Sverdlovsk Oblast, explained that other avenues for addressing the issues of economic and political responsibilities had been exhausted. On the legislative side, he mentioned the two oblast charters sent, without reply, to the Supreme Soviet. On the executive side, Rossel said that both President Yeltsin and Prime Minister Viktor Chernomyrdin had approved and were in support of a plan for the economic independence of Sverdlovsk, which had been drawn up by a group of scholars and specialists. However, Rossel noted that following approval by Yeltsin and Chernomyrdin, he had taken Sverdlovsk's project to *eighteen* ministers in Moscow, and they had all refused to work with Sverdlovsk. Given this response, Rossel asked, "Well, what are we supposed to do? The habit of everything being administered from above has to change."[7] Rossel's explanation for the necessity of the referendum suggests that the desire to seek a referendum on the status of Sverdlovsk Oblast grew out of the frustrated experience of attempting to work with the federal government.

The decision to add Sverdlovsk's question to the referendum was made by the Oblast Soviet on April 15, only ten days before the referendum. Although it did not give the oblast much time to prepare, the decision was made because, according to Anatolii Grebenkin, chairman of the Sverdlovsk Oblast Soviet, a referendum was the only constitutional way of beginning the process of changing the status of Sverdlovsk Oblast in the Russian Constitution, and it was easier and cheaper for the oblast to add a question to the all-Russian referendum then to have a separate referendum.[8] The oblast procurator (attorney general) protested the addition of the Sverdlovsk Oblast Soviet's question to the all-Russian referendum because the procurator considered the question to be illegal insofar as it concerned changing the federal structure of Russia.[9] However, the Sverdlovsk Oblast Court dismissed the protest, and the question was included on the

---

[5] Timofeev, 17 April 1993, p. 1.

[6] The question was termed *opros*.

[7] B. Timofeev, "Polozhim odno 'Da' na vosemnadtsat' 'Net'," *Ural'skii rabochii*, no. 77, 24 April 1993, p. 1.

[8] Timofeev, 17 April 1993, p. 1.

[9] B. Timofeev, "Sokhranim generalam zolotye pogony," *Ural'skii rabochii*, no. 73, 20 April 1993, p. 1.

referendum.[10] Three weeks after the referendum, the Supreme Court of Russia also dismissed the oblast procurator's protest of the referendum.[11]

On the eve of the referendum, Grebenkin and Rossel held a press conference in which they explained that the referendum would be considered valid if more than half of registered voters participated. They also clarified that if more than 50% of voters in a valid referendum approved Sverdlovsk's question on the referendum, then the Oblast Soviet, "heeding the opinion of citizens," would move forward with working to constitutionally change Sverdlovsk Oblast's status by sending a legislative initiative to the Supreme Soviet. Grebenkin also underlined that the issue was "only about socio-economic politics, not under any circumstances about 'shaking loose' the federal structure, the integrity of Russia." He explained, "we want to have the same possibilities and rights in decisions of our economic problems as other Russian republics."[12]

Despite expectations of low voter turnout, 66.7% of registered voters in Sverdlovsk participated in the referendum (compared with 62% in Russia overall). Sverdlovsk voters generally supported Yeltsin by voting according to the President's popular slogan, "Da, Da, Nyet, Da" which translated into "yes" to confidence in the president and his economic program, "no" to early elections for the president, but "yes" to early elections for the Supreme Soviet.[13] To Sverdlovsk's question 83.36% of the voters in Sverdlovsk Oblast voted "yes," in support of equal rights with republics. There was not much difference between rural and urban votes as even in the oblast capital of Ekaterinburg, 82.4% of the electorate voted "yes."[14] The interpretation of this result among the leaders of Sverdlovsk Oblast was that it constituted the first legal step toward changing the status of Sverdlovsk Oblast in the Russian Constitution. The next step would be for the Oblast Soviet to vote to send an initiative to the Supreme Soviet.

The Constitutional Conference

For regions such as Sverdlovsk, the Constitutional Conference held out hope that a solution to its claims of economic and constitutional inequality

---

[10] Press-tsentr oblsoveta, 23 April 1993, p. 1.

[11] Levin, 1 December 1993, p. 3.

[12] Timofeev, 24 April 1993, p. 1.

[13] "Referendum v Rossii sostoialsia," *Ural'skii rabochii*, no. 78, 27 April 1993, p. 1.

[14] Results given by the Sverdlovsk District Commission of the all-Russian referendum, cited in B. Timofeev, "Vybor sdelan, gospoda!" *Ural'skii rabochii*, no. 80, 29 April 1993, p. 1.

might finally be found. Eduard Rossel, Anatolii Grebenkin, and Aleksei Vorob'ev (director of the office of the head of administration and a legal scholar) participated as representatives from Sverdlovsk in the conference. According to Grebenkin, the Sverdlovsk representatives went to the Constitutional Conference with the intention of seeing to "the equality of all subjects of the Federation in terms of socioeconomic and political rights."[15]

On June 26, the participants of the conference were given a draft of the constitution for discussion.[16] The draft constitution did not grant republics their main demand, the right to secede, but it did support asymmetrical regional relations by granting numerous special rights to republics as opposed to oblasts and krais. It came as little surprise then, that on the issue of equal rights for all subjects of the Federation, Grebenkin concluded, the draft "did not succeed in solving the problem which stands before our oblast soviet, and most importantly, which faces our multinational people living in the territory of Sverdlovsk Oblast."[17]

The popular mayor of Ekaterinburg, Arkadii Chernetskii, was initially opposed to the change in status of Sverdlovsk Oblast and the creation of a Urals Republic. He later changed his position and, in an interview, explained that his initial opposition was based on a lack of information regarding the Constitutional Conference. He said that when he found out the concrete results of the conference in terms of what actual positions had been worked out, both on the federal side and on the side of Sverdlovsk representatives, he changed his mind. Most important in changing his position, Chernetskii said, was that in his opinion "the initiators of the process [to create a Urals Republic] sufficiently clearly see a line, over which it is not possible to cross." He explained:

There is no talk of full sovereignty with all its attributes: borders, customs, army, language, etc. The proclamation of the Urals Republic does not bring any damage to the integrity of Russia. But, the word "republic" in the given situation is being used as a term which in Russia according to complex traditions is connected to definitions of authority. National formations already have such authority, but unfortunately administrative-territorial formations do not.

By "national formations," Chernetskii was referring to republics with their titular ethnic groups, and by "administrative-territorial formations" he

---

[15] A. V. Grebenkin, "My budem reshitel'ny," *Oblastnaia gazeta*, no. 75, 6 July 1993, p. 1.
[16] Ibid. See "Konstitutsiia Rossiiskoi Federatsii," *Izvestiia*, no. 132, 16 July 1993, pp. 3, 4–6, for the full text of the draft constitution.
[17] Grebenkin, 6 July 1993, p. 1.

meant oblasts and krais. Chernetskii also argued that had a term other than "republic" been used, "then certainly the resonance of the decision [to proclaim a Urals Republic] would have been different."[18]

Only four days after the announcement of the draft constitution, on 1 July 1993, there was a session of the entire Sverdlovsk Oblast Soviet where a vote on changing the status of Sverdlovsk Oblast to republic was to be taken.[19] In his speech before the oblast soviet, Grebenkin said that there were two ways to solve the problem of equal rights; either give all subjects exactly the same rights or settle for the existing system but raise the status of Sverdlovsk to that of republic. Grebenkin pointed out that neither republics, federal authorities, nor other oblasts that were receiving subsidies were in favor of giving all subjects equal rights, and, for that reason, Sverdlovsk was forced to consider the latter choice of unilaterally raising its status to republic.[20] At the end of the session, 162 out of 189 Sverdlovsk deputies voted to support changing the legal status of Sverdlovsk from oblast to republic.[21]

The Sverdlovsk Oblast Soviet immediately issued a "Declaration of the Change of Status of Sverdlovsk Oblast" and an explanatory notice entitled "Regarding the Status of Sverdlovsk Oblast in the Structure of the Russian Federation."[22] In the declaration, the Sverdlovsk Oblast Soviet declared the "raising of the status of Sverdlovsk Oblast to the level of republics in the structure of the Russian Federation." The deputies also proclaimed that "laws on the territory of the Urals Republic were to be regulated by the Constitution of the Russian Federation, legislation of the Russian Federation and the Urals Republic." As for competing laws, "the Urals

---

[18] Arkadii Chernetskii, "Provozglashenie Ural'skoi Respubliki ne neset ushcherba tselostnosti Rossii," *Na smenu!*, no. 152, 17 August 1993, p. 2.

[19] For detailed analysis of the arguments for and against the Urals Republic, see Chapter 6. For additional discussion of the Urals Republic movement, see Eduard Rossel, "Ural'skaia Respublika – put' k territorial'nomu ustroistvu i upravleniyu Rossiiskim gosudarstvom," in A. V. Gaida and A. V. Ivanov, eds., *Ural'skaia Respublika i problemy stanovleniia novoi rossiiskoi gosudarstvennosti* (Ekaterinburg: Sverdlovskii oblastnoi Sovet, 1993), pp. 6–16; G. Azanov, *Ural'skaia Respublika: igra ambitsii ili neobkhodimost?* (Ekaterinburg: naucho-metodicheskim tsentrom IPPK, 1994); Gerald M. Easter, "Redefining Centre-Regional Relations in the Russian Federation: Sverdlovsk *oblast'*," *Europe-Asia Studies* 49:4 (1997), pp. 617–35; and Gilles Favarel-Garrigues, "La region de Sverdlovsk et le pouvoir du gouverneur," in Marie Mendras, ed., "Russie: le gouvernement des provinces," *Nouveaux Mondes* 7 (Winter 1997), pp. 161–91.

[20] Grebenkin, 6 July 1993, p. 1.

[21] N. Ponomareva, "Svoi prava voz'mem sebe sami," *Oblastnaia gazeta*, no. 75, 6 July 1993, p. 1.

[22] See *Ural'skii rabochii*, no. 123, 7 July 1993, p. 3, for the full text of these documents.

Republic acknowledged the superiority of legal acts of federal institutions of power taken *within the boundaries of their competency.*" Furthermore, the declaration stated that "within the boundaries of its authority the Urals Republic independently decides questions of its vital activity, implementing legislative, executive, and judicial power on its territory."[23]

The next day, the Sverdlovsk Oblast Soviet proclaimed a decision to form a Urals Republic. Sverdlovsk also invited the other four oblasts in the Urals region (Cheliabinsk, Kurgan, Orenburg, and Perm') to join in the "republic."[24] In a press conference following the vote and proclamation, Grebenkin emphasized that "we intend to take no illegal actions." In explanation for the actions taken, he said: "in our view, the oblast must possess the same rights economically and politically as the republics. We believe that relations among the components of the Federation of Russia must be built along territorial, not national lines."[25]

Anatolii Matrosov, Sverdlovsk Oblast Soviet deputy and director of the Urals Regional Association of Soviets, echoed Grebenkin's remarks in an article that he published in *Izvestiia*, a leading national newspaper, to explain the actions of the Sverdlovsk Oblast Soviet to the rest of Russia. Matrosov began his article with the following statement: "'The Urals is the cornerstone of the realm' is a fine image which everyone is sick and tired of." He then went on to say that "we therefore regard 26 June 1993 as a black day for us, since this was the day when the new Russian Federation constitution was prepared, which once again enshrines for many years the oblasts' and krais' vassalage not only to the center but also, in essence, to the national republics."[26] Moreover he wrote:

The Sverdlovsk Oblast Soviet's decision to create the Urals Republic should be regarded as a serious warning of the impermissibility of organizing Russia along ethnic lines, of the impermissibility of adopting a constitution that does not allow for equality among all the Federation's components, and of the impermissibility of adopting any legal acts of federal authority and administration affecting the interests of the Federation's subjects without their agreement. The Urals is resisting – that means it has the power to remain the Russian realm's cornerstone.[27]

---

[23] "Deklaratsiia ob izmenenii statusa Sverdlovskoi Oblasti," *Ural'skii rabochii*, no. 123, 7 July 1993, p. 3. Emphasis added.

[24] D. Usachev, "Ot oblasti do respubliki – odin shag," *Rossiiskaia gazeta*, no. 126, 3 July 1993, p. 2.

[25] *FBIS Daily Report – Soviet Union* 93:132 (13 July 1993), p. 57 [from A. Pashkov, "Urals Republic Does Not Aspire to Sovereignty," *Izvestiia*, 9 July 1993, p. 2].

[26] Anatolii Matrosov, "Uralu nekuda vykhodit' iz Rossii," *Izvestiia*, no. 128, 10 July 1993, p. 8.

[27] Ibid.

Later, in another interview, Matrosov said, "how can one talk about the creation of Russian statehood and at the same time insist on preserving inequality among integral parts of the Federation?" Finally, he concluded, "there is only one realistic path – to wrest a portion of the requisite power from the center for the regions, and to increase the authoritative status of krais and oblasts."[28]

The comments of Grebenkin, Chernetskii, and Matrosov not only highlight Sverdlovsk's desire for equal economic and constitutional rights, but they also demonstrate the contingent nature of the movement for a Urals Republic by revealing the events that transformed the idea of economic inequality into a decision by the oblast soviet to vote to change the status of Sverdlovsk Oblast.

Had the Constitutional Conference gone differently, for example, had what was to become the December 1993 Constitution been circulated at the conference, it seems unlikely that Sverdlovsk Oblast would have voted right away to change its status. In other words, it was not that those in favor of a Urals Republic had always desired republican status and were simply waiting for an opportunity to act. Rather, support for the decision to change the status of Sverdlovsk was a contingent product of the confluence of ideas regarding inequality and concrete attempts at implementation of various plans, as well as the particular institutional context of federalism in Russia in 1993.

Reactions to the Sverdlovsk Vote

The actions of the Sverdlovsk Oblast Soviet were initially met with silence by central authorities. There was no immediate statement to officials in Sverdlovsk from President Yeltsin, Ruslan Khasbulatov (chairman of the Supreme Soviet), or Prime Minister Viktor Chernomyrdin.[29] Sverdlovsk leaders took the lack of a response, especially by Yeltsin, as a sign of support for the Urals Republic. In fact, Eduard Rossel said that "support by the president for the decision of the oblast regarding the taking of economic and political independence was obvious to the naked eye."[30] Other regional leaders, especially leaders of republics, also interpreted the lack

[28] V. Petrovskii, "My ne storonniki razvala. My za edinuiu i nedelimuiu," *Rossiiskaia gazeta*, no. 144, 29 July 1993, p. 3.

[29] Usachev, 3 July 1993, p. 2.

[30] Boris Iarkov, "Ural'skaia Respublika – pishcha est', no dlia razgovorov," *Na smenu!*, no. 124, 7 July 1993, p. 1.

of reaction by Moscow authorities as a sign of acceptance of Sverdlovsk's actions. However, republican leaders did not at all support the creation of a Urals Republic. For example, the leadership in both Tatarstan and Bashkortostan suspected collusion between Moscow and the Urals, and interpreted Sverdlovsk's change in status as a means of denying rights to national republics.[31]

By July 9, Vycheslav Kostikov, Yeltsin's press secretary, finally issued a statement claiming that the formation of a Urals Republic was to be suspended. However, Anatolii Grebenkin told *Izvestiia* that Kostikov's statement was wrongly formulated as there was nothing to suspend. According to Grebenkin, in order to change the status of an oblast to a republic legally, there were three requirements: the people's will, a decision of the oblast soviet, and a decision of the Russian Supreme Soviet.[32] The referendum of 25 April 1993 was the first step; the 1 July 1993 vote by the oblast soviet was the second; and further action was in the hands of the Supreme Soviet. This was an interesting, seemingly legalistic response. However, the legal requirements, which did not seem to have any practical importance at this time, because of the near impossibility of getting Supreme Soviet approval, would turn out to be important later – that is, when the Supreme Soviet no longer existed. Here the musical chairs metaphor is apt: many many legal rules and requirements existed in 1993, but which would turn out to matter, and when, no one knew.

Reaction in Samara

On the same day as the Moscow response, July 9, the leaders of the Samara Oblast Soviet also issued a response to the events in Sverdlovsk through their press service. Leaders of the Samara Oblast Soviet noted that it was indeed true that, at the level of subjects of the Federation, "not only the form, but also the functions, authority, norms of representation, and principles of forming the power structure are unclear." Samara Oblast Soviet leaders said that these questions were raised at the Constitutional Conference, but that no definitive answer had yet emerged. The press service reported that "these circumstances demand more active politics in the interests of

---

[31] R. Batyrshin, "Nastalo vremia rasplachivat'sia za oshibku: lidery Ufy i Kazani o suverenizatsii kraev i olastei," *Nezavisimaia gazeta*, no. 125, 7 July 1993, p. 3.
[32] *FBIS*, 13 July 1993, p. 57.

the population of the regions. The most acceptable appears to be to connect all citizens to the constitutional process through the institution of a referendum. With these goals, the oblast soviet is working on a proposal regarding a local referendum." The Samara Oblast Soviet did not have a concrete question in mind but was considering several possibilities in light of the decision by Sverdlovsk Oblast. The Samara Oblast Soviet also invited readers to write in to newspapers with their opinions regarding a possible referendum.[33]

In contrast to the Oblast Soviet's response, Konstantin Titov, the head of Administration of Samara Oblast, issued his own reply both to the declaration of the Urals Republic by the Sverdlovsk Oblast Soviet and to the initiatives of the Samara Oblast Soviet. Titov declared that, in response to the referendum issue, "it is too early to put the question of creating a republic before the people of Samara." Instead, he said that "right now it is necessary to strive to solve the problem of equal rights within the framework of the Constitutional Conference."[34] These comments mirror Titov's conciliatory views on the regional economy and economic problems facing Samara outlined in Chapter 5.

Titov also disagreed strongly with the idea that multiple oblasts might unite into a single republic such as in the Urals. He said that "the creation of a republic from a few oblasts – Sverdlovsk, according to rumor, plans to unite with Perm' and Cheliabinsk – can also create rivalry amongst regional elites."[35] Actually, the other oblasts in the Urals had not initially welcomed the invitation by Sverdlovsk to join the Urals Republic, but by mid-July Cheliabinsk and Perm' had expressed support for joining the Urals Republic and discussions with the other oblasts (Kurgan and Orenburg) continued throughout the summer.[36]

One interesting aspect of Samara's position toward a movement for greater sovereignty is how relatively inchoate the position in Samara was by July 1993 in comparison to Sverdlovsk. Although the comments by Titov and the leaders of the Samara Oblast Soviet make it clear that the idea of regional inequality had at least surfaced in Samara, it never approached anything like the developed interest in Sverdlovsk. As a fellow oblast, Samara

[33] Press-sluzhba oblsoveta, "Samarskii referendum," *Samarskie izvestiia*, no. 146, 9 July 1993, p. 1.
[34] "Titov protiv krainostei," *Delo*, no. 27, 9 July 1993, p. 11.
[35] Ibid.
[36] V. Petrovskii, "My poidem drugim putem," *Rossiiskaia gazeta*, no. 127, 6 July 1993, p. 2.

was subject to almost exactly the same institutional constraints faced by Sverdlovsk. Hence, the lack of action and the lack of economic and political grievance in Samara cannot be explained by structural factors.

Crisis Between the Federal Executive and Legislature: September and October 1993

As Grebenkin had noted, following the vote by the Sverdlovsk Oblast Soviet in July, the next step in the creation of a Urals Republic was the drafting of a constitution of the Urals Republic, which after being passed by the Sverdlovsk Oblast Soviet would be sent to the Russian Supreme Soviet for final approval.[37] By September, a draft of the Urals Republic constitution had been completed and was being circulated in the oblast for revisions.

At the same time, Sverdlovsk was moving forward in discussions with the other oblasts of the Urals regarding the unification of the oblasts into a common Urals Republic. They formed an inter-regional association that was called the Association for Economic Cooperation of Oblasts and Republics of the Urals (*Assotsiatsii ekonomicheskogo vzaimodestviia oblastei i respublik Urala* or AECORU). AECORU met three to five times per year and served as a forum for regional debate and cooperation. On September 14, under the auspices of AECORU, the chairmen of oblast soviets and heads of administrations of Kurgan, Orenburg, Perm', Sverdlovsk, and Cheliabinsk met and announced that the five oblasts were ready to begin work on the constitutional and legal formation of a united Urals Republic. In a joint statement, they explained:

The formation of the Urals Republic is aimed at: preventing the collapse of the economy of Russia; decentralizing management and ensuring the rational employment of natural resources, property, and finances; the pursuit of an effective taxation policy; and the provision of more substantial social support for the population. The need to create the republic is dictated not by the desire to divest ourselves of Russia but by the aspiration to enable the productive forces of the Urals to develop effectively and the people of the Urals to fully enjoy the results of their own labor.[38]

---

[37] The drafting of a constitution for the Urals Republic was guided by a working group at the Institute of Philosophy and Law (within the Urals department of the Russian Academy of Sciences) located in Ekaterinburg. M. Sidorov, "Kolokol dlia urala," *Vechernii Ekaterinburg*, no. 185, 29 September 1993, p. 2.

[38] Aleksandr Levin, "Kto boidet v Ural'skuiu Respubliku?" *Oblastnaia gazeta*, no. 105, 17 September 1993, p. 1.

The statement is similar in tone and content to many arguments made by Sverdlovsk leaders in support of the Urals Republic. Following the AECORU meeting and announcement, Eduard Rossel gave an interview to *Izvestiia* in which he discussed some examples of the economic advantages of the Urals Republic, such as a combined industrial output that would amount to 15% of Russia's total industrial output, an amount larger than that of any other macro-region such as the Greater Volga region, or the Siberias and the Far East combined. In addition, Rossel claimed that a unified Urals region would improve efficiency, for example, by lowering transport costs.[39]

Rossel made an additional claim that given the current instability between the federal executive and legislature in Moscow, regional policy can be characterized as "divide and rule" where the interests of the regions are ignored. Rossel argued that it is not necessary for the regions to simply wait for the center, allowing inequities to persist. Rather, he argued, "a republic in conditions of crisis is a vigorous and decisive means of establishing a viable management base and halting the collapse of the state." Rossel stressed that the formation of a republic is not simply a short-term or stopgap measure aimed at gaining unjustifiable advantages over other regions but rather is a solution to the historically inadequate representation and consideration of regional interests. He said:

For us its [the Urals Republic's] creation is a means rather than an end in itself. First, this path leads to the nullification of sector and departmental priorities over common territorial interests. Second, the republic's creation is aimed at nullifying the basis of the nation-state, that is to say, disposes of the utopian thesis of "as many states as there are tribes." Third, this is the path of responsible management whereby the population of the territory itself determines the basic parameters of its activity via its own institutions of leadership. Fourth, it serves as a means of overcoming the fear that derives from remote external forces making management decisions fundamentally at odds with the interests and plans affecting the lives of the broad strata of the territorial community, of which there are countless examples. Fifth, it takes a step toward equalizing the political, social, and legal rights of citizens.[40]

In this set of remarks, Rossel touched on several traditional divisions that existed during the Soviet period between the regions and the center. His first point referred to the competition for managerial control between central

---

[39] Aleksandr Pashkov, "Ural'skaia respublika ukrepit Rossiiu," *Izvestiia*, no. 177, 17 September 1993, p. 2.
[40] Ibid.

ministries and regionally located enterprise directors,[41] and his second point referred to the Soviet practice of recognizing and privileging certain ethnic groups. Rossel's third and fourth points referenced the issue, which marked much of Soviet history, of central control over regional affairs. However, Rossel's fifth point was a novel formulation of the idea that citizens of Sverdlovsk were being treated unfairly. While similar instantiations of Rossel's earlier points could be found in various periods of Soviet history and in a variety of regional settings, the idea of particularized inequality was, I argue, a post-Soviet phenomenon.

One reason for the development of the idea of inequality toward Sverdlovsk was that coherent and consistent central government policy-making from Moscow was increasingly unattainable owing to the advancing struggle between the president and the parliament throughout 1993. And the chaos of central policy-making (or to be more precise, the lack of centralized policy-making) eventually affected every region in Russia and cast a shadow of confusion over the understanding of the proper role of federal and regional governance structures.

Even in Samara, a region that had previously not acted at all to support a movement for greater sovereignty, inconsistency and outright negligence in central government policy created the conditions for heated debate over the division of central and regional responsibilities. For example, when Samara Oblast was not given resources for purchasing seed-grain, which had been promised by the center, its oblast soviet debated various ways of trying to get resources out of Moscow, including withholding tax payments and diverting funds marked for other uses. However, during the debate, it became clear that even if the oblast wanted to withhold taxes, there was no mechanism for doing so because the oblast, unlike the republics, had neither its own treasury nor any control over the branch of the Central Bank of Russia located in the region.

At the end of a long day's discussion, an oblast soviet deputy, Pavel Elin, gave a speech in which he suggested that, "in order to be protected from the [central] government," Samara Oblast should consider "the creation of our own republic with all the consequences which follow from it." A reporter present at the oblast soviet session said that many deputies considered this proposal to be "no more than the product of a minute of short-temperedness," and that no one paid attention to the proposal – no

---

[41] See Chapter 3 for more discussion of the tension between central ministries and regional elites.

one, that is, except Konstantin Titov. Titov did not let the comment go, but instead brought the item up for discussion and "remarked that similar resistance to federal powers was hardly of any use." Furthermore, Titov declared:

Ambition of this kind can cause the oblast to be deprived altogether of credit resources; this is all the more true for a republic. Instead, it is necessary to work with Moscow, and oblast powers should work constantly, choosing agreed means, *even if it is one crumb at a time*. It is necessary to approve the new constitution in which equal economic and social rights of all regions of Russia can be secured. However, divisions which play off national cards against each other can only lead to an abyss.[42]

Titov was referring to the same draft Russian constitution so criticized by Sverdlovsk leaders (by September, the constitution had still not been approved by the Supreme Soviet). It is remarkable, in comparison with arguments made in Sverdlovsk, that Titov asserted that raising the status of the oblast would not improve the regional economy. Following Titov's statement, there was no further discussion at the oblast soviet session regarding the issue of creating a republic.

Nevertheless, Titov's strong stance against the formation of a republic did not entirely end the debate over reworking the status of Samara Oblast. On September 18, Oleg Anishchik, the chairman of the Samara Oblast Soviet, gave an interview in which he called for raising the status of Samara Oblast. However, in contrast to the arguments surrounding the Urals Republic, Anishchik primarily argued that the status of Samara needed to be changed in order to give Samara the authority to deal with issues that were currently being ignored as a result of the prevailing crisis in Moscow between the president and the Supreme Soviet, and the lack of a federal constitution. Anishchik said:

The current government turns out to be neither "the will" of the president, nor "the will" of the Supreme Soviet. As a result we observe the breakup of the budget system. Because of the deficiencies of the existing Constitution, the government turns out to be unaccountable to parliament, unlike what is accepted in all countries. There is not at all any kind of coordination. When the Supreme Soviet conducts an economic conference, the government ignores it; when the government is in session, no one from the Supreme Soviet attends, etc.[43]

---

[42] T. Voskoboinikova, "Nardepy ne rvutsia v bol'shuiu politiku. Khotiat vershit' ee v sobstvennoi respublike?" *Volzhskaia kommuna*, no. 168–9, 3 September 1993, p. 1. Emphasis added.

[43] O. N. Anishchik, "Krizis nalitso," *Samarskie izvestiia*, no. 196, 18 September 1993, p. 1.

Anishchik also said that the oblast soviet was currently working on formulating a referendum to ask the residents of Samara whether they agreed with changing the status of Samara Oblast. Anishchik's comments highlight the contingent institutional context; his views on the status of Samara in the Federation and the need for greater sovereignty were largely dependent on the extreme crisis between the federal executive and legislature.

Rather than quelling regionalist demands, Yeltsin's decision to dissolve the Russian Supreme Soviet and Congress of People's Deputies with Decree 1400 on September 21 only sparked further action. On September 24, the heads of the soviets and administrations at all levels within Sverdlovsk Oblast met and adopted a draft constitution for the Urals Republic.[44] Following this meeting, on September 29 there was an extraordinary session of the Sverdlovsk Oblast Soviet to discuss the events in Moscow and to move forward on the formation of the government and constitution of the Urals Republic.[45]

The reaction in the regions to the violent episode in Moscow over the weekend of October 3 and 4 was mixed. In Sverdlovsk, on October 5 Eduard Rossel and Anatolii Grebenkin sent a public telegram to Yeltsin saying "[we] support your resolute actions concerning the reform of the state structures. From our side we guarantee order and stability in the oblast and the support of the Urals people in carrying out this reform."[46] In Samara, Konstantin Titov supported Yeltsin, but the Samara Oblast Soviet condemned the presidential decrees and Yeltsin's use of force. In its decision, the Samara Oblast Soviet was not alone; from Yeltsin's own estimate, 50% of oblast soviets reacted in a similar fashion.[47]

The Samara Oblast Soviet also took another step, however, which was that they unilaterally declared Samara Oblast to be a "state-territorial formation" (without ever having had a referendum on the issue of changing the oblast's status). This move was opposed by both the oblast procurator and the head of the administration, Konstantin Titov. Titov opposed the oblast soviet decisions and went on TV directly after the decisions were taken accusing the deputies of moving toward the formation of a parallel administration in the oblast.[48] As it turned out, the decision by the Samara

---

[44] "Oblsovet mozhet priniat' ural'skuiu konstitutsiiu," *Kommersant'-Daily*, no. 184, 25 September 1993, p. 2.
[45] "O proekte konstitutsii Ural'skoi Respubliki," *Na smenu!*, no. 192, 13 October 1993, p. 3.
[46] *Ural'skii rabochii*, 5 October 1993, p. 1.
[47] "Oblsovet reshaetsia na konflikt c tsentrom," *Delo*, no. 37, 8 October 1993, p. 13.
[48] Ibid.

Oblast Soviet did not amount to anything because the next day, October 9, Yeltsin issued a decree liquidating the existing system of soviets and transferring their powers to the heads of administration (regional executives who had been all appointed by the president).

The movements for greater sovereignty in the Russian Federation cannot be classified as simple anti-Moscow protests. Where the movement for greater sovereignty was more developed, in Sverdlovsk, the personal support for Yeltsin was unified and strong.[49] The support for Yeltsin in Sverdlovsk runs contrary to expectations because we would expect those seeking greater sovereignty from Moscow to be less supportive of the president. The experience of Samara, on the other hand, is less surprising. There, the few deputies who voiced support for a movement for greater sovereignty were against Yeltsin, whereas Konstantin Titov, the head of administration who consistently opposed any movement for greater sovereignty, strongly supported Yeltsin. If movements for greater sovereignty in the Russian Federation were essentially anti-Moscow protests, then the movements should have been most developed in places such as Samara where there was opposition to Yeltsin rather than in Sverdlovsk where both the legislature and executive branches strongly supported the president. Another consideration is that executives might have been expected to support the president, while the oblast soviets should have supported the Supreme Soviet. This was the case in Samara, but in Sverdlovsk both the executive and oblast soviet strongly supported the president.

The Creation of the Urals Republic

While in Samara the idea of changing the status of the oblast was effectively extinguished by Yeltsin's decrees in support of regional executives over legislatures, the Sverdlovsk movement for the Urals Republic was undeterred by the events in Moscow. In fact, Yeltsin's decision to disband and bomb the Supreme Soviet actually bolstered the creation of a Urals Republic because, in so doing, Yeltsin removed the last constitutional obstacle to the Urals Republic's formation. The third step in the process of creating a Urals Republic was that the Supreme Soviet should approve the change in the Russian Constitution allowing for the upgrading of Sverdlovsk's status and the Supreme Soviet should approve the Constitution of the Urals Republic. With the

---

[49] Of course, Yeltsin was from Sverdlovsk, but Sverdlovsk has consistently supported "reformers" over communists since perestroika.

Supreme Soviet no longer in existence and the new Russian Constitution not yet in effect (it was to be voted on in a referendum on December 12), Sverdlovsk actors thought they had gained new freedom to act unilaterally.

On 27 October 1993, the Sverdlovsk Oblast Soviet voted on and adopted the Constitution of the Urals Republic. The Constitution was approved by 171 out of 189 deputies, and it was printed in full in *Oblastnaia gazeta* on October 30. The deputies voted that the Constitution would go into effect on 31 October 1993.[50] The deputies also decided to hold a referendum specifically on the Urals Republic Constitution; the referendum was to take place concomitantly with the Russian elections on December 12. The Sverdlovsk Oblast Soviet also established that the Urals Republic was to have a directly elected governor and a two-chamber legislature; these positions were also to be elected on December 12. In the interim, Rossel would serve as governor, and the Sverdlovsk Oblast Soviet would serve as the lower house of the legislature. Finally, October 27 was declared "the day of the Urals Republic."[51]

With "Ukaz No. 1" (decree no. 1) issued by Rossel on October 31, Rossel, according to the Constitution of the Urals Republic, transferred executive power in the republic from the head of the administration to the governor (himself) until December 12, when the first governor was to be elected. In the decree, Rossel also entrusted Valerii Trushnikov, chairman of the Government of the Urals Republic, with preparing suggestions for the structure of executive power during the period before the December 12 elections.[52] Although it appears that the creation of the Urals Republic was strongly driven by elites, public opinion polls taken during the period showed strong majority support for the Urals Republic.[53]

Central Reaction to the Creation of the Urals Republic

In a statement issued on 1 November 1993, Viktor Chernomyrdin denied the existence of the Urals Republic. He said that "there is no such republic for me and we shall have no contact with it" and later that "there will be no Urals Republic." In a conciliatory move, in response to Chernomyrdin's remarks, Grebenkin declared that the leadership of the Urals Republic was

---

[50] Bozhenko, 12 November 1993, p. 1.
[51] M. Sidorov, "'Da' konstitutsii," *Vechernii Ekaterinburg*, no. 207, 29 October 1993, p. 1.
[52] "Ukaz no. 1," *Vechernii Ekaterinburg*, no. 210, 3 November 1993, p. 1.
[53] Easter, 1997, pp. 623–4.

willing to seek a compromise with federal authorities, including suspending decisions on the adoption of the Urals Republic Constitution.[54]

At the same time, on November 2 and 3, Rossel took part in a meeting of the Council of Ministers of Russia, and in a meeting of leaders of republics, krais, and oblasts. Both meetings were directed by Yeltsin. According to Rossel's press service, in his presentation to the Council of Ministers, Yeltsin "devoted attention to regional politics and called the process of raising the status of a number of oblasts to the level of republic normal [*normal'no*]." The press service also reported that Yeltsin's opinion was that the widening of authority of subjects of the Russian Federation would speed and improve economic reform.[55] In addition, it was reported that Yeltsin said that "the desire by oblasts to raise their status was not due to the personal ambitions of regional elites."[56] However, one point of concern was that Yeltsin did not mention the Urals Republic by name.

Nevertheless, Rossel and others in Sverdlovsk interpreted Yeltsin's comments as fully supportive of the Urals Republic. Rossel also claimed that during the Council of Ministers meeting, Viktor Chernomyrdin "quickly crossed out paragraphs from his own speech" after Yeltsin made positive comments regarding the regions. Rossel's conclusion was that Chernomyrdin had changed his intended remarks and perhaps his opinions on the Urals Republic in light of Yeltsin's positive position toward the Urals Republic. Rossel also claimed that other officials, both from Moscow and the regions, became noticeably friendlier toward him after Yeltsin's speech.[57]

When Rossel returned to Ekaterinburg he gave a press conference in which he assured residents that although he had not personally met with Yeltsin while he was in Moscow, he had given all documents related to the formation of the Urals Republic to the president's office. Rossel also acknowledged that the new Constitution of the Russian Federation did not mention the Urals Republic, but he proclaimed: "we will build our republic *de facto* and later obtain *de jure* acknowledgment."[58] Rossel also

---

[54] *FBIS Daily Report – Soviet Union* 93: 211 (3 November 1993), p. 52 [from *Interfax*, "Sverdlovsk Official Dismisses Chernomyrdin's Remarks," 2 November 1993].

[55] "Tsentr-region: nuzhen kontakt," *Oblastnaia gazeta*, no. 127, 5 November 1993, p. 1.

[56] N. Ponomareva, "De-fakto est'. De-iure – budet!" *Oblastnaia gazeta*, no. 128, 10 November 1993, p. 1.

[57] Ibid.

[58] B. Timofeev, "Skvoz' igol'noe ushko da k solnyshku," *Ural'skii rabochii*, no. 212, 6 November 1993, p. 1.

referred to Sverdlovsk citizens as "pioneers" in creating new categories in the Constitution.[59] However, this confidence in institutional innovation was premature.

Disbanding of the Urals Republic

On November 9, the Sverdlovsk Oblast Soviet held an extraordinary session to discuss the negative reaction of key central officials (in particular, Sergei Filatov, head of the Presidential Administration, and Nikolai Medvedev, Chairman of the Russian Federation Commission for the Nationalities-Federation System and Inter-Ethnic Relations) to the creation of the Urals Republic. At the session, the oblast soviet also passed a law on the election of the governor to be held on December 12, and the deputies agreed on the question regarding the Urals Republic Constitution, which was to be put to the population in a referendum also on December 12.[60] The question was to be: "Do you accept the Constitution of the Urals Republic that establishes the equality of the Urals Republic with the other republics of the Russian Federation?"[61] The Sverdlovsk leaders correctly assumed that Yeltsin's approval was the main factor that would allow for further acceptance of the Urals Republic; however, they turned out to be seriously mistaken in their assessment of what Yeltsin's public position would be.

Unbeknownst to the deputies at the time, on the morning of the same day as their meeting, 9 November 1993, Yeltsin had signed a decree (no. 1874) entitled "On Terminating the Activity of the Sverdlovsk Oblast Soviet of People's Deputies." In it, Yeltsin decreed that the decisions of the Sverdlovsk Oblast Soviet of 1 July 1993 ("On the Status of Sverdlovsk Oblast Within the Russian Federation") and 27 October 1993 ("On the Urals Republic Constitution") "are to be considered as having no juridical force from the moment they were adopted." Moreover, Yeltsin decreed that the activities of the Sverdlovsk Oblast Soviet were to be terminated as of November 9, that the administration of Sverdlovsk Oblast (headed by an executive appointed by the president) was to oversee all functions and responsibilities of the former Sverdlovsk Oblast Soviet, and that elections for a new representative

---

[59] L. Minina, "'Budu idti do kontsa', – zaiavil zhurnalistam E. Rossel'," *Vechernii Ekaterinburg*, no. 213, 6 November 1993, p. 1.

[60] B. Timofeev, "Ukaz, kak Groznyi okrik: 'tsyts!'" *Ural'skii rabochii*, no. 214, 11 November 1993, p. 1.

[61] N. Gorodetskaia and V. Todres, "Ural'skaia respublika otmenena: bei svoikh, chuzhie budut boiat'sia," *Segodnia*, no. 77, 11 November 1993, p. 2.

institution were to be held in early 1994.[62] The Sverdlovsk Oblast Soviet received the decree by fax at the end of their session at approximately 11:00 P.M.[63]

The next day, 10 November 1993, Eduard Rossel was relieved of his post as head of the administration of Sverdlovsk Oblast by another decree signed by Yeltsin, for "failing to carry out presidential decrees and for considerably exceeding his powers." Valerii Trushnikov was appointed interim head.[64] Trushnikov had served as first vice-chairman of the Sverdlovsk Soviet Executive Committee (*ispolnitel'nyi komitet soveta* or ispolkom), and later as first vice-head of the Sverdlovsk Administration and chairman of the Government of the Urals Republic.

Upon receiving the presidential decree, Rossel and the Sverdlovsk Oblast Soviet agreed to comply, but Grebenkin noted that "there is nothing in the text of the Urals Constitution that contradicts presidential decrees." He also said that the name of the document would be changed to a "charter."[65] These comments are similar to remarks made by Grebenkin in response to criticisms by Nikolai Medvedev just after the adoption of the Urals Republic Constitution and the creation of the Urals Republic. In those remarks, Grebenkin explained that the Sverdlovsk Oblast Soviet had not exceeded its powers because the oblast is allowed to adopt a charter, and the Urals Republic Constitution was not more than "a constitutional charter." Grebenkin also "clarified" that the Urals Republic was not actually a "republic," but a "state-territorial formation."[66] The formal end of the Urals Republic did not mark the end of the pursuit of economic rights and greater autonomy for Sverdlovsk. However, as the narrative of the Urals Republic has suggested, institutional context was crucial to the development of specific political and economic interests. And as institutional contexts changed, so too did regional understandings and strategies.

This analysis highlights the role of institutional contingency in sovereignty movements because the outcome of the interaction between ideas and events or institutional context was not fixed or predetermined. Rather,

[62] "Ukaz Prezidenta Rossiiskoi Federatsii," *Rossiiskaia gazeta*, no. 211, 11 November 1993, p. 2.
[63] Levin, 1 December 1993, p. 3.
[64] *FBIS Daily Report – Soviet Union* 93: 217 (12 November 1993), p. 34 [from *Mayak Radio Network*, "Yeltsin Sacks Sverdlovsk Oblast Head," 10 November 1993].
[65] Gorodetskaia and Todres, 11 November 1993, p. 2.
[66] *FBIS Daily Report – Soviet Union* 93: 208 (29 October 1993), pp. 53–4 [from *Interfax*, "Urals Official Rejects Medvedev Criticism on Constitution," 28 October 1993].

the narrative of the development of the Urals Republic supports the concept of mutual constitution of local understandings and institutional and experiential contexts. That is, the creation and denouement of the Urals Republic in Sverdlovsk and the minimal actions toward discussion of a movement for greater sovereignty in Samara were determined by both the particular underlying ideas about the regional economy and understandings of political and economic categories, as well as by the experience of regional actors within the institutional context of 1992–3. In other words, the *imagined economies* in Sverdlovsk and Samara – those which were subjectively constructed rather than objectively given – constituted the economic basis of sovereignty movements in the two regions.

Conclusion

This book has been about the development of economic interests and movements for greater sovereignty. Using my analytic framework of imagined economies, I have examined the experience of Russian regional autonomy movements in the early 1990s and have argued that regional economic interests are intersubjective, contingent, and institutionally specific, and likewise, that the economic basis of the sovereignty movement in Sverdlovsk was a function of local understandings of the economy and particular institutional contexts.

Two last points on the role of institutional context need to be made to conclude and extend this analysis. First, I will discuss how attention to institutional context and social understandings, in particular the orthodox and heterodox interplay during perestroika, help us to understand both the timing of nationalist movements in the USSR and the end of the Soviet system. Second, I will briefly outline how the changing institutional context helps explain how regional economic demands were transformed in the post-1993 period. Finally, I will consider some implications of the imagined economies framework for further research in political economy, the constructivist paradigm, and studies of nationalism.

Timing of Nationalist Movements and the End of the Soviet System

One of the most intriguing questions of Russian and Soviet politics is why the USSR collapsed. And what explains its timing in the late 1980s rather than earlier? Systemic arguments about military pressure from the West or economic decline provide some important insight into the international context of perestroika and the long-term prognosis for the Soviet Union, but they cannot account either for the timing of Gorbachev's reforms or for

245

the institutional specificities of perestroika and glasnost, which ultimately led to the destruction of the CPSU, the introduction of elections, and liberalization.[1] Moreover, arguments that assume regional economic interests and take for granted a natural interest in greater sovereignty focus on the lowered costs of expression during perestroika or potential economic gains for pursuing greater sovereignty.[2] However, such arguments belie evidence of a lack of homogenous interest in sovereignty across territories, either in the USSR among union republics or in the Russian Federation among constituent units (republics, oblasts, and krais). And such arguments neglect the matter of how nationalist interests were constructed to begin with.

This study, focused on regionalism in the Russian Federation in the early 1990s, locates the development of political and economic interests within the broader question of the origins of nationalism.[3] Following Anderson, Gellner, Suny, and others, the process of coming to see one's group as a group, and of cognitively disconnecting the destiny of one's group from that of others, including the center, is crucially important to the development of particular interests and group-based activity, namely nationalism. To the extent that individuals think of themselves as merely interchangeable cogs in a great machine, or undifferentiated bits blown about by the winds of fate or the whims of centralized authorities, there is little space for imagining an alternative future or the possibility of taking action to shape that future. The argument of this book, which uses constructivist political economy and social theory, suggests an answer, relying on ideas and institutions, to the question of how differential understandings of regional economic and political interests could emerge from an ideologically centralized system.

While some claim that ideology was not important to the end of the USSR because the decline in the belief in Leninist ideology predated

---

[1] See for example, Stephen Brooks and William Wohlforth, "From Old Thinking to New Thinking in Qualitative Research," *International Security* 26:4 (March 2002), pp. 93–112. For an alternative argument specifically on the end of the cold war, see Matthew Evangelista, *Unarmed Forces: The Transnational Movement to End the Cold War* (Ithaca, NY: Cornell Univ. Press, 1999).

[2] Daniel Treisman, "Russia's 'Ethnic Revival': The Separatist Activism of Regional Leaders in a Postcommunist Order," *World Politics* 49:2 (1997), pp. 212–49; and D. Treisman, *After the Deluge: Regional Crisis and Political Consolidation in Russia* (Ann Arbor, MI: Univ. of Michigan Press, 1999).

[3] For an excellent and exhaustive analysis of the timing and development of nationalist movements, and the breakup of the USSR, see Mark Beissinger, *Nationalist Mobilization and the Collapse of the Soviet State* (Cambridge: Cambridge Univ. Press, 2002).

perestroika, I argue that, conceptually, perestroika was aimed at propping up Leninism, and that this very process, via the orthodox-heterodox dialectic, is what ultimately undermined Leninist ideology. That is, the ideological decay, which was clearly evident in the 1970s, inspired Gorbachev's attempt to achieve a truly Leninist system, and this ideological battle is what drove much of the institutional reforms during perestroika. In this sense, ideological and ideational factors were an important part of the institutional reforms of perestroika – this despite the fact that ultimately perestroika destroyed Leninism.

Similarly, on an institutional level, perestroika was not aimed at destroying the Soviet state or communism, although that was its result.[4] Perestroika was an attempt to *strengthen* the Soviet system. However, rather than transforming the Communist Party, perestroika and the perestroika-catalyzed heterodox movement of rasstroika conceptually and institutionally destroyed the Communist Party and, thereby, the Soviet system. Opportunities for a heterodox project that would radically upset Soviet political and economic power were not only made possible but were also seized upon at every chance by those intent on weakening central Soviet power. Thus, although it was not intended, perestroika fatally weakened Soviet political and economic institutions.

In summary, it was the combination of the ideational revolution along with the perestroika-inspired institutional devastation that proved so damaging to the USSR as a state and so crucial to the development of nationalist and regionalist interests.[5] The decentralization and increased fluidity of economic and political organization that followed the end of the CPSU created the conceptual space for novel political strategies such as nationalism and separatism. And the disordering of principles for allocation of federal and regional resources widened the field of imagination for region-specific conceptions of politics, the economy, and the regions' place in the state.

---

[4] For an analysis that focuses on the institutional bases of the end of the USSR, see Valerie Bunce, *Subversive Institutions: The Design and the Destruction of Socialism and the State* (Cambridge: Cambridge Univ. Press, 1999).

[5] For an analysis that is somewhat complementary to this one, see Steven Kotkin, "1991 and the Russian Revolution: Sources, Conceptual Categories, Analytical Frameworks," *The Journal of Modern History* 70:2 (June 1998), pp. 384–425. Kotkin identifies an interesting deficit in the historiography of the end of the Soviet Union. Most scholars turned primarily to nationalism in explaining the destruction of the Soviet Union, but in the process they mistakenly ignored the role of ideology and specifically the role of the decline of communism and class as an organizing principle.

Post-1993 Federalism in Russia

The institutionally contingent nature of economic and political interests is demonstrated not only by the tumultuous period of sovereignty movements described in this book but also by the post-1993 institutional context. The eventual state of federal relations in Russia was a contingent, rather than predetermined outcome. In addition, consideration of the post-1993 institutional context suggests how regional interests were transformed, given that new context, and thus provides further support for a contingent and contextual explanation of the timing of movements for greater sovereignty in the Russian Federation, as outlined in the imagined economies framework.

One of the clearest indicators of the uncertainty and contingent nature of the eventual form of federalism in the Russian Federation was the use of violence in the tragic Chechen wars (as well as against the Parliament). Given the center's apparent willingness to use any means necessary to control separatism, it cannot be entirely ruled out that the federal government might have acted with equally destructive force against other regions. Even though the probability of violence against Russian regions was indeed very low, the achievement of greater autonomy through peaceful means in Sverdlovsk, as well as in Tatarstan and other regions with movements for greater sovereignty, was, at the time, not the only conceivable outcome.

Moreover, the eventual path of Russian Federalism via the development of democratic, more autonomous, decentralized regional governance was also not preordained.[6] Rather than raising the powers and responsibilities of the oblasts and krais to that of republics, another option for federalism in Russia could have been recentralization through the elimination of all republican privilege and even republics themselves. This option was expressed in the idea of creating *guberniias*, which would be large multi-subject provinces with internal administrative divisions, completely blind to ethnicity. The creation of guberniias was supported by Russian nationalists, most notably by Aleksandr Solzhenitsyn and Vladimir Zhirinovskii, but also by some prominent liberals such as Gavriil Popov. Zhirinovskii publicly stated that if he and his party, the LDPR, ever came to power, on the first day of his rule he would form guberniias by decree and arrest all republican presidents.[7] On the second day, Zhirinovskii said, Russia would be

---

[6] Indeed, democracy in the regions remains questionable in most cases.
[7] The Liberal Democratic Party of Russia (which is neither liberal nor democratic, but rather extremely nationalist) was extraordinarily successful in the December 1993 elections but has since been less popular.

unified, and he would therefore create smaller administrative units within guberniias.[8]

President Putin's creation of seven federal districts (*federal'nyi okrug*) in May 2000, although sometimes confused with the guberniia concept, was essentially a reorganization of President Yeltsin's earlier system of presidential representatives. Rather than presidential representatives in each region, Putin appointed a plenipotentiary (*polnomochnyi predstavitel'* or *polpred*) in each of the seven federal districts. The federal districts correspond to existing military districts as well as the traditional macro-regions (Siberia, Volga, Urals, etc.). Initially there was much concern that five of these plenipotentiaries were military officers, but as it turns out these plenipotentiaries are mainly involved in the oversight of federal employees, rather than interfering with regional governance. Moreover, it is important to note that the federal districts are (thus far) not subjects or constituent units of the Federation and therefore do not currently represent a radical reorganization of the state-territorial units that comprise the Federation – as Zhirinovskii's guberniia concept would have.

These two points – the use of violence and the existence of radically different alternatives – highlight the role of historically specific factors in the development of Russian federalism. This contingency is realized in the specificity of institutional contexts. After 1993, as the institutional context changed, so too did the articulation of regional interests. The lack of separatism and movements for greater sovereignty in the Russian Federation after 1993 coincides with a consolidation of the boundaries of economic and political categories and the opportunities to pursue regional economic and political interests by different means. Rather than sovereignty movements, regional economic and political demands in the post-1993 period took different forms, but the forms that they took were based both on the new institutional context and the legacy of the 1991–3 sovereignty movements.

At the federal level, the Constitution and other new institutions, including most prominently the Federation Council, but more recently the Presidential State Council, have channeled the expression of regional interests away from movements for greater sovereignty. At the regional level, a range of new institutions also worked in conjunction with the new federal

---

[8] Vladimir Shlapentokh, Roman Levita, and Mikhail Loiberg, *From Submission to Rebellion: The Provinces versus the Center in Russia* (Boulder, CO: Westview, 1997), p. 119.

institutions, including the development of inter-regional associations, regional political parties, elected regional executives, bilateral treaties, and more recently, attempts at centralization of regional laws and local self-government reform. All these institutions were important to the end of sovereignty movements in Russia.[9]

Returning to the case of Sverdlovsk, the post-1993 central institutional changes, which were partially a result of the demands of the Urals Republic movement, altered the landscape of political and economic opportunities available to regional actors. In the process, Sverdlovsk actors' interest in creating a "republic" was replaced by interests in pursuing regional demands for political and economic equality through the array of new federal institutions.

More generally, the Constitution of December 1993 did not bring an end to the articulation of regional political and economic demands, but it did mark the end of formal sovereignty movements, and in that sense it went some way toward transforming regional political and economic relations in the Federation into the realm of "normal" politics. In other words, the Constitution, by promising de jure equality for all regions, was crucial in transforming interests in sovereignty into interests in pursuit of economic and political demands by other means. Along these lines, Gail Lapidus has argued that in the post-1993 era, rather than regions-versus-republics, the federalism debate in Russia has shifted to conflicts over jurisdiction and authority, and resource allocation and control.[10] Thus, the strategies for pursuing conflict have changed; rather than sovereignty movements, and in particular changing a territory's institutional status, regions and republics alike pursue greater political and economic authority within the status quo institutional bounds.

Since its inception, the Federation Council has provided a forum for the articulation of regional interests and greater regional representation in federal governance. Even the very first elections to the Council in December 1993 played this role. In Sverdlovsk, for example, in the few weeks following

---

[9] The one exception to this, of course, is Chechnia where the secessionist war continues. Because Chechnia, for a variety of reasons including ongoing war, never really participated in pre- or post-1993 federal institutions, the institutional context, which was so vital to the development of specific political and economic interests for other regions of Russia, did not apply to it.

[10] Gail W. Lapidus, "Asymmetrical Federalism and State Breakdown in Russia," *Post-Soviet Affairs* 15:1 (1999), pp. 74–82.

his dismissal, Eduard Rossel collected the requisite 65,000 signatures and registered as a candidate to the Federation Council for Sverdlovsk Oblast.[11] In explaining why he decided to run as a Sverdlovsk representative to the Federation Council, Rossel stated,

I decided to take part in the elections in order to bring the idea of regional autonomy to its conclusion via the Federation Council. It is not only a matter of our oblast, it is a question of all 68 Russian oblasts, which still have even fewer rights than the republics. That must not be, just as there should not be loved and unloved children in a family.[12]

Rossel was easily elected, and after his election, he issued a statement to the voters of Sverdlovsk in which he thanked them for voting for him and assured them that he would continue to work for the formation of a Urals Republic.[13] Both of Rossel's statements cited earlier suggest that the idea of regional inequality had not disappeared, but the understanding of the institutional categories that could address inequality had changed.

After his election in 2000, one of President Putin's stated goals was to strengthen "vertical power" in the Federation, and he has pursued this concretely through changes to the federal institutional structure.[14] In addition to the federal districts and plenipotentiaries discussed earlier, the reform of the Federation Council and the introduction of a new Presidential State Council were other important parts of the federal reforms. In the context of the decentralized and in many ways chaotic 1990s, these changes marked steps toward "normalization" of federal relations, but unlike Yeltsin's fall 1993 institutional changes (principally, disbanding soviets and introducing

---

[11] "Former Sverdlovsk Governor to Stand for Parliament," *FBIS Daily Report – Soviet Union* 93: 220 (17 November 1993), p. 68 [from *Interfax*, 16 November 1993, Moscow].

[12] Rossel used the term *oblast* to describe the 68 non-republican subjects of the federation (i.e., 49 oblasts, 6 krais, 11 AOs, and 2 federal cities). L. Tsukanova, "Nashe pole deiatel'nosti – khoroshie zakony, schitaet deputat Eduard Rossel'," *Rossiiskie vesti*, no. 7, 12 January 1994, p. 2.

[13] "Ideia Ural'skoi Respubliki zhivet," *Kommersant'-Daily*, no. 245, 21 December 1993, p. 4.

[14] For comprehensive analysis of the changes to the federal structure, see Steven Solnick, "The New Federal Structure: More Centralized, or More of the Same?" *Program on New Approaches to Russian Security, Policy Memo Series*, no. 161 (2000); and M. Hyde, "Putin's Federal Reforms and Their Implications for Presidential Power in Russia," *Europe-Asia Studies* 53:5 (2001), pp. 719–43. For a fairly comprehensive assessment of legal reform under Putin, see R. Sharlet, "Putin and the Politics of Law in Russia," *Post-Soviet Affairs* 17:3 (2001), pp. 195–234.

the new Constitution and Federation Council), Putin's reforms did not entail a fundamental reworking of the representation of regional interests in the federal government.

In addition to institutional changes at the federal level, there have also been a range of regional institutions that worked in conjunction with the new federal institutions. The development of a variety of inter-regional associations throughout the Federation represents one of the ways that regional economic and political interests have been pursued in the post-1993 context. Most of the inter-regional associations correspond to the geographic macro-regions (e.g., Urals, the Volga, or the Far East) and to the new federal districts. And therefore, in most cases, these associations are a mechanism for addressing and coordinating the interests of different types of territorial units (oblasts, republics, and autonomous okrugs) within the same geographic macro-region. While the creation of some organizations dates back to the beginning of perestroika, many have been substantially developed in the post-1993 period. For example, the Urals Republic movement brought renewed interest and a substantive agenda to the Association for Economic Cooperation of Oblasts and Republics of the Urals (*Assotsiatsii ekonomicheskogo vzaimodeistviia oblastei i respublic Urala* or AECORU), and this organization has continued to thrive after the end of the Urals Republic movement.[15]

Moreover, some of these early inter-regional organizations were the basis for new organizations that worked in conjunction with the changing federal political institutions. For example, in Samara, Konstantin Titov served two terms (until 1996) as chair of the Greater Volga Association (*Assotsiatsiia Bol'shaia Volga*), which had been created during perestroika.[16] But in 1999, Titov started an organization of governors called Voice of Russia (*Golos Rossii*). And in the Urals, AECORU was the basis for several new organizations. The day after his election to the Federation Council, Rossel said that he wanted all the deputies from the Urals region to form a "Urals Senate"

[15] The organization included five oblasts, two republics, and one AO in the Urals: Cheliabinsk, Kurgan, Orenburg, Perm', and Sverdlovsk oblasts; the republics of Bashkortostan and Udmurtia; and Komi-Permiak AO. On November 10, the day after the ordered disbanding of the Sverdlovsk Oblast Soviet, and the day of Rossel's dismissal, AECORU delegates voted to create the post of president of the association, and they elected Eduard Rossel to that position the same day. A. Levin, "Desiat' dnei v noiabre," *Oblastnaia gazeta*, no. 137, 1 December 1993, p. 3.

[16] This association included Astrakhan, Nizhnii Novgorod, Penza, Samara, Saratov, Ul'ianovsk, and Volgograd oblasts and the republics of Tatarstan, Chuvashiia, and Mordoviia.

that could serve as an unofficial representative body, while the AECORU, composed of governors of the regions, could serve as its executive body.[17] Moreover, on December 30, 1993, *Pravda* reported that an Assembly of Urals Region Deputies, comprised of both Federation Council and Duma deputies, had been founded, and the association's stated goal was to support regional interests in parliament and to work on particular methods of implementation of reforms.[18]

The creation and development of regional parties is another manifestation of the changing institutional context of the pursuit of regional interests. For example, in Sverdlovsk, in preparation for the December 1993 elections, Rossel formed a group called Transformation of the Urals (*Preobrazhenie Urala*), which was officially a "non-party social and political union," but was essentially dedicated to advancing the interests of Sverdlovsk and the Urals.[19] The party won one quarter of the seats in the oblast legislature in the April 1994 elections, and in May 1995 was expanded into an all-Russia political movement Transformation of the Fatherland (*Preobrazhenie Otechestba*).[20] In December 1995, Transformation of the Fatherland got the highest percentage of votes of any party in Sverdlovsk, 12.1%, but nationally it got only 0.5%.[21] Rossel then devoted great effort to building Transformation of the Urals as a party for the April 1996 oblast legislative elections, and the party won a majority in both houses of the legislature in those elections.[22]

Although Rossel used Transformation of the Urals for his own political purposes, including his gubernatorial electoral campaigns, the party effectively conveyed a broader cultural message focused on supporting the development of a Urals identity. The party echoed the claims of the Urals Republic movement in terms of the promotion of regional equality, and it also sought to promote Urals culture in the form of restoration of historical

---

[17] "Former Sverdlovsk Governor Elected to Federation Council," *FBIS Daily Report – Soviet Union* 93: 237 (13 December 1993), p. 61 [from *Interfax*, 13 December 1993, Moscow].

[18] "Sobranie deputatov ural'skogo regiona," *Pravda*, no. 220, 30 December 1993, p. 1. Also see Tsukanova, 12 January 1994, p. 2.

[19] *Preobrazhenie Urala*, no. 1, 1996.

[20] Vladimir Gel'man and Grigorii Golosov, "Regional Party System Formation in Russia: The Deviant Case of Sverdlovsk Oblast," *The Journal of Communist Studies and Transition Politics* 14:1–2 (March–June 1998), p. 35.

[21] Ibid., p. 37.

[22] Ibid., p. 39, Table 1. Also see "Patterns of Regional Development," *Russian Regional Report* vol. 2, no. 8, 27 February 1997.

sites like Verkhotur'e, one of the oldest settlements in the urals, and reburial of the Romanovs.[23]

Interestingly, in Samara, Governor Titov has continued to work closely with the center and with federal parties, rather than forming Samara-based parties. In 1994 Titov joined the council of Russia's Democratic Choice (*Demokraticheskii vybor Rossi* or DVR), and in 1995 he joined Our Home – Russia (*Nash dom – Rossiia* NDR), which was Prime Minister Viktor Chernomyrdin's party, and for the December 1995 parliamentary elections was the deputy leader of NDR. Later, Titov joined another national party, the Union of Right Forces (*Soiuz pravykh sil*).

Consistent with some of the implications of the imagined economies framework, Vladimir Gel'man and Grigorii Golosov have analyzed regional party development and have outlined a nuanced argument that relies heavily on process and institutional opportunities.[24] In comparing party development in Sverdlovsk, St. Petersburg, Novosibirsk, and Buriatia, they found that structural economic conditions do not explain regional party development. Instead, they argued that party development depends on constant intra-elite competition within the structure of elections and via the use of political parties to contest the elections.

Perhaps the most important political institutional development in the regions after 1993 has been the establishment of elected regional executives. The movement for a Urals Republic and the actions of Sverdlovsk Oblast played an important role in this development, but the federal executive-legislative context was also important. Moreover, the institution of elected governors and mayors has itself become an important mechanism for the pursuit of regional interests.

The debate over elected regional executives dates back to the 1991–3 period. Under the old (pre-December 1993) system, only six regions had elected heads of administration.[25] And election of the executive had been a key demand of movements for greater sovereignty in regions such as Sverdlovsk.[26] In the fall of 1993, Yeltsin decreed that initially he would

---

[23] Yaroslav Startsev, "Gubenatorial Politics in Sverdlovsk *oblast'*," *Post-Soviet Affairs* 15:4 (1999), p. 343.

[24] Gel'man and Golosov, 1998.

[25] These were Amurskaia, Briansk, Lipetsk, Orel, Penza, and Smolensk. Michael McFaul and Nikolai Petrov, eds., *Politicheskii al'manakh Rossii 1997*, vol. 1 (Washington, DC: Carnegie Endowment for International Peace, 1998), p. 125.

[26] *Ustav Sverdlovskoi Oblasti*, reprinted in full in A. D. Kirillov, B. A. Kirillov, and A. E. Ryzhkov, *Ural: stanovlenie oblastnykh zakonodatel'nykh organov vlasti* (Ekaterinburg: fonda politologicheskikh issledovanii, Ural politicheskii, 1995), pp. 145–98.

appoint all governors but that elections would be held one year later. However, when it came time for elections in October 1994, Yeltsin instead issued a decree forbidding the election of governors.

In April 1995, the Sverdlovsk Oblast Soviet challenged Yeltsin's decree banning elections in the federal Constitutional Court.[27] This court challenge was a serious threat to central authority since overturning Yeltsin's decree would open the way to gubernatorial elections in every region in Russia. However, because governors were to serve as representatives in the Federation Council, which was the new upper house of parliament, appointment by the president would have strengthened the federal executive vis-à-vis the Duma (lower house of parliament). Therefore, the issue of gubernatorial elections was intertwined in the politics of federal legislative-executive institutional power struggles.

Instead of allowing a decision by the Constitutional Court, Yeltsin and Rossel worked out a deal whereby the Sverdlovsk Oblast Soviet withdrew its formal appeal to the Constitutional Court and Yeltsin issued another decree calling Sverdlovsk an exceptional case, thereby allowing it to hold gubernatorial elections.[28] And by December 1995, Novosibirsk, Tambov, and Tver' had held elections.[29] As more and more regions got exceptions, eventually, by mid-1996 after several rounds of negotiations with the Duma as well as other regions, Yeltsin lifted his general ban on gubernatorial elections in all Russian regions.[30]

The extension of bilateral treaties, between Moscow and individual regions, represented another example of the expansion of rights previously reserved for republics to oblasts and krais.[31] The bilateral treaties also

---

[27] Gerald M. Easter, "Redefining Center-Regional Relations in the Russian Federation: Sverdlovsk *oblast*," *Europe-Asia Studies* 49:4 (1997), p. 625.

[28] For additional analysis of the struggle for gubernatorial elections in Sverdlovsk between Rossel, the oblast legislature, Aleksei Strakhov (the head of administration), Moscow, and the courts, see Easter, 1997, pp. 625–6. Also see Gel'man and Golosov, 1998, pp. 35–7.

[29] McFaul and Petrov, 1998, p. 125.

[30] Gubernatorial elections in Sverdlovsk Oblast took place in August 1995 and again in 1999, and in both cases Eduard Rossel was easily elected: in 1995 he received 59.9% of the vote in the second round, and in 1999 he received 63% in the second round. Titov remained head of administration of Samara from his appointment in 1993 until 1996 when he was elected governor with 60% of the vote against Valentin Romanov, a communist candidate.

[31] For a discussion of bilateral treaties, see E. Bukhval'd, "The Bilateral Treaty Process and the Prospects of Federalism," *Problems of Economic Transition* 43:11 (2001), pp. 30–42. On the treaties and the "contractual" rather than "constitutional" nature of Russian federalism, see K. Stoner-Weiss, "Central Weakness and Provincial Autonomy: Observations on the Devolution Process in Russia," *Post-Soviet Affairs* 15:1 (1999), pp. 87–106.

represented an additional mechanism for addressing issues of federal versus regional responsibility. The treaties affected federal economic relations because they often involved agreements over levels of taxation and subsidies, the control and use of natural resources, regional currency-equivalents (*vekselia*), and regional trade restrictions.[32] Eventually more than half of the regions of Russia would sign such treaties.[33]

However, although the treaties were a step toward institutionalization of federal relations, the process of dividing authority was ad hoc.[34] Many treaties were amended several times, and some contradicted rules set out in the Constitution. In defining spheres of authority, the bilateral treaties also competed with regional-level laws, some of which also contradicted either federal laws or the Constitution itself.[35] Therefore, the bilateral treaties did not by any means solve the general problem of federal relations, but they did represent both a novel means of addressing regional demands, and some level of institutionalization of the process of federal relations.

As the experience of the bilateral treaties demonstrates, a consistent problem of post-Soviet Russia from 1991 on has been both the outright contradiction between written laws and practice, and the selective application of law by both regional and federal officials. President Putin's 2000 introduction of legal changes, which give the president greater ability to force regional executives to follow federal law and to warn and remove or suspend regional executives for repeated violation, have addressed some of these contradictions, but the key point is that the legal battles over regional versus federal laws represent a changed context for the pursuit of regional interests – that is, through the courts, rather than through social movements.

The post-1993 institutional context demonstrates that as the relevant categories in economic relations changed – that is, with the new Constitution, the Federation Council, new regional economic associations, regional

---

[32] Lapidus, 1999, p. 79.

[33] Sverdlovsk signed a bilateral treaty (and seventeen subsequent agreements) in January 1996. See *Preobrazhenie Urala*, no. 1, 1996; and Vasilii Kononenko, "'Eduard Rossel' realizoval, nakonets, svoiu ideiu o chastichnom suverenitete Sverdlovskoi oblasti," *Izvestiia*, no. 7, 13 January 1996.

[34] For an analysis of bilateral bargaining as a path-dependent development resulting from the particularities of Soviet federalism, see Mikhail Filippov and Olga Shvetsova, "Asymmetric Bilateral Bargaining in the New Russian Federation: A Path-Dependence Explanation," *Communist and Post-Communist Studies* 32 (1999), pp. 61–76.

[35] For a summary of political and economic conflicts between the center and regions in the mid to late 1990s, see Lapidus, 1999, pp. 74–82.

parties, elected regional executives, and, bilateral treaties – the institutional context supporting the development of interests in movements for greater sovereignty had been radically diminished.

However, the legacy of the sovereignty movements' demands has not disappeared, and the future of Russian federalism will remain significantly influenced by the experience of federal relations during the early 1990s. In this respect, analysis of the first Russian Republic is crucial to any understanding of the subsequent boundaries of political and economic life in the Russian Federation. And, particular institutional contexts, as emphasized in the analysis here, will remain a crucial component to explanations of the development of regional political and economic interests. In other words, in the coming years, we should not expect further movements for greater sovereignty in the Russian Federation unless there were to be a major institutional transformation, combined with marked articulation of local political or economic grievances.

Potential for an Imagined Economies Research Agenda

In explaining the development of interests and, in particular, interests in greater sovereignty, the imagined economies framework directs attention to local understandings of the economy and particular institutional contexts. Given the institutional fluidity of the 1990s in Russia, as well as the chaotic context of information about the economy resulting from the transition from communism to capitalism, one might argue that the immediate post-Soviet context is an unusually fecund moment for diversity in economic understandings; therefore, the framework may be specific to such transitional contexts. Indeed, one might wonder if markets bring rationality both to the distribution of goods and services as well as to understandings of the economy.

Some rational choice proponents have argued that instrumental rationality arguments work best in contexts where choice is constrained, and conversely, contexts such as the Russia of the early 1990s would be too institutionally unstable for rational choice analysis. For example, Bates et al. write that "The greatest achievement of rational choice theory has been to provide tools for studying political outcomes in stable institutional settings. . . . Political transitions seem to defy rational forms of analysis."[36]

---

[36] Robert H. Bates, Rui P. de Figueiredo, Jr., and Barry R. Weingast, "The Politics of Interpretation: Rationality, Culture, and Transition," *Politics and Society* 26:4 (1998),

In these situations they argue that "interpretivism" might be required. Such arguments may suggest that the analytic framework of imagined economies is particularly suited to contexts such as the immediate post-Soviet period.

The analysis of both orthodox and heterodox critiques of the economy, however, as outlined in Chapter 2, suggests that in every economy – even in stable settings such as American voting behavior – the possibility of mediated and heterogeneous interpretations of economic conditions exists. I argue that there is strong evidence that cognitive processes, as well as elite manipulation, systemic framing, and institutions more generally, affect the way individuals and groups understand the economy. Therefore, although the post-Soviet context may have been particularly chaotic and open to a range of interpretations, as demonstrated by the discussion of the complexity of data outlined in Chapter 1, all economies are complicated, and therefore there will always be multiple possible understandings of economic conditions.[37]

As I have emphasized, however, institutions are crucially important both to the mediation of economic understandings and to the development of economic interests. In this way, stable institutions may smooth out some of the variance in heterogeneous understandings of the economy, but less heterogeneity does not take away from the basic point that, even if variance is reduced, economic meanings are still subjectively constructed, rather than objectively given. Therefore, even in institutionally stable contexts, attention to local understandings of the economy and the process by which they have developed will contribute to understanding the development of political and economic interests.

Scholars can access intersubjective understandings of the economy in a variety of sources including public opinion polls and interviews as well as historical texts and images. The analysis in this book has relied on discourse and content as well as quantitative analysis, but the imagined economies framework is not specific to any particular methodology. Cognitive mapping, experiments, formal models, or other methods may also be appropriate given the types of sources available. Therefore, the methodological

pp. 604–5. For similar analysis of "constrained" choices, see Debra Satz and John Ferejohn, "Rational Choice and Social Theory," *Journal of Philosophy* 91:2 (February 1994), pp. 71–87.

[37] For an analysis of economic decision-making that specifically considers the context of uncertainty, see Jens Beckert, "What Is Sociological about Economic Sociology? Uncertainty and the Embeddedness of Economic Action," *Theory and Society* 25:6 (December 1996), pp. 803–40.

demands of the framework are driven by the object of analysis, (i.e., local understandings and particular institutional contexts), rather than specific analytical techniques.

Implications for Political Economy

The imagined economies framework supports a broadly integrative approach to political economy. By considering a range of models of cognition and decision-making, the imagined economies framework suggests a way to account theoretically for both beliefs and instrumental rationality in the development and pursuit of economic and political interests. In addition, the framework is an attempt at greater integration of the insights of psychology and cognitive science into social scientific analysis, and in particular the application of schema theory to political economy.

Finally, the imagined economies framework specifically addresses a major question in political economy research, namely, the origins of interests. Following from orthodox and heterodox critiques of economic objectivity, I have argued that economic interests are neither structurally determined nor primordially inherent. The analysis of the Urals Republic and noted absence of activity in Samara demonstrated that there was no unvarying interest in greater autonomy amongst regional actors. The imagined economies framework suggests that interests must be considered in terms of particular categories of understanding (i.e., local intersubjective understandings) and specific institutional contexts.

Nationalism and Constructivism

The primary theoretical contributions of the imagined economies framework are the inclusion of psychology and social theory in the constructivist political economy literature and the expansion of the constructivist paradigm to economic interests in the nationalism literature. This latter extension follows from both orthodox and heterodox critiques of economic objectivity outside the field of nationalism, as well as constructivist approaches in the nationalism literature that focus on non-economic claims. Objective economic claims are one of the final frontiers of the nationalism literature, in the sense that, to date, analysis of economic interests in studies of nationalism have been treated relatively separately from approaches to economic interests in the constructivist political economy literature. The imagined economies framework is an attempt to broaden the ongoing study of the imagination of political communities to embrace the generation of economic interests as part of the conception of political identities.

The framework presented here has demonstrated that economic interests are not always determined by "objective" economic conditions. In contrast to those who would continue to debate whether regionalism is more likely to occur in economically advanced regions or economically less developed regions, my analysis suggests that economic conditions do not seamlessly produce economic interests nor the expression of political demands.

While the analysis in this book examined the economic basis of particular regional movements in Russia, the theoretical arguments developed here are not limited to Russian regionalism. The case of the Urals Republic bids scholars to consider how regional economic interests may be constructed and formed into a basis for political action. In this case, for example, the imagined economies framework can contribute to making sense of the contradictory findings regarding the role of economic conditions in the secession literature more broadly. More cases, especially those that are explicitly nationalist or separatist, which allow for controlled comparison of ethnicity and economic factors, are needed to develop this argument further, but the imagined economies framework presented here is a first step along the road to truly integrating analysis of the economy into constructivist analyses of nationalism.

Appendix Tables

Table A1 *All Subjects of the Russian Federation According to Federal Districts and Goskomstat Macro-Region Classifications*

Federal District	Goskomstat Macro-Regional Classification	Region Type	Region Name
	None	1 oblast	Kaliningrad
		2 republics	Kareliia, Komi
Northwestern Federal District (*Severo-zapadnyi federal'nyi okrug*)	Northern (*Severnyi raion*)	1 autonomous oblast	Nenetskii (Arkhangel'sk Obl.)[a]
		3 oblasts	Arkhangel'sk, Murmansk, Vologda
	North-Western (*Severo-Zapadnyi raion*)	3 oblasts	Leningradskaia, Novgorod, Pskov
		1 federal city	St. Petersburg
Central Federal District (*Tsentral'nyi federal'nyi okrug*)	Central (*Tsentral'nyi raion*)	12 oblasts	Briansk, Iaroslavl', Ivanovo, Kaluga, Kostroma, Moskovskaia, Orel, Riazan', Smolensk, Tula, Tver', Vladimir
		1 federal city	Moscow
	Central-Black Earth (*Tsentral'no-Chernozemnyi raion*)	5 oblasts	Belgorod, Kursk, Lipetsk, Tambov, Voronezh

(continued)

Table A1 *(continued)*

Federal District	Goskomstat Macro-Regional Classification	Region Type	Region Name
Southern Federal District *(Iuzhnyi federal'nyi okrug)*	Northern Caucasus *(Severo-Kavkazskii raion)*	7 republics	Adygeia, Chechnia, Dagestan, Ingushetiia, Kabardino-Balkariia, Karachaevo-Cherkeiia, Severnaia Osetiia
		1 oblast	Rostovskaia
		2 krais	Krasnodar, Stavropol'
	Volga *(Povolzhskii raion)*	1 republic	Kalmykiia
		2 oblasts	Astrakhan', Volgograd
Volga Federal District *(Privolzhskii federal'nyi okrug)*	Volga *(Povolzhskii raion)*	1 republic	Tatarstan
		4 oblasts	Penza, Samara, Saratov, Ul'ianovsk
	Volga-Viatskii *(Volgo-Viatskii raion)*	3 republics	Chuvashiia, Marii El, Mordoviia
		2 oblasts	Kirov, Nizhegorodskaia
	Urals *(Ural'skii raion)*	2 republics	Bashkortostan, Udmurtiia
		1 autonomous okrugs	Komi-Permiatskii (Perm' Obl.)
		2 oblasts	Orenburg, Perm'
Urals Federal District *(Ural'skii federal'nyi okrug)*	Urals *(Ural'skii raion)*	3 oblasts	Cheliabinsk, Kurgan, Sverdlovsk
	Western Siberia *(Zapadno-Sibirskii raion)*	2 autonomous okrugs	Khanty-Mansiiskii (Tiumen' Obl.), Iamalo-Nenetskii (Tiumen' Obl.)
		1 oblast	Tiumen'

(continued)

Table A1 *(continued)*

Federal District	Goskomstat Macro-Regional Classification	Region Type	Region Name
	Western Siberia (*Zapadno-Sibirskii raion*)	1 republic	Altai
		1 krai	Altaiskii
		4 oblasts	Kemerovo, Novosibirsk, Omsk, Tomsk
Siberian Federal District (*Sibirskii federal'nyi okrug*)		3 republics	Buriatiia, Khakasiia, Tyva
	Eastern Siberia (*Vostochno-Sibirskii raion*)	4 autonomous okrugs	Aginskii Buriatskii (Chita Obl.), Evenkiiskii (Krasnoiarsk Krai), Taimyrskii (Krasnoiarsk Krai), Ust'-Ordynskii Buriatskii (Irkutsk Obl.)
		2 oblasts	Chita, Irkutsk
		1 krai	Krasnoiarsk
Far Eastern Federal District (*Dal'nevostochnyi federal'nyi okrug*)	Far Eastern (*Dal'nevostochnyi raion*)	1 republic	Sakha
		2 autonomous okrugs	Chukotskii, Koriakskii (Kamchatskaia Obl.)
		1 autonomous oblast	Evreiskaia
		2 krais	Khabarovsk, Primorskii
		4 oblasts	Amurskaia, Kamchatskaia, Magadan, Sakhalinskaia

[a] For each autonomous okrug, the historic statistical "host" region is given in parentheses; in these cases individual AO data have usually been aggregated with the host region's data, except Chukotskii and Evreiskaia where data have been given separately.

Table A2 *Source Data for Indicators of Regional Activism Among Russian Regions, 1990–1993 (Key on p. 267)*

Region	1. Unilateral Change in Administrative Status before Oct.'93	2. Adoption of a Regional "Constitution"	3. Non-binding Referendum on Sovereignty	4. Assertion that Regional Law takes Precedence over Federal Law	5. Assertion of Economic Autonomy
Altaiskii					Iz 9/1/93
Amurskaia					EG
Arkhangel'sk	Iz 1/24/93; PAR			Iz 1/24/93	Iz 4/8/93
Astrakhan'					
Belgorod					Iz 1/15/93; Iz 7/1/93
Briansk					Iz 7/1/93
Cheliabinsk	Iz 7/15/93; K 7/6/93; K 9/30/93;[a] PAR		PAR	PAR	Iz 7/1/92
Chita	Iz 11/21/91		Iz 7/7/93; K 9/14/93		EG
Iaroslavl'					Iz 1/29/92; Iz 3/10/93; Iz 8/28/93
Irkutsk	Iz 10/26/91; Iz 11/18/91; Iz 6/23/93				Iz 7/10/91
Ivanovo					
Kaliningrad					Iz 5/12/93; K 7/7/93; K 7/8/93; K 7/17/93; K 9/10/93;
Kaluga					
Kamchatskaia					EG
Kemerovo					Iz 3/26/92; Iz 8/12/92

(continued)

Table A2 *(continued)*

Region	1. Unilateral Change in Administrative Status before Oct.'93	2. Adoption of a Regional "Constitution"	3. Non-binding Referendum on Sovereignty	4. Assertion that Regional Law takes Precedence over Federal Law	5. Assertion of Economic Autonomy
Khabarovsk					EG
Kirov					
Kostroma					
Krasnodar					
Krasnoiarsk	Iz 10/31/91; Iz 11/22/91; Iz 2/12/92; Iz 2/25/92	Iz 5/21/93		Iz 5/21/93	Iz 7/1/91; Iz 11/22/91; Iz 7/8/93; Iz 9/3/93
Kurgan	K 7/6/93; K 9/30/93[a]				
Kursk					Iz 1/15/93; Iz 7/1/93
Leningradskaia Obl.	K 9/15/93[b]		Iz 8/6/93; PAR		EG
Lipetsk					Iz 1/15/93
Magadan					FIz 6/26/93–7/2/93; FIz 7/10/93–7/16/93
Moskovskaia Obl.	PAR[c]		PAR	PAR	Iz 3/10/93
Murmansk					
Nizhnii Novgorod	EG				
Novgorod					Iz 6/3/91; Iz 6/17/91
Novosibirsk					Iz 7/1/91
Omsk					Iz 5/26/93
Orel				PAR	Iz 1/15/93
Orenburg	K 7/6/93; K 9/30/93[a]				
Penza					
Perm'	K 7/6/93; K 9/30/93[a]				

(continued)

Table A2 *(continued)*

Region	1. Unilateral Change in Administrative Status before Oct.'93	2. Adoption of a Regional "Constitution"	3. Non-binding Referendum on Sovereignty	4. Assertion that Regional Law takes Precedence over Federal Law	5. Assertion of Economic Autonomy
Primorskii	Iz 7/7/93; Iz 7/8/93; K 7/8/93;[d] PAR				K 2/13/93; K 4/15/93; K 5/25/93; K 8/20/93; K 10/13/93
Pskov			PAR		
Riazan'				PAR	
Rostovskaia					Iz 7/1/93; FIz 10/29/93–11/4/93
Sakhalinskaia			PAR		EG
Samara	PAR[e]				
Saratov		PAR	PAR		
Smolensk				PAR	
Stavropol'					
Sverdlovsk	Iz 8/3/93; Iz 9/17/93; K 7/7/93; K 7/9/93; K 9/6/93; K 9/25/93; K 10/28/93; K 11/2/93; K 12/21/93; PAR	Iz 10/28/93; K 9/25/93; K 9/30/93; K 10/28/93; K 11/02/93; PAR	Iz 8/3/93; PAR	K 10/28/93	
Tambov					Iz 1/15/93
Tiumen'	PAR				Iz 6/11/91; Iz 3/7/92

(continued)

Table A2 *(continued)*

Region	1. Unilateral Change in Administrative Status before Oct.'93	2. Adoption of a Regional "Constitution"	3. Non-binding Referendum on Sovereignty	4. Assertion that Regional Law takes Precedence over Federal Law	5. Assertion of Economic Autonomy
Tomsk	Iz 3/24/92; PAR		Iz 8/6/93; Iz 8/25/93; PAR		Iz 7/8/93; Iz 7/22/91
Tula					
Tver'					
Ul'ianovsk					
Vladimir					
Volgograd					K 2/27/93
Vologda	Iz 3/13/93; Iz 5/18/93; K 7/7/93; K 7/9/93; PAR	Iz 5/15/93	Iz 5/18/93; PAR	Iz 3/13/93	Iz 3/13/93
Voronezh	Iz 9/8/93[f]				Iz 1/15/93; Iz 7/1/93

Key:

Iz = *Izvestiia* (1990–3);

FIz = *Finansoviie izvestiia*, a joint publication of *Izvestiia* and the *Financial Times;*

K = *Kommersant'-Daily* (1993 only);

EG = Beth Mitchneck, "An Assessment of the Growing Local Economic Development Function of Local Authorities in Russia," *Economic Geography* 71:2 (April 1995), p. 159. Mitchneck lists data until June 1991 for declarations of sovereignty and free economic zones. No source information for the data is given;

PAR = Michael McFaul and Nikolai Petrov, *Politicheski al'manakh Rossii 1997.* vol. 1 (Moscow: Carnegie Endowment for International Peace, 1998), pp. 125–132, Table 1.3. No source information for the data is given.

[a] From articles about the Urals Republic saying the region intends to join the Republic in the future.

[b] Article discusses this possibility.

[c] Moscow and Moskovskaia Oblast were not distinguished in this source.

[d] The krai soviet first accepts and then rejects a declaration proclaiming the krai's sovereignty.

[e] This is not included in the index (Table 1.3) because the decision was after October 1993.

[f] The oblast soviet called for upgrading the status of all oblasts within the Russian Federation, not just its own.

Table A3 *Variable Description and Source Citations for Regional Conditions Model*

Variable Name	Description	Source
Real income	Regional market basket as % of income, as % of Rus. avg., averaged for 1992 and 1993	Goskomstat Rossii, *Tseny v Rossii: statisticheskii sbornik* (Moscow: Goskomstat Rossii, 1996), pp. 139–41.
Industrial production	Per capita regional industrial production as % of Rus. avg., averaged for 1991–3	Goskomstat Rossii, *Regions of Russia*, CD ROM, 2000 edition, Series 13.1.
Raw materials	Volume of raw materials (oil, gas, coal) as % of Rus. total volume, averaged for 1990–3	Goskomstat Rossii, *Promishlennost Rossii* (Moscow: Goskomstat Rossii, 1995), pp. 247–50.
Exports	Value of regional exports as % of Rus. total value averaged for 1990–3	Goskomstat Rossii, *Rossiiskii statisticheskii ezhegodnik* (Moscow: Goskomstat Rossii, 1995), pp. 869–72.
Defense employment	Defense Employment Index (range 0–5), 1980	Clifford Gaddy, *The Price of the Past: Russia's Struggle with the Legacy of a Militarized Economy* (Washington, DC: Brookings Institution Press, 1996), p. 155, Table 9–4. Author's estimates.
Unemployment	Regional unemployment rate as % of Rus. avg., averaged for 1992–3	Goskomstat Rossii, *Regions of Russia CD ROM*, 2000 edition, Series 3.10.
Net tax payments	Per capita net tax payments (taxes – transfers) as % of Rus. avg., 1992	Daniel Treisman data set.
Urbanization	Level of urban population in region as % of Rus. avg., averaged for 1991–3	Goskomstat Rossii, *Regions of Russia CD ROM*, 2000 edition, Series 2.2.
Education	Regional higher education level (population with higher and secondary special education) as % of Rus. avg., 1994	Goskomstat Rossii, *Rossiiskii statisticheskii ezhegodnik* (Moscow: Goskomstat Rossii, 1995), pp. 550–2.
Population	Regional population as % of Rus. avg., averaged for 1991–3	Goskomstat Rossii, *Regions of Russia CD ROM*, 2000 edition, Series 2.1.
Distance from Moscow	Region's distance from Moscow, as % of average distance from Moscow for all regions, 1991	G. M. Lappo, ed., *Goroda Rossii: entsiklopediia* (Moscow: nauchnoe izdatel'stvo Bol'shaia Rossiiskaia entsiklopediia, 1994).
Strikes	Total man-days lost to strikes as % of Rus. avg., averaged for 1990–3	Goskomstat Rossii, *Rossiiskii statisticheskii ezhegodnik* (Moscow: Goskomstat Rossii, 1994), pp. 475–6.

Table A4 *Variable Description and Source Citations for Regional Change Model*

Variable	Description	Source
Real income change	% change in cost of region's food basket as % of income, as % of Rus. avg. 1993 as % of 1992	Goskomstat Rossii, *Tseny v Rossii: statisticheskii sbornik* (Moscow: Goskomstat Rossii, 1996), pp. 139–41.
Industrial production change	% change in region's per cap. industrial production as a % of Rus. avg., 1993 as % of 1991	Goskomstat Rossii, *Regions of Russia CD ROM*, 2000 edition, Series 13.1.
Raw materials production change	% change in region's share in Rus. total volume production of oil, gas, and coal, 1993 as % of 1990	Goskomstat Rossii, *Promishlennost Rossii* (Moscow: Goskomstat Rossii, 1995), pp. 247–50.
Exports change	% change in region's share of the value of total Rus. exports, 1993 as % of 1990	Goskomstat Rossii, *Rossiiskii statisticheskii ezhegodnik* (Moscow: Goskomstat Rossii, 1995), pp. 869–72.
Unemployment change	% change in region's unemployment rate as % of Rus. avg., 1993 as % of 1992	Goskomstat Rossii, *Regions of Russia CD ROM*, 2000 edition, Series 3.10.
Urbanization change	% change in the level of urban population in the region, 1993 as a % of 1991	Goskomstat Rossii, *Regions of Russia CD ROM*, 2000 edition, Series 2.2.
Population change	% change in region's population, 1993 as a % of 1991	Goskomstat Rossii, *Regions of Russia CD ROM*, 2000 edition, Series 2.1.

Table A5 *The Effect of Economic Change on Regional Activism (OLS regression coefficients, standard errors in parentheses)*

	All	Demodernization	Economic Downturn
Real income change	0.0057335	0.0054077	0.0067148
	(0.005552)	(0.0053427)	(0.0049668)
Industrial production	0.2558872	0.2426522	0.2472316
change	(0.3102078)	(0.3026215)	(0.3009189)
Raw materials	−0.0034471	−0.0032846	−0.0034643
production change	(0.0037439)	(0.0036503)	(0.0036214)
Exports change	0.002018	0.0020478	0.0019288
	(0.0016179)	(0.0015976)	(0.0015797)
Unemployment change	0.0005401	0.0005567	0.0011977
	(0.00613)	(0.0060694)	(0.0059653)
Urbanization change	−0.0336322	−0.0363733	
	(0.0544995)	(0.0528526)	
Population change	0.0117163		
	(0.0470424)		
Constant	0.9190521	0.9129187	0.9348247
	(0.1154089)	(0.1116438)	(0.1064338)
Number of obs =	55	55	55
F =	(7, 47) 1.21	(6, 48) 1.42	(5, 49) 1.63
Prob > F =	0.3184	0.225	0.1692
R-squared =	0.1522	0.1511	0.1427
Adj R-squared =	0.026	0.045	0.0553
Root MSE =	0.71277	0.70577	0.70197

* significant at the 0.10 level, ** significant at the 0.05 level, *** significant at the 0.01 level.

Table A6 *Regional Understandings of the Economy: Fiscal Relations, Combined Source Locations*

	Affected Location		
Benefit Evaluation	Samara	Sverdlovsk	Total
Negative	33	37	70
	58%	79%	67%
Positive	24	10	34
	42%	21%	33%
TOTAL	57	47	104
	100%	100%	100%

Pearson chi^2(1) = 5.0787. Pr = 0.024.

Appendix Tables

Table A7 *Regional Understandings of the Economy: Production Issues, Combined Source Locations*

| Benefit Evaluation | Affected Location | | |
	Samara	Sverdlovsk	Total
Negative	29	83	112
	42%	58%	53%
Positive	40	59	99
	58%	42%	47%
TOTAL	69	142	211
	100%	100%	100%

Pearson chi^2(1) = 5.0281. Pr = 0.025.

Table A8 *Regional Understandings of the Economy: Price Issues, Combined Source Locations*

| Benefit Evaluation | Affected Location | | |
	Samara	Sverdlovsk	Total
Negative	21	69	90
	78%	80%	80%
Positive	6	17	23
	22%	20%	20%
TOTAL	27	86	113
	100%	100%	100%

Pearson chi^2(1) = 0.0764. Pr = 0.782.

Table A9 *Regional Understandings of the Economy: Trade Issues, Combined Source Locations*

| Benefit Evaluation | Affected Location | | |
	Samara	Sverdlovsk	Total
Negative	20	83	103
	50%	75%	68%
Positive	20	28	48
	50%	25%	32%
TOTAL	40	111	151
	100%	100%	100%

Pearson chi^2(1) = 8.3234. Pr = 0.004.

Index

Index

Index

Index